The Crusades and the Christian World of the East

THE MIDDLE AGES SERIES

Ruth Mazo Karras, Series Editor
Edward Peters, Founding Editor

A complete list of books in the series is available from the publisher

The Crusades and the Christian World of the East

Rough Tolerance

Christopher MacEvitt

PENN

University of Pennsylvania Press
Philadelphia

154800566

Copyright © 2008 University of Pennsylvania Press

All rights reserved. Except for brief quotations used for purposes of review or scholarly citation, none of this book may be reproduced in any form by any means without written permission from the publisher.

Published by
University of Pennsylvania Press
Philadelphia, Pennsylvania 19104-4112

Printed in the United States of America on acid-free paper

10   9   8   7   6   5   4   3   2   1

A Cataloging-in-Publication Data record is available from the Library of Congress

ISBN-13: 978-0-8122-4050-4
ISBN-10: 0-8122-4050-2

Contents

Note on Transliteration and Names

The names of people and places mentioned in this book have been translated and transliterated into English in a variety of ways that are not always consistent. I have attempted to render personal names in a way that reflects most closely the sound in the original language, even when that name is being used in another language. I have thus referred to the Ayyubid sultan as Salah al-Din rather than Saladin. Many names of towns and geographical features have different names in Armenian, Syriac, Arabic, Greek, Latin, Turkish, and Old French. I have generally used the name of the community that was dominant in the period under discussion, with a few exceptions for well-known places. Thus, I have consistently used Edessa for the sake of familiarity, when almost everyone in the twelfth century knew it by some variation of its ancient Syriac name, Urhay (Latin Rohas, Arabic al-Ruha, Turkish Urfa, Armenian Urha). Only a few classicizing Latin chroniclers used Edessa, but that has stuck. In transliterating Armenian into English, I have generally followed the system of transliteration of the Library of Congress. I have generally used the standard western calendar for dates, although the communities under discussion used a variety of different calendars.

The Frankish Levant, c. 1130.

Introduction

A few months after the capture of Antioch (3 June 1098), the leaders of the First Crusade wrote a letter to Pope Urban II, on whose urging they had embarked on their long, strange journey across Europe and Byzantium. The rigors of nearly two years on the march, the exhausting eight-month siege of Antioch, the euphoria of its capture, the miraculous discovery of the relic of the Holy Lance, and the astonishing victory over yet another Turkish army had left the crusaders astonished and overwhelmed. The last straw came on 1 August with the death of Adhemar of LePuy, the papal representative accompanying the crusaders. His passing left the crusaders without a guiding and unifying voice. Confused and lacking direction, the crusaders hoped a letter to Urban might elicit further guidance. After summarizing the recent events of the crusade, the letter-writers urged that Urban himself come to Antioch, which was, as they noted, the first seat of St. Peter, and that the pope then lead the crusaders on to Jerusalem. Why? The crusaders confessed that they had found some challenges beyond their military skills: "we have subdued the Turks and the pagans," they wrote to Urban, "but the heretics, Greeks and Armenians, Syrians and Jacobites, we have not been able to overcome (*expugnare*)."[1] What the crusaders wanted to do to the "heretics" is unclear: kill them as they had the Turkish inhabitants of Antioch? Expel them from the lands the crusaders had conquered? Or perhaps the crusaders' frustration arose because they did not know how to confront an issue as complex and unexpected as eastern Christianity.

For the modern historian, the letter is a glimpse at a moment of possibility, as the army's leaders gathered in Antioch on that late summer's day to consider the direction of their journey. At Antioch, the crusaders stood at the edge of the Byzantine world, a world different from their own yet more familiar than the great sweep of Islamic lands that lay open to the south and east of them. The letter from Antioch hints at their anxiety on leaving the familiar to venture into the unknown. Yet their anxiety circled not so much around the Turks or Islam; for as the writers confidently asserted, "we have subdued the Turks and the pagans." Rather, the crusaders were alarmed by the religious diversity of the Christian world of the Middle East. Turks and Muslims they were prepared for, but for Armenians, Greeks, and Jacobites they were not. The letter raises a series of questions. How would the Franks approach local Christians? What language would they use to frame their relationship? Would the Franks perceive them as a conquered community like the Muslims, or would they see them as fellow Christians, or simply as an occupied subordinate people? These inquiries have provoked strikingly divergent answers from historians of the crusades and of the Frankish East.

In one sense, the harsh attitude displayed in the crusader letter from Antioch conforms to what many would expect from a group of soldiers who believed that killing Muslims was a meritorious act—it simply extended that persecutory and violent agenda to another foreign and suspect group, indigenous Christians. Scholars and educated readers alike have seen the twelfth-century Middle East as an era dominated by crusade and jihad: a world in which conflict between Muslims and western (Latin Catholic) Christians not only expressed itself in a series of battles fought in the name of religious ideology, but formed a fundamental part of the way individuals and communities defined themselves and others. For such Christian and Muslim leaders as Bernard of Clairvaux, Nur al-Din, or Richard the Lion-heart, this may well have been true. But for communities living in the Levant, both indigenous and Frankish, crusade and jihad played little role in the way they understood or experienced the world around them. Rather, individuals and communities formed their identity through a network of families, civic relationships, professional ties, and associations with churches, shrines, and local holy places. Taken together, such identities often crossed religious boundaries.

This book examines the intersection of two Christian worlds, that of western Christians (or Franks, as they were generally known in the Middle East) who conquered Syria and Palestine as part of the First Crusade and remained to settle in the occupied lands, and that of eastern Christians over whom they ruled. The society that emerged at that intersection has been characterized as colonial and European, or as creole and orientalized; both descriptions rely on a dichotomized understanding of interreligious relations as either oppressive or tolerant. Instead, I argue for a mode of social interaction between local Christians and the Franks in twelfth-century Syria and Palestine that I call "rough tolerance," which encompassed conflict and oppression yet allowed multiple religious communities to coexist in a religiously charged land.

The Twelfth-Century Middle East

Over the period of a century (1090–1190), the Middle East underwent dramatic political change. So rapid were these changes that one Armenian chronicler believed that contemporary events "were showing us change, decay, and disappearance of what exists and revealing to us the instability of mankind on earth."[2] The north Syrian town of Marash, for example, in the course of the century fell under the rule of Armenians, Byzantines, Franks, the Seljuk Turks of Rum, and the Zengids of Mosul—in essence every major power in the Levant. This sense of instability and change underlies much of the cultural permeability of twelfth-century Syria and Palestine.

Political Change in the Levant

Two moments capture the dramatic changes the twelfth century brought. The first moment comes in the 1160s, when Franks, Byzantines, and Turks vied for political dominance. The Franks controlled the Mediterranean seacoast, having captured the last Muslim-held port, Ascalon, in 1153. The Byzantines, under emperor Manuel I Komnenos (1143–80), routinely led large armies to northern Syria to ensure their dominance there, while the Turkish leader Nur al-Din (1146–74), building on the victories of his father Zengi (1127–46), brought the important cities of Mosul, Aleppo, and Damascus under one ruler for the first time in sixty years. Notably, two of these powers were Christian. All eyes were turned to Fatimid Egypt, which, while economically dynamic and fertile, was paralyzed by political conflict. It seemed possible that any of the three could gain control of Egypt and thereby dominate the Middle East. Within twenty years, that came to pass. Nur al-Din's successor, Salah al-Din (1174–93), successfully conquered both Egypt and the Frankish principalities; never again would a Christian power based in the Levant threaten Muslim hegemony.

Yet some seventy years earlier (1090), a very different future seemed imminent. In the eyes of many, the days of a united Islamic world had returned, this time under Turkish leadership. The Byzantines had retreated to the very walls of Constantinople as Seljuk armies marched as far as the Aegean and

the Bosporus. Even Christians of the Middle East celebrated the seeming re-
newal of the ancient Islamic empire under Seljuk leadership. The Armenian
chronicler Matthew of Edessa (c. 1070–c. 1136) eulogized the Seljuk sultan
Malik-Shah (1072–92) by remembering "there was no land which did not
submit to his rule." But his authority was not based on cruel conquest, for "he
showed a fatherly affection for all the inhabitants of the lands and so gained
control of many towns and regions without resistance."[3] Iran was the center
of Turkish authority; Baghdad was ruled by the caliphs, and Palestine and
Syria were just the dusty borderlands of a vast empire sweeping almost to
India. Malik-Shah died in 1092, and was the last ruler to wield authority from
"the Caspian to the Mediterranean" for more than two hundred years.

The First Crusade

The difference between 1090 and the 1160s lies in the fragmentation of Islamic authority and the emergence of Frankish principalities in the Levant.
The two are intimately linked; the First Crusade (1096–99) did not cause the
collapse of the Seljuk empire, but took advantage of the squabbles of Malik-
Shah's successors by conquering Antioch and Jerusalem. The First Crusade
struck participants and (Christian) commentators as nothing short of miraculous. Matthew of Edessa marveled that "God protected the army as he had
the children of Israel in the past."[4] Its assorted armies traveled from western
Europe through Hungary and the Balkan territories of the Byzantine empire
to arrive in Constantinople in various groups during the winter and spring
of 1097, a journey of roughly 2000 miles which in itself was a notable achievement. With their departure from Constantinople, the crusade armies left
Christian lands, and for the next two years faced the daunting challenge of
surviving in Muslim-controlled territory. The crusaders first captured Nicaea
(19 June 1097), capital of the recently established Seljuk sultanate of Rum, and
then defeated two Turkish armies while crossing central Anatolia. The crusade nearly ended during the grueling eight-month siege of Antioch in Syria,
but the city was captured by ruse on 3 June 1098. The crusaders then immediately had to defend the city against another Turkish army sent from Mosul.
It was soon after this that the crusaders sought guidance by letter from Urban
II. After recouping their strength in Antioch for several months, the army
then marched to their final destination of Jerusalem, capturing it on 15 July
1099 with a bloody massacre. The survival of the army through three years'

march, innumerable sieges, and pitched battles with several large Turkish armies seemed possible only by virtue of divine intervention.

With the conquest of Jerusalem, the crusade ended, and the vows the crusaders had taken were fulfilled. But they were left with the question: what should be done with the cities and territories the crusaders had conquered from Antioch to Jerusalem? Rather than relinquishing the lands they conquered to Byzantium, as they had done with Nicaea and other lands in Anatolia, the crusaders established the kingdom of Jerusalem, with Godfrey of Bouillon as its ruler, with the remaining crusaders (the majority having died or returned to Europe on completion of their vows) as its new political and military elite. Bohemund of Taranto, a Norman from southern Italy, had claimed Antioch as his own before its capture, and Godfrey's brother Baldwin of Boulogne already ruled Edessa. The last Frankish principality to be created was the county of Tripoli, carved out of the Syrian coast by the Provençal nobleman Raymond of St. Gilles and his descendants after an eight-year siege of the city of Tripoli. These four polities—the county of Edessa, principality of Antioch, county of Tripoli and kingdom of Jerusalem—are often referred to as the "crusader states," an appellation that more accurately describes how they were established than how they survived. Though their protection was the motivation for crusades during the next two centuries, the princes who ruled them were not crusaders. They had conquered Jerusalem and fulfilled their vows. Their concerns were no longer about their own salvation or protection of the holy places, but those of ruling elites everywhere—to defend their lands against any threat, Muslim or Christian, and to augment and solidify their authority. While the societies they ruled are commonly discussed in books that take "the crusades" as their subject (as this book itself does), the history of the Frankish Levant only intersected with the history of the crusades proper at brief moments. For extended periods, they did not coincide at all.

Geography of the Frankish Levant

While the First Crusade may have been motivated by the religious significance of Jerusalem, the rest of the cities and regions the crusaders conquered were chosen for more prosaic, strategic reasons. The Franks did not, for example, occupy the barren Sinai peninsula, even though it contained the mountain where God gave the Israelites the Ten Commandments and Moses saw the glory of God. Instead, the Franks seized the fertile lands of the

Mediterranean coast, as well as strategic highlands and areas where Christians made up the majority of the population. At their greatest extent, the lands of the Franks covered the region now occupied by Israel, the Gaza Strip, the West Bank, the western border area of Jordan, Lebanon, the seacoast of Syria, and the southeastern coast of Turkey, as well the Turkish-Syrian borderlands stretching halfway to Iraq.[5] The area covered a variety of landscapes, from the oases of the Dead Sea to the rich farmlands of the Euphrates valley, and a large proportion of it was productive land. The crusaders first entered the area from the north, descending out of the steep river valleys of the Taurus Mountains, the chain that stretches from the Mediterranean coast inland to the Caucasus Mountains and divides the highlands of Anatolia—windswept and cold in the winter, hot and dry in the summer—from the flatter hills and plains of Syria. Their destination was the city of Antioch, which sat in the valley of the Orontes river, well-watered and humid, marshy in places but allowing cultivation of sugarcane, wheat, and barley.[6] To the north were the Syrian Gates, the pass through the Amanus Mountains to Cilicia, while the Orontes valley itself led east and then south, sheltering the cities of Apamea, Hama, and Homs, only the first of which ever came under Frankish rule.

To the east of the Orontes lay the Syrian limestone massif, a series of hills which gradually flattened out into the dry plains around Aleppo, which themselves continued as a great flat desert stretching east to Mesopotamia. The limestone hills marked the edge of Frankish power; towns and fortresses such as 'Imm and Harim allowed the Franks to overlook and at times to dominate the plains, but rarely to occupy them. To the north, however, the Franks moved much further inland, following the foothills of the Taurus Mountains east, which were home to the county of Edessa, the only entirely land-bound Frankish principality. The county had no natural boundaries to the east; similar topography and climate continued east to the black-walled city of Amida on the Tigris River and even farther, as the Taurus Mountains ran headlong into the Zagros chain, which makes up the backbone of Persia. Occupying land on both sides of the Euphrates, the county covered the rich farmlands along the river, as well as the foothills of the Taurus, which, while dry, allowed the cultivation of pistachios, walnuts, and, in the western hills, olives.

For the most part, however, the Franks preferred proximity to the coast. Not only did sea travel provide the quickest route to Latin Europe, but seaborne trade was an ever increasingly important part of the Frankish economy, as the navies from the commercial cities of Italy—Pisa, Genoa, and Venice—largely dominated the eastern Mediterranean sea routes, and allowed the establishment of mercantile colonies in many of the Frankish-controlled seaports. To the south of Antioch, the county of Tripoli stretched approximately eighty-five miles along the Levantine coast, and extended some thirty miles to the east into the Lebanon Mountains, which run north-south, parallel to the seacoast. Between the sea and the mountains was a rich but narrow coastal plain, well watered, which supported a variety of agricultural products.

The kingdom of Jerusalem was the largest of the Frankish principalities, stretching from Beirut in the north to the Sinai desert in the south. The Lebanon Mountains rumbled to an end in the fertile rolling hills of the Galilee, a region sandwiched in the thirty-four miles between the Mediterranean and the Sea of Galilee. The kingdom was largely defined by the Mediterranean coast and the Jordan River to the east, which flowed south from the Sea of Galilee to the Dead Sea. Southward, the valley through which it flowed was deep, hot, and increasingly dry, though punctuated with fertile oases. Across the river to the east rose the high hills of biblical Gilead. These rocky hills, almost cliffs, are the eastern edge of the great geological scar running all the way to East Africa, better known as the Great Rift Valley. On their heights at the southern end of the Dead Sea, the Franks built the great castle of Kerak (Krak des Moabites), which watched over the merchants and pilgrims traveling from Muslim-ruled Damascus south to Mecca and Cairo. On the other side of the Jordan rose the Judean hills in which sat Jerusalem; the hills gradually gave way to the coastal plain, which was at its widest here. To the south was the Negev Desert, over which the Franks exercised only sporadic authority.

Religious Communities of the Levant

The Syrian and Palestinian lands conquered by the crusaders and their successors were home to a wide variety of religious communities. It is commonplace to discuss the diversity of the Middle East in terms of Muslims, Jews, and Christians, yet even this simplifies its religious complexity. Each group can (and should) be considered as several different, often competing, communities. Three separate Christian communities constituted the bulk of the Christian residents of Palestine and Syria, and were formally distinguished by theological disagreement over the Council of Chalcedon, held in 451. Called

to settle debate over how Christ's divine and human characteristics were related, the council established that Christ had one human nature and one divine nature "without confusion, without change, without division, without
separation." Instead of resolving disagreements, the council only fed the fire
of controversy. Over the following century and a half, different factions
within the Christian community, particularly in Syria, struggled to ensure
the dominance of their theology, eventually leading to the establishment of
separate church institutions and hierarchies. By the twelfth century, a host of
liturgical and cultural differences also distinguished communities, and often
these were more significant than theology. The number of fingers used when
blessing oneself, the use of leavened or unleavened bread in church services,
even the words of the liturgy itself came to bear the weight of religious identity and the anxieties of Christian division. Each group claimed the name of
"orthodox," that is, "those who believe rightly"; thus, in this book I use the
names by which they were known (often polemically) by other Christians
outside their community in order to avoid repeatedly using the name "orthodox" for different communities, as well as the confusion of designations like
"Greek" or "Syrian," which sometimes signal ecclesiastical affiliation and
sometimes liturgical language.

The Melkites (Greek Orthodox) were the Christians of Syria, Palestine
and Egypt who accepted the definition of Christ's nature promulgated at
Chalcedon, and remained in communion with the patriarch of Constantinople and the emperor, once their lands and cities came under Muslim rule. At
times the Melkite patriarchs of Antioch, Jerusalem, and Alexandria were appointed from Constantinople. Their name derived from the Syriac word
"malka," meaning king or emperor, signaling their continued adherence to
the emperor of Constantinople. But Melkites themselves could be divided
into two groups, those who spoke Greek and those who spoke Arabic or Syriac. Antioch, once among the centers of Hellenistic culture in the ancient
world and under Byzantine rule from 969 to 1086/7, still had a large Greek-
speaking Melkite population in the twelfth century. In Palestine too the
Melkites constituted the great majority of the Christian population, but these
more often spoke Syriac or Arabic.

The Jacobite (Syrian Orthodox) tradition developed from the ascetic
and theological traditions of Alexandria, exemplified in Cyril of Alexandria
(d. 444) and developed by Severus of Antioch (d. c. 539).[7] The Jacobites rejected the conclusions of the Council of Chalcedon, believing the council to
have mistakenly separated Christ's human and divine qualities. Yet only a

century later, under the leadership of the bishop of Edessa, Jacob Burd'ana (or Burd'aya, Baradaios in Greek, d. 578, from whom the epithet "Jacobite" arose), did such miaphysite[8] communities begin to define themselves independently of the imperial church and ordain a separate hierarchy.[9] Jacobite communities could be found from Antioch across northern Syria and Mesopotamia, but by the time of the First Crusade were no longer the majority of the population. In Late Antiquity, Jacobites used Syriac as both a spoken and a liturgical language. By the twelfth century, however, many had shifted to Arabic as their primary language, though Syriac remained important as a written and liturgical language in many communities.

The third group of Christians was the Armenians, with whom the Franks interacted and intermarried most often. The Armenian church had a distinct tradition both politically and theologically, having been established under the independent Arsacid monarchy in the fourth century, rather than within the Roman empire as in the case of the Melkites and Jacobites. The Armenians, like the Jacobites, did not accept the Council of Chalcedon. While some Armenian councils condemned the Chalcedonian formula, proximity to Byzantium meant that Chalcedonian theology always had an appeal to some Armenians. Armenian communities in the eleventh and twelfth centuries dominated the cities and countryside in Cilicia and northern Syria, as well as in their homeland around Lake Van and the Caucasus Mountains. Jerusalem had an Armenian quarter from the early medieval period, with a cathedral dedicated to St. James that was rebuilt in the twelfth century.

Other smaller Christian communities also lived in Palestine and Syria. Perhaps the group most closely associated with the crusades in the eyes of many historians is the Maronites, who looked to the early fifth-century ascetic Maron as a founder. The Maronites developed an institutional structure separate from the imperial church only after the Muslim conquest of the Levant in the seventh century. Their leader claimed the title of patriarch of Antioch, and by the twelfth century their communities were largely concentrated in the mountains of Lebanon. Many came under the rule of the county of Tripoli, but few twelfth-century sources mention them explicitly, with the exception of William of Tyre, who believed them to be monothelite heretics, that is, Christians who believed that Christ has two natures but one will. William was delighted to report, however, that under Frankish influence they had repented of their error and had reconciled themselves to the Roman church.[10] The Maronites thus became the first "Uniate" church, in communion with Rome but maintaining a separate hierarchy, liturgy, and canonical traditions.

The Nestorians inhabited the same Syriac-speaking cultural world as the Jacobites and also rejected the council of Chalcedon, but for the opposite reason—they believed that the council had failed to adequately distinguish between Christ's divine and human natures. The Nestorians had already separated from the imperial church following the ecumenical council of Ephesus in 431. Also known as the East Syrian church, the Church of the East, or later the Chaldeans, the Nestorians flourished largely in areas under Sassanian rule in Late Antiquity.[11] The Nestorians developed close relations with the 'Abbasid caliphate, and at times served as the representative of all Christians in the empire. In the early medieval period, Nestorian missionaries and merchants traveled east along the trade routes, establishing communities as far east as China. Only a few small Nestorian communities, however, came under Frankish rule in the twelfth century.

Other Christians may have had religious communities in Jerusalem in the twelfth century. The German pilgrim Theodericus recorded that "Nubians" also had clergy in Jerusalem, but it is unclear whether this refers to Egyptian Copts or Ethiopians. Both groups were miaphysite in theology and were in communion with the Jacobites.[12] Georgians, who were in communion with the Melkites but came from the same Caucasian cultural world as Armenians, controlled the monastery of the Holy Cross just to the west of the city wall of Jerusalem, and Georgian hermits and monks could be found elsewhere in Palestine.[13]

In many areas, of course, Muslims were in the majority, but again many different communities lived in the Levant, with different attitudes towards the crusaders. The fundamental divide within the Islamic community was between groups generally called Sunnis (*ahl al-Sunna*) and Shi'a (*shi'at 'Ali*). Having its origin among supporters of the Caliph 'Ali, cousin and son-in-law of the prophet Muhammad, Shi'ism developed as a religious movement after the 'Abbasids seized the caliphate in 750, pushing aside descendants of 'Ali whom the Shi'a believed to be the rightful leaders of the Islamic community. As Shi'ism evolved from a partisan group into a religious community, adherents asserted that 'Ali received secret knowledge from Muhammad, which he passed on to his descendants and which was the basis of a variety of esoteric, mystical, and "secret" teachings. Sunna, on the other hand, designated those Muslims who accepted the authority of the first generation of Muslims and the continuity of the historical community, represented by the caliphs. This too was a flexible term, and different writers used it to encompass various schools of thought.

In many areas, the Shiʻa did not form separate communities, but inter-mingled among the Sunni population; each community formed a majority in different areas of the Muslim world. Some branches of Shiʻism, however, did strive to establish separate polities. A group of Ismaʻilis (supporters of Ismaʻil, an eighth-century descendant of ʻAli) established a Shiʻi (Fatimid) caliphate in North Africa in 909, capturing Egypt in 969 and, a few years later, southern Syria. Another group of Ismaʻilis (called Nizaris for their support of Nizar, the son of the Fatimid caliph al-Mustansir, 1036–94) seized control of a series of fortresses in western Iran shortly before the death of Malik-Shah in 1092. The Nizaris also gained castles in the 1130s and 1140s in the hills west of Hama, and boosted their relatively weak military strength by the well-planned murder of opponents, gaining them the name of "Assassins" and a fantastical reputation among Sunnis as well as Franks.[14] The Nizaris of Syria often joined in alliance with the Franks against their Sunni neighbors. Still other communities of Ismaʻili inspiration existed in the Levant. The Druze looked to the Fatimid caliph al-Hakim (996–1021) as the source of supreme religious knowledge, maintaining their doctrines in secret. Thus Shiʻa living in towns such as Tripoli, Aleppo, and Damascus could identify with or sup-port a variety of different movements.[15]

Jewish communities were among the oldest communities of the Middle East, and were established throughout Frankish territory. Rabbinic commu-nities were the largest, and documents from the Genizah collection from Cairo demonstrate that in the eleventh century important communities lived in Jerusalem, Tyre, and Tiberias, as well as other cities in Palestine and Syria. Palestine was also home to one of the three Talmudic academies of the Jew-ish world. Many Karaites, a Jewish group that rejected the authority of the Talmud, were also found in Palestine. Palestine, and particularly Jerusalem, had been a center for Karaism in the tenth and eleventh centuries, and the crusader conquest of Jerusalem devastated both the Rabbanite and Karaite communities.[16] Karaism continued to flourish in the Byzantine empire, in Egypt, and later in eastern Europe, but the crusader sack of Jerusalem in 1099 effectively ended Karaite presence in Palestine for two centuries. Rabbanite communities survived under the Franks in other cities, most notably Tyre.

Also significant in the Frankish period were the Samaritans, who ac-cepted only the first five books of the Hebrew Bible as divinely inspired, and probably emerged as a distinct group at the time of the Babylonian Exile (c. 587–539 B.C.E.), since they did not go into exile but remained on the land. In the medieval period, Samaritan communities were spread throughout the

Middle East, from Thessalonika to Cairo. The center of Samaritan worship was (and is) Mount Gerezim, outside the modern city of Nablus (ancient Neapolis), and the Jewish pilgrim Benjamin of Tudela, traveling in 1169–71, recorded a number of Samaritan communities under Frankish rule.[17]

In many ways, this enumeration of Levantine religious diversity is misleading, suggesting discrete, well-defined communities, fitting together like pieces of a mosaic. Rather, we should imagine societies in which a religious community was only one of a number of groups or associations in which a person might participate. Others were based on professional identity (doctors, for example, came from all religious communities)[18] or regional, urban, or even neighborhood identities. Middle Eastern cities were not segregated by religious community, although some might have quarters identified with certain groups (a Christian or Jewish quarter, for example). The establishment of the Frankish principality simply added another community, language, and religious identity to the mix.

Importance of Christian Communities in the Middle East

Why, the reader might ask, focus on Armenians, Jacobites, and Melkites out of all these different local communities? The most important reason is that only these Christian communities produced written sources that allow us to understand the experience and perspective of local communities who lived under Frankish authority. While considerable material survives documenting Jewish and Muslim views of the crusades and of the Frankish settlements in the Levant, it was written from the perspective of those living outside the Frankish principalities, and therefore cannot represent those who experienced Frankish authority directly.[19] Local Christian sources—chronicles, theological treatises, and letters—originated almost entirely in northern Syria, where Jacobites and Armenians made up the majority of the population. While historians have long been familiar with these texts, and many of them have been translated, they generally have been used to verify Latin texts about the Levant, rather than being analyzed for their own perspective. It is only through them that the relationships of indigenous communities and Franks can be discussed with any confidence.

The challenge of this approach is determining the extent to which local Christian experience aids the historian to understand the experience of other indigenous communities. The historiographic assumption has been that the Franks treated local Christians better than Jews or Muslims on the basis of shared faith, though they still did not treat them as equals. While such an argument has an aura of common sense to it, the underlying assumption that social groups prefer those who are similar to them and feel antagonism towards those who are most different is based largely in evolutionary psychology, and may not apply in all historical situations. In many episodes of social conflict, it is the "intimate enemy," a term which Elaine Pagels has used in discussing Jewish and early Christian intracommunal struggles, who is perceived as the greatest challenge and threat.[20] Given contemporary attitudes towards schismatic and heretic Christians in Latin Europe, it is easy to imagine that the crusaders might have viewed local Christians as more of a threat than Jews and Muslims. Samaritan communities, for example, suffered little under the Franks; their center of worship was undisturbed, and a large number of Torah scrolls survive from the period. It was under the Mamluks that their ritual center was taken from them.[21] The letter written from Antioch shows that the Franks were prepared to use the language of heresy against local Christians, and Peter the Venerable (1092–1156) notably argued that violence against Christian schismatics, heretics, and rebels was even more justified than against infidels. As Jonathan K. Smith declared about other religious groups, "the radically other is merely other; the proximate other is problematic, and hence of supreme interest."[22] This book, therefore makes no such assumptions about the *necessity* of better treatment for local Christians, or worse treatment for Jews and Muslims, but seeks whenever possible to delineate the ways in which Jewish and Muslim experiences were broadly similar to or sharply different from those of local Christians.

This study is largely restricted to the period between 1097 and 1187, that is, from the period when the crusaders first entered Syria until the conquests of Salah al-Din, which brought the vast majority of those lands back under Muslim rule for five, ten, or twenty years, or even permanently. While the Third Crusade and subsequent campaigns brought some areas back under Frankish rule, it was a slow process, and the society that was reestablished in the thirteenth century was noticeably changed.[23]

Historiography of the Crusades

Current historiography of the crusades has developed a consistent picture of the relationship between the Franks and local communities.[24] Joshua Prawer and other scholars have depicted a segregated world in which a small Frankish elite dominated Palestine and Syria, isolating themselves from the local population through discriminatory legal systems, the importation of European serfdom, and the exclusion of locals from positions of authority. This position has begun to be questioned by historians, but no alternative has been suggested.[25] This book offers new ways to think about this question; I argue that the Frankish Levant was a world in which religious and social identities were flexible, and in which violence and tolerance were not exclusive characteristics, but strategies often employed simultaneously.

The question of how the crusaders interacted with local communities became a subject of inquiry only in the nineteenth century, although the study of the crusades began much earlier, emerging almost imperceptibly from the narratives of the medieval chroniclers of the crusades themselves. The first collection of sources was the *Gesta Dei per Francos* of Jacques Bongars, which gathered many of the important Latin texts for the crusades and history of the Frankish East, but did not include sources from other languages.[26] While the study of Arabic and Syriac had been well established in Europe since the Renaissance and even before, those who knew these languages rarely applied their knowledge to the twelfth- and thirteenth-century Middle East, restricting their use to biblical scholarship and patristics. The Arabist Antoine Galland (1646–1715), translator of *The Thousand and One Nights*, first suggested the benefit of using eastern sources to better understand the crusades.[27] Edward Gibbon used some Arabic and Syriac sources in his *Decline and Fall of the Roman Empire*, and presented the social history of the Latin states as a decline from Frankish virility and freedom to oriental sloth and pleasure-seeking, while the native inhabitants yearned for the more tolerant rule of the caliphs.[28] The Armenian chronicle of Matthew of Edessa, for example, did not appear in print in western Europe until 1813, when the scholar Jacques Chahan de Cirbied published extracts from two manuscripts from the imperial library in Paris.[29]

Only with the publication of the monumental *Recueil des historiens des croisades* in the early and mid-nineteenth century did a substantial number of Middle Eastern medieval texts become available to the student of the crusades. This ambitious project began with the Benedictine Maurists of St. Germain-des-Prés about 1770, but after they were suppressed during the French Revolution (the superior-general and forty of the monks died at the guillotine), the royalist Académie des Inscriptions et Belles-Lettres took over the project.[30]

The subject of local relations with the Franks excited considerable interest during the late nineteenth and early twentieth centuries, particularly among French historians. While earlier histories of the crusades, such as Michaud's influential narrative, had focused largely on the Latin narrative of war and settlement, devoting little interest to cultural interactions with local populations,[31] this changed as French colonial ambitions in the Middle East grew. The French had cultivated close relations with the Ottoman sultans since the sixteenth century, and were the first European nation to receive special trading status within the empire. France's economic power and relationship with the Maronites were the twin tools used to expand French influence in the Middle East, particularly along the Levantine coast. Through religious missions, merchants, and consular officials, the French established a close relationship with the Maronites, as the only Christians in the Middle East who remained in communion with the Catholic Church from the medieval period, and eventually claimed the role as their protectors. Other European powers did the same with other minority communities—the Russians claimed a special relationship with Greek Orthodox communities, while the British developed relations with the Druze—but the French wielded the most influence. Further commercial treaties with the Ottomans in the nineteenth century, particularly in 1838, extended the rights of French and other European merchants to buy and sell within the empire.[32] The French particularly dominated the silk trade, which was a significant part of Lebanon's economic connections to Europe. When Napoleon III sent French troops to Lebanon to protect local Christian communities during the civil disturbances in Syria and Lebanon in 1860, he reminded the soldiers to "show yourselves the dignified children of these heroes who gloriously brought the banner of Christ to that land," that is, the crusaders. [33]

France's preeminent position in the Levant was explicitly linked to the French leadership of the crusades, and nineteenth-century French historians of the crusades reinforced this image with accounts emphasizing the close relations between the Franks and local populations, particularly Christians. In the introduction to his 1883 book entitled *Les colonies franques de Syrie aux XIIme et XIIIme siècles*, Emmanuel Rey announced his intention to examine "the causes which favored their [the crusaders'] establishment and development in the midst of a population of Orientals of all races, Syrians, Greeks, and Armenians, [which] appears to me a new subject destined to fill one of lacunae in the history of the crusades."[34] The title of Rey's book gave the Frankish settlements of the Levant a new title—"colony," which linked the Latin principalities of the twelfth and thirteenth centuries to France's colonial ambitions in Syria in the late nineteenth century. Rey asserted that the numerous offspring of mixed marriages, called *poulains* in Frankish sources, identified themselves with the local traditions and values of their indigenous mothers rather than with any aspect of their Frankish fathers.[35] Throughout his account, Rey emphasized the interactions of Franks with local Christians, whether in the realm of business, war or religion.

Interest in the local Christian influence on the crusaders was not limited to the French. Lieutenant-Colonel Claude Conder's work showed much the same interest in understanding Frankish society within the context of local Christian communities.[36] Conder led the Survey of Western Palestine in the late nineteenth century, which documented archaeological and historical sites from the Biblical through the Ottoman period, and thus saw the Franks within the context of Middle Eastern history, rather than through the lens of medieval Europe. The first American historian of the crusades, Dana Carleton Munro, agreed with the conclusions of the French school, concluding, "a study of the administration and laws shows the care the Franks took to win the goodwill of the natives."[37]

Scholars, however, began to turn away from the image of an integrated Levant as two issues gained attention: an increased emphasis on Christian-Muslim conflict, and a growing sense of the influence of French colonialism on crusade historiography. The English historian William Stevenson, writing soon after Conder, enunciated this new view of the Latin East. For Stevenson, the cultural and social history of the Frankish settlements was secondary to the crusades proper; instead, "the story is one of a contest between Moslems and Latins."[38] But it was post-World War II historians, beginning with R. C. Smail, who nailed shut the coffin on the French school of thought. Smail suggested that Frankish society segregated Europeans from native Arabs, Syrians, and Armenians, and that little significant cultural or social exchange existed between the Frankish conquerors and local populations. Furthermore, he argued that pre-war French historians such as Rey saw an integrated society where there was none in an attempt to justify colonial regimes in the Near East, particularly the French domination of Syria and Lebanon.[39]

The segregationist historiographic position that Smail advocated has remained the dominant one among crusade historians to the present day. Steven Runciman's three-volume epic *History of the Crusades*, written from his eastern perspective as a Byzantinist, concluded that "when they [the crusaders] set themselves up in the East they treated their Christian subjects no better than the Caliph had done before them. Indeed, they were sterner, for they interfered in the religious practices of the local churches."[40] As historians such as Joshua Prawer and Jonathan Riley-Smith turned their attention to the social, legal, and political structures of the Frankish Kingdom of

Jerusalem, a consensus emerged that depicted the Frankish society as largely urban and isolated from the local population by segregated cities, separate law courts, and different religious traditions.

Joshua Prawer's 1972 book, *The Latin Kingdom of Jerusalem: European Colonialism in the Middle Ages*, revived Rey's characterization of the Frankish settlements as colonies; for Prawer, however, these "colonies" displayed none of Rey's rose-tinted imperialist characteristics, and he even used the term "apartheid" to describe its judicial and legal systems.[41] In Prawer's work, the "segregationalist" model reached its fullest and most explicit development. For him, the main explanation for the lack of integration was economic. The Franks depended on a subjugated and disenfranchised local population to finance their occupation, and would do nothing to jeopardize those economic interests.

Nor has interest in or adherence to this approach diminished; Prawer's book was republished in 2001, and other recent studies on the position of the local population have emphasized the segregated nature of the Frankish Levant.[42] Carole Hillenbrand's encyclopedic work revealed the variety of Muslim responses to the crusaders, and concluded that Islamic resentment, suspicion, and ultimate rejection of the Franks outweighed other reactions.[43] Prawer also studied the position of Jewish communities under Frankish rule, and likewise saw a community which, while inevitably impacted by the political and military events of the age, remained isolated from the Franks and even other local communities.[44]

While the work of Smail and his historiographic heirs may well have been necessary to correct the colonialist agenda in older French crusade historians, their own vision of the Levant reflected late twentieth-century events in Israel and Palestine. The Zionism that founded Israel was too easily seen as a parallel to the crusades, and the failure of Israel to create an integrated society among its Jewish and Palestinian citizens and subjects has given historians a model of ceaseless conflict between immigrant and indigenous communities that was easily applied to Israel's twelfth-century counterpart. Furthermore, the desire to overturn the historiography of the earlier generation led them to apply the ideology and impact of nineteenth-century colonialism to the twelfth-century Levant.

The Crusades in the Historiography of Medieval Europe

The segregationalist position has added powerful arguments for the inclusion of the Frankish Levant as a part of the growing European world of the twelfth and thirteenth centuries. For the western medievalist, the crusades are emblematic of Europe's dynamism and expansion, a result of the religious reform movement of the eleventh and twelfth centuries, and, in the thirteenth, a part of the growth of papal power. Frankish settlements in the Levant were similarly seen as part of a larger expansion of western elites into frontier areas such as Ireland, eastern Europe, and Spain which, as Robert Bartlett has argued in *The Making of Europe*, resulted in distinctive settlement patterns, formulation of separate legal systems, and interethnic conflict. The segregationalist view of the Latin East thus matches a pattern found throughout the frontiers of medieval Europe. Bartlett argues, as his title suggests, that such experiences and processes both within Latin communities and at their borders helped to create the "Europe" of today. The "crusader" states are an example of what we might call a "failed frontier," which ultimately did not become part of "Europe" only because certain of these characteristics did not develop enough—for example, not enough European colonists settled in Palestine compared to Ireland, Sicily, or Lithuania.[45] Some historians have even linked Europe's twelfth-century Levantine colony and practice of segregation to the history of European colonies in the Americas, Asia, and Africa in the early modern period, making the conquistadors sixteenth-century crusaders.[46]

Contributing to the sense that the Frankish Levant was a segregationalist regime, a European bubble floating on a sea of Middle Eastern resentment, is the conflation of crusades with the history of the "crusader" East. Most books (and college courses) entitled "the crusades" attempt to encompass both a history of the Frankish East (the "crusader" states) and the religious ideology and subsequent military endeavors that were the crusades themselves. The latter were acts of holy war in which battle against the infidel, often with the goal of recovering or defending the Holy Land, aided the reconciliation of the sinning Christian with his god, and were part of a triumphalist and universalist Christianity, which did not acknowledge the existence of any truth other than the word of God as expressed in the Old and New Testaments and interpreted by the fathers of the church. Crusade ideology thus rarely led the warrior to think about the faith of his enemy; the crusade was not a war of conversion, concerned with the salvation of others, but about the salvation of the warrior himself. The infidel represented a path to salvation, not a focus of concern for the crusader.[47]

This is a subject that has little to do with the polities that ruled Palestine and Syria from 1098 to 1291, or the cultures and societies over which they ruled. This conflation ultimately limits the historian's ability to discuss either subject effectively. The usual compromise is to ignore or sideline crusades that are not directed against Muslim powers, as well as those after 1291, when the last Frankish city on the Levantine mainland fell to the Mamluks. Likewise it implicitly suggests that the ideology that underpinned the crusades was equally the foundation for the "crusader" states. By that definition the true crusader state was the kingdom of France under Louis IX, not the Frankish principalities of Outremer. The difference can be marked by the use of the term "crusader" versus "Frank"—I use "crusader" only for those who took a crusade oath, or who at least fought under someone who had, and had not yet fulfilled that oath. "Frank" I use to refer to western Christians (sometimes former crusaders) who settled in the Levant or visited for a period of time.

The Frankish Levant differed not only from other frontier areas of Latin Europe but also from the European heartlands. Although founded by aristocrats from Provence, northern France, Flanders, and southern Italy, the Frankish East did not participate in the political, religious, and cultural changes that Europe underwent in the twelfth century. In Latin Europe, the institutions of the Roman church, for example, grew stronger, in part driven by the conflicts of the Investiture Conflict and an urgent sense of reform sweeping through Latin Christian society. While the crusades themselves were both product of and impetus for those changes, the culture of the twelfth-century Frankish East was unaffected by concerns about the relationship of the church to secular power, or the purity of the clergy. The hallmarks of the vigorous reformist culture of the church were not found in Outremer, such as a new clerical learned elite or assertive bishops (with the possible exception of Daibert of Pisa). Nor do the darker aspects of twelfth-century European reform appear, such as the persecution of Jews and heretics through which new elites and ambitious kings secured their power and built new polities based on law and an autocratic monarch.

Nor can the historian claim that the Latin East was simply ignorant of these developments. Pilgrims, crusaders, and churchmen traveled back and forth, and were aware of what was happening in Latin Europe. The council of Nablus in 1120, assembled by Baldwin II of Jerusalem and attended by the leading ecclesiasts of the kingdom of Jerusalem, shows all the characteristic signs of the reform movement: it ensured ecclesiastical control of tithes, instituted a death penalty for sodomy (the first in the medieval period), and decreed that a man who engaged in sexual relations with a Muslim concubine should be castrated and have his nose cut off. Bigamy and adultery were also outlawed. The concern over sexual crimes is what we might expect from a small, anxious community that feared being overwhelmed by surrounding Muslim societies. Such concern with pollution, sexual in this case, is a theme that would have been familiar to many, as the theme of religious pollution was often invoked in crusade propaganda. Indeed, Fulcher of Chartres, who was living in Jerusalem in 1120 and may have even attended the council, used the theme extensively in his narrative of the First Crusade.[48] But Benjamin Kedar has shown that the statutes drafted at Nablus drew inspiration from the Byzantine legal tradition, not from western reformist trends.[49] Noticeably missing from the council were any decrees having to do with heresy or restrictions on the Jewish population, two subjects that would seem most useful to a monarchy and church hierarchy desperate to establish their authority. The Latin East, we might say, dabbled in the reformist, centralizing, and "persecuting" trends of the twelfth century, but chose not to participate in them.

The segregationalist model has also kept scholars from including the culture and history of the Frankish Levant in discussions of multiethnic societies or interethnic conflict, despite the popularity of the subject in both Islamic and medieval European studies. Over the last twenty years, historians have sought to understand the roots of European persecution of minorities, particularly Jews, producing a body of scholarship that can be useful for situating the twelfth-century Levant in a spectrum of practices of the medieval Mediterranean.[50] Perhaps the most significant work has been that of David Nirenberg, who has argued that episodes of violence between Jews and Christians in fourteenth-century Spain and France were not merely the outburst of irrational hatreds, but the expression and manipulation of local beliefs and concerns. Furthermore, Nirenberg pointed out that the modern dichotomy between "tolerance" and "intolerance" fails to account for the centrality of conflict for constructing social relations.[51] Episodic violence can be a way of establishing boundaries between communities and articulating the power dynamics between communities. In other words, it is often violence that allows communities to coexist. Nirenberg's work is particularly useful for dismantling the dichotomy of violence and coexistence. It no longer suffices to point out episodes of violence involving Franks and local populations and conclude that "tolerance" did not exist; violence must be used to explore how relationships among communities were managed, defined, and exploited. Whereas in Nirenberg's Spain symbolic or real violence was used as a tool to delineate boundaries between communities, in the Frankish Levant, coexistence was based on ignoring difference; they were not communities of violence, but communities of silence. Silence allowed different religious communities to live side by side, but also permitted the Franks to exile, oppress and even massacre local populations with little backlash.

Rough Tolerance: A New Model of Religious Interaction

Much of the reason the segregationalist model has endured for fifty years is that it is the only model available for historians to use. Without it historians are left with the nineteenth-century colonialist model of an integrated Levant, a variety of *convivencia* of the East, where content locals flourish under the benevolent rule of creole Franks "gone native." The evident errors of this vision have led historians perforce to cling to the segregationalist explanation, which at least captures the darker aspects of Frankish authority. One of the principal goals of this book is to argue that the segregationalist vision of the Frankish Levant is deeply flawed, and to present an alternative.

"Rough tolerance," as we might call it, is not the equivalent of modern concepts of multiculturalism, in part because it was not an ideology but a practice. I use the term "tolerance" because the practices of rough tolerance allowed the coexistence of diverse religious and ethnic communities without the legal or social structures of control or domination that were emerging in contemporary Latin Europe; it was "rough" because political power rested largely in the hands of the new Frankish aristocracy, who employed it against indigenous communities as they felt necessary. I do not use "tolerance" in a moral sense (some moral philosophers refer to it as the "impossible virtue" because the conditions for its full existence can never exist). Franks and others who engaged in rough tolerance were not doing so because they believed it to be a virtuous quality. If tolerance is defined as "the refusal, where one has the power to do so, to prohibit or seriously interfere with conduct one finds objectionable," we cannot be certain whether it is tolerance or indifference we are discussing.[52] All we can say is that the Frankish aristocracy allowed conduct and beliefs that would have been unacceptable in Christian Europe.

Because violence directed against indigenous communities was localized and unaccompanied by other forms of legal and social control, and because the social boundaries of local communities were porous and ill-defined, neither Latins nor locals developed the rhetoric of "us" and "them," or images of the "other" or the "oppressor." Episodes of conflict, violence, and oppression occurred frequently, yet they were often directed at specific groups within local communities in a way that used intracommunal factionalism to drain away the sense of threat to the larger community. Whereas in Nirenberg's fourteenth-century Spanish world each act of violence was loaded with symbolic meaning, in the Latin principalities of the Levant, Franks and local Christians denied that any lasting symbolic significance had accumulated around incidences of conflict.

Rough tolerance is difficult to define and describe, for by its very nature it is unspoken, undefined, and amorphous. Nevertheless, there are characteristics by which we can catch its presence, if only in silhouette or shadow. The first and most difficult sign to uncover is silence itself. Arguments based on silence are proverbially verboten for historians, yet in the case of the Frankish East, it is essential to discuss what is not present. Silence covers a variety of absences from both local Christian and Frankish sources. The most striking absence is that of local Christians from Latin texts. While they appear periodically as groups and individuals in episodes described by many chroniclers such as Fulcher of Chartres and William of Tyre, local Christians and their communities were identified only by linguistic characteristics, identities that masked the more problematic markers of religious identity. The Armenians are most easily identified, distinguished by their own language, but all other Christians were designated as either "Graeci" or "Suriani," names with only a tenuous connection to the languages the communities spoke or used in liturgy. The theological and ecclesiastical issues separating the various Christians of the Levant were rarely discussed. The Latin Patriarch of Antioch, Amalric of Limoges, for example, apparently thought it appropriate to invite Michael the Great (Michael the Syrian) to the Third Lateran Council in 1179, and solicited a refutation of the Cathar heresy from him. He ignored the fact that Michael, as leader of the Syrian Orthodoc (Jacobites), claimed the same title of patriarch of Antioch that Amalric himself held, and was thus the leader of a church that, from a Latin perspective, had a heretical pedigree as ancient as the Cathars themselves.

Absence is also a feature of local Christian sources, but not concerning theological issues. Patriarch Michael the Great, in contrast to Amalric of Limoges, was clearly familiar with the Christological beliefs of the Latin church, and willing to discuss them. Rather, the deliberate blindness of local sources concerned issues of power and governance. Although Frankish leaders repeatedly used violence and intimidation against local Christians to establish and maintain their authority, local Christians did not develop a litany of crimes which had been committed against them, nor did they develop a stereotype of the Franks, though both Armenians and Jacobites certainly had such images of the Byzantines, and to some extent the Armenians had developed one of the Turks. Michael the Great failed to even mention in his chronicle a Frankish raid on his own monastery of Mar Barsauma, despite his familiarity with other sources that mentioned it. Both local Christians and Franks chose not to know, to forget, or to overlook those aspects of the other which had the most power to control and define the other.[53]

The second characteristic that allowed rough tolerance to exist was permeability: the easy flow of persons and practices across social and religious boundaries. Permeability thus also depended on the silences discussed above. It allowed a Frankish noble such as Baldwin, count of Marash, to have an Armenian priest as his confessor without either having converted, a Latin family to build a shrine to a Jacobite saint who healed their child, or a Melkite bishop to request that he be buried as a Latin Hospitaller. For local Christians, permeability arose from the relative weakness of their elites; both Melkites and Armenians had been devastated in different ways by the tribulations of the eleventh century, and the Jacobites had long suffered from factionalism and internal conflict that made them vulnerable to external influence. Strikingly, permeability did not extend to intellectual exchange; books and ideas did not flow across communal boundaries in the Frankish Levant as they did in other multicultural societies such as Sicily and Spain. This may be due to the reluctance on the part of the Frankish elite to patronize or support educated clergy of the sort who would seek new editions of classical texts such as Aristotle, for such a group could tighten boundaries and create exactly the regimes of knowledge they were so clearly avoiding.[54]

A third characteristic of rough tolerance was localization. Rough tolerance operated only on a local level; one might say it existed only in the line of sight. Frankish military power was employed only against specific groups: this group of rebellious councilors or that warlord, or this specific community living in this one place. Both the Franks and local communities understood such violence within specific social, physical, and geographic limits. An attack on one group or individual was never interpreted as an attack on an entire community or class, nor did the Franks ever systematically attack all Armenian warlords, or all Jacobite monasteries. In part, the localization of violence was enabled by the weakened elites of local communities, by their willingness to forget, as well as by Frankish unwillingness to recognize local communities as they constituted themselves. Indigenous leaders, wielding only local authority, were thus reluctant to use a discourse of oppression as a way to bolster their own authority, both for fear of becoming targets of Frankish attack themselves, and because they did not want to give up access to sources of support coming from Frankish leadership.

Rough tolerance has its roots in early medieval western practices, not in the relationship between Islam and the *dhimmi* communities.[55] Many historians have seen Frankish toleration of other religious communities as a continuation of Islamic practices, with Muslims forced into a subordinate status alongside Jews, and in some interpretations, local Christians. Yet rough tolerance differed from the *dhimmi* system in a number of ways. Most significantly, the *dhimmi* system envisioned a society of discrete and hierarchalized communities: at the top was the community of Muslims, and beneath them, the inferior *dhimmi* communities, each separately constituted. The *dhimmi* community should be represented by a leader, often a bishop or patriarch for the Christian community, who served as the intermediary between the community and Islamic authority. The system thus required the delineation of difference between Christian, Jew, and Muslim; different communities sometimes petitioned to be recognized as entities distinct from others. For example, the Karaites in eleventh-century Cairo petitioned the Fatimid caliph to be allowed to butcher animals without Rabbanite supervision.[56] The Franks, in contrast, had no formal structures governing local communities and had no interest in defining them.

The practices of rough tolerance were about avoiding such categorization. The origin of rough tolerance was rather a development of early western medieval disinterest in categorization and difference. The experience of Jewish communities in early medieval western Europe, for example, is akin to that of local communities in the Frankish Levant. Unlike the high medieval period, Jews in France and Italy practiced a wide variety of professions, owned land, and had few legal restrictions placed on them. Yet they were also subject to violence and attack and sometimes forced conversion. Although the Christian tradition had developed a negative image of "the Jew" that pervaded exegesis and canon law, rulers such as the Carolingians showed little interest in separating, identifying, or classifying difference in the communities over which they ruled. Rather, Jews were considered members of the community on an equal footing with other groups.[57] Just as Jews were not subjected to legal restrictions, the beliefs and practices of Christians were not subjected to examination in the way that they were after the eleventh century.

The twelfth-century description of the Franks by Michael the Great, patriarch of the Jacobite church, which noted that "they never sought a single formula for all the Christian people and languages, but they considered as Christian anyone who worshipped the cross without investigation or examination,"[58] could equally be a description of Frankish kingdoms of the early medieval West.

Rough tolerance also differed from the forms of political, social, and religious interactions that existed in medieval Spain, often referred to as *convivencia*. The nature of the relationships among Jews, Christians and Muslims is still a contentious historiographic topic, but several characteristics distinguish it from rough tolerance: both the size and prominence of Jewish communities in Spain and the shared Arabic culture in which Muslims, Christians, and Jews could participate mark out the multireligious interactions in Spain as distinctly different. In particular, *convivencia* was not silent; disputation and dialogue among different groups was common.

This book approaches rough tolerance from a variety of directions. The first chapter examines the eleventh-century history of the Middle East, establishing the social and political patterns and expectations local communities developed prior to the First Crusade. Chapters 2 and 3 take the exercise of Frankish power for their subject, particularly in northern Syria, exploring how their authority was established and used both against and with the majority Christian population. It was in northern Syria that the largest concentration of local Christians lived, and that the Armenian and Syriac texts written under Frankish rule were produced. It was also here that the crusaders first came to political power in the Levant, and it was here the most important Frankish rulers had their formative political and cultural experiences. The first two kings of Jerusalem (both named Baldwin) were first counts of Edessa before ascending to the throne of the Holy City; Melisende, who ruled the kingdom with her son until 1150, was the daughter of an Armenian mother from Melitene and grew up in Edessa.

Not only do we have the best opportunity to understand the relationships between locals and Franks in the Levant through an examination of experiences in northern Syria, it was a cultural world deeply influential in the Frankish East. Chapter 4 studies the relationship between local Christian ecclesiastical hierarchies and the Franks, discussing the basis and effects of Frankish "theological ignorance," as well as the ways in which locals and Latins did learn about each other. The legal and social status of indigenous individuals under Frankish rule is the subject of Chapter 5. Using primarily

Latin charters, I argue that European serfdom was not imported to the Levant, and show that Syrians, Palestinians, and Armenians participated in Frankish governance at a variety of levels. The last chapter turns to the ecumenical negotiations that became important in the 1160s. Byzantine attempts to unite the churches of the Levant under imperial leadership paradoxically heightened the importance of sectarian identity, undermining the permeability and silence that were so vital to rough tolerance. The result is a book which presents the Frankish Levant as imbedded within a larger Middle Eastern world, and gives an explanation of interreligious relationships found elsewhere in the premodern world.

Chapter 1
Satan Unleashed: The Christian Levant in the Eleventh Century

When the Armenian communities of the Kingdom of Ani, located in the highlands of what is now eastern Turkey, experienced an eclipse and an earthquake simultaneously in 1036/7, they knew that something beyond the ken of ordinary men had occurred. King Hovhannes and the *kat'olikos* Petros, the leader of the Armenian church, seeking the significance of these omens, sent an embassy of eminent men to consult Hovhannes Kozern, a venerable *vardapet*[1] whose wisdom and piety wreathed him with the stature of an Old Testament prophet. When the emissaries from the king and *kat'olikos* arrived at the hermit's cell, they found the holy man prostrate in prayer, bathed in tears and unable to speak. After the vision that gripped him passed and his grief subsided, he explained to his alarmed audience what the ominous portents presaged. Soon overwhelming calamities would strike the Armenians, Hovhannes warned. Christians would turn away from the Church, blaspheming and ignoring God's law, forgetting the fasts, and neglecting their prayers. Even patriarchs and priests would abandon their altars, and princes and kings would grow cruel and capricious in the use of their God-given authority. Harlots and whoremongers would lead the people, and parents and children would turn against each other. The cause of these disasters, the hermit explained, was the release of Satan from the confinement in which Christ's crucifixion had placed him; the end of the world was at hand. With the strength of Satan behind them, a cursed people—the Turks—would burn the lands of the Armenians, kill their families, level their cities, and desecrate their churches.

Their sufferings would end, Hovhannes predicted, only after sixty years, when "the valiant nation called the Franks will rise up; with a great number of troops they will capture the holy city of Jerusalem, and the Holy Sepulcher, which contained God, will be freed from bondage."[2] Yet the crusaders would achieve only a temporary victory; the Turks would then return with ferocity seven-fold. After fifty years, "the Roman Emperor will be awakened as if from a sleep, and like an eagle, rapidly will come against the Turks with a very great army, as numerous as the sands of the seashore. He will march forth like a burning fire, and all creatures will tremble in fear of him."[3] His triumph over the Muslims would be complete, and once again the known world would be under the rule of the Roman emperor. Hovhannes did not explicitly predict the return of Christ, but his depiction of the ultimate triumph of the emperor drew on the apocalypse of Pseudo-Methodius, a seventh-century Syriac account. Pseudo-Methodius first described the figure of the "last emperor," who would defeat the Muslims and lay his crown on the cross at Golgotha; cross and crown would then ascend to Jesus in heaven, signaling the end of earthly dominion and the inauguration of the kingdom of God on earth.[4]

Hovhannes's vision appears in the chronicle of Matthew of Edessa, an Armenian monk living in northern Syria under Frankish rule in the early twelfth century. The vision the chronicler described was not a prediction from 1036/7, but a description of the dilemma Matthew believed Armenian communities of the Middle East, who had already witnessed the arrival of the crusaders in Syria and heard of their capture of the holy city of Jerusalem in 1099, faced in his own day. He saw his people as orphans, exiles from their motherland and abandoned by their leaders. Byzantine diplomacy had robbed Armenians of their independence, dispersed their rulers, and divided the church, while Turkish attacks ravaged their land and sacked their cities. Nevertheless, the threat that Armenians such as Matthew of Edessa perceived was not persecution or war, but the danger of integration with surrounding communities. Leaderless, their church divided by schism, and surrounded by Byzantines, Franks, and Turks, many Armenians drifted easily in the political and cultural currents of their neighbors, buoyed by values shared among the diverse communities of the Middle East.

Just as Matthew of Edessa inserted the crusaders into an apocalyptic narrative as a way to transform the unexpected into the predicted, other Levantine Christians brought their own paradigms and expectations to their initial encounters with the crusaders, which continued to underlie their relationships for decades after. This chapter discusses the origins of those paradigms and expectations, and also provides a background history of medieval Christian communities in the Middle East, a subject not widely known except to the few who study it. Such a history serves as an alternate introduction to the Frankish Levant as well, replacing the traditional western European narrative that begins in western Europe at the turn of the millennium with one that begins in the Levant in Late Antiquity, an era always haunting the collective memory of eastern Christians.

A Brief History of the Christian East

As discussed in the introduction, this book focuses on three religious communities—Melkites, Jacobites, and Armenians. For each, the events of Late Antiquity shaped their beliefs and identity, while each reacted to the emergence of an Islamic empire in different ways.

Armenians in Late Antiquity

Some readers might be surprised at the prominence of Armenians in a book about twelfth-century Syria and Palestine, for those territories are a long way from the mountains of the Caucasus and the shores of Lake Van, which were the homeland of the Armenians. However, it is difficult to speak of a distinct area called "Armenia" in the pre-modern period. The heart of Armenian territory was perhaps the Araxes River valley, which today forms part of the border between Turkey and the Republic of Armenia, as well as between Iran and Azerbaijan. Here can be found the ancient cities of Artaxata, Dvin, and Ejmiacin, the center of the ancient Armenian church. Yet the kingdoms and provinces that at various times have borne the name Armenia or some variation of it cover a range of territories across what is now eastern Turkey, Armenia, Georgia, Azerbaijan, and northwest Iran, and have expanded, contracted, and shifted from east to west over the last two millennia. The lands most often referred to by the name "Armenia" were characterized by high mountain ranges and deep river valleys, which both invited invasion and hindered conquest. The Tigris and Euphrates, the rivers of Paradise according to the book of Genesis, arise in the Armenian highlands and flow down to the fabled lands of the Fertile Crescent. The Armenian highlands were equally attractive from the west, and were often borderlands, porous to cultural influences from both directions. Fertile valleys, forests, mineral resources, and strategic mountain passes tempted Assyrians, Medes, Persians, and Romans, but the mountainous terrain made permanent conquest difficult. Nor were local leaders any more successful at imposing a unified authority over a wide area. Aristocratic dynasties (*naxarar*, pl. *naxarark'*) dominated local cantons, and Armenian lands remained notorious for brigandage into the nineteenth century.[5]

As the northernmost people sandwiched between the eastern Roman empire and the Persian kingdom, Armenians sometimes could use the near-continuous Roman-Persian conflicts of antiquity to their own advantage, but often had little role in the fate of their communities. The ruling dynasty of Armenia from A.D. 66 to 428 was a branch of the Parthian royal family (the Arsacids), and a local form of Zoroastrianism was the dominant religion.[6] The Armenians used a Persian palette to paint their world; their early literature depicts an aristocratic Iranian society of hunts and banquets.[7] The influence of the Greco-Roman Mediterranean world, however, grew from the first century B.C., when Tigranes II (the Great) conquered much of Syria, Mesopotamia, and Cappadocia. His capital, Tigranocerta, had a Greek theater for the performance of plays, and the king encouraged Greek philosophers to settle in his capital, as intellectual adornments to match the city's Hellenistic architecture.[8] Ties to the Roman empire were further strengthened when King Tiridates III converted to Christianity in 314,[9] encouraging the Christianization of Armenia that legendarily began with the apostles Bartholomew and Thaddeus. Local cults and Zoroastrianism competed for a time, but by the sixth century Armenian identity had become linked to Christianity. While Christianity in Armenia felt the impact of both Greek and Syriac influences, it quickly developed an autonomous hierarchy and distinct traditions. The Armenian patriarchate initially rested in the hands of a single family, the descendants of St. Gregory the Illuminator, from the patriarchate's institution in the early fourth century to the death of Gregory's great-great-great-grandson in 437/9.

The later fourth century saw the return of Armenia to Persian influence. A Persian victory in 363 over the Romans, resulting in the death of the Roman emperor Julian, led to a Persian invasion of Armenian lands. The armies of the shah subsequently razed many cities established under Roman influence and exiled the Armenian king Arsak II to Persia, where he committed suicide. In 387, Emperor Theodosius I and the Sassanian King of Kings Shapur III signed a treaty that formally divided Armenia between the two empires, an event that René Grousset compared to the signing of the Treaty of Verdun for the extraordinary duration of its effects.[10] The end of the Armenian kingship and the continuation of hostilities between Rome and

Ctesiphon left Armenians buffeted by two storms, whose swells and gales pushed in conflicting directions.

Armenian society was further isolated from the Romans by the theological disputes of the fifth century concerning the relationship of divine and human characteristics in Jesus, which culminated in the declaration of the ecumenical council of Chalcedon in 451 that Christ existed in two natures "without confusion, without change, without division, without separation." Many Armenians did not accept the definition of faith formulated at Chalcedon, for few Armenians participated in its deliberations. Only five months before the council, many of the Armenian clergy and aristocracy had been defeated in a rebellion against the Persians, who were attempting to impose Zoroastrianism on the portion of Armenia under their control. The Persian forces crushed the Armenian resistance on the plains of Avarayr (north of Lake Urmia in what is now northwest Iran) on 26 May 451. Many of the clergy were executed, and noble *naxarar* families wiped out.[11] However, the Armenian church did not entirely reject "Chalcedonianism."[12] Even under Persian control, the Armenian church continued to have contact with imperial Christianity, but Jacobite and Nestorian thought also had an impact on Armenian theology.[13] After the loss of the Arsacid monarchy, separation from the Roman Christian tradition, and the defeat of 451, the fourth century became in retrospective the golden era in Armenian memory, when kings converted to Christianity, inspired theologians taught the true faith to the entire Christian world, and the line between East and West did not run directly over them.

Jacobites and Melkites Under Muslim Rule

In the summer of 636, the emperor Heraklios sent a large Byzantine army south to Syria to protect the region from Arabs raiding from the south. Exhausted by a long struggle for survival against Persia that had already devastated Syria and Palestine, the Byzantines were now unprepared to face a new opponent—the Muslims—invigorated with the confidence of the newly proselytized, for it had only been four years since the prophet Muhammad had died in Medina. Islamic armies quickly conquered Byzantine Egypt, Palestine, Syria, and Mesopotamia, and soon afterward defeated the Persian Empire. Within two decades, most Jacobite and Nestorian communities had come under Islamic rule, as had three of the four eastern patriarchates of the imperial church—Antioch, Jerusalem, and Alexandria, leaving only Constantinople still under Byzantine rule. The Muslim conquest also brought into being a new Christian community, the Melkites. Unlike the Jacobites, Armenians, or Nestorians, the Melkites remained in communion with the patriarch of Constantinople, but their immersion in a new Islamic world made them distinctive from the Byzantine communities with whom they shared theology and religious practices.[14]

Under Islamic law, Christians joined Jews, Zoroastrians, and the mysterious Sabians[15] as religious communities given protected status of *dhimma*, a word which signifies the contract of hospitality and protection extended by the Islamic community. Although different regimes may have been in place in different areas, especially in the first century of Islamic rule, essential was the stipulation that *dhimmi* communities must pay the *jizya*, a tax representing their subordinate status and the superiority of Islamic authority. In addition, relations between Christians and Muslims were governed by what came to be known as the Pact of 'Umar, which claimed to be a letter written by the Christian community of Jerusalem to Caliph 'Umar (634–44), but which probably developed in the ninth or tenth century. The pact enjoined that Christians could not build new churches, restore old ones, dress like Muslims, or hold public religious ceremonies, along with a host of other restrictions that often were not enforced, but could be used against Christians when Muslim authorities felt it necessary.[16]

Melkite communities of the Middle East struggled to understand how a Christian empire could be defeated by infidels, as the permanence of the Arab victory became apparent.[17] No longer could they feel superior to pagans and Jews and praise God as King David had in the Psalms, knowing "that you love me I know by this, that my enemy does not triumph over me, but because of my integrity you sustain me and I stand before you forever" (Ps. 41.12–13). Yet Melkite communities adapted rapidly to the realities of their new Islamic world. By the early ninth century, Syriac and Arabic became the written and liturgical languages of choice, as Melkite communities relinquished the Greek traditions that were part of a vanishing Hellenistic Near East, and joined a vigorous new Islamic intellectual world. Levantine cities such as Jerusalem and Antioch and the regions around them were centers for the largest Melkite communities; but the intellectual heart of the Melkites beat in the Judean desert monasteries, most famously at Mar Saba, home to titans of theology such as John of Damascus (c. 676–749), who wrote largely in Greek, and Theodore Abu Qurrah (c. 750–c. 825), who wrote in Arabic. These and other Melkite philosophers and theologians (as well as

Jacobites and Nestorians) participated in a shared intellectual culture based on the power and expressiveness of the Arabic language, the demands of rationalist argument, known as *kalam*, and the belief in the value of applying it to religious belief.[18]

Despite intellectual exchange and still-wealthy ecclesiastical institutions, Melkites did experience a darker side to Islamic rule. The flourishing of stories of Christians, often apostates or converts from Islam, being executed for publicly advocating Christianity speaks to a sense of resentment.[19] Christian churches and monasteries were sometimes subject to attacks and pillage, and Islamic authorities were often disinclined to allow reconstruction. Even the monastery of Mar Saba came under attack several times; in 797 the monastery was sacked and twenty monks were killed.[20]

Jacobites also flourished in the early centuries of Islamic rule, at least as far as monastic and theological sources allow us to understand.[21] The Muslim conquest allowed many communities to escape periodic imperial persecution; the caliph cared little about the Council of Chalcedon and largely sought to ensure the smooth governance of the newly acquired territories. Evidence from monasteries such as Qartmin, in the Tur 'Abdin, suggests that the faithful continued to donate land and gold to the monasteries.[22] Like the Melkites, the Jacobites participated in the lively intellectual culture of the early Islamic empire. Yahya ibn 'Adi (893–974) was a Jacobite from Takrit who studied in Baghdad with a famous Nestorian philosopher (Abu Bishr Matta ibn Yunus, 870–940) and an equally well-known Muslim philosopher (Abu Nasr al-Farabi, c. 870–950). Ibn 'Adi became an influential translator of Greek and Syriac works into Arabic, as well as a theologian and philosopher. His book *Tahdhib al-aklaq*, a nonsectarian treatise on morals, led the Muslim intellectual al-Shahrastani (d. 1153) to include ibn 'Adi among the philosophers of Islam.[23]

Yet the relative tolerance of 'Abbasid authority also brought complications to Jacobite communities. Changing provincial and administrative boundaries, as when Roman Mesopotamia became caliphal Jazira, led to disputes within the community over ecclesiastical jurisdiction. Different factions appealed to caliphal authority for support, sometimes even having their opponents imprisoned, as happened to the patriarch George in 767.[24] Monasteries such as Qartmin in the east and Qenneshre in the west, once dominant in distinct regions separated by the Roman-Persian border, now competed for influence in the church hierarchy, leading to further schisms and controversy.

Armenians Under Muslim Rule

Just as in Damascus and Antioch, where Melkite Christians manned the new Islamic empire's administration as their fathers had done for the Byzantines, the initial Islamic conquest of Armenia had little impact on local political structures. Aristocratic families preserved their lands, the right to tax, and the right to bear arms. An attempted Byzantine reconquest of Armenia at the end of the seventh century, however, ushered in decades of conflict that devastated Armenian lands. After the final Muslim reconquest and a subsequent series of local rebellions in the early eighth century, Armenians lost their self-governing status. The autonomy that had existed under the Umayyad caliphs vanished beneath a lachrymose catalogue of taxes, executions, and devastation throughout the eighth century. Revolts, particularly in 703, 747/8, and 774/5 (the largest), led to the disappearance of several *naxarar* families and the settlement of Arab colonists in many areas.

Armenians regained much of their political independence in the late ninth century, as the power of the 'Abbasid caliphate declined and Byzantine forces grew stronger. Ashot I Bagratuni received the title "prince of princes" from Caliph Mutawakkil in 861, and when the patriarch Kevork II crowned Ashot king in 884, both the caliph and the Byzantine emperor eagerly recognized his self-proclaimed rank. The disappearance of a number of *naxarar* dynasties in the eighth century concentrated political power in the hands of a few aristocratic families; the Bagratuni and the Artsruni dynasties became particularly influential.[25] Other Caucasian principalities also gained independence, sometimes under Armenian "protection"; a Georgian branch of the Bagratuni family ruled Tayk', an important area north of Karin (ancient Theodosiopolis, modern Erzurum).[26] In neighboring Georgia the caliph appointed a Bagratuni prince to help control rebellious Arab emirs, such as the ruler of Tblisi.[27]

While Melkites and Jacobites participated in the bureaucratic systems of both the Byzantine empire and the young Islamic caliphate, Armenians clung tenaciously to an older system.[28] Political authority flowed through channels of kinship, alliance, and patronage. As in Ireland in the same era, power was maintained through war, raiding, and generosity to one's dependents, as well as through pursuit of blood feuds. Despite centuries of Hellenistic and Roman influence, Armenia remained a land largely without cities. Those that did exist, such as Partaw and Dvin, remained under Arab control long after Armenian lords had reoccupied the fertile valleys and stark hilltops of the Armenian countryside.[29] Bagratuni and Artsruni rulers built churches to glorify their piety and authority in small villages or rural areas, rarely in cities.[30]

The Armenian church maintained ties with other Christian communities under Islamic rule, and the ambiguous theological position of the Armenian church—neither Chalcedonian nor solely miaphysite—encouraged Melkites and Jacobites to ensure that the Armenians did not stray into the opposite camp. The Melkite theologian Theodore Abu Qurrah visited Ashot Msaker (d. 826), a Bagratuni prince, to lead him to drink from Melkite waters, but his visit provoked the Jacobite theologian Abu Ra'ita to send his disciple Nonnus of Nisibis to counter Theodore's Melkite propaganda. Nonnus was evidently the more persuasive of the two, and spent some years at the Armenian court as what Sidney Griffith called "a scholar-in-residence."[31]

Even with the reemergence of the Armenian kingship in the ninth century, Armenians maintained a complex relationship of alliance and aggression with caliphal authority in Baghdad. An Arab governor (the *ostikan*) continued to reside in Partaw or Dvin, who, although nominally representative of the caliph, often allied with Armenian princes against local rivals or against the central authority of the caliph. While dynastic chroniclers cast their Armenian patrons as holy warriors defending an embattled Christian community, in reality the Bagratunis and others were eager to keep in the caliph's good graces—most of the time. Arabic and Islamic names such as Hasan and Ablgharib became popular among the nobility. Armenians had shared their cultural world with Byzantines and Muslims for centuries, and the danger from within their own communities—from religious, political, and dynastic rivals—was often a greater source of worry than the Byzantines or Muslims.

The Tenth-Century Revival

Like the Cappadocian hero Basil Digenes, who, "taking many cities and lands of the unruly, chose to make his dwelling by the Euphrates,"[32] Armenians, Byzantines, and Jacobites in the tenth century came once again to settle in Syria and Mesopotamia under Christian sovereignty. Byzantine armies, manned with Armenian soldiers and allied with Armenian aristocrats,[33] were victorious against Muslim armies, conquering territories that had been under Muslim rule for over three hundred years. As a result, the Byzantine Empire in the early eleventh century enjoyed power and breadth of territory unmatched since the age of Justinian.

Armenians played a major role both in the Byzantine army and as allies, and their participation in the reconquest led to widespread Armenian settlement in the conquered areas. Mleh, an Armenian in Byzantine service, established the tenth-century theme (a Byzantine military province) of Lykandos on lands in Cappadocia conquered from the Muslims, and resettled it largely with Armenians.[34] The Byzantine general John Kourkuas (also of Armenian ancestry)[35] captured Melitene from its local Arab emir in 934, and demanded that the population either convert to Christianity or leave. The emirate of Kalikala (ancient Theodosiopolis, modern Erzurum in northeastern Turkey) fell in 949, and its Muslim population was replaced by Armenians and Greeks. The pace of conquest quickened between 955 and 972 as Nikephoras Phokas conquered Samosata in 958 and Germanikeia (Marash) in 962. Campaigning in Cilicia (the southern coast of modern Turkey) in 964 and 965 brought Adana and Tarsus back into the empire, and drove out much of the Muslim population of the area. Antioch, the ancient capital of Syria, succumbed to Byzantine siege in 969, and the Hamdanid emir of Aleppo agreed to pay tribute. In 975, John Tzimiskes, yet another general and emperor of Armenian descent, led his armies to capture Baalbek, Beirut, and Byblos in what is now Lebanon, and received the submission of the city of Damascus, once home of the caliphs.[36]

As a result of this Byzantine-Armenian cooperation, many of the areas reconquered from the Arabs in the tenth century were settled by Armenians. Al-Muqaddasi, a Muslim geographer from Palestine, noted that the Amanus Mountains north of Antioch were inhabited entirely by Armenians in his own day (c. 985),[37] and the eleventh-century Armenian historian Step'anos Taronets'i (Stephen of Taron) recorded the establishment of Armenian bishoprics in cities such as Tarsus in Cilicia and Antioch in the eleventh century, due to the numbers of Armenians who had migrated there during the Byzantine reconquest.[38] Jacobites also participated in Byzantine resettlement in Cappadocia and northern Syria, settling particularly in the area around Melitene. By the time of Basil II (d. 1025), many Jacobites of Melitene had grown wealthy from trade throughout the Levant and Mesopotamia. One family, the Banu Abu Imran, was wealthy enough to finance an imperial field army on the eastern frontier for an entire winter. Jacobite and Melkite Christians became officials in Byzantine administration of frontier areas, and even officials sent from Constantinople were reluctant to interfere in local affairs.[39] The Armenian kingdoms flourished as well; five kingdoms jockeyed for power in the Armenian highlands—Ani, Kars, and Lori were ruled by

Bagratuni dynasties, while Vaspurakan, between Lake Van and Lake Urmia, prospered under the powerful Artsrunis, and Siwnik', southeast of Lake Sevan, was ruled by its eponymous dynasty.

Melkite communities who remained under Muslim rule did not fare so well in this period, particularly those in Palestine.[40] The persecutions of the Fatimid caliph al-Hakim, beginning in 1009, undermined the Christian communities in Syria and Palestine through executions, taxes, discriminatory laws, and the demolition of dozens of Christian churches across Fatimid territory. Shrines such as the Holy Sepulcher in Jerusalem, St. George in Lydda, and many others were completely destroyed or suffered serious damage. While the monastery of Mar Saba escaped destruction, it was no longer the intellectual center it had been. Jacobite monasteries in Mesopotamia, on the other hand, were buoyed by the prosperity of their coreligionists in Melitene and elsewhere on the Byzantine frontiers. While the poverty of their monastery had forced the monks of Qartmin to abandon the use of the Estrangelo script by the end of the ninth century, finding that its elegant orthography required more parchment than the abbey could afford, by the turn of the millennium the script was back in use as the monastery enjoyed a financial revival.[41]

The Christian communities of Syria, Palestine, and Mesopotamia faced a changed cultural world in the tenth and eleventh centuries. The emergence of the Fatimid caliphate, first in North Africa, then in Egypt and Syria, effectively split the Islamic world in two. As the 'Abbasid caliphs lost the power to control their wide domains, military dynasties stepped in to fill the void—first the Buyids, followed by the Seljuk Turks in the eleventh century. Both dynasties came from cultural traditions quite different from those that had dominated the caliphal court previously. The Buyids came from the southern Caspian region of Daylam, an area that converted to Islam relatively late and claimed strong real or created connections to the pre-Islamic Persian past. Buyids as well as many other Daylamis converted to Shi'a Islam, in part as an expression of opposition to the 'Abbasid caliphs. Although the Buyids did not replace the 'Abbasids with a Shi'a caliphate when they came to power, they favored Persian over Arabic and patronized Shi'a clergy. The Seljuks, who took control of the Islamic Middle East in the eleventh century, were recent converts to Sunni Islam, and when they learned a language other than their native Turkish, it was more likely to be Persian than Arabic. No longer was Arabic a lingua franca that crossed religious boundaries, and Melkite and Jacobite Christians found it more difficult to participate in the intellectual world of which they had once been a part. Particularly under the Seljuks, Islam replaced Arabic as the primary common denominator of the communities united under their rule. Thus Christians, once so prominent in the caliphal court and bureaucracy, played little role in Seljuk governance or intellectual life.[42] In contrast, Christians (and Jews) in Fatimid areas continued to fill important roles within the government.

To Be or Not Be: Byzantine Annexation

Byzantine expansion in Syria and Mesopotamia ended under Basil II (976–1025), who established a new policy toward the empire's eastern frontiers. The last century's conquests had, in Basil's eyes, dangerously empowered the aristocratic families who had provided the bulk of the generals and troops for victory. Basil therefore made peace with the Fatimid caliphate of Egypt, gaining a somewhat demilitarized border in Syria. This allowed Basil to direct his attention toward the Balkans, where his victories increased imperial power, rather than benefiting ambitious aristocratic families. Ending the alliance between Armenian and Byzantine aristocrats, which had been the engine of Byzantine expansion, was crucial to his enterprise. Basil embarked on an ambitious program to encourage Armenian princes to ally with imperial interests, rather than with those of Byzantine nobles. Offering titles and lands within the empire (often seized from his aristocratic enemies), Basil cajoled and threatened many Armenian kings to accept his offers.

Some annexations were punitive. Basil II successfully annexed the large territories of the Armenian prince David Bagratuni of Tayk' after his death in 1021 as punishment for David's support of the revolt of the Byzantine aristocrat Bardas Skleros in 987. The first to accept his offer willingly was King Senek'erim of Vaspurakan in 1021, who received Cappadocian territories around Sebasteia and Caesarea in return for his kingdom.[43] The next year King Hovhannes willed his kingdom of Ani to the empire, though the resistance of his nephew Gagik II, who eventually accepted lands in Cappadocia as compensation for his lost inheritance, delayed the annexation until 1045.[44] The last to be annexed was the kingdom of Kars, surrendered by King Gagik only in 1067. He received Tzmandos in recompense, where his daughter Maria continued to rule until sometime after 1078.[45]

Although some resisted Byzantine domination, many Armenian leaders often found being an imperial client an appealing option, for beginning in 1029 Turkish groups exploiting power vacuums in Iran began raiding across Iraq and into Armenia.[46] One anonymous continuator of an Arstruni chronicle, writing in the twelfth century, was delighted by the annexation, remembering Basil as a "God-loving and pious man" under whose leadership the Byzantines, "filled with divine love, had compassion for the appeal of their children, and summoned them from their various provinces. They gave them gifts, appointed them at the royal court, gave them great cities in exchange for their cities, and in return for their castles, impregnable fortresses and provinces, villages, estates, and holy hermitages."[47] On the other hand, the Armenian cleric and historian Aristakes Lastivertts'i (d. 1070s), who chronicled the disasters of the Turkish invasion of Armenia and Anatolia in the mid-eleventh century, depicted in gory detail the destruction and murder that Basil II's invasion of Tayk' in 1021 visited upon the civilian population,[48] but also condemned Armenian princes such as Gagik of Ani for "timidity" and "lacking a mature spirit."[49] Matthew of Edessa, writing in the twelfth century under Frankish rule, saw the annexations as manifestations of Satan's growing power; both cowardly Armenian princes and avaricious Byzantine emperors were his pawns. Others, like the priest Gregory who believed this to be "the age of the servitude of the Armenians," felt only the sting of exile.[50]

The ease of the annexations, however, suggests that there was in fact little elite resistance, though the city of Ani did reject Byzantine rule and surrendered only when King Gagik II would not return; "they recognized the perfidiousness of the Armenian lords."[51] The annexations did not necessarily mean that proud aristocrats had to bend their necks to the yoke of Byzantine authority. Once organized into Byzantine themes, many of the annexed areas were still ruled by Armenians, although appointed by Constantinople. Gregory Magistros, member of the illustrious Pahlavuni family and once a leading nobleman in the kingdom of Ani, became the imperial *doux* (administrator of a large province) of Mesopotamia, and in 1051 became *doux* of Vaspurakan and Taron.[52] The Armenian dynasts who settled around Sebasteia and Caesarea were similarly granted imperial authority in their districts, receiving appointments as *strategoi* (administrator of a theme).[53] These annexations capitalized on the fissile nature of Armenian society, encouraging aristocrats long accustomed to turning to Constantinople or Baghdad for support to encourage and demand the integration of the Armenian lands into the empire.[54]

The Battle of Mantzikert and Its Aftermath, 1071–1097

The retreat of Armenian princes to strongholds in the heart of the Byzantine empire did not in the end protect them from the Turks, for the newcomers had become more than nomadic raiders—they were the new masters of the Islamic world. The Seljuk leader Toghrul-Beg entered Baghdad in 1055 as the protector of the caliph and gained the title "sultan"; his military domination was thus transmuted officially into delegated caliphal authority. Though his eponymous grandfather Seljuk was born a pagan, Toghrul-Beg now ruled the heartland of Islam, from cities such as Bukhara, perched on the edge of the great central Asian steppes, to the ancient Syrian cities of Damascus and Aleppo. Byzantine territory was a convenient source of plunder, and a useful distraction for the Turkmen warriors who might otherwise seek to elevate a new sultan just as they had elevated him. In 1059, Toghrul-Beg's nephew Alp Arslan sacked Sebasteia, the new home of the Artsruni dynasty; Caesarea, also ruled by the Artsrunis, fell in 1067. Many Armenians fled south to Syria and Cilicia, swelling the already considerable Armenian population there.[55]

On 26 August 1071, a large Byzantine army met the forces of the Seljuk sultan Alp Arslan outside the Armenian town of Mantzikert.[56] The Byzantine emperor Romanos IV Diogenes was a vigorous military leader, determined to put an end to the destructive Turkish raids into central Anatolia. He gathered an impressive army, augmented by Armenians and Frankish mercenaries, as well as Uzes, a Turkic people who lived on Byzantium's western border in what is now Romania. Although the Byzantine forces were numerically superior, Romanos did not have the full support of his aristocratic generals or some of the mercenaries. In the ensuing battle the Turkish forces triumphed, capturing the emperor. The defeat left Armenia, Anatolia, and areas farther west poorly defended. Alp Arslan, however, had little interest in a permanent conquest of Byzantine territory; he hoped only to arrange a settlement so that he might turn his attention to the great prize of the eastern Mediterranean—Egypt. The Turkmen forces that made up his troops, however, had different intentions. They could not overlook the evident opportunities for more raids and plunder in Anatolia, Cilicia, and Syria, and as a result ignored the truces and peace agreements Alp Arslan negotiated. The Seljuk sultan, for his part, was not unhappy to see his restless warriors distracted in Byzantine lands; it lessened the likelihood that they might devote their attention to his own territories. As a result a number of Turkish principalities, which owed only nominal loyalty to the Seljuk sultans, were established in Anatolia and Asia Minor by 1090.

The disaster at Mantzikert was a defeat, but not a massacre; considerable numbers of Byzantine troops and mercenaries remained active, though not under a unified imperial command. Some remained loyal to Romanos IV Diogenes, others to his stepson Michael VII Doukas, who had been elevated to the throne when word of Romanos's capture reached Constantinople. Others turned to the defense of local areas around Melitene, Edessa, Antioch, and Tarsus, where military warlords, Armenian aristocrats, and ambitious mercenaries vied for control over the cities and countryside stripped of Byzantine troops, even as Turkish war bands were sweeping farther and farther west toward Constantinople.[57] The Christian communities of Anatolia, Cilicia, and northern Syria grew accustomed to such military forces, nominally associated with Byzantine authority but of heterogeneous ethnic origin, establishing themselves as local powerbrokers, and perhaps defending local communities from Turkish attack. They were not so different, in the end, from the troops that occupied the area when it was a Byzantine frontier some fifty years earlier.

Philaretos

One of the most successful of the Christian warlords to emerge after the battle of Mantzikert was the Armenian Philaretos, a former Byzantine general.[58] The principality he established in Syria and Cilicia covered roughly the same area as the later Frankish territories of Antioch and Edessa, and his achievements are a powerful reminder that the crusaders filled a need already evident among the beleaguered Christian communities of the Levant. Philaretos was not seen by these communities as someone intent on establishing an independent principality, but rather as one who was securing a shaky border area which might later come under direct Byzantine administration. The traces of this quasi-Byzantine authority can be seen in the way other military leaders in the area accepted Philaretos's authority. Under his leadership, a Frankish mercenary, named Rmbarat in Matthew of Edessa, led a troop of westerners numbering eight hundred men who were considered one of the more potent military forces in the area.[59] With troops of that number, Rmbarat (perhaps the Armenian version of the French name Raimbaud, or perhaps referring to the Norman mercenary Roussel de Bailleul) would have been able to carve out a principality for himself—Baldwin of Boulogne did so twenty years later with only two hundred horsemen—but instead Rmbarat chose to serve under Philaretos. Basil Apokapes, another former Byzantine army officer, also chose to serve under Philaretos.[60] Basil had even greater opportunities to rule independently than Rmbarat. His father, Abukab (in Greek, Apokapes), had served in the Byzantine army and was *doux* of Edessa from 1032 to 1033,[61] and Matthew of Edessa praised him as "a benevolent and pious man, compassionate toward orphans and widows, and a benefactor and conciliator of people."[62] Yet he too chose to rule Edessa on Philaretos's behalf.

Philaretos's attempt to carve out a principality of his own not only foreshadowed the success of the crusaders but also facilitated it. Philaretos absorbed other warlords into his forces, undermined surviving Armenian dynasties,[63] and fragmented the power of the Armenian church through schism.[64] His death left a vast stretch of Christian territory leaderless shortly before the arrival of the First Crusade. This loss of leadership led local communities to look elsewhere; the chronicler Matthew had little praise for any Christian after the death of Gagik of Ani until the arrival of the crusaders, but instead looked to the Seljuk sultan Malik-Shah as a protector of Christians, declaring that "this sultan's heart was filled with benevolence, gentleness, and compassion for Christians."[65] Similarly, he considered the emir Isma'il, Malik-Shah's brother-in-law, to be "a benefactor of all the Armenians, moreover, he was an embellisher of monasteries and a supporter of monks, besides which he protected the [Christian] faithful against harassment from the Persians."[66]

Philaretos's loss of power in 1086/7, however, did not mean the end of local Christian political power and the untrammeled ascendancy of the Turks. While Antioch, the largest Christian city in northern Syria, fell to the Seljuks in 1084/5, a number of Greeks, Armenians, and Jacobites, some of whom may have served under Philaretos, seized control of regional cities and strongholds. A Greek named T'oros[67] seized power in Edessa after a short Turkish occupation. Melitene was ruled by the *kouropalates* Gabriel, an Armenian whose daughter was married to T'oros, while an Armenian lord named Constantine held Gargar (near Samosata). The fortress of Shaizar in the Orontes valley was controlled by unnamed bishop "in the name of the Romans."[68] Oshin and Levon held castles in the Taurus Mountains of Cilicia, Ablgharib in al-Bira, the three sons of the Jacobite Sanbil around Samosata, and the Armenian Kogh Vasil in K'esun.

After a century as a Byzantine frontier, followed by the disaster of Mantzikert, Turkish invasions, and the rule of Philaretos, Christian communities in northern Syria had lost much of their internal cohesion. Religious and traditional elites were scattered or forced into new roles. Towns and villages grew accustomed to a frontier mentality where political and military authority were synonymous and often invested in warlords with only the most tenuous claim to legitimacy beyond brute force. In such a world, soldiers, aristocrats, doctors, priests, and monks found religious and ethnic divisions of little significance, and Byzantine, Turkish, or warlord rule looked relatively similar. While permeability had been characteristic of religious communities even under the 'Abbasids, the devastations of the eleventh century had destroyed or undermined the religious and aristocratic elites who could provide a sense of cohesion for Christian communities.

Contact and Knowledge Between Eastern and Western Christians

Philaretos's ephemeral lordship thus prepared the way militarily and politically for the arrival of the crusaders. But how did local Christian communities view the arrival of these western armies? Some sources of the twelfth century, that is, after the capture of Jerusalem and the settlement of the Franks, emphasize the cataclysmic, even apocalyptic, effect that the arrival of the armies of the First Crusade had. The story of the *vardapet* Hovhannes Kozern recounted at the beginning of this chapter is but one example of the dramatic drumbeats used to describe the *adventus crucesignatorum*. However, this language reflected a retrospective and polemic interpretation placed upon the events by Matthew of Edessa, who knew how the arrival of the crusaders would affect the political and religious map of the Levant. In many ways the crusaders fit easily into existing paradigms of political and cultural life that had developed through the experiences of the eleventh century. Many towns and villages were already adapted to the arrival of large Byzantine, and more recently, Turkish armies moving swiftly through their territory. Nor was the fact that this army was largely western in composition particularly different. Although Franks appear infrequently in Armenian and Jacobite chronicles written before the First Crusade, Greek sources and post-crusade Armenian chronicles make it clear that Frankish individuals and troops were common in the eastern borderlands of Byzantium.

Westerners in Armenian Histories

It is striking how little interest Armenian and other local Christian chroniclers displayed in western Europe or its inhabitants prior to the crusades.

Their disinterest was not due to a lack of contact. Many Armenians traveled to Latin Europe—three bishops even participated in the evangelization of Iceland in the eleventh century[69]—and a number of Armenian holy men and bishops traveled to, or resided in, western Europe in the tenth century, such as Simon of Polirone, who settled in a monastery near Mantua.[70] Yet none of them recorded their experiences and impressions, or returned to share them with Armenian chroniclers.

The few instances where Latins are mentioned in pre-crusade Armenian texts usually concern the historical or ecclesiastical events of Late Antiquity, an era to which Armenians looked for historiographic inspiration. Biblical and early ecclesiastical histories depended on Eusebius of Caesarea, but used only those parts that concerned the eastern world. Step'anos Taronets'i (Stephen of Taron, fl. 1000) wrote his *Universal History* at the end of the tenth century. His first book established chronologies based on the Old Testament and classical history; Roman emperors appear briefly between a discussion of the Maccabees and the Assyrian monarchs, and again when their activities intersected with events occurring in the Near East, such as Julius Caesar's invasion of Egypt.[71] His second book covered classical and Late Antique history, and again the only Latin elements are brief mentions of Roman emperors such as Diocletian. His third book is the most often utilized by historians, as it discussed events contemporary with the author, a period for which there are relatively few other sources. In this section, Stephen mentioned Rome (or western Europe) only twice; and both are in a letter from the *kat'olikos* of Armenia to the Greek bishop of Sebasteia discussing the theology of Christ's nature.[72]

Not only did Armenian chroniclers show little interest in Latin Europe, they were ignorant of Latin history and traditions. Movses Daskhurants'i (fl. tenth or eleventh century), the attributed author or editor of an Armenian history of the Caucasian Albanians, believed the see of Rome was founded by the evangelist Luke.[73] Yet the name "Rome" conferred an air of legitimacy and authority. Movses stated that the prestige of the books brought from Rome by the bishop of Siwnik' was enough to make the bishopric the third-ranked in all Armenia.[74]

In the account of Aristakes Lastivertts'i, Latin Europe and its inhabitants entirely disappear, although Frankish mercenaries were a significant presence in Byzantine armies at the time. Armenians remained rooted in an eastern-focused history, where Rome hardly interrupted the continuity of Babylon, Assyria, the Israelite patriarchs, the Persian Empire, and the caliphs.

Yahya of Antioch, a Melkite Christian writing in Arabic in the mid-eleventh century, had little more to say about the West. A relative of the tenth-century patriarch of Alexandria, Eutychios, also a historian, Yahya began his chronicle with a list of recent patriarchs of the Christian world, but admitted that he was uncertain about the sequence of the patriarchs of the West—that is the bishops of Rome.[75] In the rest of his history, Yahya mentioned Latins or western Europe only once, when Amalfitan merchants in Cairo were massacred in a riot at the end of the tenth century.[76] Even the voluminous chronicle of Michael the Great (d. 1199), patriarch of the Jacobite church, which drew on earlier Syriac chronicles, rarely had anything to say about western Europe.

In contrast to these accounts, Matthew of Edessa's chronicle, written after the First Crusade, is flooded with Franks, even in the portions of his account narrating pre-crusade history. As he did with the prophecy of Hovhannes Kozern, Matthew sought to write the Franks into the sacred and secular history of the Levant. The Franks thus appear as proto-crusaders—fearless, pious, and violent, like the nameless Frank in the army of Basil Apokapes who valiantly burned down the Turkish catapult that was threatening the Armenian town of Mantzikert in 1054/5, saying "I will go forth and burn down that catapult, and today my blood shall be shed for all the Christians."[77] A sentiment worthy of a crusader indeed. For Aristakes and other chroniclers who wrote before the First Crusade, Franks were a common but unremarkable part of the human landscape. Only after living under Frankish rule for decades did Matthew come to see western Christians as more than Byzantine mercenaries.

Western Views of the Levant and Levantine Christians

In contrast, the societies in Latin Europe who would supply the vast numbers of crusaders in 1096 had intense interest in the eastern world. This interest was stimulated in three ways: by the long tradition of pilgrimage to the Holy Land, by the position Constantinople held as one of the largest cities of the Christian world, and by interest in the military and religious threat of Islam. While the Levant, its cities and shrines appear frequently in western chronicles, eastern Christians do not. Accounts of the Levant in eleventh-century northern French sources demonstrate that interest and knowledge of the eastern Church was scant.[78] Many knew of Constantinople as a beautiful and wealthy city full of holy relics, and as the residence of the Byzantine Emperor, it was also a locus of power and prestige.

Although Constantinople was famous, the city itself was better respected than the citizens therein. French chroniclers rarely mentioned individual Byzantines, even emperors, and when they did, the descriptions were rarely complimentary. The eleventh-century Burgundian chronicler Ralph Glaber mentioned Byzantium only three times in his history: the first mention was purely historical, referring to the division of the Roman empire between the two capitals, the second castigated Byzantine attempts at reconquest in Calabria and Apulia in the early 1020s and 30s, and the last condemned an attempt by the patriarch of Constantinople to be recognized as an equal of Rome. Although Glaber accused the Byzantines of the sin of "superbia,"[79] he never mentioned the liturgical and doctrinal issues that were occasionally such a stumbling block between the two churches. Indeed, Glaber gave no description of the Byzantine empire or its church. Was this because he assumed that his readers knew all about them, or because he did not consider the differences between Latins and Greeks important enough to comment upon, or because he was unaware of them? In contrast, Muslims received more attention and also a brief, though inaccurate description of their religious beliefs and how they differed from Christianity.[80] Non-Byzantine eastern Christians appear only once, when monks came from the monastery at Sinai to receive Richard II of Normandy's largesse, a story that also shows up in Adhemar of Chabannes.[81] Neither Adhemar nor Ralph suggested that the monks of Sinai were any different from the other monks who came to Richard's court, other than in the exotic location of their monastery. A similar pattern appeared in other French chronicles of the eleventh century. Such ignorance or disinterest is also found at the royal level; the French monarchy, unlike the German emperors, did not have any significant diplomatic contact with the Byzantine empire in the eleventh century.[82]

Chroniclers in other areas, particularly southern Italy, had more contact with the Byzantine and Levantine world, and correspondingly displayed more interest in and knowledge of societies and events in the East. The historian Amatus of Montecassino, writing in the great southern Italian monastery sometime between 1078 and 1086, knew something of the death of emperor Romanos IV Diogenes and the usurpation by his stepson, but believed the Greeks had "the habit of defeating their enemies through malicious ratiocination and subtle treachery," and in war were "weak as women,"[83] images of Greeks that were widespread in western Europe. Some communities in southern Italy remained predominately Orthodox, even after the last Byzantine holdout there, the city of Bari, fell to the Normans in 1071. The

Normans from southern Italy who joined the crusade thus had significantly more familiarity with Byzantine culture and religious traditions than those coming from northern France.

Even in sources where the Byzantines appear frequently, Jacobites, Armenians, and Nestorians go unmentioned. The various Levantine Christian churches were either elided with Byzantine Christians or ignored altogether. Yet western Europeans were in some ways intimately familiar with the Levant. Pilgrim traffic between the Latin West and Palestine was at an all-time high in the eleventh century. Numerous accounts of these pilgrimages survive in various forms—in chronicles, letters, and even charters. The details of these pilgrimages focused on various aspects of the pilgrimage—the difficulty in reaching Palestine, the hostility of Muslims, and the aid of saints in reaching the pilgrim's goal. One of the largest of the mass pilgrimages of the eleventh century was the one led by Gunther, bishop of Bamburg, in 1065.[84] Leading approximately six thousand Germans, Gunther, his fellow bishops, and their followers were attacked by Arab brigands near Ramla on their way to Jerusalem. The battle between the pilgrims and the highwaymen lasted several days and ended in victory for the pilgrims, after which they continued on to Jerusalem to complete their pilgrimage. Several German annals recorded the events in some detail. All focused on the interactions between the pilgrims and local Muslims, both those who attacked them and those who came to their aid. Local Christians, whom they should have met on their journey south from Lattakia, or in Jerusalem, were never mentioned. The chronicles refer to the local Muslims in various terms—*gens Arabitarum, barbarus*,[85] and *saracenus*.[86] The pilgrims, on the other hand, are referred to generally as *christiani*, leaving the reader with the sense that being Christian was synonymous with being Latin. Chroniclers, or their oral sources, found stories about Muslims, factual or otherwise, more to their taste than those about eastern Christians.

How then would the participants in the First Crusade have viewed the lands and people of the Levant? The discussion over what Urban's intentions were for the military expedition he planned at the Council of Clermont in 1095, and the degree to which that influenced the crusaders, has continued throughout the twentieth century and into the twenty-first.[87] The chronicles, letters, and charters associated with Urban II suggest that the pope had a number of goals in mind for the expedition east: bringing Jerusalem under Christian control, defending the Byzantines against Turkish attacks, liberating eastern Christians from Muslim rule and finding western Christian warriors a legitimate war in which to exercise their talents. It is misleading to mark out the single goal among these that was the "essence" of Urban's plan; each played an integral role. Eastern Christians were perhaps the most ambiguous part. According to Fulcher of Chartres, a likely participant in the Council of Clermont where the crusade was first preached, Urban II urged his audience "to hasten to carry aid to your brethren dwelling in the East, who need your help."[88] For the papacy, the "eastern brethren" of the Latins were the Byzantines. Rome still perched at the edge of the Latin world, and the city's bishops had never forgotten the far more ancient Mediterranean world of which they were still a part. Always conscious of Rome's status as the most honored of the five ancient Christian patriarchates (Rome, Constantinople, Antioch, Jerusalem, and Alexandria), the bishops maintained connections with their eastern brethren as much as possible. Although the schism of 1054 had soured the diplomatic amity of the churches, the unity of the Christian Church continued to be a constant concern for both patriarch and pope.[89]

The eleventh-century papacy, however, had far less independent contact with the patriarchates of Jerusalem or Alexandria, or with the Jacobite or Armenian churches.[90] A letter written by Gregory VII in response to one from the Armenian archbishop of Sivas (ancient Sebasteia), admonishing the Armenian on certain matters of liturgical practices and doctrine, reveals that the pope was not accustomed to receiving letters from the Armenian church (though he urged the archbishop henceforth to remain in frequent contact with Rome), nor was he very familiar with the doctrinal character of the Armenian church.[91] There is no evidence for contact with Jacobites, Copts, or Nestorians.

Urban's understanding of the crusade was not the same as that of the participants. The crusaders themselves, to judge from the charters mortgaging and donating property made out before their departure, focused entirely on the goal of liberating Jerusalem itself. Eastern Christians almost never appear as a part of lay motivation.[92] In part this may be due to vocabulary. The pope, though referring to the Christians of the Byzantine Empire, did not seem to have used the word "Greek" at any point to indicate whom he sought to aid. Although Constantinople was an amazing city, full of riches and wonders, and thus was a place worthy of defense, the "Greeks" had already earned a reputation in the West as being crafty, proud, and working against the interests of those in the West. Often, Urban referred to the "ecclesia" in reference to eastern communities. In his letter to the Flemings, written in December 1095 (within a month of the Council of Clermont), Urban spoke of "the churches of God in eastern parts" under attack, singling out "the Holy City of Christ . . . and its churches." The goal of the crusade, then, was "the liberation of the eastern churches."[93] When Urban ambiguously referred to the "eastern churches," he was referring to the community as a whole: the people, the clergy, an entire Christian society. The lay audience, on the other hand, conditioned by the stories and experiences of pilgrimage, thought not of peoples, such as the unpopular Greeks, but of places, such as Jerusalem, Antioch, and Constantinople, and more specifically of the holy churches in those cities, the buildings themselves and the relics and *loca sancta* they enshrined. As we shall see, this invisibility of local Christians continued to characterize western understanding of the Levant long after the First Crusade.

On the eve of the arrival of the First Crusade in Syria in 1097, local Christian communities were in some ways as prepared as anyone can be for the arrival of large foreign armies. The area had been a frontier or borderland for a century and a half, and had been the tromping ground of Byzantine forces, Seljuk armies, and the war bands of various local lords. The crusaders in this sense were a familiar sight. Yet their familiarity was only in a Levantine context; the conception of holy war that drove the crusaders was unknown. Local Christian communities were thus prepared for the military aspect of the crusaders, but not for the permanence of their presence or for the cultural expectations they brought with them. The crusaders, for their part, arrived in a world with which many of them were familiar through pilgrimage and story, but were focused largely on the sacred geography of Syria and Palestine and were little concerned with Christian communities so long established there. Rough tolerance was thus born out of this combination of conditions—local communities fragmented, isolated, lacking entrenched elites, and foreign occupiers strangely uninterested in the peoples over whom they ruled.

Chapter 2
Close Encounters of the Ambiguous Kind: When Crusaders and Locals Meet

According to the twelfth-century Jacobite chronicler and bishop Basil bar Shumana, his city of Edessa—Urhay in Syriac—was none other than Ur of the Chaldees, founded by Nimrod and birthplace of the biblical patriarch Abraham. "Ur," Basil recognized, was merely an ancient word for "city," and "hay" signified the Chaldeans.[1] The bishop was justifiably proud of Edessa, a city whose people, according to a well-known legend dating to Late Antiquity, believed in the divinity of Jesus before his death and before the citizens of any other city. While western eyes kept Jerusalem in sharp focus, for many eastern Christians "the city," Edessa, sparkled with a brighter light. Edessa's contemporary size and wealth as well as its associations with the remembered origins of the Jacobite and Armenian communities made it a vital center of the Christian Levant.

Most historians of the Latin East have shared the crusader fascination with Jerusalem, and have focused their studies on the Frankish kingdom that shared its name. This is in many ways sensible. The city was the intended destination of the First Crusade; its recovery after Salah al-Din conquered it in 1187 was the motivation for the Third Crusade and most of the major expeditions of the thirteenth century. Jerusalem was the capital of the only Frankish kingdom in the Levant, and its ruler was crowned in the Holy Sepulcher, the holiest shrine in Christendom. The kingdom outlasted all others established in the wake of the First Crusade, and the king served as overlord and protector of the others. The kingdom's army was larger, the land it covered more extensive, and from a historian's perspective, the primary sources concerning it survive in far greater numbers and quality. It is not surprising, then, that the history of the Frankish East is largely synonymous with the history of the Kingdom of Jerusalem.

As alluring as Jerusalem and the story of Frankish rule over Palestine might be, compelling reasons suggest that historians should cast their eyes elsewhere as well. Jerusalem was, despite its surpassing holiness for three religions, a minor city. Acre, Tripoli, and Tyre, coastal cities all, outranked it in commercial importance, and its citadel and fortifications served only to protect itself, without greater strategic significance, unlike the great castles of Krak des Moabites (Kerak) and Krak de Montreal (Shaubak) to the east, and Tell Bashir, al-Bira, or Baghras to the north. It is to Edessa we should turn, as Basil bar Shumana suggests, for the twelfth-century Near East is a different world when viewed from its citadel. The city sits upon the foothills of the Taurus Mountains, which stretch from the Mediterranean Sea east to the towering Caucasus Mountains. From its perch on the boundary between the highlands of Anatolia and the deserts and plains of Syria and Mesopotamia, the Roman empire of Justinian seems not long ago, and the idea that it might still return entirely possible. While Jerusalemites must always keep an anxious eye to the south, for armies marching from oasis to oasis across the northern Sinai from rich and populous Egypt, Edessans knew that armies arrive from the east—from Mosul, Mardin, Baghdad, even far off Khorasan. To the borders of India lay innumerable cities and peoples whose march to the Mediterranean must pass under the walls of Edessa.

The Franks, too, periodically glimpsed this vista; Baldwin, the first king of Jerusalem, titled himself at times "king of Babylon and Asia," and he ruled Edessa before coming to Jerusalem. For the historian of the Latin East as well, the perspective from Edessa is unique. The chronicles, letters, and theological treatises left behind by the Jacobites and Armenians in northern Syria offer an unparalleled opportunity to understand the experience and perspectives of indigenous communities living under Frankish rule, rather than the views of their compatriots writing amid different political and cultural situations in Constantinople, Baghdad, Mosul, Damascus, and Aleppo.

Two chronicles written by local Christians of Edessa illuminate the establishment of the Franks in northern Syria and the position of local communities both before and after their arrival. The first, and better known, is that of Matthew of Edessa, whose annal began in 952/3 and ended in 1136/7 and covered events in Edessa, the Armenian kingdoms of the Caucasus Mountains, and Byzantium as well as the Muslim world. Matthew believed that the complexities of the twelfth-century Levantine world threatened the integrity and survival of Armenian communities, particularly diasporic communities such as the one in Edessa. At the same time, however, Matthew framed his account with apocalyptic prophecies, assuring his readers that the threat of assimilation was as much a sign of Satan's presence on earth as the massacres and sieges suffered by Armenians in the days of the Turkish invasions. As a result, Matthew's portrayal of Armenian interaction with other religious and ethnic groups is paradoxical. When Armenians found themselves attacked and massacred, Matthew saw the hand of Satan. Yet should Armenians mingle with Franks, Byzantines, or Muslims in easygoing camaraderie, Matthew argued that they were equally being led by the wiles of Satan to abandon their ancestral customs and religion. While this might have led Matthew to assume uniform hostility towards non-Armenians, in fact it allowed him to be uncommitted to any particular image of Byzantines, Franks, and Muslims; each appears as ally, friend, persecutor, and enemy with no particular consistency.[2]

The second local Christian source presents the historian with the complications of redaction and compilation. The text as preserved today is referred to as *Anonymi Auctoris Chronicon ad A.C. 1234 Pertinens*, a slightly misleading title, for the text actually contains two chronicles, one devoted to ecclesiastical matters and the other to civil events.[3] Only the civil account ends in 1234; the ecclesiastical narrative ends in 1207. The two chronicles as they exist today were likely written by an anonymous Jacobite priest or monk from Edessa in the early thirteenth century, after Edessa had again come under Muslim rule. The details of his accounts suggest that the author had access to patriarchal archives, likely kept in the monastery of Mar Barsauma, near Samosata. The anonymous chronicler also drew extensively on the lost account of Basil bar Shumana, (d. 1171). Basil had intimate knowledge of both Frankish and Muslim modes of governance. He was first the Jacobite bishop of K'esun, and then became archbishop of Edessa.[4] In the latter position, Basil worked closely with both the Frankish counts of the city and the Turkish conquerors after 1144. He was the only bishop of the city to survive the Turkish conquests of 1144 and 1146; the Latin archbishop died in the siege of 1144 and the Armenian archbishop was taken captive after the Turkish recapture of the city in 1146.

Michael the Great, patriarch of the Jacobites, also wrote a chronicle covering Edessa under Frankish rule, but his world history began with creation. Michael traveled widely through the Levant, living sometimes under Frankish rule but more often under Muslim leaders.[5] While Michael's account also borrowed from Basil's and was generally interested in northern Syria and Mesopotamia, he did not have the specific focus on Edessa that both Matthew and the anonymous chronicler did.

The twelfth-century history of northern Syria was perceptively narrated by a fourth chronicler, a priest named Albert writing thousands of miles away in Aachen, Charlemagne's ancient capital in the Rhineland. Albert, as far as we know, never visited the Levant, but his chronicle is best informed about Godfrey of Bouillon and his brother Baldwin of Boulogne. Albert may have based much of his history on the accounts of crusaders who had fought under the two brothers before returning to the Rhineland; as a result his details of Baldwin's two-year rule of Edessa are unparalleled in any other source.[6] Other Latin chroniclers include Fulcher of Chartres, who was Baldwin of Boulogne's chaplain but who remained curiously silent about his years in Edessa, and Ralph of Caen, who wrote an account of the First Crusade from the perspective of Tancred, nephew of Bohemund of Taranto, though Ralph himself did not participate in the crusade.[7]

We might wonder when local communities first realized that the crusaders and their successors were not simply another army like those who had passed through the area in the previous thirty or even one hundred years, but a new group with an unfamiliar ideology. At first, they must have seemed little different from the Frankish mercenaries so often seen in Byzantine armies. Perhaps the realization came after the conquest of Antioch in early June 1098, when the crusaders refused to return the city to the Byzantines, and Bohemund of Taranto became its ruler. Yet ambitious warlords were nothing new in the area, and local communities might well have assumed that the Byzantines or Turks would bring him to heel. Bohemund in this light was not so different from Philaretos. Perhaps, then, it was when the Franks appointed their own bishops in Antioch and Edessa in 1100, establishing a Latin hierarchy alongside the Armenians and the Jacobites.[8] More likely, though, it could only be noticed in hindsight, perhaps even decades later, for the Frankish conquest of northern Syria was not achieved through the brief and generally inconsequential battles waged against the ineffectual Turkish garrisons occupying the towns and fortresses. Rather, it was a slow process, somewhat akin (on a smaller scale) to the ancient Romanization of Mediterranean society, whereby Frankish institutions and Frankish modes of social and religious thought gradually infiltrated and influenced local communities even as those same institutions and modes of thought changed in response to local demands.[9] This might seem an exaggeration, but we cannot forget that this process was cut short by the expulsion of the Franks from the Levant twice; once by Salah al-Din in 1187, and finally at the end of the thirteenth century.

The county of Edessa was the first Frankish state in the Levant. Its foundations were laid when Baldwin of Boulogne seized the castle of Tell Bashir in the fall of 1097, and solidified when he gained control of the city of Edessa itself in early March 1098. At Edessa, then, crusaders first came to terms with the local populations they were to rule, and vice versa. Thanks to Matthew, the anonymous chronicler, and to some extent Albert, the establishment of the Frankish county of Edessa ceases to be an event taking a few months, and can be understood as a process of years. It is only in northern Syria that historians can discuss this process in any detail. Even for the kingdom of Jerusalem, it can only be discussed at the level of cities and regions, rather than at the level of individuals, specific groups, or communities available for analysis in northern Syria. The process by which the Frankish county of Edessa was established allows us to peer into the "roughness" of Frankish political power. When was it used and when was it not? We can also glimpse the limitations of local authority, and how the ability of local leaders and communities to maintain autonomy was hampered by the fragmentation of the eleventh century.

Responses to the First Crusade

Though generally inconsequential in histories of the "the crusades," appearing sporadically in footnotes, introductions, and conclusions, local communities, particularly Armenian communities, gained their fifteen minutes of fame during the crusader conquest of northern Syria in 1098. For that brief moment, historians portray them as actors rather than observers, and often describe the crusader conquest almost as liberation, with grateful Armenians eagerly welcoming the Latins into their cities and helping them to conquer others.[10] Even when discussing this limited local participation in the First Crusade, historians rarely examine the events themselves, but merely accumulate a number of episodes in which Armenians or other local residents aid the crusaders, and equate this with participation in the crusade.

It is only in hindsight, and from a western perspective, that we can picture Armenians participating in the First Crusade; though Armenians certainly participated in many battles, they viewed them not as a crusade or an armed pilgrimage, but as a local series of skirmishes intended to demarcate their spheres of power. Armenians and crusaders may have fought side by side, but they did not participate in the same battles, for the ideological significance, their understanding of who the enemy was and their expectations of victory were starkly different. Nor should we overestimate how often crusaders and Armenians cooperated; the fissiparous nature of Armenian authority ensured that for every cooperator with the Franks, another would choose to cooperate with Turkish forces.

Crusaders in Cilicia: Resistance

The Byzantine defeat at the battle of Mantzikert (1071) and the fall of Philaretos (1086/7) left northern Syria and Cilicia a patchwork of petty principalities ruled by warlords. The centers of Seljuk and Byzantine power were distant, though both claimed authority over the area. In a land where everyone seemed to be king in his own castle, the arrival of the crusaders introduced yet another competitor for power, hardly welcome to anyone. It was in Cilicia (now the southern coast of Turkey) in the fall of 1097 that crusaders first attempted to hold conquered cities for themselves, rather than return them to the Byzantines, as they had sworn to Emperor Alexios I Komnenos to do. But it was not the Byzantines who were their competitors for territory in Cilicia, it was Armenian warlords. When historians of the crusades have examined this episode, they have done so entirely from a Frankish, and usually military, perspective. However, this encounter provides an opportunity to untangle the ways in which Armenians, crusaders, and historians have interpreted encounters between crusaders and indigenous communities.

Due to its mountainous terrain and location as a borderland between Anatolia and the Levant, Cilicia was notoriously difficult to control from Rome, Constantinople, or Baghdad, and often flourished as a semi-independent area.[11] Throughout the twelfth century, Cilicia was a playing field for competing Byzantine, Frankish, and Armenian forces, and it did not fall under permanent Armenian control until 1183. Curiously, the initial crusader occupation of Cilicia received only cursory attention from Jacobite and Armenian chroniclers; historians must rely instead on Latin accounts. Although western sources depict Armenians as eager allies, a careful reading of the sources within an Armenian cultural context suggests that local Christian leaders sought to deflect crusader attacks onto their Turkish and Armenian neighbors, and to avoid direct cooperation with the newcomers.

Crusaders had become familiar with Armenians before arriving in Cilicia. A certain number, relatively few but enough to be noticeable, joined the Frankish armies early on. At least one Armenian named Bagrat—about

whom we will learn more later—joined the army at Nicaea, and Fulcher of
Chartres marveled at the babble of languages, including Armenian, that he
heard around the crusader campfires during the march from Nicaea to Antioch.[12] To the crusaders, Cappadocia to the north of Cilicia was "terra Her-
meniorum," the land of the Armenians, due to the large number of
Armenians settled there.[13]

It was Tancred and Baldwin of Boulogne, two younger and ambitious
relatives of the great leaders of the crusade, who sought to conquer Cilicia for
themselves.[14] The two crusaders left the main body of the army on 14 September 1097,[15] and headed south, taking with them troops borrowed from
the forces of their uncle and older brother respectively. The area lay partially
under Turkish control, but Ralph of Caen, who wrote in Jerusalem some
years later, noted that some "Armenians preserved their freedom with great
difficulty."[16]

Tancred and Baldwin took different routes through the Taurus Mountains, only to meet outside the walls of Tarsus. Tancred arrived first and, after
defeating the Turkish garrison in a battle outside the walls, negotiated for the
surrender of the city the next day. During the negotiations, Baldwin arrived,
demanding a share of the city and its plunder. The size of Baldwin's army
perhaps compensated for his tardiness; according to Ralph of Caen, Tancred
had only one hundred knights and two hundred foot soldiers, while Baldwin was accompanied by five hundred knights and two thousand foot
soldiers.[17] Although Tancred, on the basis of his military victory and subsequent negotiation, had already been accepted by the citizens of Tarsus as
their new ruler,[18] Baldwin forced his rival to withdraw and claimed the city
as his own.

No Armenian source from the twelfth century indicated how the people
of Tarsus and surrounding areas reacted; Ralph of Caen, on the other hand,
though not an eyewitness, was confident in ascribing to the Armenians an
enthusiastic response. Even as Tancred slunk away from the city, ambassadors
from an Armenian named (in Latin) Ursinus, the lord of the nearby town of
Adana, approached him to suggest that Tancred attack the town of Mamistra, a little farther east. The Armenian emissaries implied that the city would
fall easily to the crusader, and indeed, the Turkish garrison fled upon Tancred's approach and the citizens welcomed the crusader's "paternal" authority. His victory stirred his rival Baldwin to march against him, but the citizens
of Adana and Mamistra, at Ursinus's urging, dismantled the bridges span-
ning the Sarus (modern Seyhan) River to slow his approach. Having forded

the river, Baldwin camped in front of Mamistra. The two armies, however, had little taste for battle against fellow crusaders, despite the hostility of their leaders. After a series of inconclusive single combats, Tancred and Baldwin resolved the standoff with a truce. Soon after, both crusaders rejoined the main crusader army, leaving behind garrisons in Tarsus and Mamistra.[19] Baldwin's willingness to compromise may have in part been spurred by news that his wife and children were dangerously ill in Marash, where the main crusader army had camped.[20]

Ralph gave Ursinus a prominent role in his narrative; his description of how Adana came under his power is one of the longest in the *Gesta*, rivaling the long speeches that followed the crusader capture of Jerusalem. Ursinus explained that until recently he had been "living in the mountains, free, but mourning the slavery of the Christian people no less than those who were exposed."[21] Moved by the plight of his fellow Armenians, Ursinus led his troops to liberate Adana, aided by the Christian citizens of the city. His triumph over the Turks was not only a military victory, but also a religious one, for "from this moment, *Allachibar*, which the infidels proclaimed in prayer, was silenced in the city, instead 'Christ conquers, reigns, and commands' resounded, returning as if in restoration."[22] The cries of the Christians cleansed the city of the aural pollution of Muslim prayers, echoing the concerns of crusade propaganda about "Saracen" pollution of Christian cities and shrines.[23] Ursinus was thus imagined as a "natural" crusader; without having taken the crusader vow, his goal was nonetheless to liberate Christians from the Muslim yoke. In Ralph's retelling, his eager cooperation with Tancred implicitly contrasted with Baldwin's rivalry, further revealing the shallowness of the latter's crusading spirit.

We can tentatively connect the eager Ursinus of Ralph's account with a historical figure. Édouard Dulaurier was the first to identify Ursinus with Oshin,[24] the ruler of Lampron, a castle in the Taurus Mountains.[25] Samuel of Ani, writing in the late twelfth century, recorded that in 1075/6 the prince Oshin left his ancestral lands "with his brother Halgam, with his wife and other nobles. Carrying his wealth and the finger of the holy apostle Peter, he entered Cilicia and captured from the Muslims the fortress of Lampron, at the foot of the Taurus Mountains toward Tarsus."[26] Under the crusader clothing in which Ralph dressed Ursinus was an Armenian lord who had experienced the dislocation common to many Armenians in the eleventh century. Oshin was in this sense no more a local than Baldwin or Tancred, and equally uncertain of his position.

Along with his wife, brother, and the finger of St. Peter, Oshin brought with him from the highlands of Armenia specific political instincts. As discussed in the first chapter, political success in the Armenian world came from allying with one side (which one was not necessarily significant), and using that alliance to bolster one's local standing and to undermine the standing of one's opponents. Such was the strategy that Oshin employed. Baldwin clearly posed the clearest threat. The victor at Tarsus, he and his army lay close to Lampron, which was perched in the mountains above the city. The Armenian, however, did not challenge Baldwin himself; instead he encouraged Tancred to seize Mamistra, a town to the east of Adana. Oshin was thus perched between the two armies, able to switch sides at will and hinder or help either party.[27]

If Ralph, writing more than a decade later in Jerusalem, interpreted local Christian warlords as holy warriors, how did local Christians view the crusaders? Unfortunately, local Christian sources are of little help. We have no record of how Tancred and Baldwin presented themselves to local communities, or even in what language. Tancred had the counsel of an anonymous Armenian, whose brothers lived in Tarsus, and Baldwin may have had Bagrat as an intermediary.[28] Given the experience of Christian communities over the previous half-century, they likely understood that such a large army could only be supported by either the Turks or the Byzantines. Familiar with Frankish mercenaries serving in the imperial army, most communities would conclude that the armies of the First Crusade were mercenaries hired by the emperor in Constantinople. The main crusader army was accompanied by a Byzantine detachment, which would further the impression that the crusaders fought at Byzantine behest.

Oshin's actions and their misrepresentations by Ralph make clear the gap between crusader and local Christian understanding of the Levantine world. As the crusaders mistakenly interpreted local Christians as eager to join their crusade, local Christians mistakenly saw Franks as yet more mercenaries, nominally in Byzantine service, fighting for local control, a confusion they shared with many Muslims.[29] Each group could only see their own motivation and goals in the other. Yet Ralph's narrative also shows the eagerness with which the crusaders encompassed Armenians within crusade ideology.

Northern Syria: Accommodation and Acculturation

Oshin's cautious approach was not the way all local rulers dealt with the crusaders, nor did Baldwin's and Tancred's conquest of, and conflict over, Cilician towns ensure their inclusion in a Frankish principality. For crusaders and local Christians alike, Baldwin's establishment of the county of Edessa proved to be a far more decisive encounter. Again, this series of episodes has generally been ignored by historians, who only become interested in the area when Baldwin reached the city of Edessa, or when his conquests impacted the larger body of crusaders at Antioch. After the death of his wife Godvera and their children in Marash, and scarcely a month after leaving Cilicia, Baldwin again separated from the main crusader army (17 October 1097), heading this time with one hundred knights to the "provincia sinistra," the western bank of the Euphrates River.[30] The area was ideal for Baldwin. A series of hills and isolated villages, it was bounded to the east by the fabled Euphrates River and to the south by the flat arid plains of the Syrian desert. In the early eleventh century, the area had been part of the frontier between the Byzantine empire and the city of Aleppo (a city sometimes under Fatimid rule), a legacy that left behind a number of small fortresses dotting the dusty hilltops. The valleys, irrigated by south-flowing rivers, could yield a variety of crops, from wheat near the river to olives, pistachios, and grapes on the lower hillsides.

In contrast to his previous exploits in Cilicia, Baldwin's Syrian expedition is well documented. His chaplain, Fulcher of Chartres, accompanied him to Syria (but did not join him in Cilicia), and his deeds also drew considerable attention from Albert of Aachen and a number of local Christian and Arabic sources. Each source presents a different interpretation of the events following Baldwin's foray into Syria; what follows is an attempt to make sense of the confusion, and draw some conclusions about the establishment of Frankish authority in Syria.

Much of what made Baldwin's rise to power possible was the fragmented nature of Armenian leadership in northern Syria, and the permeability of local communities. Baldwin, wittingly or not, came to power through the quarrels and animosities of Armenian warlords; he was accepted not because his claims of authority were seen as the establishment of a new religious and ethnic ruling class, but because he appeared to be the leader of a small armed group, whose cultural identity was relatively unimportant, working within an already established frontier system. It is likely that Baldwin was enticed to enter Syria on behalf of one side of an Armenian feud. Albert of Aachen attributed Baldwin's decision to abandon Cilicia for Syria to a mysterious, and in Albert's eyes, suspicious character, Pancracius.[31] As with Oshin, the historian must unearth the Armenian Bagrat from beneath the

Latin Pancracius. Bagrat was an Armenian who had once been imprisoned by Emperor Alexios in Constantinople, escaped, and joined the crusaders.[32] While Albert implied that he was merely a soldier among Baldwin's troops, Bagrat in reality was one of the petty Armenian warlords who dominated the region, a fact that may explain his presence in a Byzantine jail.[33] His brother was Kogh Vasil, who ruled the Syrian towns of K'esun and Raban. Where Oshin saw the crusaders as a threat, Bagrat saw them as an opportunity, not to liberate his homeland from Muslim domination, but to secure his position against local Armenian rivals.

Bagrat suggested that Baldwin attack Tell Bashir, a fortress on the Sad-jur River (a tributary of the Euphrates) which protected the road between Edessa and Antioch and was crucial for the control of trade and communication between the coast and the fertile northern Euphrates area. Gathering his forces, Baldwin prepared to launch an attack, when to his surprise, the gates were thrown open and the Armenian citizens streamed out to welcome him, having already dispatched the Turkish garrison themselves.[34] Following his easy victory, Baldwin next besieged Rawandan, another important site between Tell Bashir and Antioch. More a fortress than a city, it was built atop a conical hill, creating an ideal defense against siege weapons. A thirteenth-century Muslim chronicler noted that it was "a small castle on the top of a high hill, isolated in its situation. Neither mangonels nor arrows can reach it. At the foot of the hill, there is a small settlement. It is one of the strongest castles, and most favoured spots."[35] Despite its fortifications, Rawandan also fell easily into Baldwin's hands, for the Turkish garrison again fled.[36] Fulcher commented that Baldwin "took many towns by force as well as by strategy,"[37] suggesting that not all cities and fortresses opened their doors willingly; unfortunately he did not give details.

Baldwin's experience in Syria was distinctly different from that in Cilicia. Most obviously, he had no crusader competitor like Tancred, but he also had a smaller contingent of soldiers. Bagrat must also have made a difference. Familiar with the area, Bagrat could guide Baldwin in negotiations with local communities and in traversing local terrain. The warm welcome extended to them by local Armenian populations was likely facilitated by Bagrat. Albert's chronicle gives the sense that Baldwin's conquest was almost an act, a set of well-planned Potemkin villages designed to bolster the crusaders' reliance on their Armenian advisors. Certainly, Baldwin faced little military opposition; the disorganized and scattered Turkish forces were theoretically loyal to the Seljuk prince Ridvan in Aleppo, but the Turkish ruler felt far more threatened by his brother ruling in Damascus than by the conquerors of a few small towns of northern Syria.[38] The hilly area Baldwin occupied did not have the large towns that Cilicia did, nor was it on the Mediterranean coast; it lacked any larger strategic importance for the Aleppan ruler.

While the Turkish garrisons offered little resistance, local warlords proved to be a far bigger problem. The first episode of real danger to Baldwin in Albert's account came from internal conflicts that arose in the wake of Baldwin's alliance with Bagrat, not from any battles with the Turks. Two local warlords were involved; Fer (likely the Armenian name P'er) was the "praepositus" of Tell Bashir, a title which generally means "castellan."[39] It is clear that P'er held this position before Baldwin's arrival, and he was likely instrumental in the expulsion of the Turkish garrison and the opening of the gates to the crusaders. P'er may even have thought of himself as the lord of the castle, and Baldwin as a temporary ally. The second Armenian, Nicusus, was similarly ambiguous in status; he controlled "large castles and fortresses" near Tell Bashir, which apparently remained in his control after Baldwin's arrival.

But P'er and Nicusus, as influential local lords of the area of Tell Bashir, did not oppose Baldwin; rather they opposed Bagrat, accusing him of planning to betray the crusaders to the Turks.[40] Infuriated by the possibility of treachery against him, Baldwin ordered his ally seized and threatened with torture unless he surrendered Rawandan. Bagrat ordered his son to give up the fortress without delay; once the castle was safely in his hands, Baldwin ceded it to one of his own knights and released Bagrat.[41] Despite his expulsion from Rawandan, Bagrat continued to control lands and castles in northern Syria, perhaps in conjunction with his brother, a further sign of his independent standing.

It is difficult to uncover the motivations of P'er, Nicusus, and Bagrat, but the conflict had little to do with Baldwin and everything to do with a complex local Christian world of political goals, struggles, and squabbles into which Baldwin and his knights were drawn. The Turks were a red herring; local Christian leaders saw each other as the real threat. Likewise, Latin chroniclers and historians of the crusades misunderstood Baldwin's position in northern Syria, presenting him as the lord of a large territory stretching from the Euphrates almost to Antioch. The ease of conquest, and Baldwin's effortless integration into the militarized Syrian world, gave the Franks the impression that their leader was the undisputed master of the area. This interpretation, however, confused acceptance by Armenian leaders of Baldwin's presence with acceptance of Baldwin's authority over them. Armenian warlords continued to flourish until the end of the county of Edessa in 1150. At most, Baldwin's direct authority was limited to strongholds such as Tell Bashir and Rawandan; most other castles and towns remained under local Armenian control. Even Tell Bashir and Rawandan may not have been fully under his control—it is unclear what authority P'er continued to wield in Tell Bashir, or Nicusus in its environs, while Bagrat continued to hold fortresses in the area of Rawandan. Perhaps we should not be too surprised that Baldwin was so adept at navigating the complexities of a world of competing local warlords. It was not so different from the political landscape of northern France, where castellans wielded the preponderance of power on the local level.

Perhaps the most surprising aspect of the narrative is its source—Albert of Aachen. As far we know, he never visited the Levant, and his sources were likely the oral reports of returning crusaders who had fought in the service of Godfrey and Baldwin. It is thus ironic that the one chronicler who had never been to the Levant best described it. One might expect that this wealth of local detail might come from Matthew of Edessa as an Armenian familiar with local politics, or from Fulcher of Chartres, Baldwin's chaplain who was by his side throughout his conquest of Tell Bashir and Rawandan, and therefore had himself met Bagrat, P'er, and Nicusus, but these two historians are silent.

Matthew and Fulcher chose to omit these events from their accounts for different, yet linked, reasons. Matthew was not writing a chronicle of events, but an account of the signs of the coming apocalypse; the events in Tell Bashir and Rawandan contributed little to that goal. He was more willing to describe Bagrat's final dispossession by the Franks nearly twenty years later, which shows his familiarity with the warlord and his circumstances. The account of his final dispossession was set within a context of a Frankish campaign against independent Armenian lords, which illustrated, not Frankish enmity, but the overwhelming power of Satan within Matthew's world. The stories of violence in Matthew's account that involve Franks were thus not a comment on Frankish behavior, and Matthew avoided discussing Frankish power when it was wielded in more quotidian and less apocalyptic ways.

Writing from his perspective in Jerusalem some years later, Fulcher's focus was on the establishment of the kingdom of Jerusalem, not on the county of Edessa. Baldwin's entanglements with local Christian feuds were not likely to win over readers in Latin Europe looking for an image of the "crusader" East as a land of pious western warriors and their Saracen enemies. Nor were local Franks eager for a discussion of the role local Christians played in the creation and maintenance of Frankish principalities. Therefore, like contemporary Muslim chroniclers, Fulcher and other Latin chroniclers effectively ignore the presence and importance of local Christians. It is not a coincidence that the two chroniclers with the most intimate knowledge of Baldwin's earliest conquests are the most silent about it.

Antioch

Baldwin was not the only crusader to build his own principality in northern Syria. Eight months after Baldwin gained control of Tell Bashir and Rawandan, Bohemund of Taranto established himself as the ruler of Antioch, but in a quite different manner.[42] While his principality occupied the same broad cultural and geographic world as Edessa, its demographics were somewhat different. Antioch and Lattakia, the two largest cities in what would become the principality of Antioch, had been under at least nominal Byzantine rule until 1084/5, and had large Greek-speaking Melkite populations, while further up the Orontes valley larger Muslim populations, as well as populations of Jacobite and Armenian communities, were established.

Nevertheless, the establishment of the principality of Antioch was similar to that of Edessa in many ways. Like Edessa, its cities and citadels came under Frankish influence by a variety of means. Many of its cities fell to the Franks through the course of the siege of Antioch, rather than through a concerted effort to build up a principality. By June 1098, a considerable part of the area around Antioch was in Frankish hands, but little directly in Bohemund's. Some places may not have been under crusader control at all. Frankish troops first entered the town of 'Artah, which controlled important transportation routes into Antioch from Aleppo, only after the Armenian population massacred the Turkish garrison and threw open the gates to the crusaders, just as the Armenians of Tell Bashir had done. It is likely that a local warlord played a similar role to P'er here as well. While the crusaders were invited into the city, they apparently did not leave a garrison, for within a few months Frankish chroniclers believed the city was once again in Turkish hands.[43] Likewise, the Aleppan chronicler Kemal al-Din suggested that both Harim and 'Imm, cities perched on the limestone massif to the east of Antioch, lost their Muslim forces through the action of their Armenian citizens.[44] The Armenians of Rugia, farther up the Orontes valley, opened their city gates to the forces of Raymond of Toulouse.[45]

The impression that the crusaders were Byzantine mercenaries was probably even stronger in the areas around Antioch than in Cilicia or around Tell Bashir; the Byzantine force under the command of Takitios, which accompanied the crusaders from Nicaea to Antioch, was present in the area until at least February 1098.[46] Furthermore, English sailors acting under Byzantine orders seized the seaport of Lattakia.[47] For communities around Antioch, the military campaign we call the First Crusade was obviously an attempt by the Byzantines to reclaim a city that had been theirs for most of the previous hundred years. Carole Hillenbrand has suggested that it is even possible that the Fatimids had a truce with the crusaders, based on the assumption that the Franks sought to recapture Antioch, not take Jerusalem. Such a goal was appropriate for agents of the Byzantines, with whom the Fatimids were accustomed to negotiate.[48]

Bohemund himself claimed the city of Antioch through military conquest, which, no matter how sneakily achieved, allowed him the right to rule the city in a way Baldwin could not claim in Edessa. The most significant challenge to Bohemund's authority came from other crusaders, notably Raymond of St. Gilles, who was unwilling to relinquish what he had occupied in the area, rather than from local warlords like Bagrat and Oshin. Bohemund also had to worry about the Byzantines, who clearly expected the crusaders to return the city to them, and worked tirelessly to regain it for the next thirty years. Although the Byzantine claim to Edessa was nearly as strong as it was to Antioch, the Komnenian emperors focused their energies on Antioch, and seemed to assume that once Antioch was in their control, Edessa would easily follow. Nevertheless, it is likely that Bohemund did confront local leaders like Bagrat, but we lack the sources to discuss it.

Perhaps the most surprising aspect of the establishment of both Edessa and Antioch is that local Muslim warlords did not behave much differently from Armenian warlords. The Turkish ruler of 'Azaz, Omar, threw off his allegiance to Ridvan of Aleppo and allied himself with Godfrey of Bouillon.[49] Likewise, Balak (Balas in Latin), the ruler of Saruj, a town near Edessa, sought Baldwin's help in subduing his own rebellious Muslim citizens.[50] Baldwin gained control of the city of Samosata (after a failed assault) by purchasing the fortress from its Turkish ruler Balduk. Baldwin even brought Balduk into his household for a time, expelling him only when the Turk urged the Muslims of Saruj to resist Frankish authority.[51] Balduk's presence in

Baldwin's court is all the more striking when we remember that Baldwin was still technically a crusader, not having completed his journey to Jerusalem. While we might be astonished at finding a Muslim lord living in the household of a crusader, it does not seem to have been odd in anyone else's eyes.[52] Balduk in this regard appeared no different from Bagrat, who also played the role of local lord-in-residence. There is no reason to suspect Balduk was unique as a Muslim warlord; his willingness to cooperate with the Franks calls to mind the Banu Munqidh, the Shi'a family that ruled the fortress of Shaizar, on the borders of the principality of Antioch. The family's most famous scion, Usama, had an easy familiarity with Franks in the decades following the First Crusade,[53] and given changed political circumstances, it is not difficult to imagine him, or some other member of his family, becoming associates of a Frankish lord in the same manner as Balduk.

The Franks in Edessa

Baldwin's activities in Tell Bashir and Rawandan demonstrated his ability to negotiate the complicated political life of northern Syria, but he became a significant leader only after he gained control of the city of Edessa. In early February 1098, T'oros, the ruler of Edessa,[54] sent the bishop of the city and twelve councilors to Baldwin to ask for his help defending the city from the Turks.[55] T'oros knew the crusaders were coming long before Baldwin seized Tell Bashir; they had sent a letter, probably after the capture of Nicaea, to T'oros and other warlords, announcing their imminent arrival and doubtless asking for support.[56] The contents of the letters would be quite interesting. Presumably the crusaders wrote on the advice of their Byzantine allies; it is therefore unlikely that letters were addressed to the warlords as independent rulers, for Alexios would be reluctant to give them that status, and as we have seen, T'oros perhaps did not even claim it. The letters probably assumed that the addressees maintained some sort of loose association with Byzantium.

Baldwin quickly accepted T'oros's invitation, for Edessa rivaled Aleppo and Antioch in size and wealth. Accompanied by only sixty knights, he arrived on 20 February 1098 after an ambush-ridden journey from Tell Bashir. Fulcher reported that "you would have been amazed to see them [Armenians] coming humbly to meet us, carrying crosses and banners, and kissing our feet and garments for the love of God because they had heard we were going to protect them against the Turks under whose yoke they had been long oppressed."[57] Such receptions delighted Fulcher, and bolstered the belief of the crusaders that they were liberating local Christians from malevolent Muslim overlords.

Again, local Christians and the crusaders were acting with different scripts in hand. Only fourteen years had elapsed since these areas had been under the control of Philaretos. The townspeople's ostentatious procession with crosses and banners, bewailing the horrors of Turkish depredations, paradoxically suggests the absence of a Turkish garrison or governor in the town. Seljuk tolerance did not extend to sedition. The processions were not intended as joyful occasions to welcome the town's savior, but either as expressions of hope of a Byzantine military revival, or as first steps toward negotiations with the latest army to pass the town.

Further misunderstandings awaited Baldwin in Edessa, for T'oros hoped to hire Baldwin and his Franks as mercenaries, as Philaretos had employed Franks like Roussel de Bailleul and Francopoulos. Perhaps this was even how T'oros understood Baldwin's role in Tell Bashir and Rawandan, as P'er's or Nicusus's "hired help." The invitation was certainly a sign of desperation. The city T'oros ruled was scarcely able to defend itself and had been wracked with internal conflict. The city was largely Christian, with a substantial and powerful Armenian population. Factions, whose identity and motivations are difficult to uncover beyond Matthew of Edessa's vague characterization of "leaders" and "citizens," had been feuding over the leadership of the city for the past twenty years. In 1078, a group of townspeople expelled the *doux* Leon Diabatenos and murdered his second-in-command so that Basil Apukab, who was besieging the city (nominally on behalf of Philaretos), could assume control of Edessa. After Basil's death in 1083/84 (one of the few leaders of Edessa in this period to die peacefully), the populace elected Smbat, an Armenian known to Matthew as "a courageous fighter against the Persians."[58]

Although Matthew portrayed Smbat as a popular leader, the aristocracy found him less appealing. When they sought his overthrow, they again offered the city to Philaretos.[59] Upon assuming control of Edessa the warlord executed Smbat, but also put to death several leaders from the anti-Smbat faction. Nine years later, Philaretos placed Edessa under the authority of a eunuch; he was murdered by an officer named Parsama (a name which suggests a Jacobite or Nestorian background), who assumed leadership of the city by popular demand. Hardly a year later, while Edessa was once again under siege by the Turks, the townspeople rose up against Parsama, displeased with his defense of the city. Parsama fled to the camp of the besieging enemy but broke his spine while jumping from the walls to escape the rioting citizens. The Turkish leader Buzan captured the city, but when he was then killed in battle in 1094/5, the Christian T'oros seized Edessa. This complex history of plots and counterplots is to some degree a function of Matthew's own particular obsession with betrayal and violence, but also reflects the factionalized nature of Edessan political life. Like the Turk Balak, then, T'oros sought Baldwin's aid because he feared a rebellious populace.

When Baldwin arrived in the city, "the townspeople came to meet him and with great rejoicing brought him into the city." They apparently had concerns about the security of the city, for Matthew remarked that "the presence of Baldwin brought much happiness to the faithful."[60] The divisive politics of the city soon reemerged, for T'oros grew jealous of Baldwin's popularity.[61] The crusader, for his part, rejected T'oros's many gifts of gold, silver, and horses, because he saw them as meretricious payments for military service, implying that he was a hired mercenary. Baldwin had no intention of working for anyone's benefit but his own. When he threatened to leave Edessa, the panicked citizenry convinced T'oros to adopt him and share power.[62]

Reluctant though T'oros may have been to share power with Baldwin, he may also have hoped that the crusader would aid him against his populist rivals. Two years earlier, he had briefly bolstered his military strength through an alliance with a Turkish prince, named by Matthew as al-Faraj. The Turk had his own motives for trying to gain control of Edessa; his family already ruled much of Anatolia.[63] T'oros and al-Faraj did not remain allies long; the Edessan ruler poisoned his erstwhile supporter in order to protect his own life. The obvious parallels between Baldwin and al-Faraj suggest that T'oros considered the crusader a potential ally, but that T'oros was also aware of the hazards of such an alliance. The similarities between al-Faraj and Baldwin also make clear the local level at which such alliances functioned. Their connections to the wider world were not important; T'oros was not planning to hand Edessa over to the Seljuks or the crusaders. Baldwin and al-Faraj offered small, manageable military forces that could tip the balance in T'oros's favor. Also notable is the interchangeability of Christian and Muslim forces; either would serve T'oros's purposes. One wonders if al-Faraj was as popular with the larger population as Baldwin was.

T'oros had further reasons for anxiety about his position; he was not an Armenian or even a Jacobite; all sources concur in naming him a Greek.[64] T'oros's use of the title *kouropalates* and his possible association with Philaretos suggest that the *doux* may also have thought that he was exercising his authority on behalf of the Byzantine emperor, as a recent interpretation of an inscription at the Harran gate of Edessa's city wall implies. A possible reading of the fragmentary (and now vanished) pronouncement provided a date of 1094 and included the name Alexios I Komnenos. Given that this is the year T'oros seized power in Edessa, it is tempting to imagine that this inscription was his way of legitimating his authority.[65] Certainly, others accepted him as an imperial representative—the anonymous Edessan chronicler noted that under the authority of T'oros "Edessa and its citadel returned to the Romans."[66]

While T'oros hoped to gain an ally to defend the city against attack and to strengthen his own position within the city, Baldwin's motivation is less clear. Did he hope to supplant T'oros? Or to earn financial rewards? Whatever his goals were, Baldwin's presence in Edessa led quickly to T'oros's deposition and death. On 7 March 1098, less than a month after Baldwin's arrival, a group of citizens incited the town to rise against the *doux* and pillaged the homes of his officers. The enraged citizens gained control of the outer walls of the city, while T'oros held the smaller citadel by the east gate.[67] The next day he reluctantly turned it over to the rebels with the agreement that he and his wife be allowed to leave the city to join her father, Gabriel of Melitene. Although Baldwin and the citizens swore an oath on holy relics not to harm T'oros, the mob struck him down with swords as soon as he emerged from the citadel. Matthew did not record the fate of T'oros's wife, but the anonymous chronicler recorded that both she and the children were killed.[68] The crowd then acclaimed Baldwin the new leader of Edessa. Baldwin's authority in northern Syria was considerably boosted by gaining control of the city. Not only did he now control an important economic, religious, and political center, but he had also been acclaimed *doux* of the city, a position dating back to the days of Byzantine rule that gave his power a legitimate form and expression.

T'oros's violent death haunted the city for years afterward. Matthew noted that a drought and subsequent famine two years later provoked regret among many Edessans: "many said that this was a judgment from God because of the iniquitous death of the *kouropalates* T'oros." As a result of their cruel murder on the steps of a church, "the Lord God brought this affliction upon the people of Abgar."[69] Such a death, however, was not unusual in Edessan politics; the eunuch Philaretos had appointed to rule the city in 1086/7 was murdered while praying at the shrine of St. Theodore,[70] and *doux*

Leon Diabatenos's second-in-command was slaughtered while seeking sanctuary at the altar of the church of the Theotokos.[71] Perhaps T'oros's death was a greater crime in hindsight because it marked the transition of Edessa into Frankish control. Fulcher of Chartres struggled to exonerate his patron from suspicion of any involvement in the plot against his adopted father, insisting that "the citizens wickedly plotted to slay their prince because they hated him and to elevate Baldwin to the palace to rule the land. Baldwin and his men were much grieved because they were not able to obtain mercy for him."[72] Matthew of Edessa, on the other hand, believed that the plotters, a group of forty citizens, approached Baldwin and got his approval before the murder. Nevertheless, the revolt against T'oros came largely from disaffected citizens, and however much Baldwin knew, it is unlikely that he was able to orchestrate the *doux*'s overthrow in just two weeks.

Perhaps the most revealing part of this episode was the participation of Constantine, the Armenian ruler of the town of Gargar, approximately eighty miles north of Edessa, in the overthrow of T'oros. Constantine had joined Baldwin on his expedition against Samosata before T'oros's death, and according to Matthew, was part of the plot against the *doux*.[73] As we have already seen with Bagrat and Oshin, local Armenian warlords were quick to encourage outside forces to attack neighboring princes. In T'oros's death, Constantine saw not the possibility of his own fate (he died in Frankish captivity in 1117/18), but the elimination of a rival. One might have expected that Constantine would seek to take T'oros's place in Edessa, rather than supporting Baldwin's bid to be *doux*. Why he did not we cannot know, but it speaks of the limited horizons of the local lord. At least in part, Constantine feared that if he left Gargar to rule in Edessa, his subordinates would overthrow him in one place or the other, if not both. In that sense, Constantine saw his fate all too clearly in T'oros's murder.

For historians of the crusades, T'oros's dramatic death and replacement by Baldwin was the story of the foundation of the Frankish county of Edessa. In 1098, it appeared to be nothing of the sort. Indeed, even years later it still would not have been evident to most Edessans that anything had changed. From their perspective, the replacement of T'oros by Baldwin was not a change in regime, but the replacement of one strongman with vague Byzantine ties with another of the same ilk. It had been regularized by an adoption, and the new warlord appropriately integrated himself into the city, for Baldwin was T'oros's successor in more than just position. Like T'oros, Baldwin's authority in Edessa was circumscribed by his ambiguous position, wielding neither the power of a conqueror nor the authority derived from local ties. He brought with him only sixty Frankish knights (though this number increased after the crusaders captured Antioch), and therefore he depended on the support of the aristocracy of the city. He left the Armenian administration of the city undisturbed.

Baldwin also chose to articulate his relationship to the city through Armenian symbols and rituals. Baldwin swore his oath not to harm T'oros on the Holy Cross of Varag. Although he could have had his own chaplain Fulcher administer the oath with his own relics,[74] he chose to use relics that symbolized the Armenian Christianity of Edessa. According to a twelfth-century account, the cross "had been brought to the mountain of Varag [in greater Armenia], by the holy lamb and royal virgin Hrip'sime," whose martyrdom in the early fourth century was traditionally remembered as one of the events that led to the conversion of Armenia.[75] The presence of such relics in Edessa demonstrated the importance of the city as a center of Armenian culture, religiosity, and politics, but also emphasized communal ties to historic Armenia, recognizing that the Armenian community was a nation in exile. Baldwin's oath, however traduced, symbolically recognized the primacy of the Armenian tradition in Edessa, and also signaled his own willingness to live within that cultural and political world. In that sense, the count of Edessa was little more than the Byzantine *doux* with a French accent.

Baldwin, however, was not satisfied simply to acknowledge the importance of the Armenian community in Edessa; he wanted to be able to mobilize it militarily and financially for his own purposes. T'oros had adopted Baldwin at the urging of the citizens, who sought to secure Baldwin's fidelity for the city through this relationship, while T'oros also hoped (futilely) to ensure the crusader's loyalty to him. According to Albert of Aachen, the adoption ceremony included a bare-chested Baldwin enfolded within the cloak or shirt of T'oros.[76] The symbolic value of the ritual is clear, but its cultural origins are obscure. Baldwin thus not only became a part of an Edessan family, but symbolically became one in the flesh with his foster father.

Soon after his adopted father died, Baldwin developed another social relationship to foster ties to the Armenian community he ruled—marriage. In the summer of 1098, Baldwin married an unnamed daughter of an Armenian prince, named in the Latin sources as Taphnuz.[77] The benefits for Baldwin were numerous. He received a generous dowry of sixty thousand bisants and became the heir of all Taphnuz's lands.[78] Both Baldwin and the Edessans could enjoy the pleasant fiction that Baldwin was now linked to them by familial ties and oaths, an Edessan in everything but name. Essential to Baldwin's success was the sense that nothing had changed. The Franks did not institute new legal regimes, oust old elites, or do anything that would announce the establishment of a new regime.

Armenian Resistance

Although Baldwin came to power with considerable Armenian support, resistance to him began as soon as he claimed Edessa as his own. He soon began to provide food, money, and arms to the rest of the crusader army besieging Antioch, as did his Armenian allies. The crusader's onetime friend and now enemy, Bagrat, remained on his lands around Rawandan, sitting astride communication and trade routes that connected Baldwin in Edessa with the crusaders in Antioch. Nicusus, who presumably still controlled his "large castles," sent a beautifully decorated tent to Baldwin's brother Godfrey. Bagrat intercepted the tent en route and presented it to Bohemund at Antioch as a gift from himself instead. When Godfrey learned of the robbery, he demanded that Bohemund return the tent. Like Achilles, Bohemund refused. Godfrey threatened to take the tent back by force, and peace and amity were restored in the crusader camp only when the leaders of the crusade intervened and convinced a grudging Bohemund to return the tent.[79]

The "affair of the tent" had a deliberate quality to it; Bagrat likely had gotten to know all the actors in this little drama while accompanying the crusaders across Anatolia. By stealing the tent he might simply have been taking the opportunity to plunder a poorly protected messenger, and then using it to ingratiate himself with Bohemund, the new ruler of Antioch. But he had good reason to resent Baldwin (and his brother Godfrey, who had provided him with troops) and Nicusus (who had set Baldwin against him). More likely, then, the theft of the tent was a deliberate gesture by Bagrat. Whether or not he intended to provoke discord in the crusader camp, his tactic had the effect of further exacerbating tensions between the contingent from Boulogne (Baldwin and his brother Godfrey) and the Normans from Apulia (Tancred and his uncle Bohemund). Bagrat perhaps sought to remind Baldwin that, while he might now rule Edessa, his authority was still limited to specific strongholds, and Bagrat at least still stood independent.

Soon after "the affair of the tent," Godfrey and Bagrat came into direct conflict. In August 1098, after the capture of Antioch by the crusaders, Godfrey escaped the pestilence that was ravaging the city by retreating with his knights to the relative calm of Tell Bashir and Rawandan, by invitation of his brother. Further conflict with Bagrat was perhaps inevitable—Baldwin may even have asked his brother to deal with the Armenian. Godfrey soon accused Bagrat, somewhat strangely, of mistreating Armenian monks, as well as robbing his brother's servants who were carrying money to him. In response to these outrages, Godfrey burned down one fortress of Bagrat's and another belonging to his brother Kogh Vasil, and as a final insult, he blinded twenty of Bagrat's knights.[80]

The accusation that Bagrat abused groups of Armenian monks sounds like Frankish slander, although the attacks on Baldwin's messengers fit a pattern of small-scale raids. Godfrey's attack on Bagrat not only extended his brother's authority, but also would seem to be a further triumph for Nicusus, who had urged Baldwin's first attack on Bagrat nearly a year earlier, as well as playing a part in the "affair of the tent." The accusation that Bagrat harassed Armenian monks signaled either the origin of the information against Bagrat (other Armenians such as Nicusus), or Baldwin's sense that such attacks needed to be justified to the local population. Taking on the mantle of defending the Armenian church is a move we will see Baldwin make again.

Bagrat was not the only Armenian to object to the increasing power of the crusaders in northern Syria. According to Albert, the city councilors of Edessa grew resentful of the large number of Franks coming to the city and the prominent role they were assuming, finding that "it displeased them excessively that they had placed him [Baldwin] in authority over them as duke and lord of the city."[81] Just as they had done with T'oros, in December 1098 they invited nearby rivals (this time anonymous Turks) to take control of the city. As they had given Baldwin the authority to rule them, they now decided to take it away. One of the councilors, however, broke ranks and alerted Baldwin to the plans of the others. The Frankish count threw the conspirators in jail and confiscated their possessions. Hearing that the captive councilors still had considerable wealth hidden in outlying castles and estates, he offered to exchange their freedom for the money, an offer they enthusiastically accepted. Baldwin refused, however, to accept money from the two ringleaders, whom he ordered blinded. He cut off the noses, hands, or feet of the others and expelled them all from the city, actions that evoked Byzantine punishments rather than those of eleventh-century Boulogne.[82] The ferocity of Baldwin's reaction terrified his father-in-law, Taphnuz, who fled the city and retreated to a castle in the mountains, refusing to return to the city for fear that Baldwin would kill him for the unpaid balance of the dowry. Albert's closing words concerning this episode sound an ominous note: "From that day on, Duke Baldwin became feared in the city of Rohas, and his name was known to the ends of the earth, being famed for his power."[83]

Baldwin's selective use of violence against local warlords and leaders reveals the roughness of the Frankish rise to power, but also how divided and fragmented local communities were after a century of border warfare. The brutal death of T'oros, the attacks on Bagrat and the punishment of the city councilors did not provoke widespread antipathy towards Baldwin or Frankish rule in general. Indeed, as the next chapter will discuss, many local communities began to adopt notions of political loyalty from the Franks. Baldwin's ambiguous ascent to the position of *doux* was the catalyst that created the group of practices essential to rough tolerance. Many of the characteristics that make rough tolerance possible were already present in northern Syria, particularly localized elites and fragmented forms of authority. Baldwin, by perpetuating patterns of authority already established, rather than creating a new political, legal and social regime, as Franks would later do on other frontiers (notably Ireland[84] and the Baltics)—made the practices of rough tolerance the established mode through which Frankish authority operated.

Chapter 3

Images of Authority in Edessa, 1100–1150

In the early fall of 1100, Baldwin I of Edessa learned that his elder brother, Godfrey of Bouillon, first ruler of Frankish Jerusalem, had died of "a violent and incurable disease." A group of knights held Jerusalem for Baldwin, in defiance of the Latin patriarch of Jerusalem, Daibert of Pisa, who had hoped that on Godfrey's death he would gain control of the city.[1] Having visited Jerusalem just a year earlier to complete his crusader vow, Baldwin was familiar with his brother's territory as well as with the patriarch, to whom he had sworn fealty for his lands in Edessa. He gathered a small army, leaving Edessa on 2 October 1100 for Jerusalem. On Christmas Day 1100, he was crowned the first Frankish king in the Levant, in a ceremony at the ancient Church of the Nativity in Bethlehem.

It was evident to Baldwin before he departed that he could not continue to rule Edessa from Jerusalem; the distance was too great and the two principalities too new. He therefore appointed his cousin Baldwin of Bourcq to succeed him as the ruler of Edessa. Under Baldwin II (as Baldwin of Bourcq will be called in this chapter), the county of Edessa became recognizably Frankish but without alienating the local population on whom Frankish authority depended. The emergence of a distinctly Frankish principality presented a number of challenges and opportunities to local communities, particularly to warlords such as Constantine of Gargar. Some Armenian elites resisted the growing power of the Franks and the increasingly Frankish expression of their authority by articulating various alternatives—identification with the Byzantine *imperium*, assertion of independence, appeal to Armenia's royal tradition—which crafted images of authority that resisted subordination to Frankish authority, but did not challenge the validity or presence of Frankish power in the Levant. Yet this was not the only response of local communities; we find local Christians taking on Frankish ideas of political loyalty and the religious value of war against the infidels, and participating as lords and knights in the new Frankish polity.

Baldwin II ruthlessly sought to expand and solidify his authority, often at the expense of local warlords. Yet Baldwin II never targeted Armenians or other local communities as a group; even as he attacked some, he supported others. Likewise, Armenians did not perceive themselves as victims of violence; as with the fall of T'oros, warlords frequently collaborated with the Franks against local rivals. Whereas Baldwin I ruled Edessa as someone who was a successor to the previous rulers and was incidentally Frankish, Baldwin II ruled a Frankish principality in a Levant increasingly dominated by Franks. Yet he too adapted practices of power of his predecessors, making rough tolerance a particularly Frankish mode of rule.

Frankish Authority

Transferring Power: Baldwin II Comes to Edessa

The offer to succeed his cousin in Edessa must have sounded promising to Baldwin II; he was serving as commander of Bohemund 's military forces in Antioch when Baldwin became king. Count of Edessa was certainly an advancement, but what exactly did the title convey? Only the vague and perhaps unfulfillable promise that those who had been loyal to his cousin would also be loyal to him. Baldwin I had governed the area through personal relationships established on the battlefield and in *realpolitik* encounters with Armenian lords and urban communities. It is possible that Baldwin II had not even visited Edessa before his accession and knew little of the style of governance there.[2]

Baldwin II in effect received only his cousin's recommendation that he should rule Edessa—his predecessor's relationships were personal, not institutional, and therefore were not transferable without the cooperation of those governed. Nevertheless, Baldwin II never faced a rebellion against him in the city of Edessa in his eighteen years as ruler, as his cousin had, suggesting that at least Edessans accepted his authority. His authority elsewhere, however, was shaky. He had inherited small pockets of territory surrounded by lands ruled by autonomous warlords, either Armenian or Turkish. He ruled the city of Edessa itself, which was an important center of trade, and likely produced a substantial income;[3] in addition, he controlled Tell Bashir, Rawandan, and Samosata. Tell Bashir and Rawandan were separated from

Edessa by two obstacles: the Euphrates river and the Armenian lords Ablgharib and Kogh Vasil, who controlled the castles of al-Bira and Hromgla respectively.[4] These two fortresses protected the two most important crossings of the Euphrates in northern Syria; Baldwin's ability to pass between his two territories was thus dependent on the goodwill of these Armenian lords. Even those areas under his direct rule had Armenian soldiers and castellans, such as P'er of Tell Bashir. Armenians also ruled lesser fortresses, such as those of Nicusus, Bagrat, and the nameless one in which Baldwin I took refuge during his initial journey to Edessa;[5] it is unclear to what extent such warlords accepted Frankish authority. Baldwin I, through his military and political abilities, had won the grudging respect of many Muslim and Christian warlords, yet they trusted him no more than they trusted one another. Baldwin II sought to subordinate local lords; those who did not submit he replaced, usually with his own relatives.[6]

Establishing Frankish Authority

Baldwin II did not immediately institute changes; he initially followed in his cousin's footsteps as he established his authority in Edessa and beyond. Within a year of becoming count, he married an Armenian woman named Morfia,[7] the daughter of Gabriel, the ruler of Melitene.[8] The city's location on the western bank of the Euphrates as it snakes into the Anatolian highlands gave the city control of much of the communications between Syria and eastern Anatolia. It was also the last city still under Christian control as one traveled north along the Euphrates River, and was thus a bulwark against the Danishmend Turks who had settled the Anatolian highlands.[9]

With a large Jacobite population who resented Gabriel's political power[10] and a dangerous frontier location, Gabriel felt himself to be in a precarious position. Like T'oros, Gabriel had been in the market for military backup. According to the anonymous chronicler, Gabriel had first sought aid from Bohemund, and had offered Morfia's hand to him.[11] Bohemund had marched north to protect the city, but was captured in battle by Malik Ghazi Gümüshtigin ibn-Danishmend, the emir of Sivas (ancient Sebasteia).

Like Gilded Age American belles in England, Franks had power, but Armenians had the titles and entrée into what seemed to the Franks a legitimate place in the larger Syrian world. The alliance between Baldwin and Gabriel served several purposes. Baldwin had gained through his Armenian wife a sense of kinship with the Armenians of Edessa, a connection strengthened by the fact that T'oros had been married to Morfia's sister. The marriage may have given Edessans a sense of stability as they were confronted with an ever-changing leadership. Baldwin may also have married his sister to the Armenian lord Levon, son of Constantine.[12]

One wonders, however, how Morfia felt about the marriage, given that she was coming to the city where her sister had been murdered by an angry mob. Certainly, the marriage did little to protect Gabriel; he died in 1101, killed when Gümüshtigin captured Melitene.[13] His daughter fared better. If Morfia feared that her marriage would lead to her sister's fate, she need not have worried. First countess of Edessa, she later reigned as queen in Jerusalem with Baldwin, and their children married into the leading Frankish families of the Levant. By 1163, their grandchildren included the count of Tripoli and the king of Jerusalem, and two of their great-grandchildren became the prince of Antioch and the empress of Byzantium.

Other Frankish lords in northern Syria followed the example of the two Baldwins. Baldwin's cousin Joscelin married the daughter of the Armenian Constantine, son of Rupen,[14] and another cousin, Galeran of Le Puiset, married the daughter of Ablgharib, lord of al-Bira, the castle protecting the most important ford of the Euphrates in northern Syria. It is likely that Franks of lower rank in Edessa and Antioch followed their leaders' examples and married local Christian wives. Little evidence of such marriages survives, aside from Fulcher of Chartres's famous evocation of the transformation of identity for the Franks who settled in the Levant, which proclaimed that "we who were Occidentals have now become Orientals. He who was a Roman or a Frank has in this land been made into a Galilean or a Palestinian. He who was of Rheims or Chartres has now become a citizen of Tyre or Antioch." Marriage was an integral part of that transformation: "some have taken wives not only of their own people but Syrians and Armenians or even Saracens who have obtained the grace of baptism. One has his father-in-law as well as his daughter-in-law living with him."[15]

Other Frankish leaders, however, did not marry locally. Bohemund (once released from captivity) and Tancred of Antioch arranged marriages with women from the French royal family, seeking closer ties to Europe. Other Franks in the Levant married the sisters or daughters of fellow crusaders. The marriages of Baldwin, Joscelin, and Galeran suggest that the Franks of Edessa perceived Armenian families as an avenue to bolster their own political standing, perhaps to a greater extent than their peers in Antioch, Jerusalem, or Tripoli did. They also demonstrate a disinterest in the religious differences between Franks and Armenians on either side. Morfia was already a Chalcedonian Christian, but Joscelin and Galeran's Armenian wives were members of religious communities not in communion with Rome, and it is unlikely that members of either couple converted.

The Two Sieges of Saruj: Armenian and Jacobite Perspectives

Baldwin II faced his first challenge as count only months after coming to Edessa. The episode reveals the fragility of his authority, the crushing violence of Frankish power, and the perspective of local Christians on that power, as narrated in strikingly different ways by Matthew of Edessa and the anonymous Edessan chronicler. In January 1101, the Turkish emir Sokman besieged Saruj. The city, approximately twenty-eight miles west of Edessa on the road connecting the city to the ford of the Euphrates at al-Bira, had been ruled by Sokman's nephew, Balak, prior to the crusader conquest in 1098, and although Balak had invited the Franks in to help him govern the city, his uncle was determined to expel them.[16] Baldwin's attempts to defend the city ended in defeat, and Saruj stood defenseless. On these events all sources agree. The subsequent events, however, are treated in strikingly different ways, with Matthew's account emphasizing Baldwin's treachery, fear and cruelty. While the Armenian chronicler praised the behavior of Fulcher, the Frankish count of Saruj, "a brave and mighty man and a person of saintly and pure conduct,"[17] who died defending the city, he vilified Baldwin, who after his defeat slunk back to Edessa and "took refuge in the citadel of Edessa together with three men and remained there reduced to a pitiable state."[18] Matthew paralleled Fulcher's valor and Baldwin's cowardice; Fulcher was described as *surb i merats marmnoy*, "pure of bodily sins," while Baldwin was scorned as *lalagin marmnov*, "pitiful in body," within two lines of text.

Baldwin's Frankish supporters soon coaxed him from the shelter of the citadel, and the count retreated to Antioch for military support, abandoning Saruj entirely. The Christian population of Saruj, along with the Latin bishop of Edessa,[19] had retreated to the citadel of the city for greater security. According to Matthew, the citizens and the bishop, finding their situation desperate and seeing little hope of aid from the defeated Baldwin, negotiated the surrender of the city to Sokman. When Baldwin returned with troops a month later, the citizens refused to renege on their agreement with Sokman, and denied Baldwin any assistance attacking the Turks who now were defending the city. Baldwin overwhelmed the defenses of the city with his own forces; and "slaughtered the entire population of the town with the sword. They pillaged the whole town and carried off a countless number of young boys, girls, and women to the city of Edessa. Thus Antioch and all the lands under Frankish control were filled with captives, while the entire town of Saruj flowed with blood."[20] Matthew's account of the events at Saruj emphasized Baldwin's failures as a leader and his cruelty toward his Christian subjects. His accusation that Saruj's citizens were either massacred or sold into slavery was shared by the Arabic chroniclers Ibn-Qalanisi,[21] Abu'l-Fida,[22] and Ibn al-Athir.[23]

Yet Matthew's narrative, despite its similarity to Arabic narratives, is inconsistent. Why would the Latin bishop of Edessa urge the citizens to cooperate with the Turks and oppose Baldwin? Why would Baldwin massacre a population acting under the advice of his own bishop? Matthew's story exemplifies the theme of betrayal he found fascinating, but does not best explain the events at Saruj.

The anonymous chronicler's version of events was quite different. Like Matthew, he recorded the defeat of Baldwin and his flight to Edessa "in fear."[24] Once abandoned by Baldwin, however, the Christian inhabitants did not negotiate; instead, they retreated to the citadel where they continued to resist the Turkish forces with "Papias, the Frankish bishop of Edessa." Baldwin then returned to Saruj with the forces he had gathered in Edessa and Antioch, attacked the Turkish besiegers, and with the cooperation of the Christians within the citadel, defeated them. The Muslim inhabitants of the city, fearing reoccupation by the Franks, seized the town gates and walls and continued to resist Baldwin, despite the defeat of Sokman's army. The Franks urged the Muslims of the city to surrender, saying that they had no desire to kill them. When they refused, Baldwin ordered the Christian inhabitants of the city to wear badges with the sign of the cross. The Frankish forces broke into the city and massacred the inhabitants, sparing only those with crosses. To the anonymous chronicler's dismay, "the populous city was destroyed and the Christians left gathered round the citadel and lived there in poverty."[25]

The Jacobite tale of a city divided between rival groups, each allied to an army outside the city, reflected the fissile and localized nature of identity in the twelfth-century Middle East. The account noted the massacres that Matthew and Ibn al-Qalanisi described, yet placed the events in a far more intelligible light.[26] While both Matthew and the anonymous chronicler referred to the presence of the Frankish bishop of Edessa among the Christians of Saruj, only the Syriac account reconciled his presence with the destruction of the city, which appeared contradictory in Matthew's narrative.[27] The anonymous account furthermore emphasized the close cooperation between the local Christians and the Franks, of which the Latin archbishop's leadership was emblematic.

The anonymous account of the events at Saruj show how differently local Christians interpreted moments of conflict with their new Frankish overlords, and the degree to which Matthew of Edessa's narrative of betrayal and violence has been accepted by historians as simply descriptive. The Jacobite account, however, suggests a far more complex world where local Christians were confronted with difficult choices, the consequences of which were never clear. Should the Jacobites of Saruj support the Latin bishop, or Sokman, whose family had once ruled the city? Should they support their Muslim neighbors, or their new Frankish Christian overlords? Who was here to stay?

The story also illustrated the tenuous nature of Frankish authority shortly after the transition from Baldwin I to Baldwin II. Fulcher, count of Saruj, did not seem to have anyone among his soldiers (Frankish, Armenian, or Jacobite) who could step into his place in a time of need; the burden of defending the city fell to the Latin archbishop. Nor did Baldwin II have many resources following his defeat by Sokman. None of the local lords (Constantine of Gargar, Bagrat, Kogh Vasil) seem to have participated in the battle on either side, and Baldwin was forced to go to Antioch, hat in hand, to find the troops necessary to regain the city.

Baldwin's response to the disaster at Saruj was to establish his own relatives in positions of authority within the county. It must have been soon after the incident at Saruj that he established his cousin, Joscelin of Courtenay, as the lord of Tell Bashir and Rawandan. Joscelin had come to Syria with the disastrous expedition of 1101.[28] The territory Baldwin granted him was at least a third of the county of Edessa at that point, and the grant immediately made Joscelin one of the most powerful Franks in northern Syria. Joscelin, in return, was fiercely loyal to Baldwin. Another Montlhéry cousin, Galeran of Le Puiset, became lord of al-Bira in 1116, after marrying the daughter of its lord, Ablgharib. As Jonathan Riley-Smith has pointed out, both cousins were Baldwin II's maternal kin, of the Montlhéry family of northern France, and their establishment in the Latin East under Baldwin's patronage led to their domination in both Edessa and Jerusalem for much of the early twelfth century.[29]

Armenian Authority: A Response to the Franks

As the Franks consolidated their authority in Edessa and Antioch and began to distribute lands and villages to their Frankish (and Armenian) followers, local lords responded with complementary and sometimes conflicting articulations of their own authority. Warlords like Kogh Vasil and Constantine of Gargar faced challenges that were often less military in character than cultural and competitive. While warlords and Franks did occasionally confront each other on the battlefield, the greater threat to local leaders was competition for military manpower, and the seduction of clear and confident articulations of authority. Some local lords in response encouraged conflict between the Franks in Edessa and Antioch, as we have already seen with Oshin and Bagrat. Such a tactic not only undermined Frankish unity, but also exposed the cracks in the ideology of Frankish power. Others retained Byzantine titles and viewed their political authority as a stand-in for imperial power, although the Byzantine empire maintained only a tenuous political position in northern Syria in the first decade of the twelfth century.[30] The continued use of imperial titles, such as *kouropalates* and *protonobelissimos*, reveals the enduring cultural presence of Byzantium long after political relationships with the imperial court were lost. For many in the Levant, both Christians and Muslims, the Roman empire was eternal, and many Christians believed that a revival of the Byzantine empire was part of God's plan for the end of the world, as the prophecy of Hovhannes Kozern suggested. Furthermore, the articulation of Byzantine authority gave some lords a language of power that could compete with crusader claims of divine support. Some Armenians looked to the period of Armenian independence in the Bagratuni period as inspiration, while others joined the Franks, served in their armies, and perhaps adapted Frankish cultural ideas to their own ends.

For most historians, the price Armenians paid as a result of the establishment of Frankish institutions in northern Syria was dramatic and tragic. Matthew of Edessa insisted that Baldwin II "gradually and successively overthrew the Armenian princes, dealing with them more harshly than with the Persians. Moreover, he harassed those Armenian princes who were still free from the domination of the ferocious Turks, and with unheard of cruelty compelled all of them to go into exile."[31] Having listed the tortures inflicted upon the princes expelled by Baldwin, Matthew sighed, "We would like to write further about their [the Franks'] many malicious deeds, but dare not, since we are under their authority."[32] His list encompassed most of the Armenian lords he mentioned in the course of his chronicle—Constantine of Gargar, Vasil Dgha (adopted son of Kogh Vasil), Ablgharib of al-Bira, and the infamous Bagrat. Latin sources complement Matthew's account by naming Frankish lords ruling in those places forcibly vacated by Armenians. By 1120, Baldwin II's cousin Galeran ruled al-Bira, and Geoffrey of Marash ruled K'esun. It seems a simple conclusion that Baldwin II systematically replaced autonomous Armenian lords with new Frankish lords loyal to him.

Two problems undercut the argument. The first is that the standard argument produces a narrative of relations between Franks and local Christians which repeatedly switches from one extreme to the other: during the First Crusade, local Christians embrace Franks with open arms, then soon afterward local Christians resent Franks for usurping power, then a decade later local Christians again embrace the Franks, risking their lives to rescue them from captivity, following them into battle, particularly under Joscelin of Courtenay, and finally pining for Frankish rule once Edessa is conquered by Zengi. The second is that this narrative relies almost entirely on the testimony of Matthew of Edessa, which historians of the crusades have taken as descriptive and normative. As discussed above, Matthew was not interested in composing a description of historical events, but crafted his text around the evidence he could find of the approach of the apocalypse and the renewed activities of Satan in the world. Matthew was therefore not interested in producing a consistent picture of Armenian-Frankish relations, and thus he happily accused the Franks of the cruelest deeds and praised them for piety on the same page.[33] Matthew's chronicle nevertheless is a critical document for understanding Armenian attitudes toward the Franks. It is not to his descriptions of moments of betrayal and conflict that historians should look, but to his general tone of competition and anxiety over loss of Armenian identity, so symptomatic of rough tolerance. To understand the growth of Frankish power and its impact on local lords, we must piece together information and perspectives from a variety of sources.

Armenian Lords, Byzantine Titles

T'at'ul, an Armenian ruling Marash, responded in what was likely the most common way of articulating political authority—through vague association with the Byzantine *imperium*. Greek, Syriac, Latin, and Armenian sources all paint different pictures of Marash in the early twelfth century, a confusion that may reflect the ambiguities of local authority. It was ruled by Philaretos, and Michael the Great believed it was ruled by his sons after his death. The crusaders camped at the city in the course of their march toward Antioch in the fall of 1097 and found a Turkish garrison who fled on their approach.[34] Matthew believed that the crusaders returned Marash to the control of Byzantium, as they were obliged to do by their oaths sworn in Constantinople.[35] Yet none of these accounts are about permanent control of the city, merely about armies passing through. Each passage does not necessitate a change in the ruler of the city, simply an ability to be accommodating. Bohemund of Antioch and his cousin Richard of Salerno returned to besiege the city in 1101, at which time it was defended by an Armenian named T'at'ul.[36] The siege failed, but in 1105/6, Matthew recorded that "the city of Marash was taken from the Greeks; for the Prince of princes [T'at'ul] left this city and gave it to Joscelin. For a large sum of gold he sold an icon of the Theotokos to the great prince T'oros, the son of Constantine, son of Ruben; then he went to Constantinople."[37] Rather than surrendering the city to another Armenian such as T'oros of Vahka or Kogh Vasil, both of whom held territory adjacent to the city, he gave it to Joscelin. Again, Armenian lords preferred to trust the Franks rather than others of their own kind.

T'at'ul appeared only in Matthew's chronicle, and there his authority was vaguely dependent on Byzantine power, perhaps resembling the ambiguous relationship T'oros of Edessa had with the *imperium*. Matthew referred to T'at'ul as a "Roman general," and also gave him the unusual title *ishkhan ishkhanats'*, literally "prince of princes."[38] This title, which Armenian leaders first received from the 'Abbasid caliphs in the ninth century, was also employed by Byzantine emperors to reward Armenian princes allied to the empire. T'at'ul left behind his own form of self-identification, not in the pages of a text but inscribed in lead on the seal he used to identify himself in documents. The seal listed two of his Greek titles, "archon ton archonton" (the Greek version of prince of princes) and "protonobelissimos."[39] The two Greek titles, together with the seal itself, associated T'at'ul with imperial authority. Yet neither Greek nor Latin chronicles support the idea that he commanded Byzantine troops, or that the titles he held gave him authority over Marash.[40]

Rather than suggesting that he was a Byzantine functionary, T'at'ul's titles were an attempt to foster an image of an autonomous Armenian prince allied with Byzantium. T'at'ul could thus have his cake and eat it too. As the sources of Armenian power in Syria arose largely from the military muscle of the warlords, they were often dismissed as brigands or usurpers. Claiming the emperor as the source of his authority enhanced T'at'ul's status among the population he ruled and gave him greater legitimacy in Frankish eyes. At the same time, the title of "prince of princes" evoked the heady days of Bagratid Armenia, when Armenians ruled in royal glory. The glimmer of that vanished prestige perhaps helped T'at'ul to attract military support from other Armenians through a language of power that rose above that of other warlords. The ambiguity of his claims also gave him a certain flexibility when dealing with the varied armies that marched past Marash. Although we do not know when he came to power, T'at'ul possibly accommodated a Byzantine army under Alexios's generals Montras and Butumides in 1104, and certainly a Turkish garrison sometime before the First Crusade and the crusader army itself in 1097. Nor were Christians the only ones to evoke Byzantine titles and images to assert their authority. The Turkmen emir of Sivas, Gümüshtigin, did the same through coins that featured a nimbused Christ on one side and a Greek inscription on the other, entitling him "the great amir," a form that deliberately echoed Byzantine coins.[41]

Kogh Vasil: Evoking the Glories of the Past

Other Armenians sought to establish their authority independently of both the Byzantines and the Franks. Kogh Vasil, the Armenian ruler of K'esun, Raban, and other Syrian towns, identified himself with the great kings of Armenia's past. We know far more about Kogh Vasil than about T'at'ul because Kogh Vasil had a propagandist—Matthew of Edessa, who settled in K'esun sometime after Kogh Vasil had died.[42] Kogh Vasil's territories lay between Antioch and Edessa, a position that left him vulnerable to Frankish attacks, yet also made him an important potential ally for both.[43] Matthew did not record how Vasil came to power; he first mentioned the Armenian when Vasil helped to raise the ransom money in 1103 to gain Bohemund's release from Emir Gümüshtigin. Michael the Great suggested that he was an associate of Philaretos and gained power after his fall.[44]

Unlike T'at'ul, who used the image of Byzantine authority, Kogh Vasil cultivated the traditional qualities of Armenian royalty and was portrayed by Matthew of Edessa as a successor to the Bagratuni kings of Armenia. Although Vasil himself arose from humble origins (*kogh* means "robber"), he claimed the majesty and proud heritage of the ancient Armenian aristocracy through his wife, who Matthew suggested belonged to the Kamsarakan family.[45] The Kamsarakans were once one of the leading princely lineages of early medieval Armenia, descendants of the ancient royal Arsacid dynasty and of the founder of the Armenian church, St. Gregory the Illuminator, but perhaps equally important was the connection such a heritage gave Kogh Vasil in the early twelfth-century world. The Pahlavuni family, who controlled the Armenian katholicate throughout the twelfth century, also claimed descent from the Kamsarakans.[46] The relationship was "invented" or emphasized in order to connect Vasil to ancient Armenian glory, and to the current patriarchs. Being able to claim an aristocratic heritage, even if through his wife, enabled Vasil to assert his power in the wider Armenian context of Cilicia and Syria without being seen as a tyrant and usurper, as Philaretos was—or so Vasil hoped.

Vasil further demonstrated his regal qualities by becoming patron and protector of the Pahlavuni patriarchs (his putative Kamsarakan relatives), and by extension of the Armenian church, the only surviving institution from the days of past Armenian glory. His greatest competitor for this role, however, was not another Armenian lord but Baldwin II himself. In 1103/4, the Armenian patriarch Barsegh Pahlavuni left the semi-ruined city of Ani. "The Frankish count Baldwin received him with great honor, as is befitting a patriarch. Moreover, the count gave him villages and various other presents and had a very high regard for the Armenian patriarch."[47] Baldwin reaped political benefits from this act of religious patronage and strengthened his ties to the Armenians of Edessa. However, Barsegh was not the sole Armenian *kat'olikos*. Barsegh's uncle Gregory II, also *kat'olikos*, had taken up residence in K'esun under Vasil's protection sometime before he died in 1106. He was the elder patriarch, having been ordained patriarch in 1065/6, the first of many Pahlavunis in the position.[48] Having secured one *kat'olikos*, Vasil then invited Barsegh to leave Edessa and join his uncle under his protection. By the time Vasil himself died in 1112, Barsegh had done so, and was Vasil's "spiritual advisor and father confessor."[49] Baldwin was left patriarchless.[50]

Martial prowess was also part of Kogh Vasil's image. Matthew of Edessa emphasized that while the Franks of Edessa suffered defeat after defeat at the hands of the Turks in the first decade of the twelfth century, Vasil was defending Christians and winning victories at Turkish expense. Vasil "brought together a regiment of Armenian troops; and brave as lions or lion cubs, these soldiers rushed against the infidels."[51] Matthew listed some of the great fighters in Vasil's army: his adopted son Vasil Dgha, his nephew Peter, and Aplasat' and Tiran. The image was one of a great warrior-king and his heroic retinue, an image long associated with kingship and power, ultimately deriving from Persian sources.

Vasil used the geographical position of his territory, located in the foothills that connected Edessa to Antioch, to ensure that his principality was not overrun by the Franks, as can be seen in his actions while Bohemund was held captive by the Turkish emir of Sivas, Gümüshtigin. Tancred, Bohemund's nephew, who had assumed control of Antioch during his uncle's captivity, showed little enthusiasm for working toward Bohemund's release.[52] Instead, Baldwin I, Bernard, the Latin patriarch of Antioch, and Kogh Vasil contributed money for the prince's release. Vasil's contribution implicated him in the brewing conflict between Bohemund and Baldwin II.[53] According to Matthew of Edessa, Kogh Vasil cemented his role as Bohemund's savior by adopting the Norman as his son.[54] In a strategy similar to that of Oshin of Lampron, Vasil encouraged conflicts between the two Franks so that neither could dominate northern Syria. By working for Bohemund's release, Vasil contributed to a chain of events that separated the Franks of northern Syria into three mutually hostile factions. Bohemund's return meant that Tancred lost the regency over Antioch. Kogh Vasil's alliance with Bohemund tacitly supported the Norman's claim to be overlord of all northern Syria, including Edessa, a claim Baldwin not surprisingly resented. While such scheming may make Kogh Vasil appear unnecessarily Machiavellian, it fits a pattern of behavior shared by Oshin, Bagrat, and others.

Vasil's interest in fostering discord is evident in his response when conflict between Tancred and Baldwin II became war. Tancred in 1108 (again acting as regent for Bohemund) attempted to force Baldwin II to become subject to Antioch. Although Vasil had previously maintained close ties to Bohemund and Tancred, he took this opportunity to ally with Baldwin;[55] the conflict also drew in local Muslim lords. The issue had no direct relevance to Vasil; his concern was that neither party grow too powerful, and to that end, he allied with Baldwin, the weaker party. Tancred won the battle, but Baldwin I of Jerusalem intervened and forced Tancred to accept Edessa's independence from Antioch.

For a decade, Vasil was the most powerful leader among the Armenians, and a rival to the Franks in terms of prestige and military might. When he died in 1112, "there was profound grief throughout all Armenia." Matthew testified that "around this prince were united remnants of the Armenian [royal] army, members of the Bagratid and Pahlavid families, sons of the kings of Armenia, together with the military aristocracy."[56] His death led to a rapid collapse of his principality, in part because his successor, his adopted son Vasil Dgha, could not play Edessa and Antioch against each other as his father had. Tancred had died at the same time as Vasil, and was succeeded by his nephew Roger,[57] who in 1116 married Baldwin II's sister Cecilia,[58] ending the years of feuding between Edessa and Antioch. One of the agreements that accompanied the marriage may have been that Roger would no longer support Armenian lords against Baldwin, for soon after the marriage, Baldwin II attacked Raban, one of Vasil's most important towns. Vasil Dgha sought support from other Armenian leaders, and himself married the daughter of Levon, son of Constantine. Levon, however, already had ties to Edessa—his sister had married Joscelin, lord of Tell Bashir, and he himself may have married another of Baldwin II's sisters. Like Constantine of Gargar and others, they sided with the Franks against a fellow Armenian lord. Levon's brother seized Vasil and handed him over to the Franks. According to Matthew of Edessa, Baldwin tortured him and forced him to hand over his territories. The young lord eventually fled to Constantinople, the haven for all exiled and defeated Armenians.[59]

Armenian Lords in Cooperation with Franks

The fate of both T'at'ul and Kogh Vasil give support to Matthew's accusations that Franks systematically eliminated Armenian warlords. Jacobite sources suggest, however, that a number of other Armenian lords continued to hold power under the Franks. Matthew lamented the death of Constantine of Gargar in a Frankish prison in 1116/7, a victim of an earthquake, but the anonymous chronicler revealed that his son Michael still ruled Gargar in 1122, the year the city passed into Frankish hands.[60] Michael gave up the citadel, not under pressure from the Franks, but because he was no longer able to defend it against Turkish attacks. Nor did the Franks retain Gargar for themselves—Joscelin sold it to Vasil, brother of the Armenian *kat'olikos*, who remained lord there until 1149/50, when he was captured by Mas'ud, sultan of Rum.[61] As compensation for the loss of Gargar, Joscelin, successor to Baldwin II as count of Edessa, gave Michael control of Dülük, a town just to the north of Aintab (modern Gaziantep).[62] Dülük (in Latin, Tuluppa) is better known as Doliche, the classical cult site of Zeus Dolichenus. Set on the largest hill in the area, Dülük dominated the land around Aintab, and protected the road connecting Marash to al-Bira. After Michael moved to Dülük, we do not hear from him again.[63] The later history of the fortress, however, gives some sense of its importance within the county. By the 1130s, it was the site of a Latin archbishopric (transferred from Muslim-ruled Manbij, ancient Hierapolis).[64] Not only did local warlords survive until the final conquest of the county in 1150, but the Franks even gave them new lordships in the strategic center of their lands.

The vital fortress of al-Bira, which protected the most important crossing of the Euphrates in northern Syria, came under Frankish rule in a way that left its Armenian lord in an ambiguous position. Galeran of Le Puiset, first cousin of Baldwin,[65] married the daughter of its lord, Ablgharib. According to Matthew, the marriage took place under strained circumstances, for Baldwin II and Galeran were besieging the city at the time. Following the marriage, Ablgharib left al-Bira and settled in Anazarba in Cilicia.[66] Again, Matthew's account is suspect. The principal motivation for the marriage was to harness Ablgharib's authority for Galeran's benefit, and to ensure that Frankish authority had legitimacy in the city. Neither goal was served through the events as Matthew recounted them. How would Ablgharib in exile strengthen Galeran's position? Why marry the daughter of a man you intend to send into exile? Anazarba, furthermore, was controlled by Levon, who, as we have already seen in the case of Vasil Dgha, preferred to cooperate with his Frankish in-laws than with other Armenian lords. Clearly, Galeran benefited the most from the marriage. A time-consuming and expensive siege was ended, and he could hope that as the son-in-law of the city's former lord, he might enjoy the loyalty and military support of its citizens. Possession of al-Bira and its environs elevated Galeran as one of the Frankish leaders in northern Syria, and meant that control of northern Syria was firmly in the hands of the Montlhéry family. Yet the marriage must have preserved Ablgharib's position to some extent, or he would have had little incentive to surrender both his castle and his daughter to Galeran.

Other cities may have remained in the hands of local Christian lords ignored by Matthew. Michael the Great mentioned several other lords who held territory under the Franks whose ultimate fate is unknown—listing the Jacobite brothers Constantine, Tavtoug, and Kristopher, who ruled in the mountains near the Jacobite monastery of Mar Barsauma, and the Armenian Ohannes, who ruled at Kahta.[67] When Vasil in Gargar (who ruled there until the end of the county of Edessa) and Michael in Dülük are put together with other lords whose fates are unknown, it becomes evident that local warlords continued to control substantial strongholds in the county of Edessa until its final conquest. What we do not know is how Michael, Vasil, Kourtig,

Ohannes and others articulated their authority. Did they consider themselves independent lords as Kogh Vasil had? As clients of the Byzantines? Or, more likely, did they identify themselves with Frankish authority?

Local Christians Exercising Frankish Authority

Many Armenians shared in the new Frankish polity, and continued to identify with it even when the Franks were not prospering. Baldwin II and his budding principality faced their first serious threat in 1104. Two Turkish emirs, Shams al-Daulah Chökürmish of Mosul and Baldwin's old enemy Sokman ibn-Artuk, now of Mardin, marched on Edessa in the spring. Baldwin sought support from Joscelin, Bohemund (recently released from captivity), and Tancred; the Frankish leaders decided to attack Harran, a city still under Turkish control yet only twenty-three miles from Edessa. The Turkish forces defeated the Franks and captured Baldwin II, Joscelin, and Benedict, the Latin archbishop of Edessa, depriving the county of its three most prominent Frankish leaders. The response of the county's local population is striking. In the eleventh century, such a defeat and capture of a *doux* of the city would have been followed quickly by his deposition and replacement, as happened to Parsama during a Turkish siege of the city.[68] Instead, Albert of Aachen asserted that the Armenian citizens chose Tancred to rule "until they saw if Baldwin could be ransomed or freed."[69]

The response of the Edessans was in contrast to the response of others in northern Syria, particularly those living under Bohemund of Antioch. Even though the battle took place in Edessan territory, and the Frankish leadership of that county was captured, it was Bohemund who suffered the loss of territory.[70] The Armenians of 'Artah, who had massacred their Turkish garrison on the approach of the crusade army only six years earlier, now invited the Seljuk prince Ridvan of Aleppo to reintroduce his troops.[71] The citizens of Tarsus, Adana, and Mamistra likewise expelled their Frankish garrisons and welcomed in the Byzantines.[72] While the Turks of Aleppo and the Byzantines gained territory as a result of the Frankish defeat, Armenian lords did not—that is, none of the Armenian populations in Edessa or Antioch invited Armenian leaders to replace the Franks. In this most concrete sense, the articulations of authority expressed by Kogh Vasil and others failed. For local populations, religious and ethnic identities did not trump all other considerations. In the fluid twelfth century, few assumed that a ruler from one's own community was necessarily the best choice. Perhaps Byzantine, Turkish, or Frankish rule gave local populations access to wider networks of trade or information, or perhaps some element we can no longer recover was involved. Whatever it was, it is clear that Armenian warlords did not have it.

Bohemund was so disheartened by the defeat and loss of territory that he decided that only large reinforcements from western Europe would allow Antioch to survive. He again appointed Tancred as regent, and sailed west. Tancred in turn left Edessa in the hands of his cousin and brother-in-law, Richard of Salerno.[73] Neither Richard nor Tancred made any effort to secure the release of Baldwin and Joscelin, and both Armenian and Jacobite sources agree that Richard exploited the county for his own profit. The anonymous chronicler considered Richard to be "a bad, tyrannical, unjust man, and greedy. . . . He inflicted on them [the Edessans] cruel tortures, imprisonments, and disgrace. He gathered much money, especially as he knew that he was a destroyer and a passer-by, not the true lord and heir."[74] Matthew similarly complained that Richard had "caused the ruin of many people."[75] According to Matthew, Richard's attempts to defend the city against Turkish attacks ended in the defeat of the city's forces, and on one occasion, Turkish troops even entered the city, massacring four hundred citizens.[76]

Even the brutality of Richard's regency, however, did not lead Edessans to turn to an Armenian leader such as Kogh Vasil or Constantine of Gargar, but instead served to heighten loyalty to the captive Baldwin (released through the efforts of Joscelin, who had obtained his freedom in 1106 or 1107). Edessans' anger toward Richard was expressed in the accusation that he was taking what rightfully belonged to their lord—Baldwin II.[77] This loyalty to the count not only was indicative of Baldwin's success in establishing his authority, but also shows the degree to which local Christians, in a city where power was previously granted through election, appointment, or conquest, had internalized the Frankish concept of political authority as a personal and increasingly transferable possession.

Franks, however, also adopted Armenian cultural and religious expressions, as Baldwin I had done in swearing his oaths on Armenian relics. The military forces of the county were perhaps where Franks and local Christians rubbed shoulders most often; local Christians fought alongside Frankish knights as equals. The Arab aristocrat Usama ibn Munqidh, whose family ruled the castle of Shaizar near the principality of Antioch, casually noted that the knights that his family held as hostages were both Armenians and Franks. Usama was a keen observer of the status of the knight in Frankish society, a subject he found fascinating, so he cannot be accused of confusing their status.[78] Furthermore, holding Armenians as hostages suggests that they were individuals of high prestige, whose redemption would be a high priority for the Franks.

Matthew of Edessa also noted the mixed character of the armies defending Edessa; when the Franks prepared to confront the forces of Mawdud, atabeg of Mosul in 1110, they were joined by the soldiers of Kogh Vasil and Ablgharib of al-Bira. The mixed army followed the Holy Cross of Varag, which "the troops of Edessa fastened to the end of a lance and carried it before them."[79] Just as the cross had served as a symbol of Baldwin I's acceptance of Edessa's Armenian character in 1097, now it served as a symbol of military cooperation, and the hope of divine support. Its use in battle recalls the Holy Lance, discovered in Antioch, which helped to convince the crusaders that, despite a lack of food, men, and horses and being besieged in a semi-destroyed city, they would defeat the enormous Turkish army outside the walls. Similarly, only a month after the capture of Jerusalem in 1099, the Franks discovered the True Cross of St. Helena, and bore it into battle, winning a momentous victory over the Egyptians at Ramla.[80] The Holy Cross of Varag, however, was not "found," as the Holy Lance and True Cross had been. The cross of Varag was already venerated by the Armenians of Edessa and the surrounding area before the arrival of the First Crusade and provided a reminder of their status as a people in exile.

Roughly contemporary with these events, Baldwin II issued a new coin that appears to represent the Holy Cross of Varag. The copper *folles* shows a figure in armor (presumably Baldwin) with a sword on his left hip, and holding a cross in his right hand. The inscription reads "ΒΑΛΔΟΥΙΝΟC ΔΟΥΛΟ CΤΑΥ[ΠΟ]," "Baldwin, servant of the cross."[81] The combination of the issue of this new coin with the use of the cross of Varag in battle suggests a deliberate campaign to ensure Armenian loyalty to the Franks. The use of the cross as a military symbol was a distinctively Frankish gesture, but the use of the Holy Cross of Varag created a synthesis of different religious traditions in order to protect the city. Perhaps Armenian priests even participated in religious ceremonies for the army before its departure for battle. The issue of the coin made the cross the new symbol for Frankish power in northern Syria, thus linking Baldwin's authority and Armenian piety to combined military strength.

The comparison of the cross of Varag with the cross of Jerusalem illustrates the frustrating one-sided character of textual sources from twelfth-century Syria and Palestine. While we can discuss the significance of the cross of Varag to Armenians, we do not know how Franks viewed the cross that led them into battle. Did they know of its association with the monastery of Varag and with Hrip'sime, one the founders of Christianity in Armenia? Or did they connect it directly to the cross of Jerusalem? Likewise, we have little sense of how indigenous Christians of Jerusalem viewed the cross that led the Franks into battle there. According to Albert of Aachen and other chroniclers, the cross in Jerusalem was found when a local Christian revealed its hiding place to the Franks.[82] The cross, then, was never lost, and the local Christian community that protected it may have attached to the cross any number of stories and meanings which have not been preserved, due to the lack of twelfth-century local Christian sources from Palestine.

The battle with Mawdud has a tragic postscript. The Edessan and Turkish armies largely avoided direct conflict, but at a vulnerable moment when the Frankish army was crossing the Euphrates, the Turkish army fell on the Armenian rear guard of the army, still on the east side of the river. Among the soldiers were many civilians who had fled Edessa and the surrounding area due to the siege and ensuing famine. Fulcher sadly reported, "they seized many of our people who were on foot and carried them off to Persia, particularly the helpless Armenians whom they had already wickedly pillaged."[83] Matthew of Edessa similarly recalled that "the Frankish forces, who were on the other side of Euphrates River, witnessed all these horrible things which were happening to all the Christians, but were unable to assist them in any way and so wept bitterly."[84] Even Matthew, who was usually suspicious of Frankish motives, acknowledged the sincerity of their grief.

Edessa Under Joscelin I

Baldwin II had come to power in Edessa through the beneficence of his cousin Baldwin of Boulogne, and when his cousin, now king of Jerusalem, died childless in 1118, Baldwin II took up his place in Jerusalem. He in turn invested his cousin, Joscelin of Courtenay, lord of Tell Bashir and Rawandan, as the next count of Edessa. Upon his accession to power, Matthew remarked that "Joscelin, abandoning his former cruel nature, now adopted a very humane and compassionate attitude toward the inhabitants of Edessa,"[85] and indeed, much of Matthew's hostility toward the Franks evaporated once Joscelin took power. While Baldwin II had built up the internal structure of the county, Joscelin was a vigorous military leader intent on expanding the county's boundaries. Even on his deathbed, he was carried on a litter at the head of his army to confront the Seljuk sultan of Rum, Kilij Arslan, who was besieging K'esun. On hearing of Joscelin's advance, the sultan retreated, all too aware of Joscelin's reputation on the battlefield.[86]

Evidence from the period of Joscelin's rule gives us a sense of other forms of authority that local Christians wielded under the Franks. An Armenian inscription preserved near the East Gate of Edessa, dated to the year 1122, attested that an Armenian named Vasil held the office of *terapahutuin*, which literally means "protector of the place" in Armenian, and indicated that Vasil's position was something like governor of the city of Edessa, or perhaps regent while the count was absent.[87] The prominent position of the inscription near one of the main gates of the city, and the public use of Armenian instead of Latin, indicate that the Armenian population of Edessa retained a large measure of political power and esteem even after two decades of Frankish rule. Similarly, Michael bar Shumana, brother of the chronicler and bishop Basil, held the Syriac title of "medabberana" of Edessa in 1129,[88] a title which suggests that Michael held the same position as Vasil. Both titles convey significant authority over the city, perhaps second only to the count himself.

Perhaps one of the most striking expressions of loyalty between Armenians and Franks was the rescue of Joscelin and King Baldwin II. Joscelin and his cousin Galeran of al-Bira were first captured in 1122 near Saruj by Balak of Harput, an ironic turn given that he was the Balak who was the former ruler of Saruj. King Baldwin II of Jerusalem, formerly count of Edessa, was already regent over Antioch for the underage Bohemund II, and now he also took his old county under his protection and marched north to free his cousins. Balak, however, captured the king as well, and imprisoned all three rulers in his stronghold of Harput, leaving the whole Frankish East effectively leaderless. In a daring raid recorded in astonishment in Latin, Armenian, Syriac, and Arabic chronicles, a group of fifteen Armenians from Behesni planned their rescue, "a deed to be remembered forever."[89] Disguising themselves as monks (according to one report), they managed to enter the castle and seize it from its Turkish garrison. Baldwin remained with the Armenians to hold the fortress, while Joscelin returned to Tell Bashir with two companions, crossing the Euphrates, William of Tyre tells us, with the support of two inflated wineskins. He hastened to Antioch and Jerusalem in search of troops to aid Baldwin, while Balak, at that time in Aleppo, quickly returned to Harput and besieged it. After the Turkish leader undermined the walls of the fortress, Baldwin surrendered. Balak executed the Armenians who had rescued Baldwin, and transported the king and Galeran to Harran, also under his control. The emir died soon after, and Baldwin was eventually ransomed from his heir Timurtash.

The bold rescue attempt by the Armenians of Behesni was an unprecedented gesture. Being held hostage was not an unusual experience for Frankish leaders. Both Baldwin and Joscelin had been taken captive in 1104, and Bohemund I was a hostage in 1100. The situation posed little threat to the well-being of the hostage; the captors generally sought money and sometimes territorial concessions but rarely executed their hostages. We cannot know what motivated the rescuers—hope of reward,[90] loyalty to Joscelin, or antagonism toward Balak—but we can note how their actions were perceived by Armenian, Frankish, and Jacobite chroniclers. William of Tyre called the rescuers "faithful and valiant," and recorded the tortures they suffered upon their capture by Balak. Matthew of Edessa considered it a "very courageous feat," and despite his interest in the betrayal and suffering of Armenians, he did not emphasize that it was the Armenians who were executed when the castle was surrendered.

It was not only Joscelin among the Franks who enjoyed close relations with Armenians under his rule. Baldwin, count of Marash, is perhaps the individual who captured the complexity of the northern Syrian world the best. His origins are unclear; the Armenian chronicler Gregory the Priest and Baldwin's own Armenian confessor believed that he was the brother of Raymond of Antioch, and therefore a son of William IX of Aquitaine, though no Latin sources confirm this identity.[91] By the 1130s, however, he was the most powerful lord in the county of Edessa. Gregory the Priest, who continued Matthew of Edessa's chronicle, praised his military prowess and skill as a ruler; noting that while Raymond of Antioch "was a man of tremendous power and might; however, he was not as skillful in the art of ruling as Baldwin, who was lord of K'esun and Marash and territories dependent on these two towns, comprising an area from the borders of Melitene to the gates of Antioch. This Baldwin was young in age but old in experience and agreeable in the eyes of God by all his deeds of prowess."[92] Baldwin had close relationships with Armenians under his rule. The *dux* of K'esun under Baldwin was an Armenian named Vahram, a name which evoked the Pahlavuni family which had long resided in the area. His Armenian confessor Barsegh noted that he spoke Armenian fluently.

Much of what we know about Baldwin derives from the funeral oration that Barsegh wrote to commemorate his death in 1146, and the oration exemplifies the complexity of relations between the Frankish elite and Armenian communities. Barsegh's eulogy was equal parts grief for a lost leader and fierce denunciation of Frankish injustice. Barsegh speaks of the lamentation of the Christians of Baldwin's realm at the "senseless and accursed death" of "this mighty champion and well-known soldier of Christ, my beloved Baldwin."[93] Like Matthew of Edessa, Barsegh delighted in the description of the coexistence of good and evil. He described Baldwin in paradoxical hyperbole, calling the Frank "this incorrigible and abandoned deceased leader, this irredeemable captive, this person who has disappeared from sight, a handsome young man, a brave and mighty warrior, an ingenious, wise, and prudent prince whose life was so short, this gallant and charming man."[94]

Yet as much as he mourned the loss of such a soldier, Barsegh intended his oration as a warning to the Frankish leadership, for Baldwin was "an example to the unrepentant, arrogant, and wicked leaders of the western forces." Barsegh had tried to guide Baldwin to the path of virtue, and to warn him of his "impending destruction," and in the funeral oration took upon himself the task to "publicly declare and record in writing his errors, as if I attributed them to myself."[95] In Baldwin's voice, he continued to speak of his "innumerable, endless and merciless injuries and blasphemies," and to list his covetousness, pride, and evils acts.

Yet Barsegh reassured his audience that "all of Baldwin's sins have been forgiven, and he has been made whole through his ceaseless confession and afterward through the shedding of his blood in the great battle."[96] Baldwin died while attempting to recapture the city of Edessa from Nur al-Din in 1146, and Barsegh reported that "the merciless nature of his heart was redeemed on that day, because by his compassion and commiseration he agonizingly suffered for those he saw perish miserably."[97] Like the anonymous Frank in Matthew of Edessa's account who, when daringly attempting to destroy the Turkish catapult besieging Mantzikert, announced that "today my blood shall be shed for all the Christians," Barsegh believed that "this land was redeemed by the sole effusion of Baldwin's blood, which he willingly shed for the Christians."[98] As a result, "he has obtained remission of all his sins from the Lord, and on the frightful day of Judgment, when all the righteous will receive their recompense, he will be crowned by God together with the pious princes and brave martyrs; for we know and believe that his is the fate of those among the Christians who fall in battle by the sword of the infidels."[99]

Barsegh's impassioned and seemingly contradictory account encapsulates the complexities of the attitudes that regulated relationships between the ruling Franks and local Christians. Many others, including many Armenian soldiers, shared the occasion of Baldwin's death, yet Barsegh chose Baldwin, for whom he nourished "a spiritual love," to eulogize. Despite his willingness to detail Baldwin's numerous crimes, many of which were seemingly suffered by Armenian communities under his rule, Barsegh redeemed his prince in a uniquely Frankish way—although not having taken the oath of a crusader, Baldwin achieved salvation through death in battle. If Baldwin had become culturally Armenian in language and ecclesiastical allegiance, then his chaplain had become theologically Frankish. Although Barsegh never detailed Baldwin's many misdeeds, he left his audience with little doubt that the count had used his authority to oppress, undermine, and impoverish the Armenian community he governed. Yet the priest did so only within the confines of praising Baldwin and describing his ultimate salvation. While the count's rule was clearly "rough," his immersion in a culturally Armenian world is equally evident.

Baldwin died in a battle to regain Edessa for the Franks. Zengi, the Turkish ruler of Mosul, had captured the city on Christmas Eve, 1144, while Joscelin II had taken his army to aid his Artukid ally, Kara Arslan of Hisn Kaifa. The defense of the city was left in the hands of the three bishops of the city—Hugh the Latin, Basil bar Shumana the Jacobite, and John the Armenian. They held the city for four weeks as Joscelin sought reinforcements from Jerusalem and Antioch. When the walls of the city were breached, the citizens fled to the citadel; in the panic many died, included Hugh, the Latin archbishop. The citadel, under the command of a Jacobite priest named Barsauma, surrendered three days later. Zengi's troops executed all the Frankish men and sold the women into slavery, but left local Christians largely unharmed.

Yet the local population, largely Armenian and Jacobite, were not willing to accept Zengi's rule. Two years after the conquest, a group of Armenians revolted against his lieutenant, Kutchuk Ali, who executed the leaders and expelled part of the Armenian community from the city. Zengi himself died shortly afterward, killed by a Frankish eunuch whom he caught drinking from the sultan's own wine supply. Joscelin thought this a ripe opportunity to recapture his capital, and having gained the support of the Armenians and

Jacobites of the city, broke into the city with Baldwin of Marash and a small army on 27 October 1146. The Turkish troops were prepared for him, however, and he was not able to gain control of the fortifications. Zengi's son Nur al-Din approached the city with a large army, and Joscelin decided to withdraw, followed by a large portion of the city's Christian population. The Turkish forces attacked, the Franks were defeated and scattered, and the Armenian and Jacobite citizens were massacred. It was in this battle that Baldwin of Marash died.

This battle was a fatal blow to the county. The Armenian bishop John was captured and taken to Aleppo; in 1150, Joscelin was also captured and taken in captivity to the same city. The anonymous chronicler declared that he was blinded, and he died nine years later, still in captivity. His last confession was made to Basil bar Shumana, the Jacobite archbishop of his former capital city. With his capture, his remaining lands rapidly fell into the hands of Nur al-Din and Mas'ud, the Seljuk sultan of Rum. Only one stronghold remained in Christian hands. Joscelin's widow Beatrice sold the castle of Hromgla, once held by Kogh Vasil, to the Armenian *kat'olikos*, Gregory III Pahlavuni. This last remnant of the county of Edessa remained in Armenian hands for the next century and a half, falling to the Mamluks only in 1292, a year after they conquered the last Frankish stronghold of Acre.

Edessa and the Frankish East

The short life of the county of Edessa, and the lack of Latin sources, has left it generally neglected historiographically, under the assumption that whatever happened there did not affect the larger Levant, particularly Palestine and Jerusalem. Yet it is hard to see how the county of Edessa could not have influenced the rest of the Frankish Levant. Certainly, the differences between northern Syria and Palestine were considerable. In Syria the Franks ruled over a largely Christian population whose local elites still held considerable power, land, and wealth. In Palestine, Muslims dominated politically and socially; correspondingly, local Christian communities had much less power, and were less numerous. Nevertheless, Christians may have constituted the majority in Palestine as well. The Christian population was concentrated in particular areas of the kingdom, particularly between Jerusalem and Nablus, along the coast between Acre and Tyre, and around Krak de Montreal (modern Kerak).

The political geography of Palestine, however, linked Syria and Palestine together. While Palestine never experienced the Byzantine reconquest of the tenth century (which in part explains why Armenians and Jacobites did not settle there in large numbers), it did share with Syria the dislocations and un-certainties inherent in being a frontier zone. In the late tenth century, the Fa-timids and Byzantines effectively divided the Levant between them, with the border somewhere around Aleppo; Palestine was firmly within the Fatimid world. In the eleventh century, however, both empires crumbled before Seljuk and Turkmen armies, and Jerusalem was prey to the same sort of war-lords as Antioch and Edessa. In the 1070s, Jerusalem fell to a Turkish warlord named Atsiz. In 1098 it was reconquered by the Fatimids, whose forces the crusaders faced in 1099. Thus it is likely that Melkite communities underwent fragmentation and loss of local leadership similar to that we have already seen in the Armenian and Jacobite communities.

Despite the many differences between Syria and Palestine, the Franks saw them as one area, part of a the same land of Syria or "Outremer," with as-sociations with sacred biblical history. Antioch was not holy on par with Jerusalem, but its association with the earliest days of Christianity gave it a status that shared in the same biblical sacrality. The crusaders who wrote to Urban in 1098 already associated Antioch with its fame as the first place where the followers of Jesus were called Christians. An anonymous pilgrim of the twelfth century connected the city with a litany of early Christian ref-erences, noting that it was the birthplace of St. Luke as well as the location of the shrine of the seven sons and their mother martyred by King Antiochus in the time of the Maccabees.[100]

Yet northern Syria and Palestine were bound together in other ways, no-tably by the experience of shared Frankish leadership. The first two kings of Jerusalem, the two Baldwins, were also the first two counts of Edessa before coming south, and their experiences in the north among the competitive and powerful Christian communities there formed a reference library on which they could draw when dealing with communities in their new realm. Like-wise, Tancred (d. 1113) had experience in ruling the Galilee, Antioch, and for a brief period Edessa. Even after he left Edessa, Baldwin II spent a consider-able portion of his time in the north. He was *bailli* (regent) of Antioch from 1119 to 1126, and similarly protected Edessa while Joscelin was in captivity from 1122 until 1123, and spent much of his time in those years in the north. Likewise his successor Fulk was *bailli* of Antioch from 1132 to 1135. Melisende, daughter of Baldwin II and regent of the kingdom after his death in 1131 until her son seized power in 1152, was born in Edessa and raised there by her Armenian mother Morfia. Her sons Baldwin III and Amalric both succeeded her, and both married Byzantine princesses. The rulers of Jerusalem could never ignore the significance of eastern Christianity, whether it was through experience in governing Antioch and Edessa, or through later alliance with the Byzantine empire.

The next two chapters show that Jerusalem was not a different world from Edessa, especially in Frankish eyes. Local Christians wielded considerable authority there as well, even if they were a smaller portion of the population. In fact, much of the power they wielded came from the Franks themselves, a result of the practices of rough tolerance in use.

Chapter 4

Rough Tolerance and Ecclesiastical Ignorance

For the chronicler Albert of Aachen, the triumph of the armies of the First Crusade at Antioch found its clearest expression not on the battlefield but in the religious ceremonies that followed the defeat of Kerbogha's army on 28 June 1098. The fifth book of his *Historia Hierosolymitana* began with the description of the cleansing of the cathedral church of St. Peter of the "iniquities" of the Turks, the rebuilding of ruined altars, the rediscovery of hidden icons and statues of Jesus and the saints. The restoration of physical buildings and sacred objects was only preparation for the spiritual celebration of the Christian community, now united in praise and thanksgiving to God. Albert described processions through the city streets, which culminated in the reenthronement of the city's Greek patriarch, John V the Oxite, an act that affirmed his authority over all Christians, Greek and Latin, in the city.[1]

John's enthronement is a moment worthy of some consideration. Despite having chosen not to return the city to Byzantine control, the crusaders did choose to restore John, the Byzantine patriarch Albert praised as "a most Christian man." At this moment at least, it seemed that the crusaders shared Urban's goal of liberating their "eastern brethren," not just cleansing the holy places of infidel pollution. Albert emphasized John's authority over all Christians; Greeks and Latins were united under his authority. Armenians and Jacobites, at this moment of Albert's historical imagination, did not exist. This celebration of a shared (yet exclusionary) Christian identity becomes all the more intriguing when contrasted with the letter the crusaders wrote to Pope Urban II from Antioch just three months later, declaring "we have subdued the Turks and the pagans; but the heretics, Greeks and Armenians, Syrians and Jacobites, we have not been able to overcome."[2]

Two words stand out in the crusaders' letter: "heretics" and "Jacobites." "Heretic" in particular is a loaded word. Particularly when used to gain the attention of the pope, the word evoked the program of eleventh-century western reformers, and suggested that it should be applied to the Christian East. The rhetoric of heresy could be an effective weapon for the consolidation of either secular or ecclesiastical authority, as contemporaries of the Franks realized. Thus the Franks had the language of heresy and submission at hand to use against local Christians, or Franks who associated with them, even as they were founding Antioch and other principalities in the Levant. They chose, however, not to use it.

The description of local Christians as "heretics" in the Antioch letter was unmatched in twelfth-century sources of the Latin East; it is the only such use of the term (with one exception discussed below) I have found before the writings of Jacques de Vitry, archbishop of Acre from 1216 to 1228, over a century later.[3] The term does appear briefly in some twelfth-century sources, but never in reference to the Christian communities of the Levant. Chroniclers of the First Crusade mentioned a "castle of heretics" the crusaders encountered in the Balkans, but they were clearly not Melkites, Jacobites, or Armenians.[4] The anonymous *Gesta* several times mentions "publicani," a term often used for heretics, as well as "azymites" and "agulani," whose meaning is more obscure but may derive from the Arabic *ghulam*, which could mean a warrior of servile origin. They appear, however, only in descriptions of Turkish armies, and are never explicitly called heretics, but are labeled one of the "gentes" or "nations" of the pagans.[5] The term "azymite" particularly shows the vagueness of this terminology, as it is a Greek term for heretics—namely, for Latins and Armenians. Again, nothing suggests that the author was referring to Greeks, Armenians, or Jacobites. William of Tyre used "heretic" to characterize Byzantines once in the last book of his history, when describing the massacre of Latins in Constantinople in 1182; though he discussed the Byzantines at many other points in his chronicle, only in this moment of tragedy did he loose a full volley of recriminatory language. He did not use "heretic" to describe Christians under Frankish rule, though this condemnation of the Byzantines implicitly categorized them as heretics too.[6]

The language of heresy never became a frame for characterizing indigenous Christians, nor a way to appeal for support from Latin Europe. Instead, over the following decades the Franks backed away from acquiring explicit theological and cultural knowledge about local communities, and refused, at least textually, to make them objects of categorization, investigation, or study. Thus, regarding local Christian communities, the Frankish regime was one of silence. Instead of categorizing them by language, customs, and religion or law,[7] as was the most common way to qualify difference, the Franks only recognized linguistic difference, thus obscuring the theological divisions through which the communities themselves articulated their identity.[8]

Local Christians from a Latin Perspective

If we rely only on Latin sources to examine the position of local Christians in the Frankish Levant, we get a vague and misleading picture, one that even deliberately obfuscated local Christian identity. The principal terms for local Christians employed by the Franks in accounts like Fulcher of Chartres, Albert of Aachen, and William of Tyre were "Graecus," "Surianus" along with its variants ("Syrus," "Surus"), and "Armenus." All three terms were apparently linguistic markers; Graeci were Christians who spoke Greek, Suriani were Christians who spoke Arabic or sometimes Syriac, and Armeni were Christians who spoke Armenian. The terms were thus accurate in terms of languages, but were theologically skewed. Surianus in particular was fuzzy; a Christian who spoke Arabic could be Melkite, Maronite, Jacobite, or Nestorian.[9] The terminology also separated into two groups some Christians who were united ecclesiastically and theologically—Melkites, who whether they spoke Greek or Arabic, shared the same beliefs and the same churches, but in Frankish imagination were divided into Graeci or Suriani.

The most common way to refer to local Christians in twelfth-century Latin text was as *Graeci et Suriani*. Yet this pairing was misleading. By the twelfth century, the Greek-speaking population of Jerusalem was a pilgrim and immigrant one. Jerusalem had once had a large indigenous Greek-speaking population, but by the tenth century the local population spoke almost exclusively Arabic. The eleventh century had brought renewed Byzantine influence in Jerusalem with the rebuilding of the Church of the Anastasis (the Holy Sepulcher) under Constantine IX Monomachos; the emperor as a result had greater influence over the patriarch and clergy of the church, and consequently more Byzantine-born clerics were found in the city. The Graeci who thronged the streets alongside the Suriani in Latin descriptions were in reality a few Byzantine pilgrims and clerics who had settled in Jerusalem. Knowledge of Greek as a literary and liturgical language survived, but it had died as a mother tongue.[10] Nor is sensible to consider "Graeci" and "Suriani" as terms to designate communities identified by liturgical languages. While both Arabic and Greek were used in Melkite liturgical services, it is unlikely that the Franks were so aware of the church-going practices of local Christians that they would know whether any particular Melkite attended services at a church with Greek or Arabic liturgy. The term *Graeci et Suriani*, then, was intended to evoke the multiplicity of local Christian liturgy and customs without explicitly describing them.

Yet the terminology, for all its vagueness, was subtly coded. Latin sources rarely used Suriani to describe Christians from the county of Edessa, where Jacobites far outnumbered Melkites, reserving the term for Christians from Antioch, Tripoli, and Jerusalem, where Melkites made up the bulk of the population. However, because Jacobites, Melkites, and even Nestorians in small numbers could be found throughout Frankish lands, a reader can never be certain to which community any particular Surianus belonged.

If Latin sources show Graeci appearing where they no longer existed, then they also failed to show Jacobites where they did flourish. Jacobites were effectively erased from Latin representation of the Levant. If we had only Latin chronicles as evidence, we would never how numerous and important the Jacobites were in northern Syria, or indeed that they were significant at all. Like the term "heretic," "Jacobite" (or any equivalent) is a rare beast in the thickets of the literature of the Frankish Levant, appearing only three times. One chronicler of the First Crusade used the term as a synonym for "Israelite"—clearly not a reference to Christians.[11] All other references to Jacobites come from pilgrimage texts. John of Würzburg noted that Jacobite monks celebrated services in the church of Mary Magdalene in Jerusalem, and included them in a long list of Christians in the Holy City, alongside Syrians, Nestorians, and Armenians, but also with Ruthenians, Britons, Irish, Hungarians, Bulgarians, and the unidentifiable Capheturici (perhaps a reference to Copts). It is unclear, therefore, whether John considered them a group distinguished by language and culture or by ecclesiastical identity.[12]

Another pilgrim, Theodericus, included the Jacobites in a list that did seem to be about separate religious groups, listing Latins, Syrians, Armenians, Greeks, Jacobites, and Nubians, but distinguished Jacobites from other Christians only by their name and by the claim that they used trumpets in ecclesiastical services in the style of the Jews.[13] A third reference comes from the late twelfth-century *Tractatus de locis et statu terre ierosolimitane*, which, as Benjamin Kedar has noted, is an early example of the shift from a pilgrimage narrative to a description of land, inhabitants, and local flora and fauna. The anonymous *Tractatus* is the most systematic of all pilgrim accounts, but expresses some confusion about local religious communities. In particular, the writer believed that Jacobites shared heretical beliefs with Nestorians, and that the Assassins were derived from a Jewish sect.[14]

That the only references to Jacobites come from pilgrims, visitors not accustomed to the ways of the Frankish Levant, rather than from Franks who had made Syria and Palestine their home, further illustrates the silence of those who likely knew the most about the Jacobites. Indeed, we would hardly know that Jacobite communities even existed in the Frankish East if we had only the evidence from the Frankish side.

Only in the thirteenth-century *Historia Orientalis* of Jacques de Vitry did a Frankish resident in the Levant define the Jacobites in Frankish imagination, as well as giving more precise descriptions of other local Christian communities. Jacques, who began his history in 1219, noted that the Jacobites had long ago been excommunicated by Dioscoros, patriarch of Constantinople. He explicitly labeled them heretics, the first to do so since the Antioch letter a century earlier, and described them as having all the characteristics of heretics: founded by a heresiarch, after whom they are named, Judaizers, who circumcise their children and thus make a mockery of baptism. In addition, they do not confess their sins to a priest, and erroneously believe that Christ has but one nature, and subsequently bless themselves with only one finger. Jacques also provided the first clear definition of "Surianus." The Syrians, according to Jacques, cover up their wives like the Saracens, and use Arabic in daily life. In culture and liturgy they are like the Greeks; and are thus "a perfidious people, full of duplicity and ruses like foxes in the fashion of the Greeks." Jacques also provided definitions of Nestorians, who appear in even fewer Latin sources than do the Jacobites, as well as of Maronites, Armenians, Georgians, and even Mozarabs.[15] Strikingly, Jacques did not separate "Graeci" out as a group distinct from the "Suriani," a choice that further suggests that the twelfth-century division of "Graeci" and "Suriani" was artificial. The thirteenth century, then, was willing and able to break the silence of the twelfth century, and categorize local communities by cultural and religious habits and beliefs, as well as by language, destroying the fiction of Graeci and Suriani as the two constituent Christian groups.[16]

Two descriptions of local beliefs and practices of local communities survive from the twelfth century that are similar to Jacques de Vitry, and both come from the pen of William, archbishop of Tyre and chancellor of the kingdom of Jerusalem. Both are exceptional in their detail and interest in defining and categorizing local religious communities. The first was a description of a Muslim group known among the Franks as the Assassins, who in the twelfth century controlled an independent principality on the borders of Frankish lands.[17] William repeated certain scandalous rumors about the group that also circulated among Sunni Muslims, but he presented them as a group that lived outside Frankish rule. His interest in them may derive from his lost work on the history of the Islamic Middle East, or it may arise because William saw the Assassins as potential converts to Christianity. The second group were Christians who did live under Frankish rule—the Maronites. William triumphantly included them in his chronicle because they had recently joined in union with the Roman Catholic church. Thus the Maronites were singled out as a group with distinct beliefs and practices only after those differences had effectively been sanitized by union with the Catholic church.[18] William's interest in the converted Maronites only emphasizes his disinterest in discussing Jacobites, Armenians, or Melkites in the same systematic way.

The refusal to know was in a sense a rejection of power, especially when such willful ignorance was embodied in texts such as the *Historia* of Fulcher of Chartres or the *Chronicon* of William of Tyre, which were intended to create an identity for Franks in the Levant, as well as to craft an image of the Frankish Levant for consumption in Latin Europe.[19] This disinterest can only be attributed to texts: letters from princes, chronicles commissioned by Frankish kings and ecclesiasts, and charters detailing property transfers and legally binding agreements, all of which were involved in the maintenance of Frankish authority on some level. The "private" knowledge of aristocrats, rulers and citizens of diverse cities and rural areas is unrecoverable and was probably detailed in regard to the identity, practice and theology of local communities, as will be discussed below. Significantly, they did not choose to perpetuate, spread, or codify that knowledge.

Although Palestine was a different world politically, culturally, and geographically from northern Syria, the Franks approached relations with local Christian communities in much the same way in both areas. By refusing to consider Melkites in theological terms, the Franks could treat them as they had the Armenians and Jacobites in northern Syria, as a community separated from them by culture and language, but not by theology. The various Levantine communities of Jews and Muslims were as invisible to the Franks as Jacobites, if not more so. Latin chronicles rarely mention Muslim and Jewish communities under Frankish rule (through they do appear in narratives of cities conquered and sacked), nor did the Franks evince any interest in the various groups among them. In charters, "Saracenus" and "Judeus" were sufficient designations. Despite the "ignorance" of the textual sources, Franks did have close relations with a variety of Melkite, Jacobite, and Armenian church leaders, an intimacy about which local Christian sources were not silent. Franks and local Christians also learned about each other through less formal means, through worship in shared churches and devotion to common saints.[20]

Local Priests and Patriarchs in the Frankish Levant

Frankish leaders did not treat local patriarchs, bishops, or monks as the crusader letter to Urban presented them—that is, as representatives of heretic and rival religious institutions that challenged the authority of their own. Nor did they ignore them as Latin chronicles suggest. Instead, the Franks treated them almost as they did the landscape itself—as peaks whose position and purview could become part of the bedrock of Frankish power, but that must be built upon before someone else usurped the position. Christian clergy, on their part, often chose to cooperate closely with royal and comital authority in order to harness Frankish power for their own benefit.

Patriarchs and Patronage in Northern Syria

For Jacobite bishops and patriarchs, the support of Frankish leaders was a resource not easily ignored, especially when they were faced with conflict within their community. From a Jacobite perspective, the Franks were little different from any other local potentates. The career of Athanasios VII, the Jacobite patriarch of Antioch from 1090 to 1129, gives a complex picture of how the Franks intervened in Jacobite affairs, leaving little doubt that, on the ground, Frankish leaders were intensely involved in the Jacobite community.

The Franks first became involved with the Jacobite community as a result of a dispute within the hierarchy of the church, specifically a conflict between the patriarch, Athanasios, and the bishop of Edessa, Basil. Two different accounts survive of this conflict—one by Michael the Great, who, as a successor of Athanasios as patriarch, naturally took the point of view of his predecessor, and the second by the anonymous Edessan chronicler, who likely here depended on Basil bar Shumana, bishop of Edessa, and therefore was partial to *his* predecessor's position. Each author emphasized different parts of the story. Athanasios, like many patriarchs of the medieval Middle East, was peripatetic—he had no fixed see or church. Over the decades of his patriarchate, he traveled largely within an area bounded by three places— Amida (modern Diyarbakir) in Mesopotamia to the east, the monastery of Mar Barsauma to the north, and Antioch to the west. Edessa lay approximately in the center. The death of the bishop of Edessa in 1101 seemed a golden opportunity for Athanasios to establish his patriarchate there, in one of the most important cities of Syria. As the anonymous Edessan chronicler wrote, "he did not have a place in Christian lands which agreed better than Edessa."[21] The citizens of the city, however, were not enthralled by the patriarch's plan and insisted on exercising their right to choose their own bishop, a request to which the patriarch Athanasios resentfully acceded. He ordained their choice, Abu Ghalib bar Sabuni, as bishop only on the condition that he return valuable gospel books that had belonged to a previous patriarch and had remained in Edessa. Abu Ghalib, who took the episcopal name of Basil, came from a well-known Jacobite family; his brother was Sa'id, the mourned and martyred bishop of Melitene. According to Michael, "the two brothers were famous in Syria, for their theological and secular learning, and also by their writings in two languages [Greek and Syriac] and by their arguments against the heretics."[22] It may have been Basil's status more than the missing gospel books that was the problem, in Athanasios's eyes. Tensions mounted on both sides, and before long Athanasios had anathematized the new bishop and the whole town.[23]

Once the patriarch and the bishop had turned against each other, one might expect that other leaders within the Jacobite community might mediate. Instead, the two clerics approached a number of Frankish leaders to help them resolve the crisis. The bishop Basil first sought the support of Baldwin II, the Frankish count of Edessa, who urged him to send a formal complaint to the Latin patriarch of Antioch, Bernard of Valence.

When Bernard questioned the two parties about the dispute, the translator misinterpreted one of Athanasios's statements, telling Bernard that the dispute was over money Basil owed the patriarch for the privilege of becoming bishop. The Latin cleric was horrified, assumed that the patriarch engaged in simony, and promptly imprisoned him. Athanasios's supporters, including a Melkite theologian named 'Abd al-Masih,[24] sought help from yet another Frankish leader—Roger, the prince of Antioch. Convinced by a hefty bribe, Roger told the Latin patriarch, "You should not judge the Syrians, because this power does not belong to you,"[25] and had Athanasios released. Thus Roger sided with Athanasios against his own patriarch. Unsurprisingly, this sequence of events made Athanasios disinclined to remain in Edessan territory, and unwilling to acquiesce to any further Frankish requests that he lift his excommunication of Basil.[26]

Significantly, it was the Jacobites who sought Frankish intervention in their affairs. Their appeal to ruling authority was born of long patterns of interaction with Muslim rulers. Appeals to caliphs, sultans, and emirs were commonplace among the Christian communities of the Islamic world. Bishops and patriarchs often denounced rivals and urged the imprisonment of those who challenged their authority, requesting Muslim rulers to step into struggles within the community. Athanasios VII himself had gone to the 'Abbasid caliph about 1096 to gain support against 'Abdur, his rival for the patriarchate.[27] Under the Franks, however, the rules had changed. Unlike the Muslims, the Franks did not forbid the head of the community to discipline his own flock by corporal punishment or imprisonment. The Jacobite patriarchate, however, had not developed the institutions of discipline that would have allowed Athanasios to bring Basil to heel by himself. Thus the conflict discussed above can in some senses be seen as the Jacobites working their way through the Frankish political and ecclesiastical system, attempting to probe its hierarchy and distribution of authority in order to discover who had the power to resolve the conflict they faced.[28] The answer seemed to be—nobody. Jacobite appeals to Frankish authority resulted in neither the cancellation of the excommunication of the bishop, nor the return of the gospel books, nor the replacement of the bishop by someone more agreeable to the patriarch.

Joscelin, Baldwin II's successor as count of Edessa, manage to resolve it more than a decade later, but again the initiative for Frankish involvement came from the Jacobites. Athanasios had spent the years following his conflict with the bishop of Edessa in a variety of places, including the monastery of Mar Barsauma at the borders of the county of Edessa, where "the monks were always in rebellion,"[29] but particularly in Amida, his birthplace, "the particular diocese of the patriarchal seat."[30] After some time in the environs of Amida, Athanasios again desired to move, but the ruler of the city prevented his departure, in part because Athanasios had excommunicated a locally influential deacon.[31]

Now Athanasios needed Frankish help. He appealed to Joscelin, who sent Michael bar Shumana, a prominent Jacobite resident of Edessa (and brother of the future archbishop), who was also the "administrator of the city and second in command to the ruler Joscelin,"[32] to demand the release of the patriarch. The emir reluctantly allowed the patriarch to leave out of fear of military attack. Athanasios spent some time with Count Joscelin at Tell Bashir and then returned to the monastery of Mar Barsauma.[33]

The death of Athanasios VII in 1129 finally gave Joscelin the opportunity to resolve the conflict. The count quickly seized from the monastery of Mar Barsauma the ritual objects necessary to consecrate another patriarch, ensuring that the election would not take place without his participation.[34] The bishops who assembled under his direction for the election were gathered largely from territories ruled by Franks and Armenians—not from Muslim lands. They elected a new patriarch, John, who had formerly been an abbot of the monastery of Dovair near Antioch, who was then consecrated in the Latin church at Tell Bashir, with Joscelin and other Frankish lords in attendance. One of the first acts of the new patriarch was to absolve Basil, the bishop of Edessa, from the anathema under which the previous patriarch had placed him, but the bishop died before the letter of absolution reached him.[35] The new patriarch, John, then took up residence in K'esun, a town under Joscelin's rule, "for some people advised the patriarch to make K'esun the patriarchal residence, in place of Amida, seeing that the city was in the empire of the Christians."[36] While in K'esun, the new patriarch ordained three new bishops,[37] probably with Joscelin's approval.

While Frankish involvement can be seen as a result of Jacobite demands, it is clear that under Joscelin in particular a competition developed between the rulers of Edessa and Amida for patronage and control of the Jacobite patriarch. When the new patriarch, John, died soon after his election, the next patriarch was elected in Amida, under pressure from that city's Muslim ruler. Some Jacobites suggested to Joscelin that the election was invalid, and that perhaps Joscelin should organize a synod to elect another patriarch canonically. In response, the new patriarch made haste to visit Joscelin, confirming the Frankish count's choice for Jacobite archbishop of Edessa and in return receiving back the chrism and instruments of ordination Joscelin had earlier seized from Mar Barsauma.[38]

As we look over this thirty-year period of patriarchal peregrinations, excommunications, conflicts, and their resolutions, a few significant elements emerge. The first is the eagerness with which the counts of Edessa engaged with their Jacobite bishops and patriarchs. Contrary to the ignorance displayed in Latin texts, it is clear that the Jacobite church was an institution of keen interest to the counts. They actively supported the Jacobite bishop of Edessa against the patriarch, and once Joscelin gained influence over the patriarch himself, equally advocated for the resolution of internal Jacobite disputes, the reconciliation of excommunicated bishops, and the restoration of a strong patriarchate—one that would reside in the county of Edessa, of course. Implicit in this was the counts' willingness to manipulate, control, and even compel patriarchs and bishops as suited their advantage. The counts' frequent meetings with the patriarchs, close relations with the archbishop of Edessa, and attendance at Jacobite saints' shrines and patriarchal enthronements gave them, and their associates and advisors, ample opportunity to gain familiarity with Jacobite theology and practices. The silence of Latin sources was not a result of a lack of knowledge or interest on the part of Frankish leaders, but a deliberate silence that allowed continued Frankish domination of local clergy.

Melkite Bishops in the Levant

For the historian, the shift from Syria to Palestine entails much more than a change in geography, climate, and history—it is a shift to a very different set of sources to answer questions about local communities under Frankish rule. Gone are the Syriac and Armenian texts, and in their place are Latin charters, chronicles, and legal texts, as well as a number of extant buildings and excavated archaeological sites, all of which are lacking for northern Syria. This lack of non-Frankish sources has complicated the ability of historians to discuss the place of local communities under Frankish rule. Given the deliberate silence of the Frankish sources, we have fewer ways of uncovering their experience.

The largest Christian community in Palestine (perhaps the largest among all groups) were the Melkites. Historians have concluded that the Franks treated the Melkite hierarchy differently from Armenian and Jacobite clergy, based on the theological notion that while Armenian and Jacobites were heretical groups, Melkites were members of the same church as the Franks, separated only by a temporary schism. Therefore Franks believed only one bishop could be the head of the communal body of orthodox Christians.[39] Accordingly, Joshua Prawer explained, "the establishment of the Latin church in Syria and Palestine was accompanied by the destitution of the Greek and Melkite hierarchies and by an almost wholesale spoliation of

the Byzantine sanctuaries. . . . Byzantine bishops were replaced by Latins."[40]
Yet the Franks did not think about local Christians in a theological framework, as we have already noted, but instead in a linguistic and cultural one.
They did not, by and large, treat Melkites any differently from Armenians
and Jacobites.

In most cases, the crusaders did not actually need to make a decision
about whether to replace a Melkite bishop with a Frank. Few Melkite bishops
were in office or in residence in Palestine when the crusaders arrived, a decline that had begun with the attacks of the Fatimid caliph al-Hakim and
continued during the struggle between the Fatimids and the Seljuks over
Palestine in the later eleventh century.[41] Although we have few sources for
this period, it appears that the number of Palestinian bishops dropped dramatically in the later eleventh century. On the eve of the arrival of the First
Crusade, no firm evidence places any Melkite bishop resident in his see in
Palestine. The patriarch of Jerusalem, Simeon II, had already fled for Byzantine Cyprus by the time the crusaders reached Antioch.[42] By the late eleventh
century, many Melkite bishops had left their sees and had become *syncelloi*,
administrators at the patriarch's court in Jerusalem. Most if not all of them
probably accompanied the patriarch into exile. Praised as a *vir sanctissimus*
by Latin chroniclers, Simeon died in Cyprus about the time the crusaders
captured Jerusalem.[43] Albert of Aachen's eagerness to point out that he was
indeed dead by the time the crusaders elected a replacement reveals some
concern about the legitimacy of supplanting Melkite bishops with Latin
ones. Other Melkite bishops appear briefly in sources but cannot be pinned
down, either chronologically or geographically. Anastasios of Caesarea flourished sometime in the later eleventh century, although we have no proof he
was resident in the city.[44] Gaza had a bishop in 1056, but he was martyred,
perhaps after having written "A Dialogue with Achmed the Sarracen."[45]

We find scarcely any more bishops in Syria, despite Byzantine efforts to
maintain them in office. Even Edessa, which spent much of the eleventh century under Byzantine rule, did not have a Melkite bishop.[46] As already discussed, the crusaders enthroned the Greek patriarch of Antioch in the
cathedral there, recognizing his authority over Latins and Melkites alike.[47]
He left the city only in 1100, when a war between Bohemund, prince of Antioch, and the Byzantine emperor Alexios I Komnenos made Latins suspicious
that he might be a Byzantine sympathizer. Despite having been expelled from
the city, John was later recognized by William of Tyre as a true man of faith
who perhaps should have been treated a little better by the Latins.[48] John V,

then, is the only example we have of a Melkite bishop being ousted from his see and replaced by a Latin, and it is evident that the issue was imperial claims to Antioch, rather than theological conflicts. Whenever the Byzantines had political advantage over Antioch, they insisted on the reinstatement of a Melkite patriarch, equally a sign of political dominance, not of ecclesiastical unity.

More Melkite bishops could be found throughout Palestine after the crusader conquest than had been there in the previous fifty years. Although the evidence is often fragmentary, it suggests that Melkite bishops flourished in Tyre, Caesarea, Sidon, Tiberias, Gaza, and Lydda. For a time, Melkite patriarchs may have continued to reside in Jerusalem alongside their Latin counterparts. Bernard Hamilton has argued that John, bishop of Tyre, and then Sabas, bishop of Caesarea, were successively appointed patriarchs of Jerusalem by the Franks in the early twelfth century, intended to serve as liaisons for Melkite priests and communities. John and Sabas, however, did not appreciate the limitations of their assigned role, and eventually retired to Constantinople. There emperor John II Komnenos used their presence as an opportunity to establish a separate patriarchate in exile, and apparently appointed a successor to John about 1122.[49]

For many Melkite bishops, however, we only have brief records of their existence. A Melkite bishop of Tiberias served as a mentor to the hermit Leontios in Constantinople in the mid-twelfth century. According to the hermit's vita, the bishop returned to Palestine at the same time as Leontios joined the monastery of Saint John the Theologian at Patmos.[50] The colophon of a Greek manuscript written for the priest Gerasimos in 1152 confirms the existence of a Melkite bishopric of Tiberias.[51] Paul, bishop of Sidon, is known only through his theological treatises in Arabic, and some scholars have suggested that he lived in the mid-twelfth century.[52] Lydda had a Melkite bishop in 1192 who visited Richard I Lionheart during the Third Crusade, giving him a piece of the True Cross. A Latin chronicler noted that the bishop had placed his flock under the protection of Salah al-Din when he first conquered the area around Jerusalem, suggesting that the bishop held office under Frankish administration.[53]

Meletos of Gaza and Eleutheropolis

But it is Meletos, monk and Melkite bishop of Gaza, who gives us the chance to see Melkite bishops interacting with their Latin peers in more detail. In

1173, Meletos negotiated an agreement with Josbert, the grandmaster of the Hospitallers, in which Meletos received the monastery of St. George at Bethgibelin (modern Bet Guvrin or Beit Djibrin, ancient Eleutheropolis).[54] The charter was written in both Greek and Latin, and in both sections Meletos was titled the archbishop of Gaza and Eleutheropolis.

Gaza may have been the bishop's principal seat; it came first in his title and was the larger city. Baldwin III conquered the city in 1149, and soon afterward turned it over to the Templars. Although William of Tyre indicated that the city was uninhabited when the crusaders refortified it, it seems likely that at least a nucleus of an urban population existed before the city was rebuilt.[55] Over the next two decades, a vibrant city grew up under the protection of the Templar castle, until Salah al-Din's forces burned and looted the town in 1170. Salah al-Din returned in 1187, and the city was never again under Frankish rule.

Although the Franks ruled the city for only thirty-eight years, impressive architectural remains show significant investment in the city. A substantial church still stands in the center of the city, and is now the Friday mosque. While its eastern apse has disappeared, its graceful arched aisles reveal its past as the Latin parish church of the city.[56] Built at approximately the same time was a smaller single-nave church in the traditional Christian quarter of the city, now dedicated to St. Porphyrios.[57] Today it serves the Melkite population of the city, as it probably did in the twelfth century. Other than a textual reference to a castle built by Baldwin III, we have little other information about the Frankish city. No archaeological excavations have been undertaken in the city, and the enormous influx of refugees into Gaza in the mid-twentieth century has obscured most of the topographical outlines that might give us clues to the layout of the medieval city.[58]

Where did Meletos fit into this cityscape? Despite the impressive size of the Latin church in Gaza, the city oddly had no Latin bishop. The Franks certainly had plenty of reasons to appoint one. The city had a Melkite bishop into the eleventh century, and the appointment of a Latin bishop would have encouraged Frankish settlement and integration into the kingdom. The fact that the see of the neighboring city of Ascalon had been transferred to Bethlehem makes the absence of a Latin bishop in Gaza all the more surprising, for he would have been the only one on the Palestine coast south of Caesarea.[59] The explanation for Gaza's bishopless state can be found with the Templars. Introducing a bishop into a city ruled by a religious order would only have created ecclesiastical complications, due to the necessity to collect

tithes and apportion ecclesiastical property.[60] Meletos may have been the so-
lution. As archbishop of Gaza, his authority was limited, according to the
charter, to "the Greeks and Syrians," leaving the Temple to serve the Latin
population.[61] (Again, one wonders how many native Greek-speakers there
were in Gaza and Bethgibelin by the late twelfth century). Perhaps even more
important was that this system left the Templars in control of parochial
tithes, for obligatory tithing was not a part of the Melkite tradition. While the
Latin patriarch of Jerusalem had received the rights and revenues of all abandoned bishoprics that had formerly existed within his patriarchate from
Pope Alexander III in 1167, neither Gaza nor Eleutheropolis was mentioned
in the list of relevant cities, even though they fitted the criteria the pope set
out.[62] Clearly, in the mind of the Latin eccliastical establishment, the see of
Gaza was not abandoned but under the care of Meletos and the Templars.

What then was Meletos's position in Bethgibelin? The ecclesiastical situation was much the same as in Gaza, for the Hospitallers, another military
order, controlled that town. It was smaller than Gaza, and the only church
found there to date is the large chapel within the Hospitaller fortress. The
only other church to appear in the historical record is the monastery of St.
George, mentioned in the charter discussed above and given to Meletos by
the Hospitallers. Meletos may have come to Bethgibelin as a result of Salah
al-Din's sack of Gaza in 1170. The Hospitaller charter dates to 1172, and may
signal that Meletos was newly settled in the town. Whether the Melkite
bishop was invited by the Hospitallers or came of his own accord is unknown, but we may be able to see an architectural trace of his presence. The
chapel in the Hospitaller castle was not contemporary with the construction
of the fortress, but was inserted sometime after 1153, and its size (approximately 30 by 16.5m) necessitated that the southeast corner tower be demol-
ished, undermining the strength of the fortress.[63] It is possible that the
chapel was built to accommodate the Latin population of the town, while
Meletos served the local Christian community at the monastery of St.
George.

The charter between Meletos and the Hospitallers reveals the close ties
that could exist between local clerics and the Latin establishment. Far from
considering indigenous Christians to be heretics or schismatics, Frankish
clergy incorporated local hierarchies into their own. This closeness extended
beyond administrative convenience, for the charter stipulated that when
Meletos died, he would be buried as a *confrater* of the Hospital. If either
Meletos or Josbert was aware of the theological and liturgical issues that the-

oretically should have separated them, they showed no evidence of it. For the Hospitallers and Templars, a Melkite bishop was better than a Latin one, for someone like Meletos presented no challenge to their own authority over the Latin population, would not claim the right to tithe, and could serve as a liaison to the local Christian communities they governed.

Curiously, Meletos's charter with the Hospitallers provides the fullest information about the Melkite clergy of Jerusalem as well. Witnessing the charter were Theoktistos the abbot, Ioannes, priest and prior, Georgios the deacon, Stephanos the priest, and Abramios the deacon. This group was smaller than the group of Latin clergy at the church; if we compare Meletos's charter to one from the chapter of the Holy Sepulcher in 1175, we find five canons, two deacons, and two sub-deacons listed for the Latin clergy.[64] The use of the Jerusalem priests as witnesses for Meletos's charter points out the absence of Melkite clergy directly associated with the archbishop of Gaza and Bethgibelin. Were there no Melkite clergy serving in Gaza or Bethgibelin other than Meletos? Were there no monks in the monastery of St. George to serve as witnesses? Meletos's connection with Jerusalem's Melkite clergy suggests that Meletos, while holding the title of archbishop of Gaza and Eleutheropolis, may have been responsible for supervising the Melkite clergy and laity over a wider area, perhaps the whole southern portion of the kingdom of Jerusalem.

Easter 1101: The Crisis of the Holy Fire

A religious crisis in 1101 gives us a brief and rare look into the way Melkite priests could clash and cooperate with royal, patriarchal, and even papal authority in the holiest shrine of Christendom, the Holy Sepulcher. By long tradition, the Easter festivities at the site of Christ's death and resurrection were marked by an annual miracle as dependable as the annual flooding of the Nile—the descent of Holy Fire from heaven to light the lamps at the tomb of Jesus, signaling to priest and pilgrim alike that the True Light had reentered the world. In 1101, to the consternation of the waiting crowd of Christian faithful, the Fire failed to appear. The missing miracle drew wide attention. Matthew of Edessa attributed it to Frankish sin and the introduction of women into the Holy Sepulcher and the monasteries of Jerusalem, and the subsequent expulsion of Armenian, Greek, Syrian, and Georgian monks.[65]

The year 1101 was also the first Easter that Baldwin I ruled Jerusalem, and it is to him and to a complex series of political events that we should look for an explanation of the crisis. Baldwin gained control of Jerusalem in November 1100, claiming the city as the heir to his brother, Godfrey of Bouillon. He was opposed by the (Latin) patriarch of Jerusalem, Daibert of Pisa, who sought either the establishment of an ecclesiastical principality under his rule, or perhaps the establishment of Bohemund or Tancred in Godfrey's place.

Originally the archbishop of Pisa and perhaps a papal legate, Daibert had arrived in the Holy Land in the summer of 1099 with a fleet of one hundred and twenty ships. He aided Bohemund's siege of Lattakia, then traveled south with him and Baldwin to Jerusalem in December of the same year. The arrival of the Pisan fleet and Antiochene troops came at a crucial time for Godfrey, who was facing attacks by the Fatimids with few forces under his command. Together Bohemund and Daibert used their influence to depose Arnulf of Chocques as patriarch of Jerusalem, and elect Daibert in his place.[66] Following his elevation, Bohemund, Baldwin and Godfrey all received their lands from the new patriarch. This was a decided advantage for Bohemund, for his claim to Antioch was still contested by the Byzantines, and ecclesiastical recognition of his claim could only help. Furthermore, Daibert in Jerusalem had no direct authority over Antioch, which had its own patriarch, and the Pisan would not be able to exercise much influence at such a distance. For Godfrey this act of homage was far more risky. While he may have seen it as a simple confirmation of his election as ruler of Jerusalem, Daibert, as a participant in the Gregorian reform movement, knew the importance of asserting sacerdotal authority over secular. He could and likely did perceive it as an acknowledgement that Godfrey's power should be dependent on that of the patriarch. Yet Godfrey had little choice. He needed Daibert's fleet to conquer strategic seaports; Daibert thus had the upper hand.

When Godfrey died unexpectedly on 18 July 1100, Daibert was well placed to play kingmaker. He wrote to Bohemund in Antioch, urging him to convince Baldwin not to come south, and to use force to prevent him if necessary. Fortunately for Baldwin, the letter never reached Bohemund, as he had been captured by the emir of Sivas, Gümüshtigin, within weeks of Godfrey's death. Baldwin himself did not hear of his brother's demise until he returned from his attempt to rescue Bohemund near Melitene; his chaplain Fulcher wryly remarked that on hearing the news "he grieved somewhat at the death of his brother but rejoiced more over his inheritance."[67]

Daibert, however, had supporters other than Bohemund, who were near at hand and not in captivity. Tancred, Bohemund's nephew and Baldwin's longtime rival, had been energetically establishing himself in the Galilee, capturing Tiberias, Nazareth, Mount Tabor (site of the Transfiguration), and Beisan (ancient Scythopolis), and at the time of Godfrey's death was attempting to capture Haifa as a seaport with Daibert in his entourage. His principality rivaled Godfrey's in size, and he was the most logical successor to Godfrey, at least in terms of proximity and experience. The patriarch, however, was unable to persuade Tancred to challenge Baldwin, and Godfrey's brother easily came into his inheritance, leaving Daibert little choice but to recognize him as Godfrey's successor. On Christmas Day 1100, the patriarch crowned Baldwin king in the Basilica of the Nativity in Bethlehem.

Again, the event could be interpreted in radically different ways by the two participants. The patriarch could note with pride the parallel with the Holy Roman Emperors and the popes; Daibert crowned Baldwin three hundred years to the day after Pope Leo III crowned Charlemagne the first emperor in the West since the fall of the Roman empire. Given contemporary assertions of papal superiority over the empire, Daibert likely felt that he had asserted his authority over Baldwin. Furthermore, holding the coronation in Bethlehem allowed the patriarch still to hope that he might gain full control over Jerusalem. Baldwin, however, saw that he had been crowned and anointed king by the patriarch, an honor his brother never achieved, and furthermore, he was crowned in the birthplace of both Jesus and King David, his predecessor as anointed ruler of the Holy Land.

While Baldwin and Daibert may have patched up their differences, it was only a truce, not a permanent resolution. Baldwin needed a patriarch on whom he could rely, and the incident of the Holy Fire conveniently discredited Daibert. Mid-March 1101 brought two crucial events; Baldwin journeyed to Haifa, where Tancred handed over to the king his Galilean principality. He did so because he had been invited to be regent of Antioch during Bohemund's captivity. He insisted, however, that should he return within three years, Galilee would be returned to him. The second event came a week later, when a Genoese fleet harbored in Haifa, carrying Maurice of Porto, a papal legate, perhaps the only figure with the undisputed authority to depose a patriarch. On his return to Jerusalem, Baldwin "without delay" accused Daibert of plotting with Bohemund to kill him and to hand over Jerusalem to the Norman, and had the patriarch suspended from office (15–17 April 1101).[68] Daibert nevertheless managed to be reinstated the next day in order to perform the Easter liturgy, by dint of pleading and a judicious bribe.[69]

Easter that year fell on 21 April, and on Easter Saturday, the pilgrims and resident Christians gathered at the Holy Sepulcher to witness the annual miracle of the Holy Fire. The church at the time consisted primarily of the great Constantinian rotunda, rebuilt by the Byzantine emperor Constantine IX Monomachos after the destruction by al-Hakim. When the Fire did not appear in the ninth hour, as it traditionally did, the crowd grew restless, and the praying grew more intense.[70] Finally, Daibert himself knelt in prayer within the tomb, hoping that his rank might win God's favor and bring about the anticipated miracle. An anonymous writer recalled that "when, however, his fervent prayer and supplications were prolonged, and when with downcast face he at last came out of the Sepulcher without having obtained the grace he sought, a powerful feeling of despair took possession of everyone there."[71] This moment when the patriarch should appear at his greatest glory, celebrating the resurrection of the Lord, only revealed his own impotence and God's dissatisfaction with him.

The Latin priests, however, were not the only ones serving at the Sepulcher. Melkites were there as well, and the Holy Fire only appeared on Easter Sunday after Daibert and his clergy left the Holy Sepulcher to pray at the Templum Domini (the Dome of the Rock), leaving the Melkite priests behind to pray in peace and bring about the anticipated miracle. The success of the Melkite priests at summoning the Holy Fire demonstrated to the watching Christian community that God did not consider Daibert the true patriarch, worthy to officiate at his Holy Sepulcher.[72] It also showed the Franks that the Melkite clergy were still a powerful force in the Holy City. The role of local clergy in bringing about the delayed miracle was widely noted. Matthew of Edessa was pleased to noted that the miracle occurred only after the Franks restored the clerics and monks to their rightful places. In his eyes, however, it was not just the Melkites who summoned the Holy Fire—"after this, the five nations of the Christian faithful began to pray, and God heard their prayers."[73] For Matthew, then, the miracle is itself ecumenical, requiring the presence of Armenian, Syrian, Greek, Georgian, and Frankish clerics to achieve.

As this is one of the few instances when the Holy Fire failed to appear, the cause is unlikely to have been accidental. Collaboration between Baldwin and the local clergy, motivated by their common interest in removing Daibert from office, is reminiscent of Baldwin's ascent to power in Edessa, where he similarly associated himself with local factions and elites to establish his authority. Fulcher of Chartres, his chaplain and chronicler, recorded that when Baldwin first arrived to claim Jerusalem in November 1100, "everyone came out to meet Baldwin, clergy as well as laity, Greeks also and Syrians, with crosses and candles. They conducted him to the Church of the Holy Sepulcher with great joy and honor, and praising God in ringing voices."[74] Such a procession was as much a demonstration of the importance of the Melkite clergy in Jerusalem as it was a welcome for Baldwin, who was unlikely to miss the message. The benefits to the new king of the collaboration between him and the local clergy are clear, but what the local clergy achieved for themselves is less obvious. Possibly confiscated land was returned to them, or perhaps they were just as pleased as Baldwin to be rid of the authoritarian Daibert.

Following Daibert's humiliation in front of the population of Jerusalem, Baldwin continued the attack, accusing the patriarch of embezzling money intended for the defense of the Holy Land. The patriarch's personal property was seized, and he fled to Jaffa, and then to Tancred in Antioch. But this was not the last that Baldwin saw of Daibert. In the fall of 1102 Daibert returned to Jerusalem with Tancred and Antiochene soldiers again behind him, and Baldwin needed their military support just as much as his brother had in 1099. Tancred insisted that Daibert be reinstated before he would agree to aid the king. Baldwin acquiesced, but shortly thereafter (7 October 1102), Daibert was again deposed by a council headed by Robert of Paris, another papal legate. His successor was the humble Evremar, whom Albert of Aachen described as "a clerk who was well-esteemed; he was most generous and good-natured in giving alms to the poor; he was devout and had a good reputation."[75] Evremar's patriarchal seal is the earliest surviving; it was embossed with two concentric inscriptions one reads EVREMARUS PATRIARCHA HIERUS(A)L(E)M, the other "'Ο 'ΑΓΙΟΣ ΤΑΦΟΣ ΚΥΡΙΟΥ ΙΗΣ(ΟΥΣ) Χ(ΡΙ)Σ(ΤΟΣ)," (the holy tomb of the Lord Jesus Christ)."[76] This bilingual sign of authority was perhaps a tacit recognition of the presence and quiet influence of the Melkite canons of the Anastasis. Indeed, by the 1150s the Latin patriarchs of Jerusalem had abandoned the traditional western designation of the shrine as the "Holy Sepulcher" and now referred to it as the church of the Holy Resurrection, a direct reflection of the Greek nomenclature.[77]

We should not, however, imagine the two separate hierarchies serving in the holiest of Christian shrines interacting only with members of their own communities. In times of crisis, the various clergy of the city would process together around the city. Fulcher of Chartres reports that in 1123 after Baldwin II had been captured by Balak, emir of Aleppo, and a Fatimid invasion was threatening the city, "we who remained at Jerusalem, Latins, Greeks and Syrians alike, did not cease to pray for our brothers who were thus placed in tribulation, to bestow alms on the needy, and at the same time to visit piously in barefoot procession all the churches of the Holy City."[78] (Again notice the absence of Jacobites and Armenians, though they too had churches in the city.)

The multiplicity of liturgies being performed in Jerusalem—even within the Holy Sepulcher itself—allowed for a jostling sense of the diversity of the Christian tradition. Yet this diversity of language and liturgy was a Frankish innovation. Under the Muslims, the Melkites alone had authority over the Holy Sepulcher, and did not admit Jacobites or Armenians. With the arrival of the crusaders, the liturgy was initially performed in both Greek and Latin by both clergies.[79] Sometime in the twelfth century, however, the Latins admitted other Christian clergy. The pilgrim Theodericus, who visited the Holy Sepulcher sometime between 1169 and 1174, noted "these are the traditions or sects which celebrate their office in the church in Jerusalem; the Latins, the Syrians, the Armenians, the Greeks, the Jacobins and the Nubians. All have differences in their rule of life and also in their divine office. The Jacobins during their feasts use trumpets, according to the practice of the Hebrews."[80] Theodericus later informed his readers that the Armenians had a chapel directly north of the Rotunda, where today the Latin sacristy is,[81] as well as another in the southern eleventh-century Byzantine wing of the Holy Sepulcher.[82] Given the vital importance of the Holy Sepulcher to the Christian concept of Jerusalem and the Holy Land, the decision to share such valuable space with others is telling.

Easter 1105: A New Modus Orandi

Four years after the failure of the Holy Fire, a Russian abbot named Daniel visited the Holy Land, and his memories are a snapshot of the Easter ceremonies in quieter times. Daniel visited the Holy Land in 1105/6, stayed at the guesthouse of the monastery of Mar Saba in Jerusalem, and even had a Sabaite monk as his guide for his visits to the holy places throughout Palestine during his sixteen-month pilgrimage.[83] The Russian was friendly with Baldwin I, who, he recounted, "knew me well and loved me greatly, for he is a kind and very humble man and not in the least bit proud."[84] Daniel even joined the king on a military expedition toward Damascus, taking advantage of the security of the royal entourage to visit holy sites in the Galilee. It was from Baldwin that the abbot asked permission to place his lamp on Christ's tomb on Good Friday, so that the miraculous Holy Fire might light it with the others on Easter Saturday; the lamps of the Melkite priests hung where Jesus' head lay, and the Melkite monastic lamps were at chest level, while Daniel humbly hung his at Christ's feet. The Latin lamps, however, hung higher on the tomb than the others,[85] but Daniel noted that they were never lit by the Holy Fire.

On Holy Saturday Daniel joined the royal procession to the Holy Sepulcher as a member of the party of the abbot of Mar Saba. The king clearly wished to enter the Holy Sepulcher in the company of leading Melkite clergy. Once at the Holy Sepulcher, the king stood on a dais next to the main altar in the now-destroyed western apse. It is less clear where Daniel and the abbot of Mar Saba stood. Daniel wrote of being "above" the tomb, opposite the great altar, yet able to see into the tomb itself; he was perhaps in the second-story gallery of the Rotunda. With him were also some of the Melkite priests.

Daniel's account gives a few clues about the ecclesiastical situation in Jerusalem in 1106. Most noticeable is the lack of a patriarch in the ceremonies; both Daibert and his replacement Evremar were in Rome, seeking confirmation of their claims to the patriarchal throne from the pope. Nor is there any mention of a Melkite patriarch or bishop. In their absence, Baldwin played a prominent role in the Easter ceremonies. He gave orders that Daniel's lamp be suspended on the sepulcher; he sat on the right of the great altar, and the doors of the tomb were sealed with the royal insignia. Baldwin's candle was the first lit once the bishop had come out of the tomb with the Holy Fire; from his Daniel and all others lit their candles.

Although Daniel did not criticize the Latins directly at any point in his account, some signs of resentment filtered through in his description of the events of Easter Saturday. Daniel suggested that the Latins "mumbled" their responses to the Holy Liturgy; he pointed out that the lamps of the Franks hanging on the outside of the tomb were never lit by the Holy Fire; and he mentioned that the Latin bishop had to check three times before the Holy Fire appeared.[86] Given the little contact that Daniel had with Latins before his pilgrimage, these ecclesiastical critiques may well be derived from his monastic hosts, or from the Melkite clergy of the Anastasis.

Yet his account also makes clear that the Melkite clergy had an established and prominent role in the Easter liturgy of the Holy Sepulcher, as did the abbot of Mar Saba and other monastics and ascetics. Furthermore,

Daniel links their presence to royal patronage. The Melkite monks were present as part of the royal retinue, not as part of the ecclesiastical hierarchy. The bonds between the royal family and the monastery of Mar Saba were reinforced by gifts made to the monastery by the royal family. The archives of Mar Saba and other Melkite monasteries have not survived, but a charter from the archives of the Latin canons of the Holy Sepulcher recorded that in 1163 or 1164, Meletios, the abbot of Mar Saba,[87] sold to the Latin canons of the Holy Sepulcher three *gastinae*[88] for the sum of four hundred and eighty bizants. The charter further records that the three *gastinae* had been given to the monastery by Queen Melisende (ruled 1131–1153, d. 1161) so that the monks might distribute twenty-four loaves of bread to the poor every Saturday.[89] We can only suspect that these were not the only gifts the royal family gave to the monastery. As Melisende's maternal family were Chalcedonian, her patronage may reflect her own private piety. However, supporting the monastery may also have been a pragmatic political decision, intended to garner support for the Frankish monarchy. Melisende herself had been born in Edessa, and her father, Baldwin II, had been count there for eighteen years. Her mother was the daughter of Gabriel, the hapless ruler of Melitene. Of them all, Melisende had the greatest appreciation for the role local Christian communities could play in the new Frankish Levant.

The Jacobite Church in the Kingdom of Jerusalem

Melisende supported other local Christian religious communities as well,[90] most prominently the Jacobites. The largest Jacobite communities were in northern Syria and Mesopotamia, but a bishopric and small monastic settlement had maintained a tenuous existence in Jerusalem.[91] A series of colophons from twelfth-century Syriac manuscripts describe a continuing legal dispute the monastery had with a Frank, resulting in royal intervention. The claims of each party went back to the conquest of Jerusalem in 1099. When the crusaders captured the Holy City, the Jacobite community had already fled to Egypt, escaping the persecution of the Artukid rulers of the city, just as the Melkite patriarch Simeon II had fled to Cyprus. As a result, their property fell to individual crusaders, who considered it abandoned. Two villages in particular, Beit 'Arif and 'Adassiyya, fell to a Frankish knight named Geoffrey of the Tower of David. Soon after 1099, the monks and the knight swapped places. Geoffrey was captured in battle by the Fatimids, and found himself imprisoned in Egypt, while the Jacobite community returned to

Jerusalem from exile in the same place. The Jacobite monk Michael, from the monastery of Mar Georgios on the Black Mountain near Antioch, recalled that the patriarch Athanasios VII (1090–1129) came to Jerusalem, and with the bishop of the city, Cyril, visited King Baldwin I. In order to regain their property, "they exhibited the deeds of sale of the said villages and they brought some of the old men of the place as witnesses, both believers and Muslims, so that the king and his chieftains were convinced that these places belonged to the Church and that he (Geoffrey) had taken them unlawfully." Their documents and witnesses had the intended effect; "the king gave back those places to our blessed father, the aforementioned bishop, though our father had to pay out a great deal of gold to the king and to many others for this reason."[92] Baldwin may have well encountered Athanasios VII earlier while he was still count of Edessa. In any case, the king's interest in the helping the Jacobite monks was a part of a larger pattern of cultivating close relations with local Christian communities.

Some thirty years later, an elderly Geoffrey was finally released from captivity and returned to Jerusalem. The Frankish community was astonished to have one of the original conquerors of Jerusalem returned to them, and when the old man petitioned to have his property restored, King Fulk (1131–43), husband of Melisende and co-ruler of the kingdom, enthusiastically agreed. What was the Jacobite community to do? A second colophon recorded that the bishop Ignatios then "sent word to the queen (Melisende)—long may she live and enjoy favor deservedly—who [had learned] the fear of God from her mother the queen and who [was full] of mercy for our Church."[93] Although Melisende may have been eager to help the monks, she had other reasons to be offended at her husband's decision. She insisted on her right to be included in all royal decisions, for, according to the will of her father Baldwin II, she was to rule equally with Fulk. The queen immediately sent a messenger to her husband, and after a round of negotiation, the properties were again returned to the monks. A third colophon detailed how Melisende and her son Baldwin III helped the Jacobites gain control of a third village in 1148.[94]

The colophons that detailed these property disputes reveal a close connection between royal authority and local Christian clerics and monks over three generations. In both cases, the Jacobites appealed directly to royal authority; even when the king had already ruled against them, the monks addressed the queen rather than anyone outside the royal family. The colophons also reveal a fundamental enthusiasm on the part of the Jacobites for the royal family and the political authority they represented The first colophon referred to the king as "our victorious king, the king of the believing people of the Franks, Lord Fulk, with the queen and their children protected by God."[95] A third Syriac colophon described the events of the Second Crusade as signs of "divine zeal."

The royal family showed equal enthusiasm for the Jacobites, choosing to support a group of "heretical" monks over Geoffrey, a hero of the First Crusade. Local monasteries were clearly a valuable source of support for the monarchy, and equally important, not a liability in the eyes of the Frankish aristocracy, on whom the royal family also relied. Royal cultivation of local monastic support shows that politically, spiritually, or both, the monasteries wielded considerable influence within the Frankish kingdom.

The royal judgments concerning the property of the monks suggest that the Franks saw their regime, at least in a legal sense, as linked to their predecessors. In contrast, Robert Bartlett has argued that in many frontier areas such as Ireland, the date of conquest represented the beginning of a new legal regime. An English royal decree pertaining to Ireland in the thirteenth century declared "that if any plaintiff bases his plea upon the seisin of his ancestors before the conquest by the English and makes no mention of seisin . . . after the conquest, he shall fail in his case and lose his right by that very fact."[96] By this standard, the crusader Geoffrey would have undoubtedly have remained in control of the villages, and the Jacobite monks would have been left out in the cold. But Palestine was not a *tabula rasa* for the Franks, nor did they imagine that their conquest overrode the integrity of local traditions and laws.[97]

The royal family served as patrons to local Christian secular communities as well. In the coastal city of Ascalon, a three-aisled late antique basilica measuring 11.2 by 12.9 m, with a single apse and perhaps six bays, has been excavated close to the eastern city wall. The archaeological evidence suggests that at some point in the pre-crusade period the church was converted to a mosque, but after the Frankish conquest of Ascalon in 1153, the building was again rebuilt as a four-columned cross-in-square church—a typically Byzantine design unlike any built for a Latin congregation. The Melkite character of the church is further emphasized by the frescoes executed in a Byzantine manner depicting four churchmen holding Greek scrolls.[98]

The excavators identified the church as St. Mary of the Green, a Melkite church of the late antique and the early Islamic period. The Melkite chronicler Yahya ibn-Sa'id, writing in tenth-century Antioch, recorded that a

Muslim and Jewish crowd destroyed the church in 939. Petitions to rebuild the church were denied, and the bishop decided to settle in Ramla.[99] The pillaged church then became a mosque, probably the "Green" mosque of Ascalon. The excavators have argued that Ascalon's Fatimid rulers had a deliberate strategy of harassment of the Christian population, perhaps because of the city's strategic location at the border between Egypt and Palestine. As a result, Ascalon lost its Christian population by the late eleventh century. If the church can indeed be identified with the Green mosque, then Latin charters allow us to trace its history a bit further. Following the Frankish conquest, the mosque was initially given to the canons of the Holy Sepulcher, who then transferred it to Amalric, count of Ascalon and future king.[100] Most likely, then, Amalric either paid for the church's reconstruction himself or donated it to local Christians, who then rebuilt it. In either case, Amalric, the son of Queen Melisende, hoped to encourage local Christian settlement in Ascalon. In doing so, he was not supporting an already established Melkite community, but actively trying to create one. Like other leading Franks, he perceived indigenous Christians as an important constituent part of his city's prosperity.

Archaeological evidence suggests that other local monasteries also had Frankish patrons. The ruins of a monastic complex survive today in the town of Dair al-Asad, located in the foothills east of Acre, on the road to Safad. The first twelfth-century reference to the village comes in a charter of 1179, in which Baldwin IV granted custody of Dair al-Asad to his uncle Joscelin III of Edessa, who had married the youngest daughter of the previous owner.[101] Archaeological evidence suggests that the monastic complex was constructed in the twelfth century, although textual sources do not mention a monastery there until the thirteenth century.[102] In the twelfth century, the Franks knew the village as the "terra que dicitur de Sancto Georgio," which suggests some ecclesiastical association.[103] It is likely that the village took its name from the monastery. A thirteenth-century pilgrim recorded the existence of a monastery dedicated to Saint George on the road between Acre and Safad, noting that it housed Greek monks.[104] Certain decorative techniques, such as the molding, linked the building to other Melkite churches in Palestine.[105] Furthermore, Ronnie Ellenblum pointed to later Islamic evidence that a monastery continued to exist at Dair al-Asad after the Islamic reconquest, further proof that it was a Melkite monastery.[106]

Parts of the monastery have been incorporated into the modern village; a full investigation of the site has yet to be carried out. Although no direct evidence links the monastery to a specific Frankish patron, its location in one the largest Frankish seigneuries of Acre suggests that, given the size of the monastery, it would not have been built without the support of the village's lord, who was perhaps Joscelin III. Thus patronage of local monasteries was not limited to the royal family; other Frankish aristocrats also found local monasteries to be a source of political support and religious comfort.

Architecture and Liturgy

The monastic ruins at Dair al-Asad draw our attention away from the royal court and the cities of Palestine, and into the Levantine countryside. It was here that the majority of the population lived, and recent archaeological research has shown that it was also home to extensive Frankish settlement, contrary to the segregationalist understanding.[107] Through archaeological evidence in the countryside that it is possible to see how Frankish and local laity interacted, and to understand how, beneath the veil of textual ignorance, Latins gained personal understanding of indigenous communities.

Shared Space in Rural Churches

It was in smaller towns and rural communities that Latins and indigenous Christians attended the same small churches, even attending the same services. The traces of such interaction can be faint. A charter from 1178 records an agreement between Gerald, the bishop of Tiberias, and John, the abbot of St. Mary of Jehosaphat, located at the tomb of the Virgin just outside the walls of Jerusalem. The issue at hand was the church of St. George near Tiberias, which had been granted to the abbey in 1109.[108] When a Latin bishop was appointed for Tiberias about 1144,[109] he soon came to resent the church that was within sight but outside his jurisdiction. The charter of 1178 was designed to resolve this tension. The document stipulated that St. George's would not serve any of the bishop's parishioners, or anyone the bishop had excommunicated. Furthermore, neither Latins nor Syrians could be baptized, married, or purified there, as these were privileges reserved for churches under the authority of the local bishop. The church was, however, allowed to bury brothers and servants of the abbey, as well as Syrians.[110]

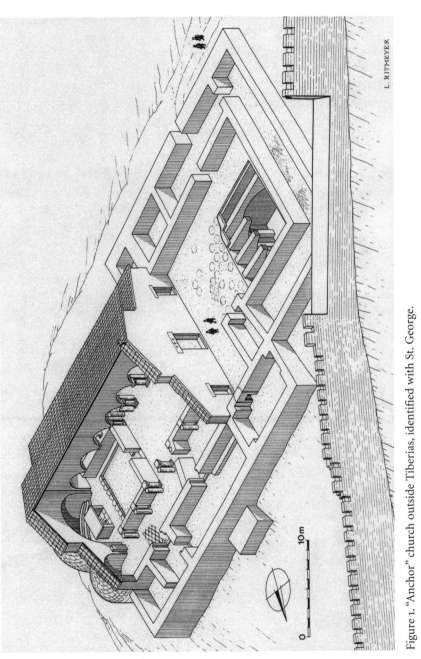

Figure 1. "Anchor" church outside Tiberias, identified with St. George.

L. RITMEYER

0   10m

Denys Pringle has suggested that the church excavated in 1991 outside the walls of Tiberias, on Mount Berenice, can be identified with the St. George of the charter[111] (see Figure 1). It is known as the "anchor" church for the half-ton basalt stone carved in the shape of an anchor found under the altar, originally a Bronze age cult object transformed into a Christian relic. The church was originally built under Emperor Justinian in the mid-sixth century. It was destroyed by an earthquake in 749, but rebuilt soon after. The new church, while following the older floor plan, had an interior height half that of the original church. The columns were apparently cut in half and doubled to support the arcading that separated the nave from the aisles. As Yizhar Hirschfeld has pointed out, this was not the result of poor planning or poverty on the part of the church, but echoed secular and sacred Islamic architecture such as the 'Abbasid palace of Ukhaidir in Iraq and the mosque of Damghan in Persia.[112] Further changes were made inside the church in the 'Abbasid period—the sanctuary was fully enclosed by walls, and benches were added along the side. Two small rooms were formed in the western ends of the two aisles by walls that encased the columns. The Franks, on the other hand, made little impact on the church, adding only buttresses to the exterior as well as a bell tower.

The church was located a kilometer south of the city in the Frankish period and perhaps halfway up the hillside above the city, convenient for those who lived outside the walls of the city; it obviated the need to descend to the bottom of the hill to attend services in town. The insistence of the charter that neither Latins nor Syrians should be baptized or married there suggests that, at least prior to the conclusion of this agreement, members of both communities were in the habit of using the church for just those ceremonies.

The layout of the excavated church raises further questions. Could both the Latin and Melkite rites have been practiced in the same church plan? It is not easy to decipher the correlation between liturgy and architecture in this setting. Robert Taft has noted that the history of the liturgy of Jerusalem has yet to be written,[113] so we are not even certain as to the demands of the liturgy the Melkites would have been performing in the twelfth century. What evidence we do have suggests that the Jerusalem liturgy had been influenced by Constantinopolitan liturgy, but was still distinct. At best, then, we can hypothesize that the architectural requirements of the local Palestinian liturgy may have been similar to that of Constantinople. Although the church was under the authority of the Latin abbey of St. Mary of Jehosaphat, the church continued to have a layout that facilitated the performance of the Melkite liturgy. Most prominently, the chancel was blocked off from the rest of the church by a high wall (similar to a modern iconostasis), pierced only by a doorway. This arrangement allowed for the liturgical practices of the local Melkite community, where the clergy would process, emerging from a door on the north side of the chancel, and enter the sanctuary through a door aligned with the nave. The monastic liturgy of the monks of Jehosaphat could also have used the space, but it is clear that the charter is concerned with the performance of secular, not monastic, services. Despite the disputes of the Latin hierarchy over the building, it is likely that the church and its congregation continued to be served by the local Melkite priests using the same liturgy as before the arrival of the crusaders. Perhaps the only thing that had changed was that now the local community included Franks as well.

Nor was the "anchor" church at Tiberias the only such church, as Ronnie Ellenblum has shown. On a promontory above al-Taiyiba, a Christian village resting in the Judean hills north of Jerusalem, the Franks built a fortified settlement on the hill above the local village, and at the same time partially rebuilt the older Byzantine church in the village. The church, perhaps dedicated to the prophet Elijah, was the only one in either the local village or the Frankish *castrum*, and thus was used by both locals and Latins.[114] The Franks did not restore the entire church, for it was apparently too large for even their combined twelfth-century needs. Instead, they constructed a church within the older Byzantine church, using two or possibly three of the apses. The southern apse preserves slots for a chancel screen and posts, the possible remains of which were found on the site.[115] Such a setup suggests that the Latin liturgy was performed in one apse, while the Melkite liturgy was said in the next, performed side by side. Other villages in the region around Jerusalem, such as 'Abud, Tekoa, and Jifna, show similar signs of mixed use by both Franks and locals.

The churches themselves were architectural statements of Frankish attitudes toward local Christian traditions. As discussed in Chapter 1, Latin Christians thought about the Holy Land in terms of holy places and the churches built to protect and commemorate them. The construction and restoration of churches was thus particularly important for the Franks. The Franks rebuilt churches that had been damaged or destroyed, such as the shrine church at Bethany, where Lazarus was raised from the dead. Like so many other churches in the Holy Land, it was originally built in the early Byzantine era. The church seemingly survived destruction by the Persians in the seventh century, but at least parts of the church were damaged by the time of the First Crusade. Unfortunately, this church did not survive to the twentieth century, and what little that remains is buried beneath the new Franciscan church, built in the 1950s. Little stratigraphy was recorded during excavation and construction of the new church, so analysis of the remains has been relatively general in nature. The Franks rebuilt the roof of the church, replacing wood beams with masonry vaults, and restored the dome over the church, which pilgrims in the fourteenth century recorded seeing again in ruins.[116]

In restoring the church, the crusaders made no apparent changes to the structure of the building, other than what was necessary to support the new stone vaulting. As the layout remained that of the early Byzantine church, with a central apse and two pastiphoria on each side in a centrally planned cross-in-square church, the shrine of SS. Mary and Martha remained ideal for Melkite liturgy throughout the twelfth century. The church belonged to the Abbey of St. Lazarus, built for Melisende's sister Ivetta; their mother was Morfia, whose family followed the Byzantine tradition. It is quite possible, then, that Melkite priests continued to serve at the sanctuary, with or without Latin priests. The church was intended for use by pilgrims; a separate church built according to a Latin plan was for the use of the nuns.[117]

We cannot dismiss the rebuilding of Byzantine churches as simply the easiest way to maintain the churches of the Holy Land, considering it a decision without ideological content. At some shrines, such as Nazareth, the Franks pulled down the preexisting church and built a new one.[118] At Mount Tabor, the crusaders apparently destroyed a functioning monastic church to replace it with one more to their liking.[119] The deliberate reconstruction of churches in older Byzantine styles, as at Bethany and Ascalon, suggests both that the Franks worked with local master masons, and that they consulted local populations about how churches should look. As we have already seen with legal traditions, the Franks deliberately linked their regime to the Byzantine and local Christian past of Syria and Palestine. The choice to do the same with pilgrimage shrines was a deliberate and explicit message signaling Frankish participation in a shared Christianity.

Melkite Critiques of the Latin Clergy

The cooperation and close contact between Melkites and Franks should not blind us to local frustration and resentment against the Latin ecclesiastical establishment. The pilgrimage text of John Phokas, a Byzantine pilgrim in 1185, allows us to travel with someone who interacted extensively with Melkite priests and local Christian communities. John was a soldier who had fought in the armies of Manuel I Komnenos in Cilicia, and therefore had faced the Franks in battle. While John's attitudes were not necessarily those of Palestinian Christians, it is still possible to catch glimpses of the experiences of local Christians, particularly the clergy, through his eyes. At the church of St. George in Lydda, John heard a story telling how St. George protected his shrine from the priests serving there. Although he did not describe the religious background of the priests telling the story, the account they related to him of a Latin bishop who presumptuously opened the tomb of St. George and was scorched as a result suggests that they were not Latins, but Melkites who could speak Greek with John.[120]

The architectural remains at St. George hint at how Melkite and Latin priests might have shared the shrine. Like so many other churches in Palestine, St. George was originally an early Byzantine basilica, but was largely destroyed in the early eleventh century by the anti-Christian campaigns of the Fatimid caliph al-Hakim. A small secondary basilica survived, however, and the Christian community of Lydda held services there throughout the eleventh century while caring for the tomb of St. George in the ruins of the old church. Denys Pringle has proposed that when the Franks rebuilt the main church, they allowed the local Melkite community to continue to use the smaller basilica for their services.[121] Another possibility also presents itself. The crusaders rebuilt the main church on its Byzantine foundations, with three apses that would have allowed for the practice of the two liturgies at separate altars in the same church, as at al-Taiyiba. In either case, the Latin priests took control of the tomb of St. George, which formerly had been in the care of the local clergy, who as was discussed earlier included a Melkite bishop. The story John heard might capture some of the resentment felt by the local bishop and clergy at the Latin usurpation of control of the tomb of the saint.

When it suited them, the Franks did appropriate Melkite property and churches. On Mount Tabor, the Franks apparently ousted the Melkite monks long established there and installed Latins instead, eventually pulling down the existing church to build one on a Latin plan. At some point, the Melkite monks were allowed to establish themselves at a separate location on the mountain.[122] Thus, shared sacred space and royal and aristocratic patronage did not mean that local communities were powerful or able to protect their churches from seizure, attack, or even demolition. The lack of boundaries between Latins and locals paradoxically left local communities with no structures or guidance on how relations with the dominant power were to be regulated. Unlike their compatriots' situation in Muslim lands, there was no "Pact of 'Umar" that laid out the rights and responsibilities of each party. The permeability and integration of rough tolerance was in this sense no better and no worse than other contemporary forms of managing multireligious societies.

Pilgrimage

Evidence from western pilgrim texts can also indirectly point to the existence of mixed Latin-local communities in Palestine. Benjamin Kedar has already discussed a number of shrines shared by Christians and Muslims in the Middle East, particularly those in the Holy Land such as the shrine of John the Baptist in Sebaste, in the crypt of the Frankish cathedral, the shrine of 'Ain al-Bakar, the spring near Acre from which God created cattle, and the Tomb of the Patriarchs in Hebron.[123] The western pilgrim accounts of the pre-crusade era had generally consistent narrative interests. Focusing almost exclusively on biblical events, they directed their readers to visit the same holy places, often based on the accounts of Bede and Jerome. In the period of the crusades, however, a new pattern emerged. Western pilgrim accounts show an increased interest in nonbiblical sacred events in the Holy Land, such as the lives of late antique saints. The source of this interest in local saints was the increased contact between resident Franks and local Christians.

The monastery of Mar Saba, for example, drew greater attention from western pilgrims in the twelfth century, resulting in greater knowledge of the life and miracles of St. Sabas among pilgrims. Pre-crusade western pilgrims did sometimes visit the monastery, but they knew little of its history. Willibald, nephew of St. Boniface and one of the first English pilgrims to the Holy Land, visited Sabas's tomb in the mid-eighth century, but recorded little about the saint.[124] After the crusader conquest, pilgrim interest in the saint grew. Saewulf, another English pilgrim who visited the Holy Land in 1102/3, showed more interest in the life of the saint, informing his readers (inaccurately) that Sabas was one of the seventy-two disciples of Jesus.[125] Saewulf likely got his information from older pilgrimage texts or from gossip from other pilgrims on the road. An anonymous Latin text from the mid-twelfth century, however, displays a far more accurate understanding of the life of Sabas. Among other details, this pilgrim had learned of the miracles Sabas had performed in Jericho, for example, transforming broth into wine.[126] His narrative closely followed the story as told in Cyril of Scythopolis's sixth-century *vita* of Sabas, mentioning even the same names of the men who sat with Sabas that evening.[127] By the later twelfth century, Sabas had been incorporated into the liturgy of the Holy Sepulcher, which on his feast day included a procession to a church dedicated to him within the walls of Jerusalem, perhaps associated with the guesthouse of the monastery near the Tower of David.[128]

The Latin pilgrims who recorded these stories about Sabas must have heard them orally, either from the monks of Mar Saba themselves, or from a resident Frank who was familiar with the cult of St. Sabas.[129] Monasteries such as Mar Saba were therefore places where Latin pilgrims and local Franks would mingle and meet Melkite monks and priests as well as pilgrims from other communities. These meetings were not silent, with the parties performing their devotions separately, but were personal, and involved telling stories, worshipping during the same religious ceremonies, and creating a temporary community. Pilgrimage routes of different traditions shared many of the same sites, so that in the time that a pilgrim spent in the Holy Land, which might be months or even a year, the faces of fellow pilgrims, whether Latin, Armenian, Jacobite, or Melkite, became familiar, as did the local priests and monks who controlled some shrines and welcomed the pilgrims.

The legend of St. Mary the Egyptian also crossed over from eastern traditions to western pilgrims through stories told at *loca sancta*. Although St. Mary was well known in Europe before the crusades,[130] her story did not become linked to physical places in Palestine until the twelfth century. Living in fourth-century Egypt, Mary the Egyptian felt such strong sexual desires that she slept with innumerable men without accepting payment. According to her vita, she came to Jerusalem for the Feast of the Exaltation of the Cross, simply for the sake of large numbers of men gathered together in one place. When she attempted to enter the Holy Sepulcher, an invisible force prevented her. She quickly understood that it was her sinful life that thus precluded her from seeing the tomb of the Savior; overcome by repentance, she prayed to an icon of the Virgin in the courtyard of the church. She lived the remainder of her life in repentance in the desert.[131]

The story had a well-established place in eastern pilgrimage traditions. Epiphanios Hagiopolites, a Byzantine monk writing in the eighth or ninth century, mentioned the icon and its connection to the saint.[132] In contrast, western pilgrims did not include it in their accounts. The Piacenza pilgrim, visiting the Holy Land in the late sixth century, mentioned an icon of the Virgin Mary at the Holy Sepulcher, but did not associate it with the story of Mary the Egyptian.[133] In the twelfth century, however, her story suddenly surfaced in Latin pilgrim accounts. Saewulf, who arrived in Palestine in 1102, believed that this image, by which Mary was converted to the monastic life, remained at the door of the Holy Sepulcher.[134] Two anonymous twelfth-century pilgrim accounts mentioned the same image in connection with the saint, and also pointed out that the icon was very close to a local Christian chapel (variously identified as Jacobite, Syrian, or Greek).[135]

Why did western pilgrims show such a sudden interest in St. Mary the Egyptian? It is not that any new information has been provided, as was the case with St. Sabas. Rather, someone, perhaps the Syrian priests in the chapel of the Holy Cross near the icon of Mary, or perhaps resident Franks who had become familiar with the local traditions of the image, told western pilgrims about the icon and its connection to St. Mary the Egyptian. The story was not told just once, but again and again, so it became a familiar part of the sacred history of the Holy Sepulcher. Although eastern Christians had honored this image for centuries, it is not until the crusader period that Latins stopped to listen to their story.

Steven Runciman claimed that "when they [the Franks] set themselves up in the East they treated their Christian subjects no better than the Caliph had done before them. Indeed, they were sterner, for they interfered in the religious practices of the local churches."[136] Runciman's ire toward the Franks derived from his sense that they were at least partly to blame for the decline of eastern Christianity. Perhaps in a larger sense this is true, but for the twelfth century what we find is that the crusaders revitalized local Christian communities, reestablishing local bishoprics and monasteries, restoring older churches, and building new ones. A small notice in Michael the Great captured this well. When Athanasios VII excommunicated the bishop of Edessa, the Jacobite citizens of Edessa began to have their children baptized in the Latin church, fearing that the ordination of their own priests was invalid due to the controversy.[137] Yet they had no qualms about the validity of sacraments dispensed by a Latin priest, nor did they choose to attend an Armenian church, with whom the Jacobites had long lived and with whom they shared similar theology. Although theoretically separated by belief and practice, Frankish, Armenian and Syrian laity found churches and monasteries, priests, and monks to be conduits of divine grace irrespective of theology. On a daily basis, in rural churches, in pilgrimage shrines, on building sites, and in scriptoria, local Christians, resident Franks and pilgrims, met, rubbed shoulders, swapped stories, and shared in the common Christian heritage of the Holy Land and Syria.

Chapter 5
The Legal and Social Status of Local Inhabitants in the Frankish Levant

In 1175, Baldwin, lord of Rames (Ramla), donated a local Christian peasant to the Hospitallers. He was to remain "with all things of his and of his heirs of either sex, forever in the authority of, and under the power of, the Hospital alone."[1] Johannes Syrianus, as the charter calls him, was distinguished by a blemish in one eye, and evidently was once in charge of the cisterns of Caffer [Kafr ed-Dik], a small village tucked away in the olive groves southwest of Nablus. The ancient pools John might have cared for can still be found on the outskirts of the village today. This brief notice is perhaps the fullest description of a Palestinian peasant in the twelfth-century documents of the Frankish Levant. This simple transaction, a common one in the charters of the Frankish Levant, raises questions about Frankish authority and the status of local communities. John the Syrian, as we might call him, is quite a different figure from other Syrians and Palestinians we have encountered thus far. Yet the vast majority of the indigenous population of Palestine (as well as northern Syria), whether Muslim, Christian, or Jewish, were peasants. What then was their experience of Frankish rule? Did the pattern of rough tolerance shape their lives as it did the Armenians of Edessa, or the monks and clergy of the Jacobite church? The donation of John by a Frankish lord to a Latin Christian religious institution was a direct expression of authority, yet what specifically happened in the exchange?

Historiography

As discussed in the introduction, crusade historians over the last fifty years have laid out a clear and surprisingly detailed model of the society John the

Syrian lived in, the conditions under which he worked, and what the donation described above indicated about local communities, based on the assumptions of the segregationalist model discussed in the introductory chapter. According to scholars such as Jonathan Riley-Smith, Joshua Prawer, and Claude Cahen, John, and all indigenous peasants whether Christian or Muslim, were serfs, a legal and social status the Franks brought with them from Europe. They lived in small villages, often of a dozen families or less, and owed half the produce of their lands to their Frankish overlords. Overseeing the lord's interests was a village headman, often called a *ra'is*, who, though a serf like the other villagers, enjoyed privileges commensurate with his authority.

According to the segregationalist model, John the Syrian would have rarely seen his lord, or any other Franks, for they dwelt in the great cities of the kingdom, like Jerusalem, Acre, and Tyre, among a mixed population of local Christians, Muslims, and Jews. Though free from the servile status of their rural cousins, the indigenous city-dwellers were nonetheless also at a disadvantage compared to their Frankish neighbors. All non-Latins had to pay the *capitatio*, a sign of their second-class status, just as all non-Muslims once paid the *jizya* when Palestine was ruled by Muslims. This second-class status also prevented the indigenous population, irrespective of their social status, from joining the ruling elite, which was based on knighthood and Latin Christianity. Unless he converted to Latin Christianity, a local Christian could not give testimony in the High Court of the Kingdom, nor could he be one of the king's men, or even a knight in a lord's service. Although the crusaders had ostensibly come to free eastern Christians from the yoke of Muslim tyranny, the segregationalist argument emphasized that they had replaced a Muslim elite with a Frankish one, leaving local Christians in the same, or even a worse subjected position.[2]

Yet the last four chapters have shown that, despite conflicts and discrepancies of power, daily interactions between Franks and local Christians formed an essential part of communal life in the Latin East. This chapter argues that the twelfth-century status of local Christians in Latin Palestine was considerably different from the well-researched and plausible model presented above. This chapter is largely restricted to the kingdom of Jerusalem, as it is only there that sufficient evidence survives to discuss the status of local Christians. In a broad sense, however, the conclusions reached here can be applied to Tripoli, Antioch, and Edessa, though their legal traditions may have been somewhat different. By relying on twelfth-century documents and excluding those that reflect the very different thirteenth-century world, we find that the conditions of Palestinian peasants differed in several ways from those of European serfdom, and that local Christians and Franks lived under the same laws and under the jurisdiction of the same courts. The permeability that characterized rough tolerance was limited neither to northern Syria nor to religious identity and behavior. Local Christians and possibly Muslims became knights, served the kings of Jerusalem as marshals, and held a variety of other important offices in the kingdom.

The segregationist model is built on three inaccurate premises. The first is outlined above, the belief that the Franks imported European serfdom into Syria and Palestine. Palestinian peasants were tied to the land, but they had little else in common with European serfs. The second is the notion of strict legal separation between Latins and the various eastern Christians. As we have seen in Chapter 4, Franks and local Christians received sacraments from each other's priests, and worshipped at each other's churches. The theological differences between them were rarely acknowledged, and little evidence from the twelfth century supports the notion that Franks expected local Christians to go through a ritual of conversion before receiving sacraments from a Latin priest, or vice versa. Indeed, considerable evidence supports the opposite. It is unlikely that Barsegh the priest was a priest in the Roman church, and even more unlikely that Baldwin of Marash converted to Armenian Christianity. Nor is it likely that conditions in northern Syria were in this matter so different from those in Jerusalem, given the many political, social, and familial ties between the two areas. The Frankish laity of Jerusalem recognized that local Christians employed different liturgies and had distinct traditions of priesthood, but did not consider these incongruities a sign of fundamental difference, any more than a Castilian would consider that the Mozarabic tradition excluded that community from communion with those following the Roman rite.

The final, and most significant, notion is that one had to be a Latin Christian to participate in governing the kingdom. This concept is derived largely from the writings of thirteenth-century jurists like John of Ibelin, a Frankish aristocrat who wrote an extensive commentary on the laws of the kingdom of Jerusalem in the 1260s. According to John, "these are those who are not able to give testimony in the High Court, and who cannot bring a motion before the court: perjurers, the insane, traitors, bastards, adulterers, those whose champion has been defeated in the field [of judgment], those who have served the Saracens and fight against Christians, or Greeks or people of such birth who are not obedient to Rome."[3] Nor does this assertion appear only in John of Ibelin; the thirteenth-century legal texts of the kingdom of Jerusalem take it as axiomatic. Indeed, such texts share no part of the "regime of silence" that characterized the twelfth century and cannot be applied to the period under study.

Thirteenth-Century Texts, Twelfth-Century World

Most of the evidence for the three inaccurate premises listed above comes from the large collection of thirteenth-century legal texts and commentaries from the Kingdom of Jerusalem. The earliest is the *Livre au roi*, compiled about 1200; most were written in the latter half of the thirteenth century. While the texts sometimes refer to laws promulgated in the twelfth century, they are not the laws themselves, and no original legal texts or commentaries survive from the twelfth century. Historians have generally accepted that the *Assises de Jerusalem*, as the texts are known as a group, applied to the Kingdom of Jerusalem as a whole, but recent research suggests that they reflect a particular thirteenth-century reality. Furthermore, the cultural and social world of the twelfth-century Levant was markedly different from that of the thirteenth.

The Battle of Hattin on 4 July 1187, when the armies of Syria and Egypt, united under Sal al-Din, annihilated the assembled knights of the kingdom of Jerusalem, has long been fetishized by historians as a transformative event in the history of the Frankish Levant, and for good reason. With the Muslim victory, the Franks lost their cities, lands, and churches; the few surviving leaders were scattered. Many of the aristocracy fled to newly conquered Cyprus; they subsequently intermarried with ambitious new arrivals to the Latin East, such as the Lusignans, Montbéliards, Briennes, and Montforts.[4] It was decades before a substantial part of Palestine returned to Frankish control, and many of the leading families of the kingdom survived only through offices and properties held in Cyprus—an interlude that exposed them to a quite different social and political milieu.

Even the rulers of what remained of the kingdom—Guy of Lusignan (1186–1190), Conrad of Montferrat (1190–1192), Henry of Champagne (1192–1197), Aimery of Lusignan (1197–1205), John of Brienne (1210–1225), and finally the absentee Hohenstaufen—were of a distinctly different cast from their predecessors. Most of these men had little previous experience in the Latin East before assuming control, and often had closer ties with other recent émigrés than with the remnants of the local aristocracy.[5]

Some historians have adopted the title "kingdom of Acre" to refer to the polity born through the Third Crusade and subsequent military ventures and negotiations in order to distinguish it from its earlier incarnation. The same distinction exists on the levels of lordship and individual landownership. As a result of conquest, reconquest, and changes in aristocracy and population, we cannot know that the taxes and services owed by a particular village in 1229 were the same as in 1129. In the intervening time, the village had likely been under Muslim control for perhaps as long as forty years. Even if the same family who owned it in the twelfth century regained control in the thirteenth, the family's idea of itself and its relation to local Palestinians and Syrians would have been influenced by the cultural and political changes in Europe. The Mediterranean in the thirteenth century grew to be an internationalized world for the aristocracies of western Europe, where a man might marry a bride from Aragon, have territory in Cyprus, serve under the Latin emperors of Constantinople, and be a royal officer in Sicily. Particularly through time spent in Cyprus and Latin Constantinople, and direct contact with the knights of the Third Crusade and other military campaigns, a Frankish lord might establish different customs in the village in 1229 from those of the twelfth century.

One can only imagine the slow process whereby a family attempted to reassemble their patrimonial lands. They had to reestablish authority over the villages, and rebuild granaries, mills and other physical tools that allowed them to measure, collect, and tax the produce of the land. In many places, peasant families may have left or been killed and new families settled in their place. What rights did the lord have over this new population? The thirteenth-century recapture of Palestine was just as much a conquest as that of the First Crusade, with the attendant opportunity to institute new taxes, customs, and exactions from a populace worn down by war. The thirteenth-century charters, for example, reflect the post-conquest realities of Latin Palestine, and we cannot assume that they accurately reflect the twelfth century.

Changes in the heartland of Europe also helped differentiate the "new" Latin kingdom of the thirteenth century from the "old." The papacy, whose influence and power had grown far beyond what Urban II had wielded when he initiated the First Crusade, insisted on greater conformity and obedience to Rome. The centralizing ideals of the papacy, culminating in the administration of Innocent III, were brought to the Latin East by aristocrats such as John of Brienne and by churchmen such as Jacques de Vitry, appointed bishop of Acre in 1216. Such changes reflected not only increased papal power, but also a changed sense of what it meant to be a Latin Christian and what the proper relationship between the sacred and temporal should be. It is telling that the first analytical categorization of local Christian churches, detailing their differences from the Catholic Church, came from the pen of Jacques. Greater consciousness of the importance of these differences can be seen in the works of John of Ibelin and other thirteenth-century jurists, who repeatedly use the phrase "men not of the rule of Rome" to categorize all non-Catholics, a phrase never seen in twelfth-century documents. The age of "theological ignorance" was over.

It was to this thirteenth-century world that John of Ibelin belonged. He was a member of the preeminent Frankish family of the Levant, the Ibelins. His paternal grandfather was Balian of Ibelin, who had surrendered Jerusalem to Salah al-Din, and his paternal grandmother was the formidable Queen Maria Komnena, widow of King Amalric. More important, his uncle was John of Ibelin, known as the "Old Lord of Beirut," the leader of the aristocratic Frankish opposition to Frederick II's claims in Cyprus and Jerusalem. John's legal writings served a number of purposes, the most important of which was to establish the legal customs of the Frankish Levant in written form, as the oral tradition on which John drew was inferior, in thirteenth-century eyes, to written legal forms.[6] John's legal learning thus became a weapon in his family's arsenal for use against Hohenstaufen domination of the Frankish Levant.

John, however, did not have access to the original laws of Jerusalem themselves. According to another thirteenth-century jurist, they were kept in a locked box in the Church of the Holy Sepulcher, and as a consequence, were called *les letres dou Sepulchre*. They were lost when Salah al-Din conquered Jerusalem in 1187. Peter Edbury has recently argued that they never existed, at least in the form described.[7] The *letres* were thus a historical fiction, a miniature version of the Donation of Constantine, intended to give the thirteenth-century customs of the Frankish Levant a venerable origin with Godfrey of Bouillon, the now legendary founder of the kingdom of Jerusalem.

John of Ibelin based his treatise on "what I have heard, learnt, and received from the wisest men of my time. I have heard these men speak of the *assises* and usages of the kingdom and the pleading in the court. Because I have seen them in action, I have embarked on writing."[8] Sadly for the historian, it is impossible to distinguish the original laws of the kingdom from the oral customs that developed around them. Relatively few portions of John's work or of other thirteenth-century legal texts can accurately be rooted in twelfth-century material or memory, and those that can have nothing to say about the status of the indigenous population.[9] Yet John's thirteenth-century theoretical assertion about the status of non-Latins has been applied to the twelfth century without context or explanation, although the dangers of this have been noted.[10] The richness of these legal sources makes them irresistible to the historian, particularly when the twelfth-century material is so tauntingly vague and incomplete. While Joshua Prawer and others have shown persuasively how little these texts represent the twelfth-century realities of Frankish burgesses and knights,[11] historians have yet to question their validity when speaking of the local Christian population.

The Peasantry

The vast majority of the indigenous population of Palestine were peasants, especially following the sieges and massacres that devastated the cities during the First Crusade and led to the death or emigration of a large portion of the urban population. Although little work has been done on conversion to Islam in Palestine and Syria, the limited evidence we have suggests that a significant proportion of the population remained Christian, and in some areas, such as the land between Jerusalem and Nablus, Christians were the majority.[12] The reliable sources for the status of the peasantry in the twelfth-century Latin East are the cartularies of the Hospitallers and a few other ecclesiastical institutions. Created to describe a contemporary transaction, written with standard formulas, the charter hews as close to description as a historian can hope to find. Yet the charter was still a document of the Frankish elite, and its forms and formulas linked it to the vast corpus of charter collections that survive in western Europe. The charters addressed similar concerns—transfer of rights and property, largely in an agricultural setting. It is understandable that the Franks would continue to use the same phrases and language to describe their new possessions in the East as for their properties in Europe. The use of the same specialized language, however, did not mean that the same conditions prevailed in both places.

Joshua Prawer has remarked that "for the peasant the Crusader had the ready-made formula of serfdom."[13] But ready-made formulas do not fit every circumstance. Although the Franks did indeed employ the language of serfdom to describe the Palestinian peasant, the application of the formula to a non-European agricultural regime is another matter entirely.[14] Even within

Europe, serfdom was an idiosyncratic institution, with services and duties varying in accordance with local geography, history, and climate.[15] Yet European serfdom, for all its variety, had common roots in the widespread slavery of the early medieval period, and in shared cultural development later. "Serfdom" has a defined meaning, developed in a European context, which is misleading when used to describe conditions in the Frankish Levant. Just as the utility of the term "feudalism" has been degraded by its use to describe economic and political systems from Japan to England to Tonga, "serfdom" is facing a similar fate. The rural regime of the Latin East must be described and discussed within its own development, not linked needlessly to Europe. A close examination of the status of Palestinian peasants shows that the only legal characteristic they shared with European peasants was that both were in some sense tied to the land. Other Mediterranean lands, such as Sicily, offer better comparison than the areas associated with serfdom, such as northern France.

Palestinian Peasants Under Islamic Rule

While John the Syrian probably was not old enough to recall the days when Palestine was under Islamic rule, his grandfather likely lived under the rule of the Egyptian Shi'a caliphs, the Fatimids. What was his status under Islamic administration, and how did conditions change under the Franks? Given the lack of archival sources, the legal and social position of rural communities in pre-crusade Palestine is difficult to uncover, particularly given the political upheavals in the latter half of the eleventh century. It is clear, however, that Islamic law did not have a category that was similar to the quasi-free status of the European serf. Individuals were either slaves or free. Muslim society of the eleventh century did recognize various states of dependency, including *dhimmi* status for non-Muslims, but these were constituted by personal ties; they never degraded a person's juridical status as free.[16]

Some historians have pointed to the institution of *ikta'* as an Islamic form of landholding that reduced the peasantry to a form of serfdom, thus allowing the easy introduction of Frankish concepts in the twelfth century.[17] Although *ikta'* varied from place to place and evolved throughout the medieval period, in essence it was the bestowal of administrative authority over large tracts of territory that included the right to collect land taxes.[18] In other words, the grant did not convey ownership of the land or any direct administrative or judicial rights over its inhabitants. Nizam al-Mulk (1018–1092), vizier of the Seljuk sultans Alp Arslan and Malikshah, wrote in his guide to governance that "officers who hold assignments [*ikta'*] must know that they have no authority over the peasants except to take from them—and that with courtesy—the due amount of revenue which has been assigned to them to collect."[19]

The evidence for where the *ikta'* was instituted is also vague,[20] and we cannot be certain that it was widespread in Palestine. The struggles over Palestine, first between the Fatimids and local tribal dynasties, then later with the Turkmen invasions of the eleventh century, would suggest that the *ikta'*, usually an absentee form of tax farming, would not have been an effective institution. The disruptions of invasion and the lack of an established local administration would have made it difficult for military officers to collect taxes with the regularity necessary to ensure a regular income. In the twelfth and thirteenth centuries, many Turkish warlords were able to usurp ownership of public and private lands using their authority as holders of *ikta'* grants, and through a combination of force and financial burdens, to tie the peasantry to their land.[21] Although this inevitably altered the peasant's social status and access to justice, he legally remained a free man. The *ikta'* in this form, however, was largely an innovation originating in the domain of the twelfth-century Zangid emirs of Mosul, and chronologically could not be an Islamic precursor to Frankish serfdom, but it can be seen as a parallel development.

Peasants in the Twelfth-Century Kingdom of Jerusalem

On 28 September 1110, King Baldwin I confirmed a number of charitable donations that had been made to the Hospitallers.

The villeins and lands, which Hugo and Gervase gave in Tiberias, and three villeins which the bishop of Nazareth gave, and one from William de Tenches, and another from Paganus Vacca, and another from Drogo, and another from Dominic, and Guitbert de Salinas another, and Pagan of Cayphas another with lands and houses in Cayphas and in Caphernaum, and another villein who Roman of Puy gave, and another who Baldwin gave with lands and houses in the town of Rames; all of these, just as they are written above, I concede and confirm to the above-mentioned Hospital.[22]

This charter, written only eleven years after the capture of Jerusalem, already reveals a startling variety of donations. None of the villeins were named; some gifts referred only to villeins, and others to both land and peasants. Some refer to villeins who live in towns such as Ramla (Rames) and others who are simply designated as "alium"—another one. The meaning of such a document is further confused when compared to others where the names of the donated villeins are spelled out at great length.[23] Donations of a single peasant—named or unnamed—became a common way for the aristocracy of Jerusalem to support religious institutions, and often land or even location was not mentioned. The gift of a single serf was relatively uncommon in northern Europe. The practice in Palestine may reflect local landholding traditions of dividing common village property among the villagers every year or two, called *musha'*.[24] Due to scarcity of evidence for agricultural regimes in Palestine and Syria in the medieval period, we have no direct evidence concerning *musha'* before the Ottoman period. The custom of donating a single villein, without reference to any gift of land, may be a way to denote revenue in areas where farm boundaries were not fixed, and was not intended to convey concrete authority over a single peasant. Alternatively, the donation of particular peasants may be a way to donate land without detailing the exact borders of the property, as is the case in charters from eleventh- and twelfth-century Norman Sicily.[25]

The terminology of the charters also suggests significant differences from European practices. The peasants of the Latin East in twelfth-century charters were never called *servus*, the term found so often in European documents; Frankish charters use *villanus* or often simply *surianus* if they were Christian, or *sarracenus* if they were Muslim. The difference in terminology may be because the term *servus* was reserved to describe actual slaves, of whom there were a great number in the kingdom of Jerusalem.[26] The slaves of the Latin East were largely urban, domestic slaves, and thus rarely appeared in the twelfth-century charters. There seems to be little chance that the two categories would be confused. The Franks may also have deliberately chosen the term *villanus*, which in northern France could mean either a villager or a serf whose ancestors were free, because it may have more accurately conveyed the higher status of peasants in the Latin East. It may also suggest that the Franks conceived of local peasants as holding servile land tenures rather than being personally unfree.[27]

European serfdom was primarily characterized by three conditions: non-free legal status, attachment to the land, and performance of servile duties and payment of servile impositions, such as *chevage, mainmort,* and *formariage.*[28] Did these or similar conditions exist in the Latin East? *Mainmort* signified that a serf had no heirs of the body; his lord was his heir and theoretically had the right to receive all his belongings at his death. In practice, however, families were generally allowed to inherit land and belongings, while the lord often received the best cow or pig as a sign of his right to take everything. The charters of the Frankish Levant frequently mentioned the heirs of *villani* and never mentioned *mainmort*, suggesting that the villeins owned their belongings with full legal possession.[29] Even the thirteenth-century legal treatises do not provide any impediment to full inheritance. Anecdotal evidence suggests the same. Ibn Jubayr, a Muslim pilgrim, noticed that the Muslim peasants he visited near Acre in 1184 were left in full possession of their houses and personal belongings.[30] Nor did peasants pay *chevage*, the head tax that in western Europe was a sign of non-free status.[31]

Although marriage between peasants of different estates was a concern, we do not have evidence for *formariage*, the payment by a serf if he wished to marry outside his lord's domain. The issue of intermarriage between peasants of different estates did not appear in twelfth-century sources. However, John of Ibelin devoted two chapters to this thorny issue. According to the jurist, should such a marriage take place, the lord of the husband must provide a replacement for the married woman, who presumably moved to his estate—but only if he agreed to the marriage.[32] In no circumstance did the peasants themselves have to pay for the privilege to marry. John of Ibelin's main concern was to maintain the agricultural workforce rather than emphasize the servility of the peasantry. Given that villages were sometimes divided among different lords, such marriages may have been common, and therefore something like John's system was needed, even if his remarks apply only to the thirteenth century. Another reason *formariage* might not have been imposed in the Latin East was that it would interfere with local religious authority. As will be discussed later, non-Latin religious courts flourished under Latin rule, and marriage fell to their jurisdiction. Local clergy would have resisted any attempt by a Frankish lord to interfere.

The only similarity between European serfs and Palestinian peasants was that both were tied to the land, although under different conditions. The primary concern of Frankish landlords was to retain a productive workforce on their lands, not to emphasize the servility of their peasants. Villeins abandoning the land could be a problem—in the 1150s a group of Hanbalis, a sect of pietist Muslims, abandoned their villages near Nablus and fled to Damascus.[33] This, however, is the only documented example of peasants fleeing Latin areas after conquest, and was motivated as much by religious ideology as by Frankish oppression. We can glimpse Latin concern over this issue in a few documents, such as a charter from 1186, where Bohemund III and the

Hospitallers agree to return to each other any peasant they find on their land who had come from the other's land.[34] Yet the charter of 1186 did not necessarily indicate that villeins were tied to the land in the European sense. The agreement is better understood as a noncompetition contract between landlords worried about losing their peasants to nearby estates offering better terms. Indeed, the only issues that appear even in John of Ibelin's thirteenth-century work concerning villeins relate to peasants leaving their lord's lands. John therefore provided a framework for the return of the villein, or compensation to his or her lord. John, however, was not concerned about peasants leaving the land to go to the cities, suggesting that a lord had no legal recourse in that situation. Limiting the freedom of peasants to leave their land was a response to local labor conditions, not the imposition of European ideas of serfdom.

Here again Norman Sicily provides a useful comparison. An Arabic document from 1177 recorded the resolution of a dispute between the abbey of San Giovanni degli Eremiti in Palermo and three brothers: Jabrun, Ibrahim, and ʿAbd al-Rahman. The three acknowledged that they were *rijal al-jara'id*, an Arabic term that indicated that they were individuals inscribed as part of the abbey's estate. They had, however, abandoned the land and settled elsewhere without permission. The abbot had seized their property in an attempt to force them to return, a tactic that was apparently successful. The document was evidence of their submission to the abbot; he in turn restored their property and agreed to submit to the abbey's chapter their request that they be allowed to live where they chose. Jeremy Johns suggests that the three brothers were prosperous; he calculates their land-holdings as between 281 and 422 acres, and that they probably had farmers working the land on their behalf.[35] Thus the brothers were legally tied to the estate, but owed no services. While we have no similar documents from the Frankish Levant, the conditions under which our Johannes Syrianus lived was much more akin that of Jabrun, Ibrahim, and ʿAbd al-Rahman than western European serfs.

A few charters detailing the donation of specific individuals living in cities further complicate our understanding of what it meant to donate an individual. A charter from 1183 recorded the donation of a number of Greeks, Armenians, Jews, and even a Frank.

I, Bohemund, by grace of God prince of Antioch, son of Prince Raymond, . . . give, and in perpetual charity I concede these men, whose names are written below, to God and to the holy house of the poor of the Hospital of Jerusalem, and to brother Roger de Molins. These are the names: from the Greeks: Afanas, Sergius, a bricklayer, and his children, Leo, a barrel-maker, Mambarak and his children, Mambarak, a shoe-maker, Leo. From the Armenians: Hanes, a butcher, Castor, a baker, Hanes, an archer, Hanes, a blacksmith, Vasil, a blacksmith. From the Jews Bolcaran, Zao, Bolchae, and his brother, Temin, Bolshassen, Stellator. And in addition to these Hugo Straigot. These above-mentioned men, whether Latins or Greeks or Armenians or Jews, the Hospital owns, holds and possesses in perpetuity, in peace and without challenge, freely and peacefully from all tallage.[36]

This charter is in many ways inexplicable, and its Antiochene origin further complicates attempts to understand it, as the legal and social conditions in Antioch differed from those in Jerusalem. These men, all craftsmen (and a soldier) and not farmers, were residents of Lattakia, a city on the coast of Syria. The charter never refers to them as *villani* or even *servi* or *sclavi*, al-though other historians have interpreted it to mean that individuals re-mained serfs even when they came to the cities.[37] However, in doing so they discounted the presence of Latins on the list, though the inclusion of the name "Hugo" and the listing of "Latins" alongside the other categories sug-gests that this was not simply a scribal slip. Similarly confusing are charters that donate knights alongside peasants, again suggesting that services or por-tions of incomes were being donated or exchanged, rather than unfree indi-viduals.[38] Our inability to understand in what way these men were donated to the Hospital, and what conditions this imposed on them, should caution us from easily categorizing other donations as signs of European serfdom.

The silence of Muslim travelers to the Latin East on this issue is also sug-gestive. The imposition of a European institution on Muslim peasants which degraded them from free to semi-slave might provoke some comment from Muslims. Usama ibn Munqidh, despite boundless curiosity about social sta-tus in the Frankish principalities, and numerous visits to the kingdom, did not mention any change in the status of peasants under the Franks, and nei-ther did the Muslim pilgrim Ibn Jubayr, although he spent the night in the house of a Muslim *ra'is* near Acre in 1184. Ibn Jubayr is well known for his comment that "the Muslim community bewails the injustice of a landlord of his own faith, and applauds the conduct of its opponent and enemy, the Frankish landlord, and is accustomed to justice from him."[39] Ibn Jubayr's praise of the Franks may have a polemical purpose intended to shame Mus-lim landlords into better treatment of their peasants; yet such a tactic would not be effective had Palestinian peasants actually lost status as a result of the crusader conquest.

The most decisive factor that separated John the Syrian from his European counterpart was that the Palestinian peasant was not obligated to perform *corvées* or other servile unpaid labor.[40] The wide variety of customs that prevailed in the Latin East suggests that in each locale the duties owed by the peasants were created through a fusion of older local customs combined with new Latin expectations. From the twelfth-century charters, we can see that the peasants paid a certain percentage of their crop yield, anywhere from one-quarter to a half, to their lord. Ibn Jubayr reported that the Muslim peasants around Acre gave half of their crop and paid a poll-tax of one dinar and five qirat per person, plus a light tax on produce from trees.[41] Thirteenth-century charters suggest that the financial burden upon the peasantry may have grown, perhaps in response to the diminished incomes of many Frankish lords following the conquests of Salah al-Din and the Third Crusade.

Thus, of the many servile conditions that defined European serfdom—*chevage, mainmort, formariage, corvées*, and being tied to the land—only the last could be found in the Latin East. These differences between the status and service of European and Palestinian peasants militate against the use of the term "serf" in the Latin East. "Indentured peasant" may more accurately convey their personal freedom along with the requirements to remain on the land.

Local Rural Landowners and Administrators

The Latin charters of the twelfth century have also preserved the buying, selling, and donation of land by local Christians. Using the same legal form (the charter) as Franks, these men and women cannot be grouped together with the agricultural workers so often donated in the same kind of legal documents, as earlier scholarship has effectively done.

The group of local landowners who have received the most attention are the *ru'asa* (singular *ra'is*, Arabic for "leader, chief, or mayor"), who helped the Latins administer their estates and govern local communities. Jonathan Riley-Smith divides these leaders into two different types: the *ra'is* of the town and of the village,[42] concluding that the latter was a serf and the former free. We have already argued that the term "serf" was misapplied to the Levant, especially in the twelfth century. Given the lack of evidence for serfdom, we will stick closer to the evidence if we accept the *ru'asa* as a single group, living sometimes in towns and sometimes in smaller communities, but always legally free.

The *ru'asa* were not merely henchmen working under Frankish orders, but local landowners worthy of respect from locals and Latins alike. A charter from 1174 documented the gift of three-quarters of the village of Meserafe that 'Abd al-Masih, the *ra'is* of Margat (Marqab), made to the Hospitallers. The son of 'Abd al-Masih, George was like his father also *ra'is* of Margat; he continued to own a fourth of the village, and was witness to the charter.[43] This family may well have owned other villages (indeed, it would surprising if they gave away most of their property to the Hospitallers all at once), and thus were as wealthy as many a Frankish knight. 'Abd al-Masih is unusual in that he donated his property to a Latin ecclesiastical institution, rather than selling it. Yet we have no reason to assume that his charity signaled a conversion to Latin Christianity; support of the Hospitallers could be strategic or could signal that 'Abd al-Masih's family had been influenced by Latin concepts of sanctity, just as Barsegh the priest had come to believe that salvation could be found on the battlefield. The *ra'is* Melenganus was more typical; he sold to the Knights of St. Lazarus three pieces of land near Bethlehem in 1150.[44] Guido Raicus, or Guy the *ra'is*, who witnessed charters in Nablus in 1178,[45] owned half the lands of the village of Mesdedule, which he had received directly from King Amalric.[46] In 1185, Guy sold them to the monks of St. Mary of Jehosaphat, for four thousand fifty bezants, a transaction that took place in the royal court.[47] It is impossible to tell whether Guy was Frankish, a local Christian with a Frankish name, or even a Muslim convert. In any case, a *ra'is* with a Frankish name hints at a rural world where locals and Latins occupied the same offices, or where local inhabitants identified with their Frankish neighbors and their culture through the assumption of Latin names. The possibility of a Frankish *ra'is* further emphasizes that the *ru'asa* were free, and that the office, whether rural or urban, was one of substantial authority and position.

Yet this evidence for a group of wealthy local Christian landowners should not lead us to think that their economic relationships with the Franks were a sign of goodwill and harmony between different communities. As we have seen already in northern Syria, the existence of a local rural elite may actually signal greater tensions between Latin immigrants and indigenous communities. In a religiously based social hierarchy, such as that described by Riley-Smith and Prawer, where a clear distinction divides society into two groups—the ruling elite and the powerless peasants—there is less chance for conflict, for the two groups hardly interact. However, the situation in Palestine was messier. Some local leaders might not have looked upon the Franks with much favor. We get a hint of the possible tension in a charter from the *ra'is* Morage, who was forced by his debts to the king to sell a mill to the Holy Sepulcher.[48] While we have no idea how Morage became so indebted to the king (though this in itself is suggestive of high status), it is clear that the Latin ecclesiastical establishment benefited.

Local Authority in Palestinian Cities

The role of the *ra'is* in the town is more difficult to establish. The traditional picture of the kingdom of Jerusalem placed the town *ra'is* as the presider over the *Cour des Syriens*, which, according to John of Ibelin, had authority over disputes that arose within the local "Suriani" community. He ascribed the origin of this court to Godfrey of Bouillon.

After this [the establishment of the High Court and the Burgess Court], the Syrians came before the king of the realm [Godfrey] and beseeched and requested that he would see that they would be governed by the traditions of the Syrians, and that they might have a chief and jurors of the court, and that by this court they would be governed according to their usages concerning the complaints that arose among them. And he consented to the said court without jurisdiction of that which pertains to loss of life or limb, or jurisdiction of the bourgeois; which would be pleaded and determined before him or before his viscount. And the chief of this court is titled *ra'is* in Arabic.[49]

It is possible that the situation John of Ibelin describes in the 1260s was also true a hundred fifty years earlier, but we have no twelfth-century evidence for the existence of such courts, though we know the names of a large number of twelfth-century *ru'asa*.[50] However, presiding over local courts is not the only possible task of the *ru'asa*. The position of *ra'is* was a common one throughout the Arabic-speaking world. Another possible role for the *ru'asa* was as leaders of local troops, as they were in twelfth-century Aleppo and Damascus. We know from other sources that local Christians participated in the defense of the kingdom of Jerusalem; William of Tyre recorded that Fulk of Tiberias had a placed a castle on the east bank of the Jordan under the command of Syrian officers.[51]

Perhaps the basis for John of Ibelin's memory was the continuation of local ecclesiastical courts with authority over religious matters such as marriage and wills, for which some evidence does survive. In keeping with west-

ern European legal traditions, the Franks themselves maintained separate ecclesiastical and secular courts. Yet for local communities, whether Jewish,
Muslim, Melkite, Jacobite, or Armenian, one legal tradition encompassed
matters that in the Frankish system were divided between ecclesiastical and
secular jurisdictions.[52] Legal disputes within indigenous communities,
whether involving secular or religious issues, probably were resolved in front
of the local *qadi*, rabbi, or priest. For example, the rabbinic court of Acre (c.
1170) heard testimony from a Christian over the death of a Jewish husband,
and corresponded with the famed scholar Maimonides, then living in Egypt,
in order to resolve the issue.[53] A Greek manuscript in the library of the Greek
Orthodox patriarchate of Jerusalem was copied for Georgios, "magistrate
and judge of the Holy City and treasurer and keeper of the sacred vessels of
Holy Christ our God of the Anastasis."[54] Georgios was thus both a priest
of the Holy Sepulcher and a judge, probably for the Melkite community of
Jerusalem. Given his dual roles, he was likely a judge for religious matters
such as marriage. Even nonreligious conflicts in a community may have been
handled without recourse to the Frankish legal system. Such a court was not
created by the Franks, nor even sanctioned by Godfrey. Rather, John of Ibelin
was giving such courts, which existed independently, a fictional Frankish
origin.

For matters such as the sale of property, however, local Christians used
the same courts as their Frankish neighbors. A charter of 1125 recorded the
purchase of a house by Bernard de Châteauroux and his wife Havidis from
George the *ra'is*. The sale was finalized in the court of the viscount of
Jerusalem, Anschetinus, and was witnessed by twenty-one burgesses.[55] This
court fits the description of the one described in the anonymous thirteenth-
century *Assises de la cour bourgeois*. Yet the elaborate descriptions of which
Christian could testify against another (for example, a Nestorian cannot give
testimony against a Jacobite) are out of place in a twelfth-century world
where Nestorians go unmentioned in every other source. The tone and language of the text find their closest parallels with the thirteenth-century work
of Jacques de Vitry and others.[56]

Nor were the *ru'asa* the only indigenous officials of the Frankish administration. Another office was that of *scribanagium*, a position of more prestige than that of *ra'is*, but whose incumbents often performed similar tasks of
administering rural estates. This office could be filled by Franks or locals. In
a charter of 1176, Baldwin, lord of Ramla, confirmed the sale of the village of
Bethduras (Giv'ati) to Constance, the countess of St. Gilles. Specifically ex-

cluded from the sale was the *scribanagium* of George of Betheri (Khan et-Tira, near Nablus), whose name suggests that he was Christian.[57] The next year George sold the office, as well as the income or lands attached, to Constance for two hundred and fifty bezants. It is a sign of the wealth and importance of this office that the sale required confirmation in separate charters by King Baldwin IV, Baldwin, lord of Ramla, and Sybilla, countess of Jaffa, heiress to the throne.[58] By the thirteenth century, the position was sometimes held in return for military service.[59]

Indigenous Knights

Local Christian integration into the Frankish social structure extended beyond the small-time landowners and administrators such as Guy, George, and others. Local Christians were able to become a part of the ruling military elite.[60] The assumption of historians has been that these individuals converted to Latin Christianity. Yet there is no evidence that they did, and considerable evidence, discussed above, that different Christian communities did not consider the boundaries between Latin, Jacobite, and Armenian rites to be crossable only through formal acts of conversion. While we do not have clear evidence in either direction, the best route would not lead us to assume conversions that contemporary texts do not support.

The majority of evidence for indigenous knights comes from the early twelfth century. One of the earliest to appear is "Barda Armeno," a witness to a charter of William of Bures, prince of Galilee in 1126.[61] His name is clearly a Latinized version of Bardas the Armenian, and he may well have been originally a companion of Joscelin of Courtenay, who, before he became count of Edessa, was prince of Galilee (1113–1118/9). By witnessing charters in the company of other knights and owning more than one village, Bardas shows himself to be not a *ra'is* or other minor functionary, but a knight.[62] In 1129, he donated the village of Coketum to the Hospitallers,[63] demonstrating not his conversion to Latin Christianity, but his adoption of the cultural values of Frankish knighthood, exemplified in the military orders. His donation was an assertion of status, rather than of religious identification. Another knight, surnamed "Armeno" with the first name George, was serving under Walter, lord of Caesarea in 1145.[64] Peter Hermenius, clearly another Armenian and possibly a son of either George or Bardas, witnessed two charters in Jerusalem in 1161,[65] and was listed under the *milites* in another charter of 1163.[66] Given the paucity of secular Armenian settlements in Palestine, it is likely that these Armenians were originally from Antioch or Edessa, and were serving in the forces of Baldwin I, Baldwin II, or Joscelin and accompanied their leaders south.

Perhaps the best-known and most prominent local family in the service of the Franks were the Arrabi family, who began as knights in the service of the Ibelins.[67] The progenitor of was Moses Arrabi; his last name may be an epithet meaning "enraged" rather than a comment on his ethnic origins. His grandson John Arrabi was still in the service of Ibelins in 1166.[68] What is perhaps most enlightening about the Arrabi family is not that they served as knights under Frankish lords, although this is important, but how they integrated into Frankish society. Moses' grandsons were named John, Peter, and Henry, and were it not for their distinctive surname, as Jonathan Riley-Smith has pointed out, we would assume they were Franks.[69] For some historians, this name shift and their high status is proof that the Arrabi family converted to Latin Christianity. If this were indeed the case, we might expect that Moses himself might have been given a different name upon emerging from the baptismal font; Moses must have had a distinctly Jewish or Muslim sound to Frankish ears. It is less surprising that, after three generations of service with other Peters, Henrys, and Johns, the Arrabi family adopted such names as their own. Other local Christian knights probably lurk in Latin charters, hiding under deceptive names like Baldwin, Guy, or Fulk.[70] This disappearance of distinctive local names among indigenous knights may be part of the reason we have relatively little evidence for native knights in the 1170s and 1180s.

In addition to the Armenian knights and the Arrabi family, a number of other names appear on witness lists that likely belonged to local Christians. The marshal of Jerusalem from 1125 to 1154 was Sado, a name that occurs rarely in western Europe and may be the Arabic name Sa'd or Sa'id.[71] We find the similar name "Sade" among peasants on the estates of the Holy Sepulcher.[72] In some of the charters Sa'd witnessed, he is listed as one of the barons of the realm.[73] It is impossible to tell whether Sa'd was a Christian or a Muslim,[74] but either shows the opportunity for Palestinians to achieve high office under the Franks. As marshal, Sa'd may have commanded the *turcopoles*, troops composed of indigenous archers on horseback, or even the Frankish knights of the kingdom.[75] Whatever his origins, his name makes clear that he had not converted to Latin Christianity, and his title is evidence for his high standing. A certain David the Syrian held a cave in the mountains of Lebanon, which in time came into the hands William of Krak; his lands were referred to as was called the "*raisagium* of the mountains."[76] We do not know what happened to David, but it is clear that the cave, plus its surrounding territories, was a valuable military possession that remained in the hands of a local Christian until 1142.

Other names survive as witnesses in charters that suggest that they were local Christians or even Muslims: among the *milites* of Margat were the *domini* Zacharias, Georgius, and Theodorus, all names common among eastern Christians.[77] Other names include Salem,[78] Vahram,[79] Michael son of Molkim, Ibrahim son of Sucar,[80] and another Ibrahim.[81] Seardus, a Syrian from Hebron, was witness to a charter in 1148. His rank is not given, but his name is between a Latin resident of Jerusalem and a Hospitaller knight, names suggesting he was of equal status with them.[82] A charter of 1155 reveals that the villages of Odadbeb and Damersor [Dayr Muhaysin] belonged to two Arab knights.[83] There is no evidence that any of these individuals converted to Latin Christianity, nor is there any evidence that it was necessary that they do so in order to be knights. Many if not all of these indigenous knights may have participated in the Haute Cour of the kingdom,[84] but where their influence was mostly likely felt was in the court of the great lordships of the kingdom, where the leading barons consulted their knights. Again, the kingdom of Jerusalem does not look as different from Edessa and Antioch as previously thought, where locals continued to hold land and rule towns under Frankish sovereignty. If there were fewer indigenous lords and knights in Jerusalem, this was due to the different social conditions that prevailed in each area prior to the crusader conquest, not to Frankish decisions to relegate the indigenous population to second-class status.

The Levant of the peasant John the Syrian, Sa'd the marshal, and the Arrabi family was both a great deal less Frankish than historians have suspected, and at the same time a great deal more. It is less so in the sense that the institutionally Frankish character of the kingdom of Jerusalem was less extensive than previously argued. The western semi-free status of the serf did not make a sudden appearance in the Levant. Peasants continued to be legally free, as their fathers and mothers had been before the First Crusade, though some of the taxes and financial exactions they had to pay may have changed. Nor were the elite of the kingdom exclusively Frankish and Latin; local Christians served as marshals, knights, and *ru'asa*, wielding political and legal authority on a variety of levels. Yet in a cultural sense it was also more Frankish than previously thought. The spread of the Frankish values embodied in knighthood and the support of military orders spread beyond the western immigrants to indigenous communities. The Frankish presence may have even created a class of local Christian (and even Muslim) warrior elites that previously did not exist. But the relatively small numbers of such men (though there may be more of whom we have no record or who are unrecognizable due to Frankish names) remind us that the kings who ruled over the land called themselves "rex Iherusalem Latinorum"—king of Jerusalem of the Latins, showing that it was still a society focused on its western origins.[85]

Chapter 6

The Price of Unity: Ecumenical Negotiations and the End of Rough Tolerance

In 1169, the Basilica of the Nativity in Bethlehem received on its nave, transepts, and bema a new cycle of wall mosaics. The church was one of the oldest still standing in the Holy Land; built under Justinian, it escaped destruction during the invasions and persecutions that destroyed other Christian shrines. As the birthplace of Jesus, it was holy to Christians and Muslims alike, but its thick Roman walls enclosed a host of other tombs and sacred associations: the remains of the irascible church father Jerome lay in its crypt alongside those of his lifelong companion, the Roman noblewoman Paula, as well as her daughter Eustochium. Although only five miles from Jerusalem, the church was the center of its own constellation of holy places, such as the Shepherds' Field and the monastery of Mar Saba. Yet the new mosaics did not draw on any of these venerable associations. Instead, they depicted early councils of the church; on the south wall are the seven ecumenical councils, while the north wall shows six provincial councils, events central to the theological definition of the Christian community, but with little connection to Bethlehem.[1] Beneath the councils were images of Christ's ancestors, which did have a specific meaning, given that Bethlehem was the birthplace of both Jesus and his most illustrious ancestor, King David. The mosaics were the gift, not of any member of the Frankish elite of the kingdom of Jerusalem, but of the Byzantine emperor Manuel I Komnenos (1145–80), a fact prominently announced by a dedicatory inscription included with the mosaics and by an imperial portrait in the sanctuary of the church.[2] The mosaic program proclaimed to pilgrim and local alike the unity of the Church, grounded in the ecumenical councils under the authority of the emperors—a particularly Byzantine vision of ecumenism. Even the text of the creed accompanying the Second Council of Constantinople (553) was written to Byzantine specifications, that is, without the "filioque" clause of the Latin credo. Nor was Bethlehem the only church under Frankish control that benefited from the generosity of the emperor. Manuel also donated gold to cover the stone slab within the Holy Sepulcher on which Jesus' body had lain, thus establishing himself as patron of the holiest shrine in Christendom and the coronation church of the Frankish kings.[3] As in the days of Constantine and Helena, the Christian shrines of the Holy Land were once again liberally bedecked with Byzantine gold.

Manuel's patronage was in some ways a continuation of traditional imperial concern for the Holy Places, but the emperor could no longer claim a special role as guardian as Constantine IX Monomachos had done in the eleventh century,[4] for in the twelfth century the Frankish kings of Jerusalem claimed that honor. Yet in the 1160s, Manuel I Komnenos reclaimed it with an ecumenical twist. It is surprising that the Franks let such a pious, ancient, and politically advantageous role slip back into the emperor's hands. Not only was Manuel the monarch of a neighboring, and often rival, state, but the emperor was also, from a Latin perspective, a schismatic. The basilica of the Nativity (like the even more important Church of the Holy Sepulcher) was like Times Square and the Lincoln Memorial rolled into one—a place of high traffic, prestige, and sacrality. Why then did Amalric the king and Ralph, the bishop of Bethlehem, give Manuel this unparalleled opportunity?

Manuel I Komnenos and the Mediterranean World

The answer arises from the political situation of the mid-twelfth century. The accumulation of power and territory by Nur al-Din (1146–74), ruler of Mosul, Aleppo, and Damascus, threatened the security of the Frankish principalities. Whereas their neighbors were once a number of competing Muslim and Christian warlords, Nur al-Din had effectively united Syria. By 1155, the Franks were effectively surrounded by just three powers: the Byzantines to the north (who had temporarily subordinated the Armenians of Cilicia), the Turks to the east led by Nur al-Din, and the Fatimid caliphate in Egypt to the south. The failure of the Second Crusade to effectively stem Nur al-Din's growing power led the Franks to believe that crusades from Latin Europe was unlikely to hold back the Turks.[5] Instead, it was Manuel, heir of the great Byzantine emperors of the past, wealthiest of all monarchs, and leader of one of the largest armies in the Middle East, who was seen as the protector and savior of the Holy Land and the Christian communities settled in it. Yet Manuel was an unlikely and unwelcome savior. Many Franks blamed him for the failure of the Second Crusade, believing that he had colluded with the Seljuks to destroy the crusading army.[6] Furthermore, Manuel, his father John II, and his grandfather Alexios I had long sought to reassert Byzantine authority over Antioch, a goal inimical to the Franks.

Nor were the Franks wrong to see in Manuel an ambition to dominate the Frankish Levant. He, however, had a different strategy from those of his his predecessors; he abandoned earlier attempts to reconquer Antioch, and instead sought to be overlord and protector of the Frankish Levant. For Manuel, however, this was only part of a much larger plan to reestablish the power of the Byzantine empire. As ambitious as Justinian, Manuel hoped to be the sole Roman emperor in both East and West. The emperor therefore set out to woo three groups—the papacy to achieve union between the Constantinopolitan and Roman churches and papal recognition of Manuel as the sole emperor; the Frankish principalities of the Levant to induce them to recognize him as overlord; and the Armenian and Jacobite churches to bring religious unity to the new Byzantine Mediterranean world he sought to create. The period from 1158 to 1172 saw intense diplomatic and military efforts to achieve these goals.[7]

Manuel's quest to create a unified Byzantine world in the Mediterranean paradoxically resulted in heightened consciousness of the differences separating different Christian communities, as well as in insistence on maintaining those divisions. Whereas in earlier chapters we have seen that relationships between the different communities were driven by local circumstance and selective ignorance, allowing rough tolerance to flourish, Manuel's initiatives pushed communities to respond beyond the local level, to articulate and analyze their identity and to define how it differed from others. The Byzantine mosaics in the Church of the Nativity were thus the material expression of imperial ambitions that could be politically and culturally felt throughout the eastern Mediterranean. Although the mosaics suggested a unified Christian world, in reality the ecumenical ideal they embodied brought schism, confusion, and controversy to Armenians and Jacobites alike. Rough tolerance disappeared in part because the Byzantines, not the Franks or local communities, believed that the clear, straight path of negotiation would lead to Christian unity faster than the dark and quiet way of rough tolerence. They were wrong.

Manuel and the Papacy

The scope of Manuel's ambition was most obvious in his attempts to reach an agreement with the papacy. The Latin and Greek churches had been separated since the mutual excommunications of Michael Kerularios, patriarch of Constantinople, and Humbert, cardinal of Silva Candida, in 1054, but neither the popes nor the patriarchs considered that to have been in any way final. Pope Urban II had pursued cautious negotiations with Alexios I, which opened channels for communication.[8] Under Manuel, the initiative came from the Byzantine side. In 1166, Manuel sent Jordan of Capua to Rome to negotiate for the union of the churches, and to obtain papal recognition of Manuel as the sole emperor. He chose an opportune moment. Pope Alexander III (1159–81) was eager for Manuel's support, as he feared that Emperor Frederick I Barbarossa (1155–90) was planning an invasion of Italy to enthrone the anti-pope Paschal III (1164–68) in Alexander's place. While Jordan of Capua was welcomed warmly by the pope, he received no clear answer to his proposals. The following year Frederick captured Rome, and Alexander sent Ubald, bishop of Ostia, and John, the papal vicar of the city of Rome, to Constantinople for further negotiations, which continued throughout the 1160s and 1170s.[9]

Manuel and the Frankish Levant

Manuel was more successful in asserting Byzantine leadership over the Frankish Levant. He was no stranger to the area; he had accompanied his father, John II, on campaign in Cilicia in 1143, and John had intended the area to become an independent principality for Manuel.[10] Following John's death that same year, Manuel abandoned his father's intention to win Cilicia from the Armenians and Antioch from the Latins through conquest, and instead asserted his authority through diplomacy, marriage, and displays of military strength. In 1157, he concluded an alliance with Baldwin III of Jerusalem (1143–62), who married his niece Theodora. The following year Manuel led a large army to Cilicia, which he used to "encourage" Latin and Armenian submission. The emperor presided over the ritual humiliation of Reynald, prince of Antioch (1153–63), who came to his camp barefoot and clad in a short woolen tunic to apologize for pillaging Byzantine Cyprus. Manuel insisted that the citadel of Antioch be surrendered to him. As a fully public sign of his authority, Manuel enjoyed an imperial triumphal entry into the city. The Byzantine chronicler John Kinnamos proclaimed that "the entire foreign and outland populace was astonished, observing in addition to these things Reynald and the nobles of Antioch running on foot around the imperial horse, and Baldwin, a crowned man, parading a long way behind on horseback, but without insignia."[11] Manuel thus did not depose Reynald and install a Byzantine governor in the city, but merely forced a public recognition of his own superiority.

Despite disagreements over military strategy, the alliance of Manuel and the Franks was strengthened by a series of marriages between the Komnenoi and the ruling families of the Levant. Manuel married Maria of Antioch, daughter of Constance and Raymond of Poitiers, in 1161; Baldwin III of Jerusalem (1143–62) married Theodora Komnena in 1158; his brother Amalric of Jerusalem (1162–74) married Maria Komnena in 1167; and Bohemund III of Antioch (1163–1201), Maria's brother, married another Komnenian bride about 1176. Bohemund III, following his release from captivity at least in part due to Manuel's efforts, traveled to Constantinople to thank the emperor and returned with a Byzantine patriarch in tow. Athanasios I Manasses (1157–70) was promptly installed in the cathedral in place of the Latin patriarch Aimery; his presence in the city was a constant reminder of Manuel's domination.

The alliance with Manuel left the Franks confident enough to confront Nur al-Din's advances in Egypt; between 1163 and 1169, Amalric I led troops to Egypt several times, both to prevent Nur al-Din's domination and to extract tribute from the Fatimids. In 1168, Amalric joined with Manuel to conquer Egypt, but set out before negotiations with the Byzantines were completed. He was defeated by Nur al-Din's lieutenant Shirkuh, and by the end of 1169 Egypt was firmly under the control of Shirkuh's nephew, Salah al-Din. A combined Frankish-Byzantine army attempted to dislodge him in 1169, but failed. Amalric even traveled to Constantinople in 1171 to keep the alliance afloat, but no further joint military ventures were forthcoming.

Ecumenical Dialogue with the Armenian Church

At the same time that Manuel was pursuing negotiations with the papacy and joint military ventures with the Franks, he was also pursuing the union of the Armenians with the imperial church. Manuel probably intended this to help subordinate the leaders of Armenian Cilicia to his authority. The negotiations between Manuel and the Armenian patriarchate began in 1165, but twelfth-century sources hint that some ecclesiastical contact between Byzantium and local Christian leaders had already begun in the 1140s, laying the groundwork for Manuel's later initiatives. Latin ecclesiastics in the Frankish Levant, on the other hand, evinced little interest in the theological beliefs of local Christians, as discussed above, and therefore had little interest in resolving issues that from their perspective did not exist. Michael the Great's praise of Frankish tolerance would have rung true for many local Christian communities. The Jacobite patriarch noted that "the Franks, that is to say the Romans, who occupied Antioch and Jerusalem, had, as we have already explained, bishops in their states. And the pontiffs of our church were among them, without being persecuted or attacked." Michael was aware that their theological beliefs did not match his own; "although the Franks were in accord with the Greeks concerning the duality of Christ's nature . . . they never sought a single formula for all the Christian people and languages, but they considered as Christian anyone who worshipped the cross without investigation or examination."[12] A Jacobite reader would immediately see in Michael's praise of Frankish tolerance a condemnation of the Byzantines, who had repeatedly sought a "single formula" for Christians everywhere, and did so again under Manuel.

The Council of Jerusalem, 1141

What little evidence we do have for Latin interest in local Christian belief in the twelfth-century Levant came from the papacy, not from local Franks. In 1141, the papal legate Alberic of Ostia came to the Latin East, sent by Pope Innocent II to depose Ralph of Domfront, patriarch of Antioch.[13] Following the successful conclusion of the council in Antioch, Alberic journeyed to Jerusalem to attend the Easter celebrations at the Holy Sepulcher. While in the Holy City, the legate attended the formal consecration of the Dome of the Rock as a Christian church (the *Templum Domini*), and held a council on Mt. Sion. According to William of Tyre's vague description, the synod was intended "to address matters which seemed especially pertinent at the moment," which in some way involved the presence of "the great bishop of Armenia, or rather, the prince of all the bishops of Cappadocia, Media, Persia, and the two Armenias, a distinguished teacher who is called the *Catholicos*."[14] This bishop, to whom William ascribed such widespread authority, was Gregory III Pahlavuni, grand-nephew of his predecessor Gregory II

Vykaser and cousin of Barsegh I. The doctrinal differences between the Armenians and the Latins were discussed, and, according to William of Tyre, "the great bishop" promised reforms.

William's account leaves the reader confused. Why was the council called? Why was Gregory, an Armenian patriarch, attending a Latin council? We are fortunate that Michael the Great gave a much longer account of the council. He did so in part because the Jacobite bishop of Jerusalem, Ignatios, was also in attendance, though his presence was conveniently ignored by William of Tyre, but also because Michael himself was involved in similar ecumenical meetings some twenty years later. In Michael's view, the synod had nothing to do with Jerusalem, and everything to do with the legate and the Byzantines. The presence of the Armenian patriarch, and perhaps of Ignatios as well, was a result of the charge of heresy "certain malicious Greeks, accustomed to evil" had made against the Armenians and the Jacobites to Alberic, perhaps while he was still in Antioch. The legate had forced Gregory to accompany him to Jerusalem,[15] and summoned the Greeks to the council so that they might explain their accusations of heresy. Their response denied the validity of the council, saying, "we will not come, because our emperor is not there."[16] Ignatios and Gregory, however, presented statements of faith, which the council pronounced orthodox. The Latin bishops, furthermore, "demanded from the Armenians and the Syrians oaths that they did not hold in their hearts different doctrines; the Syrians made it with joy, but the Armenians did not agree to this, and they [the Latins] discovered that they were phantasiasts and simoniacs," stock accusations Jacobites made against Armenians.[17]

Michael's narrative leads his readers to the startling conclusion that there was no theological barrier to full communion between the Latins and Jacobites. Michael himself knew this was incorrect; only some twenty pages earlier he had solemnly informed his readers that "the Franks were in accord with the Greeks on the duality of the nature [of Christ],"[18] and thus at odds with the Jacobites' miaphysite theology. Michael's account thus tarred the Greeks as persecutors, the Armenians as heretics and liars, and the Latins as dupes. Nevertheless Michael, in agreement with William of Tyre, linked the council directly to the papal legate, leaving local Frankish leaders no role. The Greek accusation of heresy may represent Michael's perception of Byzantines as persecutors of the Jacobites, or it may signal Byzantine attempts to break Frankish silence around theological issues among Christians in the Levant.[19]

Armenians at the Papal Court

Although Michael cast the council of 1141 in a negative and persecutorial light, the events that followed suggest that the Armenians at least had an equal interest in ecumenical dialogue, and Gregory III may have attended the council in Jerusalem of his own accord. The arrival of Armenian delegates from the *kat'olikos* in December 1145 at the court of Pope Eugenius III in Vertralla was witnessed by Otto of Freising. The German chronicler was impressed by the envoys, astonished that they had come from the "utter East" on a journey lasting a year and a half. Like William of Tyre, he overestimated the power and influence of Gregory III, proclaiming that he had "countless numbers of bishops under him."[20] Although the purpose of their visit was to meet with the pope, Otto suggested that what the Armenians were really interested in was the Byzantine Church. "These reasons [for their coming] were as follows. In the administration of the Eucharistic rite they agree in certain respects with the Greeks, in certain other respects they differ from the Greeks. . . . Since they differed in these and in other matters they had chosen the Roman Church as arbiter."[21] The Armenians may also have been in Italy to call attention to Edessa, which had fallen to Zengi a year earlier, but the concerns Otto recorded remained focused on the ecclesiastical world of the eastern Mediterranean.[22] As in Michael's account of the Jerusalem council of 1141, the Latins are the arbiters, but not the initiators or the focus of the ecumenical activity. Both the council in Jerusalem and the meeting in Vertralla suggest that the Byzantines were attempting in the 1140s to institute contact with at least the Armenians, and perhaps the Jacobites as well, and that it was the Armenians who hoped to draw the Latins into the dialogue.

Nerses Shnorhali and the Byzantines

We thus have fleeting references to some sort of contact among the Armenian, Jacobite, Latin, and Byzantine churches in the 1140s, but the causes and contexts of these early discussions remain obscure. Beginning in 1165, however, we find a substantial body of textual evidence concerning ecumenical negotiations between the Byzantines and the Armenians and Jacobites that extended over several years.[23] According to a colophon written that year, Nerses Shnorhali, brother of *kat'olikos* Gregory III, met in Mamistra the *protostrator* Alexios Axouch, Byzantine governor of Cilicia and nephew-in-law of Manuel I Komnenos. Alexios told Nerses, "I had wished for a long time to speak to you about the Scriptures and to study the cause of discord in the one church of Christ."[24] Nerses responded to the *protostrator* with a profession of faith, which has been preserved in the collection of Nerses's letters. While the colophon suggested that these negotiations developed from the chance meeting of Alexios and Nerses, it is more likely that the initiative came from the emperor Manuel.

Nerses's letter reveals that the Armenians were also eager for these negotiations; the *kat'olikos*'s statement of faith effectively argued that Armenians and Byzantines shared the same beliefs about the nature of Christ, despite different theological formulations. Nerses stated that Armenians believe "in one nature in Christ, not mixed, as Eutyches argued, but as Cyril of Alexandria who in his books of commentaries, said against Nestorios, that 'The nature of the incarnated Word is one, as the Fathers have said.' "[25] While this may sound firmly miaphysitic, Nerses continued to explain that "thus whether it is said, 'one nature from an indissoluble and inseparable union, not from confusion,' or it is said, 'two natures which are unconfused and inalterable, not from division;' both are within the boundaries of orthodoxy."[26] Nerses here argued that the traditional miaphysite Armenian definition and the Byzantine Chalcedonian position were synonymous.[27] It was thus the Armenians who were engaging in the theological work that might allow union.

Nerses's letter sparked an epistolary exchange between the Armenian and Manuel that continued for the next several years. The emperor's reply, dated September 1167, accepted Nerses's profession of faith and urged a meeting between delegates.[28] By the time the emperor's letter arrived, however, Nerses had succeeded his brother as *kat'olikos*. As patriarch, Nerses replied with another statement of faith, and a defense of Armenian ecclesiastical practices, for those proved trickier than reconciling theological formulations.[29] Having established a firm basis for negotiations through this volley of letters, Manuel informed Nerses in his next letter of 1170 that he was sending two envoys, a theologian named Theorianos and a Chalcedonian Armenian abbot named John Outman, to discuss unification directly.[30] Nerses's meeting with the two ambassadors produced another letter to Manuel,[31] and an account of the discussion itself, preserved in Greek.[32]

In 1172 the dialogue resumed when Theorianos returned to Cilicia with nine propositions which, if they were accepted by Nerses, would constitute unification. The nine issues include both theological concerns, such as Christological definitions, and ritual matters, such as the use of azymite (unleavened) bread in the Eucharist.[33] Nerses died in 1173, before a synod could be held to consider the proposal, but the negotiations were continued by his nephew, *kat'olikos* Gregory IV. In 1179, a synod approved union with the Byzantine church, but the death of Manuel the following year left it a meaningless agreement.[34] Instead, the Armenian church in Cilicia signed a union with the Latin church in 1193 that had an enduring impact on Armenian liturgy and practice, and lasted through various political intrigues and religious disagreements until 1375.

We have already discussed Manuel's interest in ecumenical negotiations, but Nerses's motivation is harder to uncover. The Armenian patriarchate had been established in Hromgla,[35] a castle on the Euphrates donated by Beatrice of Edessa in 1150, which fell under the authority of Nur al-Din and his successor, Salah al-Din. Nerses was thus free of direct political pressure from the Byzantines, Armenian lords, and even Franks. The patriarch's response was instead a response to expectations and competition within the Armenian church. The role of the patriarch had changed dramatically in the eleventh century. With the disappearance of the royal houses and many of the aristocratic families of Armenia, the patriarchate lost its traditional sponsors. Like so many other Armenians, the *kat'olikoi* had abandoned the Armenian homeland, and until settling in Hromgla in 1150, continued a peripatetic existence. The disorder of the late eleventh century had seen the establishment of as many as six rival patriarchates, a sign of the fragmentation of authority both within and outside the church.

The Pahlavuni family, beginning in 1065/66, had successfully monopolized the office through a chaotic century, in part due to their ability to adapt to rapidly changing political and ecclesiastical circumstances. They were one of the few Armenian dynasties in Cilicia and Syria who could trace their roots to the Armenian kingdoms of the tenth century. One of the ways that the Pahlavunis maintained their position was through impressive literary and theological achievement. Gregory II, the first Pahlavuni patriarch, was known in Armenian as "vykaser," that is, "martyrophile," because of his voluminous translations of saints' lives from Greek into Armenian. His father, Gregory Magistros, was one of a group of Armenians known as the "philhellenes"; he wrote letters in ornate Greek and translated Plato into Armenian.[36] The Pahlavunis thus remade the patriarchate from an institution that found its support in the Armenian royal dynasties into one that looked to the *vardapets*, the teachers of the Armenian church, as a new source of authentication. Prominent within the Armenian hierarchy and influential within Armenian society, the *vardapets* were teachers and priests who could serve as theologians, ascetics, poets, or even prophets. Constituting a clerical rank within the Armenian church with no specific liturgical or ritual duties, the *vardapet*s had no parallel in other churches.[37] The Armenian church did not have a strong episcopate; instead, the monastery held a prominent place with both church and society, and it was often within monasteries that the *vardapet* worked.[38] Nerses's epithet was Shnorhali, a name that meant "grace-filled." The title referred to both Nerses's divinely inspired theological knowledge and his education in the monastery of Karmir Vank' (the Red Monastery) outside K'esun, whose graduates often took the title "shnorhali" as a sign of their connection to the monastery, and as a sign of prestige among the *vardapet*s.

Nerses's negotiations with the Byzantines were in part a show performed for the *vardapet*s; the discussions were held at Hromgla, the patriarchal residence, not in Constantinople or some other neutral city. Confronting the Byzantines on an even theological playing field gave Nerses a forum to display his intellectual virtuosity before a home audience. The patriarch's goal, then, was not necessarily to achieve union with the Byzantines, though that might result. Rather it was for Nerses to strengthen support for the Pahlavuni patriarchate among the intellectual elite of his church. The crucial judges of the merits of his arguments were not Theorianos or his imperial master, but the gathered *vardapet*s, and it was their support Nerses intended to win. Rather than promoting union with the Byzantine church, his actions reaffirmed the unique character of the Armenian hierarchy by appealing for support to the one group of clerics who could not be assimilated into a Byzantine structure—the *vardapet*s.

Jacobite Patriarch Michael and the Quest for Legitimacy

The Jacobites under patriarch Michael the Great also became involved with negotiations with the Byzantines soon after the Armenians, and like Nerses, Michael used the negotiations to strengthen his position within his own community. But the Jacobite patriarch regarded the Byzantine offer of negotiations as more a threat than an opportunity; his relations with the Latins were far friendlier, and he joined the ecumenical discussions largely to forestall Manuel from cultivating another more amenable leader to replace him.

Michael became the Jacobite patriarch of Antioch in 1166. The bishops who assembled following the death of patriarch Athanasius VIII (1138–66) put the names of three candidates together and selected the slip containing the name of Michael, at that time the archimandrite of the convent of Mar Barsauma. A group of bishops arrived after the election and contested the results, protesting that it should not have proceeded without them. Others made their opinions known through letters and messengers. The bishop of Jerusalem, with tepid enthusiasm, wrote that Michael was one of only two possible candidates the bishops should consider. Those who objected to the election grudgingly accepted Michael as patriarch as support for him trickled in from elsewhere.

Michael, however, refused to be consecrated until the assembled bishops promised to conduct themselves according to the canons of the fathers, and swore to avoid simony, stop combining two bishoprics into one, and stop transferring from one bishopric to another. These demands gave many of the bishops pause, and several wanted to consider another candidate until Dionysios bar Salibi, bishop of Amida, spoke in favor of reform of the church. A further controversy erupted over who should consecrate Michael—the *maphrian* of the East, who had consecrated the two preceding patriarchs and was second in authority to them, or the head of the council, who was the bishop of Edessa. Finally, it was agreed that the *maphrian* would impose his hands on Michael while the bishop of Edessa would say the Mass.

This narrative, taken from the chronicle of the thirteenth-century Jacobite historian Gregory bar Hebraeus, was probably based on Michael's own account, and presented his election as supported by the majority of bishops and monks, and as a triumph over simony and ecclesiastical corruption.[39] The considerable debate his election engendered, as well as the suggestion that those who opposed him were guilty of simony and corruption, suggests that it was a hard-won fight. His first years in office, then, were devoted to securing his position against any would-be challengers, for it was not uncommon in Jacobite ecclesiastical politics for a contested election to be followed by the emergence of counter-candidates and anti-patriarchs.

Soon after his election, Michael went on tour, visiting Edessa and the monasteries nearby. The following year he traveled to Cilicia, Antioch, Lattakia, Tyre, and then Jerusalem for Easter. There he met with the Latin patriarch of the city, Amalric of Nesle, "and was treated by him with honor."[40] It was perhaps through this meeting that the Jacobites came to join the Latins, Melkites, and Armenians as Christian groups who had clergy serving in the Holy Sepulcher.[41] Michael then returned to Antioch, where he visited the Latin patriarch of Antioch, Amalric of Limoges, who was in exile outside the city, for the patriarchal throne was occupied by Athanasios I, the Byzantine patriarch successfully introduced by Manuel in 1166.[42] Michael was again "welcomed with joy" by the Latin patriarch, but refused to visit Athanasios.[43] He remained in Antioch for a year, perhaps at the invitation of the exiled Latin. Their friendship lasted long afterward; Amalric invited Michael to attend the third Lateran Council in Rome in 1179, a sign that he considered Michael's theology orthodox and his character worthy. Michael chose not to go, but wrote a treatise against the Albigensians to help the council in its fight against the heresy.[44]

This "Grand Tour" of Syria and Palestine was clearly designed to bolster Michael's shaky position after a contested election. From his perspective, ecumenical visits to Latin prelates gave him greater status and ammunition against those who might question the validity of his election. To his detractors, Michael could point to his achievement in gaining a chapel for the Jacobites in the church of the Holy Sepulcher, a privilege his church had never before enjoyed. Only through his unparalleled closeness with the Latin patriarchs was he able to achieve it. In Chapter 4, we saw the example of Basil, Jacobite bishop of Edessa, who appealed to the Latin patriarch of Antioch to resolve a dispute with his own patriarch. Michael, then, was not the only one who viewed Latin ecclesiastics as a source of support during conflicts within the Jacobite church. Michael enjoyed a long and esteemed career, earning him the title of "the Great" among the Jacobites.[45] While his reputation doubtless was based on his character and role as a theologian and administrator, his closeness to the Latin hierarchy apparently only added luster to his reputation.

Jacobite and Byzantine Negotiations

While Michael visited the Latin patriarchs on his own initiative, the same was not true of the Jacobite patriarch's interactions with the Byzantines. As with the Armenians, the Jacobites had contact with local Melkites before beginning talks with imperial representatives. While he was resident in Antioch, Michael wrote a pamphlet explaining the essentials of his faith, which he wrote in response to "the Greeks," probably a veiled reference to Athanasios I or his clergy. The unknown recipient of the letter in turn sent it to Manuel I Komnenos, who then wrote back to Michael.[46]

The emperor's motives are clear enough; including the Jacobites in his ongoing negotiations with the Armenians was a logical extension of his interests. Michael's response should be seen in the context of his contested election and subsequent search for support in Edessa, Antioch, and Jerusalem. The unique situation where the Latin, Jacobite and Greek patriarchs of Antioch were all resident in the city or its environs at the same time is not accidental, particularly on Michael's part. The Jacobite patriarch sought Byzantine acknowledgment of his patriarchate to forestall any possible competitors. This was a serious threat. Theodoros bar Wahbun, Michael's own student, attempted to replace his former teacher as patriarch in 1185 by offering to unify the Jacobite church with both the Latins and the Greeks if they would recognize him as patriarch. Theodoros received some support at that time from Mesopotamian bishops, and he traveled to Jerusalem, Hromgla, and Cilicia in the hope of gaining further support, replicating Michael's own search of validation after his election.[47] The invasions of Salah al-Din and his own death shortly thereafter cut short his quest to replace Michael, but the early support of the bishop of Amida, one of the more important Jacobite sees, signaled that Theodoros's claim was taken seriously.[48] His attempt not only points out Michael's vulnerability, but also shows the appeal ecumenism had among at least part of the Jacobite episcopate.

Having sought Byzantine support, Michael was obliged to respond to the emperor's ecumenical interests, and the letter exchange between Michael and Manuel in Antioch soon led to the Jacobites being included in the ongoing negotiations with the Armenians. Theodoros bar Wahbun, the future anti-patriarch, and John, the Jacobite bishop of K'esun, attended meetings with Nerses and Theorianos, perhaps in 1170.[49] After negotiating with Nerses in 1172, Theorianos proceeded to meet separately with the Jacobites. At K'esun, a city formerly ruled by the counts of Edessa but now controlled by Nur al-Din, Theorianos met Theodoros, whose knowledge of Greek, Armenian, Arabic, and Syriac made him the ideal representative.[50] According to the Greek account, the negotiations were supposed to be held at the monastery of Mar Barsauma (Balsamon in Greek), where Michael was in residence, but Theodoros advised Theorianos that travel to the monastery was too dangerous because a local emir was planning to ambush him. Theorianos therefore remained in K'esun and merely sent a letter to Michael, who sent a reply containing yet another confession of faith. The Byzantine theologian considered the whole of the profession orthodox, except the patriarch's assertion that Christ had only one *hypostasis* (substance) and one *ousia* (nature).

The discussion between Theorianos and Theodoros was recorded in Greek, perhaps as a transcript for Manuel, and Greek was likely the language of negotiation, as we know Theodoros was fluent. Their meeting did not last long; the Byzantine envoy refused to negotiate with Theodoros because the Jacobite insisted on introducing Aristotle into a discussion that Theorianos felt should be based on Christian authorities. Theodoros left, and was replaced by John, bishop of K'esun. John seemed more willing to avoid the subject of Aristotle, and the rest of the discussion was devoted to the problem of Christ's divine and human qualities.

The absence of the patriarch from the negotiations is a sign that he participated for different reasons from the Armenians. Michael's excuse that he could not negotiate directly with Theorianos because of unsafe travel conditions was likely a pretext. We have seen that the Jacobite patriarch traveled extensively when it suited him, and given Nur al-Din's respect for Manuel's military might, it is unlikely that he would have molested Theorianos, his official ambassador, or Michael, had he chosen to travel to K'esun. Michael thus put the negotiations in the hands of Theodoros, allowing the patriarch to claim credit for any positive outcome, but also to deny knowledge of anything that might taint his reputation. These negotiations, however, were far less conclusive than the Byzantine discussions with Nerses, and did not continue. Their failure to achieve union does not render the negotiations insignificant, however, for they are a further sign of Michael's insecurity in his office, and help explain conflicts and arguments within the Jacobite church.

Cultural Consequences of Ecumenical Negotiation

While these negotiations had limited ecclesiastical and political results, they engendered considerable confusion within the Armenian and Jacobite communities. For Michael and Nerses, these negotiations were both an opportunity and a threat. While some advantages might accrue as a result of the negotiations, simply by discussing union with the Byzantines each opened himself up to attack from conservatives within his own community. To ignore the Byzantine overture was equally dangerous, for this left an opening for others to challenge his leadership, as the example of Theodoros's attempt to challenge Michael shows; his hopes of becoming patriarch may well have their origin in his role in the negotiations with the Byzantines.

Participating in the negotiations could also pose a political threat. In 1173, an Arabic-speaking scribe named Alexander went to Nur al-Din and accused Nerses, Michael, and Athanasios, the Jacobite bishop of Edessa, of having received letters from Manuel concerning a plot to deliver control of

Edessa to the Byzantines. Athanasios, along with a number of Armenians and other citizens of Edessa, was brought to Aleppo to be questioned. Following an investigation, the Muslim authorities determined that Alexander was an impostor, and the charges were dismissed.[51] Accusations involving the exchange of letters between Manuel and the leaders of the Armenian and Jacobite churches suggest, however, that he misinterpreted the ecclesiastical negotiations for something more directly political. Nur al-Din would not have been entirely wrong to be suspicious of these negotiations. They were certainly intended to strengthen Manuel's position in Cilicia and northern Syria, and had they resulted as Manuel hoped, they would have been a threat to Nur al-Din's own power.

Edessa was the city where the effects of the negotiations on the lower clergy and laity were mostly clearly manifest. The city held the largest concentrated population of both Armenians and Jacobites, and it was the cultural and religious center of northern Syria. Because it was not the seat of either patriarch, Edessa was often the center of separatist movements and challenges to patriarchal power. Thus it was in Edessa around the same time as the negotiations were going on, that a group of Armenian *vardapets*, led by a man named Ausig, accused Nerses of simony. It was an odd accusation, given that Nerses achieved his rank through nepotism rather than bribery. Rather, the accusations were a reflection of fears that Nerses was in effect "selling" the katholicate to the Byzantines—part of the Byzantine proposal for union would have placed the authority to choose the *kat'olikos* in the hands of the emperor. Perhaps Ausig and his supporters even believed that Nerses was receiving financial support from the Byzantines in return for his cooperation in uniting the churches.

Yet Ausig and his followers were more than just disgruntled Armenian conservatives. The Ausigites, as Michael called them, were soon expelled from the city, and their fate indicates the confusion that reigned in Armenian religious communities as a consequence of the Byzantine negotiations. Two of the Ausigite priests came to the Jacobites in bewilderment, complaining about Nerses and the Christological debates that had engulfed the Armenian church. In particular, they were baffled by the writings of the Alexandrian bishops and saints, Athanasios and Cyril, who sometimes seemed to argue for the double nature of Christ, and sometimes for a single nature. Michael kindly explicated the true meaning of the holy fathers. Having cleared this matter up, Michael wrote to Nerses and gained the two priests readmittance to the Armenian church. Other Ausigites remained alienated from the Armenian church; some ended up in Jacobite monasteries, while their leader Ausig traveled to Antioch and joined the Melkite church.[52] The extremity of these choices—fully miaphysite or fully Chalcedonian—reveals the confusion engendered by the reanimation of Christological issues that had long seemed settled within the Armenian church.

The Theological Treatises of Dionysios bar Salibi

The possibility of union with the Byzantine church also provoked a flurry of Jacobite theological treatises. Dionysios bar Salibi, bishop of Amida and supporter of the patriarch Michael, wrote a series of treatises against other Christians, Jews, Muslims, and pagans, which may have all been part of a larger book on heresy.[53] The one group he did not attack were the Franks. Dionysios was born in Melitene, became bishop of Marash in the 1150s, later was transferred to Amida, one of the most important sees in the Jacobite hierarchy, and died in 1171.[54] While he never lived under Frankish or Byzantine rule, as a Jacobite bishop he likely was familiar with both and traveled to their lands for synods and to visit other Jacobite clergy.

Two of his polemics, those directed against the Melkites and the Armenians, react to the ongoing negotiations with the Byzantines. But his polemic on the Melkites was not directed at Manuel, the patriarch of Constantinople, the local Melkite hierarchy, or even Michael for engaging in negotiations. Rather, it was provoked by a letter Dionysios had received from a Jacobite monk, Isho', who had become a Melkite or was considering doing so. The treatise was a personal rebuttal of Isho''s claims; in it Dionysios referred to a more general polemic he wrote against the Melkites as well as to another letter to Isho', both of which are apparently lost.[55] Although we do not have Rabban Isho''s letter, Dionysios quoted portions of it in his response.

While the meat of Dionysios's work was a defense of Jacobite beliefs and practices, from subjects such as how many fingers one should use in the sign of the cross to ultimate Christological questions, the underlying issue was the value of ecumenism and the possibility of union. Isho', for his part, alternated in his letter between asserting the superiority of Melkite tradition and arguing that Christians should overlook the differences between different Christian communities. The monk seemed particularly eager to avoid making explicitly theological arguments; thus, when advocating the Chalcedonian definition of the nature of Christ, he made no theological truth-claims, but pointed out that this belief was widespread throughout the Christian world, while miaphysite belief was limited to Jacobites, Armenians, and, curiously, "a few Franks."[56]

Isho''s frequent reference to the majority of the Christian world was a product of the widened horizons of Levantine Christians in the wake of the crusades. Dionysios's response is telling: "Further, how did you assert that all Christians believe in two natures except us and the Armenians, while the Egyptians, Nubians, Abyssinians, the majority of the Indians, and the country of Libya which in the time of Dioscorus was composed of one thousand and five hundred parishes, accept the faith of the great Severus?"[57] The bishop's view of the Christian world was that of Late Antiquity, where a miaphysite Christian could survey the oecumene and proudly note that a large part of the ancient and populous eastern world—Syria, Egypt, Mesopotamia—believed in the single nature of Christ. Yet this was not the world that Isho' saw. His list of Chalcedonian peoples showed that he was looking westward, to the groups of "barbarians" converted after the Late Antique period—the Russians, Hungarians, and Alans.

Isho' wished others would follow his lead and avoid theological argument. The monk claimed, "we (Syrians) constitute ourselves the judges of Christians; some of them we make pagans and some others heretics. What would be better for us to do would be to live in peace with everybody."[58] Yet his conversion to the Melkite church (or flirtation with that possibility) suggests that, in contrast to his rhetoric of unity and coexistence, he felt considerable anxiety over the differences that separated Jacobites from fellow Christians. His letter, at least the parts quoted by Dionysios, gives the impression of someone theologically confused and uncomfortable with the evident differences among Christians, differences that were all the more evident in the midst of ecumenical dialogue.

Dionysios, however, argued vociferously for the superiority of his tradition with every theological and historical fact he could muster. His introduction emphasized the importance of avoiding "ambiguity," and referred to Isho''s letter as "conciliatory" and "standing between truth and falsehood in order not to hurt anyone's feelings." He challenged the monk, asking "are the Syrians right or are they wrong? And if they are right, why do you not reject the Chalcedonians?"[59] The energy Dionysios put into his treatise suggested that much more was at stake than one confused and conciliatory monk. The danger Dionysios feared did not come from the casual daily contact that prevailed among Christians throughout the Levant; nor did Isho''s confusion.

Instead, it arose from a new situation where the fundamental markers of identity were challenged by ecumenical negotiations.

Dionysios thus rejected Isho''s attempt to equate union with inclusivity, reminding the monk of Byzantine injustice.[60] "I warned them several times to let everyone go his own way without recrimination against his neighbour of another creed, but they showed no desire to heed our advice. I wrote chapters concerning their habits, and also on the fact that we should be permitted to enter their churches, and be allowed to pray for them and they for us."[61] The bishop insisted that Byzantine attitudes toward Jacobites were not conciliatory and friendly but malicious and dangerous. "Now repair in your imagination to the city of their pride. You will see that it contains a mosque for the Mohammedans, but it has no church for the Syrians and the Armenians."[62] Dionysios thus effectively argued that Byzantine ecumenism was a sham, and the very idea of rapprochement meaningless.

The bishop's discussion of the Franks made clear that his objections and arguments against the Melkites were not theologically based, but were a response to Byzantine ecumenical pressure. Although the Franks shared with the Byzantines belief in the two natures of Christ, Dionysios was careful not to include the Latins in his denunciations. He pointed out that the Byzantines have no right to call themselves "Romans," because that name truly belonged to the Franks. Their correct name is "Hellene," "pagan," and he dismissed their claim of divine authority for the emperor, saying no man can serve two masters.[63] In any event, "the true kingdom is that which is established in orderliness and virtue, as in the times of Constantine, Theodosius, and the rest of the Roman kings, that is to say the kings of the Franks."[64]

Dionysios's treatise against the Armenians was also a reaction to Manuel's ambitious ecclesiastical plans. His polemic against the Armenians denigrated their theological understanding, portraying them as a people easily led astray by heresy. The title of Dionysios' work is "Book against the heresy of the Phantasiasts from which sprang the creed of the Armenians, and against the practices in which the latter indulge."[65] From the outset, Dionysios linked the Armenians to the heretical Phantasiasts, who were docetic Christians who taught that Christ's humanity was imaginary and that he was entirely divine.[66] A few pages into the text, however, Dionysios admitted that this heresy was no longer widespread among the Armenians.[67] Throughout the Jacobite's polemic, however, he portrayed the Armenians as easily led into heresy, and as confused on a number of important Christological points from which they are frequently rescued by the Jacobites. The ignorance of the Armenians extended even to their origins—"it is we who have enlightened your authors and revealed to them that you are descended from Togarma, who was from the children of Japhet."[68] The Armenians also followed a number of "Jewish" habits, such as sacrificing a lamb at Passover and placing its blood on their thresholds, a further sign of their ecclesiastical ignorance.[69]

Such a portrayal was intended to drain away the prestige of the negotiations, in which the Armenians played such a prominent role. Theodoros and John of K'esun had gone to the *kat'olikos*'s residence at Hromgla for parts of the negotiations, and Dionysios thought it was inappropriate for the Jacobites to be playing second fiddle to the Armenians. While theoretically the Armenian and Jacobite churches shared a common theology and were in communion, in fact the two communities differed considerably. The period of Armenian domination of Cilicia and northern Syria in the late eleventh and early twelfth centuries placed a considerable number of Jacobite communities under Armenian rule, a condition many did not find comfortable. Michael the Great complained about Armenian brigands attacking Jacobites, and Kogh Vasil had seized the Red Monastery outside K'esun and given it to the Armenian patriarchs. According to the thirteenth-century Jacobite chronicler and *maphrian* of the East, Gregory Abu'l Faraj Bar Hebraeus, Dionysios himself had once been kidnapped by the Armenians when he was bishop of Marash.[70]

The pilgrim who arrived in Bethlehem in the late 1160s or early 1170s would find at the birthplace of Jesus the mosaics of the early ecumenical councils, and might think them to be clear statements of irenic ecumenism. Yet what the images signaled was the disappearance of the "rough tolerance" of the earlier period. As Manuel I Komnenos sought to subordinate the churches of the Levant to the church of Constantinople, local Christian clergy, both Jacobite and Armenian, began to see their daily interactions with other Christians in a new light. The very idea that they might somehow be joined with the church of Constantinople, of the emperor, the same that was in countless stories of oppression and martyrdom, made it an urgent task to emphasize what was distinct and separate about the Jacobite or Armenian tradition. Yet at the same time, there was an undeniable urge on an individual level to engage in these negotiations, for they brought prestige from outside. Furthermore, they offered the opportunity for rival leaders within religious communities to challenge those in power, as the example of Theodoros demonstrated. The negotiations thus engendered competition both within church hierarchies, and between the Armenian and Jacobite churches. The reconsideration of the late antique Christological debates stirred further anxiety as long-held divine truths were subjected to scrutiny and compromise. Priests, monks, and even laity began to question the place of traditional doctrines in their beliefs and identity. The conversion of Ishoʻ and some of the Ausigites was the result. The increased emphasis on maintaining sectarian identity foreshadowed the changed religious atmosphere of the thirteenth century, when confessional standing began to affect the legal status of Christians under Frankish rule. The mosaics of Bethlehem were a monument, not only to Manuel's aspirations of Christian unity under Byzantine leadership, but also to a new era of sharpened and defined boundaries among Christians of the Levant, bringing to an end an era of unspoken compromise and unacknowledged ecumenism.

Conclusion

In the prophecy of Hovhannes Kozern with which we began this study, the Frankish dominion over the Holy Land was predicted to be a temporary triumph, a foreshadowing of the final conquests of the Roman emperor, who would reconquer all lands from the Muslims. Matthew of Edessa's repeated use of different versions of this prophecy, given voice by a number of different *vardapets*, was a testament to its power to express the anxieties, frustrations, and hopes of Armenian communities. Following the fall of Edessa to Zengi in 1144, Nerses Shnorhali wrote a lament for the fallen city. After pages of poetry describing the destruction of the city and the horrors perpetrated on its citizenry, Nerses turned to the old prophecies, and crafted from them a new vision of the future of the Levant, in which Edessa would be redeemed from its devastation. For the Muslims who had desolated the fair city of Edessa, Nerses had this warning: "Anew the Frank is on the move/ Unfathomable numbers of horsemen and foot-soldiers."[71] The new crusaders would conquer the whole of the Islamic world from Cairo to Khorasan, razing Mecca to the ground, and throwing the Ka'aba into the Red Sea; "for all Christians they will be the rescuers from the unbelievers."[72] Nerses was far clearer than Matthew as to what would follow the final triumph of Christianity:

The realm of the Christians will be rebuilt,
filled with endless, immeasurable goodness,
It will be abundant in fruits

Of many seeds and of all kinds of fertility.
People will be rejoicing in merriment,
Fattened by eating and drinking.

Yet this new world the Franks would create would be more than an earthly paradise—it would be the heavenly Jerusalem.

There under the veil
The holy priests, initiated
In the divine temple,
Will stand to offer mass.
There will rest the flocks of sheep
The troops of innocent and holy lambs.
You will eat the bread, descended from heaven.
You will dwell in green places,
You will drink from the waters of rest,
From the immortal holy sources
And from the celestial clouds,
From the apostles, the prophets
From the holy words of the doctors
Dancing together with the celestial ones,
Singing with the angels
About the thrice holy Seraphs,
Songs to the Trinity on High.[73]

Unlike the prophecies recorded by Matthew, this vision had no place for the Byzantine emperor. Despite the power of Manuel I Komnenos, and his ambition to achieve at least some of what Nerses described, the Armenian placed the crown of future victory on the head of the Franks. Nerses probably knew that the Second Crusade was being planned as he wrote; a group of Armenian bishops was with Pope Eugenius III when he issued the crusading bull—Nerses may even have been one of them. But the failure of the crusade to live up to Nerses's predictions did not render the vision meaningless. It was a sign of the profound shift in the shape of the world as the Armenian communities of the Levant constructed it. Gone was the looming figure of the emperor, menacing in his power yet comforting in the unity he brought. Local Christians in the twelfth century more often took the venerable name of "Roman," long synonymous with the Byzantines and those who ruled "New Rome," Constantinople, and instead applied it to the Franks. By the end of the century, the Armenian rulers of Cilicia would turn to the Hohenstaufen emperors of Italy and Germany for their crown, rather than to the *basileus* in Constantinople.

The impact the Franks had on local Christian communities from northern Syria to southern Palestine has been depicted in quite different ways, from the nineteenth-century image of a colonial utopia to twentieth-century interpretations of decline and oppression. Perhaps the least recognized image, yet fundamental to all, was the historiographic imposition of modern ideas of religious identity. While boundaries between different religious communities did exist, they were permeable and elastic markers that allowed for a variety of religious encounters. The importance of traditional church hierarchies enforced a certain communal identity as Latin, Armenian or Jacobite, but other identities existed side by side. Adherents of the cults of Mar Barsauma or Mar Saba might find shared meaning by regular religious devotions to the saint, while those Franks who admired the asceticism and learning of the Armenian *vardapet*s might find closer identification with the Armenian elites who served as their patrons, as Baldwin of Marash did. Politically the Franks could play a variety of roles. Nerses's apocalyptic Franks stand beside a gallery of other images of the rulers of the Levant; they appear as tolerant Christians, as men of greed, as pious worshippers of local saints, oppressors, and military leaders. Frankish sources provide a similar survey of local Christians as heretics, grateful citizens, opportunists, pious leaders, or betrayers. Yet one image never held the symbolic weight of a stereotype; each had meaning only within circumscribed contexts. Discussions of the eventual defeat of the Frankish principalities of the Levant can no longer depend on the argument that their fall was caused by their lack of roots in their new home, or because of the antagonism of the people they ruled. Like the constantly changing image of "Frank" and "local," a new vision of the Latin East must be crafted. It was only at the end of the twelfth century, with the Byzantine negotiations for ecclesiastical unity, the conquests of Salah al-Din, and the development of a new thirteenth-century Mediterranean world that the boundaries between religious communities become solid, traversable only through formal acts of conversion.

Notes

Introduction

1. The only copy of the letter is found in the account of Fulcher of Chartres [Fulcherius Carnotensis], *Historia Hierosolymitana*, ed. Heinrich Hagenmeyer, p. 264; trans. Frances Rita Ryan in Fulcher of Chartres, *A History of the Expedition to Jerusalem, 1095–1127*, p. 111 (hereafter Fulcher, *Historia*; Ryan, *History*). Fulcher included the letter only in the first version of his chronicle, which may have been intended to stir support for Bohemund's planned crusade against Byzantium. A papal letter to clergy and people of Lucca suggests that Urban may have been planning to travel east, perhaps in response to the letter. Heinrich Hagenmeyer, *Epistulae et chartae ad historiam primi belli sacri spectantes*, #17, p. 167.

2. Matt'eos Urhayets'i (Matthew of Edessa), *Zhamanakagrut'iwn*, p. 282; trans. Ara Edmond Dostourian in Matthew of Edessa, *Armenia and the Crusades: Tenth to Twelfth Centuries: The Chronicle of Matthew of Edessa*, p. 184 (hereafter Matt'eos Urhayets'i, *Zhamanakagrut'iwn*; Matthew of Edessa, *Chronicle*).

3. Matt'eos Urhayets'i, *Zhamanakagrut'iwn*, pp. 234–35; Matthew of Edessa, *Chronicle*, p. 153.

4. Matt'eos Urhayets'i, *Zhamanagrut'iwn*, p. 263; Matthew of Edessa, *Chronicle*, p. 170.

5. This of course is just a vague approximation of what the Franks controlled. Any solely geographical description is necessarily inaccurate; see Ronnie Ellenblum, "Were There Borders and Borderlines in the Middle Ages? The Example of the Latin Kingdom of Jerusalem," in *Medieval Frontiers: Concepts and Practices*, ed. David Abulafia and Nora Berend, pp. 105–19.

6. Claude Cahen, *La Syrie du Nord à l'époque des croisades*, p. 473.

7. Patrick Gray, "Theological Discourse in the Seventh Century: The Heritage from the Sixth Century," *Byzantinische Forschungen* 26 (2000): 219–28.

8. "Miaphysite" has become the preferred term to describe theology dependent on Cyril of Alexandria, for both historiographic and modern ecumenical reasons. "Monophysite" is now used for the theology of Eutyches, with its greater emphasis on the oneness of Christ's nature, rather than its unity, emphasized in miaphysitism.

9. For a clear discussion of the emergence of miaphysite communities in the sixth century, see Lucas Van Rompay, "Society and Community in the Christian East," in *The Cambridge Companion to the Age of Justinian*, ed. Michael Maas, pp. 239–66.

10. Willelmus Tyrensis, *Chronicon*, ed. R. B. C. Huygens, 22: 9, p. 1018; trans. in William of Tyre, *A History of Deeds Done Beyond the Sea*, trans. Emily Atwater Babcock and A. C. Krey, 2: 458–59. For further discussion of William of Tyre's depiction of the Maronites, see Chapter 4.

11. William Baum and Dietmar Winkler, *The Church of the East: A Concise History*. Sebastian Brock argues persuasively that the title "Nestorian" for the Church of the East is inaccurate and misleading, but unhelpfully does not give a useful alternative. "The 'Nestorian' Church: A Lamentable Misnomer," *Bulletin of the John Rylands University Library of Manchester* 78, 3 (1996): 23–35.

12. *Peregrinationes Tres: Saewulf, John of Würzburg, Theodericus*, ed. R. B. C. Huygens, Corpus Christianorum: Continuatio Mediaevalis 139, p. 152; E. van Donzel, "Were There Ethiopians in Jerusalem at the Time of Saladin's Conquest in 1187?" in *East and West in the Crusader States II*, ed. Krijnie Ciggaar and Herman Teule, pp. 125–30.

13. Johannes Pahlitzsch, "Georgians and Greeks in Jerusalem (1099–1310)," in *East and West in the Crusader States III*, ed. Krijnie Ciggaar and Herman Teule, pp. 35–51.

14. William of Tyre did not know the origin of the word "assassin," but claimed that they had formerly been the strictest of Muslims. *Chronicon*, 20:29, pp. 953–54; trans. Babcock and Krey, *History*, 2: 391.

15. Marshall G. S. Hodgson, *The Venture of Islam*, 3 vols.

16. Marina Rustow, *Toward a History of Jewish Heresy: The Jews of Egypt and Syria, 980–1100*.

17. Benjamin attests to Samaritan communities in Caesarea (pop. 200), Mt. Gerezim (pop. 1000), and Ascalon (pop. 300). *The Itinerary of Benjamin of Tudela*. See also Benjamin Kedar, "The Frankish Period" in *The Samaritans*, ed. A. D. Crown, pp. 82–94.

18. See Etan Kohlberg and B. Z. Kedar, "A Melkite Physician in Frankish Jerusalem and Ayyubid Damascus: Muwaffaq al-Din Ya'qub b. Siqlab," *Asian and African Studies* 22 (1988): 113–26.

19. Only two other chronicles existed written in the eastern Mediterranean under Frankish rule: the now-lost chronicle of Hamdan b. 'Abd al-Rahim, a resident of al-Atharib; see Carole Hillenbrand, *The Crusades: Islamic Perspectives*, p. 258; and Leontios Makhairas, writing in fourteenth-century Cyprus, *Recital Concerning the Sweet Land of Cyprus entitled "Chronicle"*, ed. and trans. R. M. Dawkins, 2 vols. Another possible addition are the Hanbali religious texts, which, while composed in Damascus, reflect the experiences of refugees from the area around Nablus, most recently discussed by Daniella Talmon-Heller, "*The Cited Tales of the Wondrous Doings of the Shaykhs of the Holy Land* by Diya' al-Din Abu 'Abd Allah Muhammad b. 'Abd al-Wahid al Maqdisi (569/1173-643/1245): Text, Translation, and Commentary," *Crusades* 1 (2002): 111–54. Some Samaritan chronicles were written under Frankish dominion, but they rarely mention the Franks, and shed little light on the interaction of indigenous communities with the newcomers. Kedar, "The Frankish Period."

20. Elaine Pagels, *The Origin of Satan*, p. 49.

21. Kedar, "The Frankish Period."

22. Jonathan K. Smith, "What a Difference a Difference Makes," in *"To See Ourselves*

as Others See Us": *Christians, Jews, "Others" in Late Antiquity*, ed. Jacob Neusner and Ernest S. Frerichs, p. 5.

23. This argument is further discussed in Chapter 5.

24. For a broad overview of crusader historiography, see Giles Constable, "The Historiography of the Crusades," in *The Crusades from the Perspective of Byzantium and the Muslim World*, ed. Angeliki Laiou and Roy Parviz Mottahedeh, pp. 1–22.

25. Ronnie Ellenblum's archaeological work *Frankish Rural Settlement* was the first book to present clear arguments against the segregationalist position. Other historians recognize its failings; see Christopher Tyerman, *Fighting for Christendom: Holy War and the Crusades*, pp. 156–70. See also recent work engaging the concept of "multiculturalism" in the Frankish Levant: Marie-Luise Favreau-Lilie, "'Multikulturelle Gesellschaft' oder 'Persecuting Society'? 'Franken' und 'Einheimishe' im Königreich Jerusalem," in *Jerusalem im Hoch- und Spätmittelalter*, ed. Dieter Bauer, Klaus Herbers, and Nikolas Jaspert, pp. 55–93; Benjamin Kedar, "Convergences of Oriental Christian, Muslim and Frankish Worshippers: The Case of Saydnaya," in *De Sion exibit lex et verbum domini de Hierusalem: Essays on Medieval Law, Liturgy and Literature in Honour of Amnon Linder*, ed. Yitzak Hen, pp. 59–69.

26. Jacques Bongars, *Gesta Dei per Francos*.

27. Robert Irwin, "Orientalism and the Early Development of Crusader Studies," in *The Experience of Crusading*, ed. Peter Edbury and Jonathan Phillips, 1: 214–30; Raymond Schwab, *L'auteur des Mille et une Nuits: vie d'Antoine Galland*, p. 40.

28. Edward Gibbon, *The History of the Decline and Fall of the Roman Empire*, 6: 59, p. 347.

29. Chahan de Cirbied cites an earlier publication of his entitled "Recherches curieuses sur l'histoire ancienne de l'Asie," but I have not been able to locate a copy, as well as an edition of the Armenian text published in Madras in 1775. Chahan provided a translation of the table of contents from manuscript no. 95, and of extracts discussing the Franks, in Armenian and in French translation. Manuscript no. 99 also contained a copy of "The Life and History of St. Nerses the Great," from which Chahan de Cirbied also provides brief extracts with commentary. Jacques Chahan de Cirbied, "Notice de deux Manuscrits Arméniens, de la Bibliothèque impériale, nos. 95 et 99, contenant l'histoire écrite par *Mathieu Eretz*, et Extrait relatif à l'histoire de la première croisade," in *Notices et Extraits des Manuscripts de la Bibliothèque impériale, et autres bibliothèques*, 275–364. Joseph Michaud, in his 1829 collection of crusade sources, used extracts of Chahan de Cirbied's translations, as well as comments and selected extracts from Nerses Shnorhali's poem, "Lament on Edessa." (For more on this poem, see Chapter 6.) Joseph Michaud, *Bibliothèque des croisades*, 3: 481–504.

30. Irwin, "Orientalism," pp. 214–30.

31. Joseph Michaud, *Histoire des croisades*, 7th ed.

32. Leila Tarazi Fawaz, *Merchants and Migrants in Nineteenth-Century Beirut*, pp. 73–76.

33. Leila Tarazi Fawaz, *An Occasion for War: Civil Conflict in Lebanon and Damascus in 1860*, pp. 22–25; quote translated on p. 115.

34. Emmanuel Rey, *Les colonies franques de Syrie aux XIIme et XIIIme siècles*, p. v.

35. Rey, *Les colonies franques*, p. 61.

36. Conder, however, looked askance at intermarriage. Like Gibbon, he noted that "the degeneracy of later generations is traced to marriage with native women." Claude Conder, *The Latin Kingdom of Jerusalem, 1099 to 1291 A.D.*, p. 181.

37. Dana Carleton Munro, *The Kingdom of the Crusaders*, 107.

38. William Stevenson, *The Crusaders in the East*, p. 5.

39. R. C. Smail, *Crusading Warfare* (1097–1193), pp. 40–57.

40. Steven Runciman, *A History of the Crusades*, 3: 474.

41. Joshua Prawer, *The Latin Kingdom of Jerusalem: European Colonialism in the Middle Ages*, p. 524.

42. A recent example is Favreau-Lilie, "'Multikulturelle Gesellschaft' oder 'Persecuting Society'?"

43. Carole Hillenbrand, *The Crusades: Islamic Perspectives*.

44. Joshua Prawer, *The History of the Jews in the Latin Kingdom of Jerusalem*.

45. Robert Bartlett, *The Making of Europe*. For the variety of meanings ascribed to "frontier" in medieval studies, see David Abulafia, "Introduction: Seven Types of Ambiguity, c. 1100–c. 1500" in *Medieval Frontiers: Concepts and Practices*, ed. Nora Berend and David Abulafia, pp. 1–34.

46. Angeliki Laiou, "The Many Faces of Medieval Colonialism," in *Native Traditions in the Postconquest World*, ed. Elizabeth Hill Boone and Tom Cummins, pp. 13–30.

47. This is of course a simplification, and particularly characteristic of the ideology of the First Crusade. See Benjamin Z. Kedar for the many ways in which missionizing and crusading conflicted and coalesced. *Crusade and Mission: European Approaches Toward the Muslims*.

48. Penny Cole, "'O God, the Heathen Have Come into Your Inheritance' (Ps. 78.1): The Theme of Religious Pollution in Crusade Documents, 1095–1188," in *Crusaders and Muslims in Twelfth-Century Syria*, ed. Maya Shatzmiller, pp. 84–111.

49. Benjamin Z. Kedar, "On the Origins of the Earliest Laws of Frankish Jerusalem: The Canons of the Council of Nablus, 1120," *Speculum* 74 (1999): 310–35.

50. Robert Moore, *Formation of a Persecuting Society: Power and Deviance in Western Europe, 950–1250*.

51. David Nirenberg, *Communities of Violence: Persecution of Minorities in the Middle Ages*.

52. See the articles in David Heyd, ed., *Toleration*. Nor do I intend to suggest that a principle of tolerance was widespread in the twelfth-century Middle East. See Cary J. Nederman and John Christian Laursen, eds., *Difference and Dissent: Theories of Tolerance in Medieval and Early Modern Europe*. Rather, I am interested in the practices that lead to tolerance. For the basis of some forms of tolerance in canon law, see James Muldoon, "Tolerance and Intolerance in the Medieval Canon Lawyers," in *Tolerance and Intolerance: Social Conflict in the Age of the Crusades*, ed. Michael Gervers and James M. Powell, pp. 117–23. I have only in the final editing process become acquainted with Robert Hayden's concept of "antagonistic tolerance," a concept which while differing in notable ways from "rough tolerance," shares in interest in the role of multireligious societies. Robert Hayden, "Antagonistic Tolerance: Competitive Sharing of Religious Sites in South Asia and the Balkans," *Current Anthropology* 43 (2002): 205–31.

53. Matthew of Edessa did recount a number of Frankish atrocities against local

Christians, but, as I have argued elsewhere, he did not use them to critique Frankish authority. Instead, he wanted to show the revitalized presence of Satan in the world. See Christopher MacEvitt, "The *Chronicle* of Matthew of Edessa: Apocalypse, the First Crusade and the Armenian Diaspora," *Dumbarton Oaks Papers* 61 (2007): 254–96.

54. This is not to challenge the interesting recent work showing the ways the Frankish Levant did participate in the intellectual world of the twelfth century. See, for example, Benjamin Z. Kedar, "Gerard of Nazareth, a Neglected Twelfth-Century Writer in the Latin East," *Dumbarton Oaks Papers* 37 (1983): 55–77; Rudolf Hiestand, "Un centre intellectuel en Syrie du Nord? notes sur la personalité d'Aimery d'Antioche, Albert de Tarse et *Rorgo Fretellus*," *Le Moyen Age* 100 (1994): 7–36.

55. Recent work holds, in comparison, that Muslim tax practices did not form the basis for Frankish taxes. Paul L. Sidelko, "Muslim Taxation Under Crusader Rule," in *Tolerance and Intolerance: Social Conflict in the Age of the Crusades*, ed. Michael Gervers and James M. Powell, pp. 65–74.

56. Rustow, *Toward a History of Jewish Heresy*.

57. Kenneth R. Stow, *Alienated Minority: The Jews of Medieval Latin Europe*, pp. 41–101.

58. Michel le Syrien (Michael the Syrian, or the Great), *Chronique*, trans. and ed. J.-B. Chabot, vol. IV, p. 607 (inside column), trans. vol. III, p. 222 (hereafter Michel le Syrien, *Chronique*).

Chapter 1. Satan Unleashed: The Christian Levant in the Eleventh Century

1. A *vardapet* is a unique rank in the Armenian church. It is essentially a scholarly position, invested with the authority to teach, second only to that of the bishop. While the position did not have any sacramental duties attached to it, the title did convey the power to excommunicate. Some historians have linked the institution to the office of the *herbad*, which fulfilled an analagous role in Zoroastrianism. Robert Thomson, "*Vardapet* in the Early Armenian Church," *Le Muséon* 75 (1962): 367–84. The role of the *vardapet* will be discussed further in Chapter 6.

2. Matt'eos Urhayets'i, *Zhamanakagrut'iwn*, pp. 66–74; Matthew of Edessa, *Chronicle*, pp. 56–60.

3. Matt'eos Urhayets'i, *Zhamanakagrut'iwn*, p. 73; Matthew of Edessa, *Chronicle*, p. 60.

4. Matthew of Edessa actually used this apocalyptic vision twice. He first employed this prophecy at the death of the Byzantine emperor Basil II (Matt'eos Urhayets'i, *Zhamanakagrut'iwn*, pp. 52–55; Matthew of Edessa, *Chronicle*, pp. 47–49). This version, however, had only the approach of the grim apocalypse of the Turks without the redemption by the crusaders or the revivified Byzantine empire. For Pseudo-Methodius and the last emperor, see Paul Alexander, *Byzantine Apocalyptic Tradition; Die Apokalypse des Pseudo-Methodius die Ältesten Griechischen und Lateinischen übersetzungen*, ed. and trans. W. J. Aerts and G. A. A. Kortekaas, Corpus Scriptorum Orientalium 569, Subsidia t. 97, 2 vols. For more on Matthew's apocalypticism, see

Christopher MacEvitt, "The *Chronicle* of Matthew of Edessa: Apocalypse, the First Crusade and the Armenian Diaspora," *Dumbarton Oaks Papers* 61 (2007): 254–96. Robert Thomson also briefly addresses this theme in Matthew of Edessa in "'History' in Medieval Armenian Historians," in *Eastern Approaches to Byzantium: Papers from the Thirty-Third Spring Symposium of Byzantine Studies, University of Warwick, Coventry, March 1999*, ed. Antony Eastmond, pp. 89–99, as well as in "Crusades Through Armenian Eyes," in *The Crusades from the Perspective of Byzantium and the Muslim World*, ed. Angeliki E. Laiou and Roy Parviz Mottahedeh, pp. 74–75.

5. A. E. Redgate, *The Armenians.*

6. James Russell, *Zoroastrianism in Armenia.*

7. Nina Garsoïan in her numerous publications has sought to emphasize Armenia's Persian heritage, arguing against a long tradition which saw Armenia largely within a western Roman context. *Epic Histories Attributed to P'awstos Buzand*, pp. 51–55.

8. Sirarpie Der Nersessian, *The Armenians*, p. 27.

9. The traditional date for Tiridates's conversion was 301, making him the first Christian monarch (ignoring claims of the third-century Roman emperor Philip the Arab to that honor), but recent scholarship has redated his conversion to after Constantine's. Redgate, *Armenians*, p. 116.

10. René Grousset, *Histoire de l'Arménie, des origines à 1071*, pp. 163–66.

11. Sirarpie Der Nersessian, *The Armenians*, p. 31. Also see Aram Ter-Ghewondyan, *The Arab Emirates in Bagratid Armenia*, trans. Nina G. Garsoïan.

12. Chalcedonian formulations were rejected at several councils, including the Council of Ani in 969. Nina Garsoïan, "Quelques precisions preliminaries sur le schisme entre les églises Byzantine et arménienne au sujet du concile de Chalcédoine II: La date et les circonstances de la rupture," in *L'Arménie et Byzance: histoire et culture*, pp. 99–112. For a different take on the connections between Chalcedonian belief and Armenian identity, see V. A. Arutjunova-Fidanjan, "The Ethno-Confessional Self-Awareness of Armenian Chalcedonians," *Revue des études arméniennes* 21 (1988–89): 345–63.

13. Nina Garsoïan, *L'église arménienne et le grand schisme d'Orient*, Corpus Scriptorum Christianorum Orientalium 574, Subsidia, t. 100.

14. Sidney Griffith, "The Church of Jerusalem and the 'Melkites': The Making of an 'Arab Orthodox' Christian Identity in the World of Islam (750–1050 CE)," in *Christians and Christianity in the Holy Land: From the Origins to the Latin Kingdoms*, ed. Ora Limor and Guy G. Stroumsa, pp. 175–204.

15. Christopher Buck, "The Identity of the Sabi'un: An Historical Quest," *Muslim World* 74 (1984): 172–86; Michel Tardieu, "Sabiens coraniques et Sabiens de Harran," *Journal Asiatique* 274 (1986): 1–44.

16. For more on the form of the pact, see Mark R. Cohen, "What Was the Pact of 'Umar? A Literary-Historical Study," *Jerusalem Studies in Arabic and Islam* 23 (1999): 100–157. For an example of a caliphal rescript appointing the leader of the Christian community in Baghdad, see A. Mingana, "A Charter of Protection Granted to the Nestorian Church in A.D. 1138, by Muktafi II, Caliph of Baghdad," *Bulletin of the John Rylands Library* 10 (1926): 127–33.

17. For Christian, Jewish, and Zoroastrian reactions to the advent of the Islamic

empire, see Robert G. Hoyland, *Seeing Islam as Others Saw It*, Studies in Late Antiquity and Early Islam 13.

18. For the Melkite communities of Palestine, see the voluminous writings of Sidney Griffith, especially his article, "'Melkites,' 'Jacobites' and the Christological Controversies in Arabic in Third/Ninth Century Syria," in *Syrian Christians Under Islam*, ed. David Thomas, pp. 9–55; idem, "Faith and Reason in Christian Kalam: Theodore Abu Qurrah on Discerning the True Religion," in *Christian Arabic Apologetics During the Abbasid Period (750–1258)*, ed. Samir Khalil Samir and Jørgen S. Nielsen, pp. 1–43. For more on the religious debates between Christians and Muslims, see Griffith, "The Monk in the Emir's *Majlis*: Reflections on a Popular Genre of Christian Literary Apologetics in Arabic in the Early Islamic Period," in *The Majlis: Interreligious Encounters in Medieval Islam*, ed. Hava Lazarus-Yafeh, Mark R. Cohen, Sasson Somekh, and Sidney Griffith, pp. 13–65.

19. Mark N. Swanson, "The Martyrdom of 'Abd al-Masih, Superior of Mount Sinai (Qays al-Ghassani)" in *Syrian Christians Under Islam*, ed. Thomas, pp. 107–29.

20. Gérard Troupeau, "Églises et chrétiens dans l'Orient musulman" in *Évêques, moines et empéreurs (610–1054)*, Histoire du christianisme des origins à nos jours 4, ed. Jean-Marie Mayeur et al., pp. 375–456; see also Amnon Linder, "Christian Communities in Jerusalem," in *The History of Jerusalem: The Early Muslim Period 638–1099*, ed. Joshua Prawer and Haggai Ben-Shammai, pp. 121–62.

21. L. I. Conrad, "Varietas Syriaca: Secular and Scientific Culture in the Christian Communities of Syria After the Arab Conquest," in *After Bardaisan: Studies on Continuity and Change in Syriac Christianity in Honour of Professor Hans J. W. Drijvers*, ed. G. J. Reinink and A. C. Klugkist, pp. 85–105.

22. Andrew Palmer, *Monk and Mason on the Tigris Frontier*, pp. 165–69.

23. Sidney Griffith, "The 'Philosphical Life' in Tenth-Century Baghdad: The Contribution of Yahya Ibn 'Adi's *Kitab tahdhib al-akhlaq*," in *Christians at the Heart of Islamic Rule: Church Life and Scholarship in 'Abbasid Iraq*, ed. David Thomas, pp. 129–49.

24. Palmer, *Monk and Mason*, p. 177.

25. Redgate, *The Armenians*, pp. 175–84.

26. For the complex relationship between Armenians and Georgians (K'art'velians), see Stephen H. Rapp, Jr., "Christian Caucasian Dialogues: Glimpses of Armeno-K'art'velian Relations in Medieval Georgian Historiography," in *Peace and Negotiation: Strategies for Coexistence in the Middle Ages and the Renaissance*, ed. Diane Wolfthal, pp. 163–78.

27. Ronald Grigor Suny, *The Making of the Georgian Nation*, pp. 29–30.

28. Unlike "barbarian" societies developing in France, England, and Germany, Armenians largely refused to incorporate Roman concepts of government into their own system. Whereas the Roman empire had largely disappeared from the western Mediterranean (with the exception of Justinian's brief reconquests and an extended Byzantine presence in Sicily and southern Italy), it (as the Byzantine empire) remained a powerful neighbor ever seeking ways to bring Armenians under its influence. Thus the "barbarian" kingdoms of Europe had a freer hand to adapt Roman law and other pieces of imperial flotsam to their needs. Had the Armenians adopted

Roman practices, they probably soon would have found the weight of Byzantine political power not far behind Roman legal codes and bureaucratic traditions.

29. The one exception is Ani, seat of a Bagratuni kingdom and a city of 50,000 to 100,000 people. H. A. Manandian, *The Trade and Cities of Armenia in Relation to Ancient World Trade*, trans. Nina G. Garsoïan, pp. 149–50.

30. Christina Maranci, *Medieval Armenian Architecture*; Lynn Jones, "The Church of the Holy Cross and the Iconography of Kingship," *Gesta* 33, 2 (1994): 104–17.

31. Griffith, "Melkites," 39–40.

32. John Mavrogordato, ed. and trans., *Digenes Akrites*, p. 217.

33. Peter Charanis, *The Armenians in the Byzantine Empire*, 28–53; Alexander Kazhdan, "The Armenians in the Byzantine Ruling Class Predominantly in the Ninth Through the Twelfth Centuries," in *Medieval Armenian Culture*, ed. Thomas J. Samuelian and Michael E. Stone, pp. 439–51.

34. Gérard Dédéyan, "Mleh le Grand, Stratège de Lykandos," *Revue des études arméniennes* 15 (1981): 73–102.

35. For other members of the Kourkuas family, see Jean-Claude Cheynet, *Pouvoir et contestations à Byzance (963–1210)*, p. 216.

36. Paul E. Walker, "The 'Crusade' of John Tzimisces in the Light of New Arabic Evidence," *Byzantion* 47 (1977): 301–27.

37. Al-Muqaddasi, *The Best Divisions for Knowledge of the Regions*, trans. Basil Anthony Collins, p. 172.

38. Stepʿanos Taronetsʿi, *Patmutʿiwn*, ed. M. Malchasian, 258; trans. in Étienne Asolik de Taròn, *Histoire universelle*, trans. Frédéric Macler, pp. 141–42.

39. Catherine Holmes, "'How the East Was Won' in the Reign of Basil II," in *Eastern Approaches to Byzantium*, ed. Anthony Eastmond, pp. 41–56. Gilbert Dagron sees a change from a tolerant Byzantium in victory to one that persecuted Christian minorities in defeat, "Minorités ethniques et religieuses dans l'Orient byzantin à la fin du Xe au XIe siècle: l'immigration syrienne," *Travaux et mémoirés* 6 (1976): 177–216.

40. The issue of when Muslims became a majority in Syria is debated; see J. L. Boojamra, "Christianity in Greater Syria: Surrender and Survival," *Byzantion* 67 (1997): 148–78; John C. Lamoreaux, "Early Eastern Christian Responses to Islam," in *Medieval Christian Perceptions of Islam*, ed. John Victor Tolan, pp. 3–32. See also the collected essays in Michael Gervers and Ramzi Jibran Bikhazi, eds., *Indigenous Christian Communities in Islamic Lands: Eighth to the Eighteenth Centuries*, Papers in Medieval Studies 9. For a recent critique of conversion debate, see Tamer el-Leithy, "Coptic Culture and Conversion in Medieval Cairo, 1293–1524, A.D.," pp. 14–33.

41. Palmer, *Monk and Mason*, pp. 189–90.

42. Jean Maurice Fiey, *Chrétiens syriaques sous les Abbasides surtout à Bagdad*, Corpus Scriptorum Christianorum Orientalium 420, Subsidia t. 59, pp. 215–16.

43. Such transfers were a common Byzantine practice, applied to whole populations as well as to aristocrats. For example, in 878 the Armenian Kʿurdik surrendered his fortress of Lokana, on the Byzantine borderlands with the Arabs, to Basil I, and received in return imperial titles and lands within the empire.

44. Jean Gouillard, "Gagik II, défenseur de la foi arménienne," *Travaux et mémoirés* 7 (1979): 399–418.

45. Jean-Claude Cheynet, "La résistance aux Turcs en Asie Mineure entre Manzikert et la Première Croisade," in *EYψXIA: mélanges offerts à Hélène Ahrweiler*, pp. 131–47; Gérard Dédéyan, "Immigration arménienne en Cappadoce au XIe siècle," *Byzantion* 45 (1975): 41–117.

46. Claude Cahen, *Pre-Ottoman Turkey*, trans. J. Jones-Williams, pp. 67–68.

47. Tovma Vardapet Artsruni, *Patmut'iwn Tann Artsruneats'*, ed. K. Patkanov, p. 307; trans. in Thomas Artsruni, *History of the House of the Artsrunik'*, trans. Robert W. Thomson, p. 370.

48. Aristakes Lastivertts'i, *Patmut'iwn*, pp. 16–18; Aristakes de Lastivert, *Rècit des malheurs de la nation arménienne*, trans. Haïg Berbérian and Marius Canard, pp. 13–15.

49. Aristakes Lastivertts'i, *Patmut'iwn*, p. 51; Aristakes de Lastivert, *Rècit des malheurs*, 50.

50. Dédéyan, "Immigration arménienne."

51. Matt'eos Urhayets'i, *Zhamanakagrut'iwn*, pp. 96–97; Matthew of Edessa, *Chronicle*, p. 73.

52. Maurice Leroy, "Grégoire Magistros et les traductions arméniennes d'auteurs grecs," *Annuaire de l'Institut de philologie et d'histoire orientales* 3 (1935): 263–94.

53. Dédéyan, "Immigration arménienne."

54. Scholars cite a number of reasons why Armenian kings gave their realms to the empire. Sirarpie Der Nersessian believed that it was extorted through Byzantine military pressure, *The Armenians*, 39–40; but Michael Chamchiam, the Gibbon of Armenian history, suggested that it was in response to Turkish raids, *History of Armenia*, trans. Johannes Avdall, 2: 115. Mark Whittow argues what has been described above, emphasizing the need to control the Armenian *naxarar* because of their alliance with Byzantine military families, rather than a desire to conquer Armenian territory. See Mark Whittow, *The Making of Byzantium, 600–1025*, pp. 383–86. Andrew Sharf discusses the tensions between Armenian familiarity with the Byzantine world and Byzantine discomfort with Armenian ecclesiastic and cultural independence. "Armenians and Byzantines in the Time of Alexios I Komnenos," in *Confrontation and Coexistence*, ed. Pinhas Artzi, Bar-Ilan Studies in History 2, pp. 101–22.

55. It is important not to overemphasize the migration of Armenians into Byzantine territory, even during the Turkish invasions. Only the royal and *naxarar* families and their supporters found it expedient to move to Cappadocia, Cilicia, or Syria in the eleventh century, largely due their familiarity with the Byzantine world. Peasants, as one might expect, remained to suffer whatever might come under Seljuk rule. Claude Mutafian, *La Cilicie au carrefour des empires*, 1: 364–65; Nicholas Oikonomides, "L'organisation de la frontière orientale de Byzance aux Xe-IXe siècles et le Taktikon de l'Escurial," in *Actes du XIVe Congrès international d'Études Byzantines*, 1: 285–302; Gérard Dédéyan, "Le rôle des arméniens en Syrie du nord pendant la reconquête byzantine (vers 945–1031)," *Byzantinische Forschungen* 25 (1999): 248–84. See also Dagron, "Minorités ethniques."

56. Jean-Claude Cheynet, "Mantzikert: un désastre militaire?" *Byzantion* 50 (1980):

410–38; Michael Angold, "The Byzantine State on the Eve of the Battle of Manzikert," *Byzantinische Forschungen* 41 (1991): 9–34; Eva de Vries-van der Velden, "Psellos, Romain IV Diogénès et Mantzikert," *Byzantinoslavica* 58 (1997): 274–308.

57. Cheynet, "Résistance aux Turcs."

58. Much of his power derived from his position in the Byzantine army before its defeat at Mantzikert. The Byzantine historian Michael Attaliates (c. 1035–c.1090) recorded that Diogenes gave Philaretos "the greater part of the army of the East" not long before Mantzikert; Michael Attaleiates, *Historia*, ed. Immanuel Bekker, Corpus Scriptorum Historiae Byzantinae, p. 132. Anna Komnene (1083–1156) believed him to be *domesticos* of the East; Anne Comnène [Anna Komnene], *Alexiade*, ed. and trans. Bernard Leib, VI, 9, vol. II, p. 64, a position that would have put him in charge of all armies in the eastern portion of the empire. Cheynet wishes to identify Philaretos with an aristocratic family, Jean-Claude Cheynet and Jean-François Vannier, *Études prosopographiques*, pp. 57–74. For further discussion on Philaretos and his activities, see Nicolas Adontz, *Études arméno-byzantines*, pp. 147–52; J. Laurent, "Des Grecs aux Croisés: Étude sur l'histoire d'Édesse entre 1071 et 1098," in *Études d'histoire arménienne* (Louvain: Éditions Peeters, 1971), pp. 61–128, first published in *Byzantion* 1 (1924): 367–449; also published in the same volume is Laurent's article, "Byzance et Antioche sous le curopalate Philarète," pp. 148–59. This article was first published in *Revue des études arméniennes* 9 (1929): 61–72. More recent is C. J. Yarnley, "Philaretos: Armenian Bandit or Byzantine General?" *Revue des études arméniennes* n.s. 9 (1972): 331–53, as well as Gérard Dédéyan, *Les Arméniens entre grecs, musulmans et croisés: études sur les pouvoirs arméniens dans le Proche-Orient méditerranéen (1068–1150)*, vol. 1.

59. Mattʻeos Urhayetsʻi, *Zhamanakagrutʻiwn*, pp. 207–8; Matthew of Edessa, *Chronicle*, p. 138.

60. In 1077/8, Philaretos sent Basil to capture Edessa, which was ruled by Leon, the brother of a former *doux* of the city. He besieged the city for six months until the citizens killed Leon themselves and welcomed Basil into the city (Mattʻeos Urhayetsʻi, *Zhamanakagrutʻiwn*, p. 216; Matthew of Edessa, *Chronicle*, pp. 142–43). Although Matthew despised Philaretos, labeling him "the first-born son of Satan" (Mattʻeos Urhayetsʻi, *Zhamanakagrutʻiwn*, p. 206; Matthew of Edessa, *Chronicle*, p.137), this did not reflect badly on Basil, which suggests that Philaretos did not appear often in Edessa. Basil was the face of authority for the city. Ibn al-Athir shared Matthew's distaste for Philaretos, calling him "a wicked ruler." Ibn al-Athir, *The Annals of the Saljuq Turks: Selections from al-Kamil fi'l Ta'rikh of 'Izz al-Din Ibn al-Athir*, trans. D. S. Richards, p. 217.

61. Mattʻeos Urhayetsʻi, *Zhamanakagrutʻiwn*, p. 64; Matthew of Edessa, *Chronicle*, p. 55. Basil defended the city of Mantzikert against the Turks in 1054-55 and also served on the western frontier, fighting the Uzes near the Danube (Mattʻeos Urhayetsʻi, *Zhamanakagrutʻiwn*, pp. 119, 151; Matthew of Edessa, *Chronicle*, pp. 87, 105–6).

62. Mattʻeos Urhayetsʻi, *Zhamanakagrutʻiwn*, p. 216; Matthew of Edessa, *Chronicle*, pp. 142–43.

63. According to Matthew of Edessa, Philaretos played a role in the death of

Tʻornik of Sasun (Mattʻeos Urhayetsʻi, *Zhamanakagrutʻiwn*, pp. 206–10; Matthew of Edessa, *Chronicle*, pp. 137–39) and the former king of Ani, Gagik (Mattʻeos Urhayetsʻi, *Zhamanakagrutʻiwn*, pp. 218–20; Matthew of Edessa, *Chronicle*, p. 144, see p. 323 note 4).

64. Philaretos also attempted to dominate the Jacobite church; the twelfth-century patriarch and chronicler Michael the Great recorded that Philaretos imprisoned ten Jacobite bishops from the area around Melitene in an attempt to pressure them into voting for his candidate for patriarch. Michel le Syrien, *Chronique*, vol. IV, pp. 581–82; trans. vol. III, pp. 175, 177.

65. Mattʻeos Urhayetsʻi, *Zhamanakagrutʻiwn*, p. 234; Matthew of Edessa, *Chronicle*, p. 153.

66. Mattʻeos Urhayetsʻi, *Zhamanakagrutʻiwn*, p. 247; Matthew of Edessa, *Chronicle*, p. 160.

67. Called an Armenian in most modern texts. His identity is discussed further in Chapter 2.

68. He was soon replaced by ʻAli ibn Munqidh, as Michael the Great recorded. *Chronique*, vol. IV, pp. 583; trans. vol. III, pp. 178.

69. Yaroslav Dachévytch, "Les arméniens en Islande," *Revue des études arméniennes* 20 (1986–87): 321–36.

70. Also tantalizing is the existence of a tenth-century manuscript from Autun containing a Latin-Armenian glossary. H. Omont, "Manuel de conversation arménien-latin du Xe siècle," *Bibliothèque de l'école de chartes* 43 (1882): 563–64.

71. Stepʻanos Taronetsʻi, *Patmutʻiwn*, 17–18; trans. in *Des Stephanos von Taron Armenische Geschichte*, trans. Heinrich Gelzer and August Burckhardt, p. 12.

72. Stepʻanos Taronetsʻi, *Patmutʻiwn*, 216, 220; Stephen de Taron, *Histoire universelle*, 92, 97.

73. Movses Kaghankatuatsʻi, *Patmutʻiwn Aghuanits Aghkharhi*, ed. Varag Arakelyan, pp. 272–73, trans. in Movses Dasxuranci (Daskhurantsʻi), *History of the Caucasian Albanians*, trans. C. J. F. Dowsett, p. 175. Almost nothing is known about the author, which accounts for the variations in his surname.

74. Movses Kaghankatuatsʻi, *Patmutʻiwn*, pp. 320–22; Movses Dasxuranci, *History*, p. 211. Dowsett assumes that "Rome" mentioned here is actually New Rome, Constantinople, but I believe the books speak of the founding of Rome under Romulus indicate that Old Rome is meant.

75. Yahya ibn-Saʻïd, *Histoire d Yahya-ibn-Saʻid d'Antioche, Continuateur de Saʻid-ibn-Bitriq*, ed. and trans. J. Kratchkovsky and A. Vasiliev, Patrologia Orientalis 18, ed. R. Graffin and F. Nau, fasc. I., pp. 706–8.

76. Yahya ibn-Saʻïd, *Histoire de Yahya d'Antioche*, fasc. II, ed. and trans. J. Kratchkovsky and A. Vasiliev, Patrologia Orientalis 23, pp. 447–48.

77. Mattʻeos Urhayetsʻi, *Zhamanakagrutʻiwn*, p. 120; Matthew of Edessa, *Chronicle*, p. 87. The Byzantine chronicler Michael Attaliates also recounts this incident, but without the Christlike quote. *Historia*, 46–47. For another example of a valiant Frank dying heroically, see Mattʻeos Urhayetsʻi, *Zhamanakagrutʻiwn*, 159; Matthew of Edessa, *Chronicle*, 109. Many other Franks appear in Matthew's chronicle, some even by name, but not all of them measure up to Matthew's ideal. Matthew accused the

Norman mercenary Hervé, in the Armenian sources named Francopoulos, of betraying his Byzantine employers in a battle with the Turks near Amida in 1063, for which he was drowned in the Mediterranean by the orders of Constantine X Ducas. Matt'eos Urhayets'i, *Zhamanakagrut'iwn*, p. 144; Matthew of Edessa, Chronicle, pp. 100–101. Byzantine chronicles of the period mention Francopoulos and his involvement in battles in Armenia, but do not record the same violent death Matthew described. Georgius Cedrenus, *Historiarum Compendium*, ed. Immanuel Bekker, Corpus Scriptorum Historiae Byzantinae, 2: 616–19. For a general discussion of Franks in military service in the empire, see R. Janin, "Les Francs au service des Byzantins," *Echos d'Orient* 29 (1930): 61–72.

78. Michael Angold, "Knowledge of Byzantine History in the West: The Norman Historians (Eleventh and Twelfth Centuries)," *Anglo-Norman Studies* 25 (2002): 19–33.

79. Rodulfus Glaber, *Historiarum libri quinque*, ed. and trans. John France and Paul Reynolds, III: 1; p. 98.

80. Rodulfus Glaber, *Historiarum libri*, I: 4; pp. 20–23.

81. Rodulfus Glaber, *Historiarum libri*, I: 5; pp. 36–47. See also Robert Lee Wolff, "How the News Was Brought from Byzantium to Angoulême; or, The Pursuit of a Hare in an Ox Cart," *Byzantine and Modern Greek Studies* 4 (1978): 139–89; Nancy Sevcenko, "The Monastery of Mount Sinai and the Cult of St. Catherine," in *Byzantium, Faith, and Power: Perspectives on Late Byzantine Art and Culture*, ed. Sarah Brooks.

82. Krijnie N. Ciggaar, *Western Travellers to Constantinople*, pp. 168–69.

83. Amato di Montecassino, *Storia de' Normannni*, I: 15, 21, p. 20, 27; Amatus of Montecassino, *The History of the Normans*, trans. Prescott N. Dunbar, pp. 48–49, 71.

84. Einar Joranson, "The Great German Pilgrimage of 1064–5," in *The Crusades and Other Historical Essays*, ed. Louis Paetow, pp. 3–43.

85. *Annales Altahenses Maiores*, ed. Wilhelm von Giesebrecht and Edmund von Oefele, Monumenta Germaniae Historica, Scriptores 4, p. 67.

86. Lambert von Hersfeld, *Lamperti Monachis Hersfeldensis Opera*, ed. Oswald Holder-Egger, Monumenta Germaniae Historica, Scriptores 38, p. 98; 14.

87. D. C. Munro, "The Speech of Pope Urban II at Clermont, 1095," *American Historical Review* 11 (1905–6): 231–42; Carl Erdmann, *The Origin of the Idea of Crusade*, trans. Marshall W. Baldwin and Walter Goffart, pp. 306–71; H. E. J. Cowdrey, "Pope Urban II's Preaching of the First Crusade" *History* 55 (1970): 177–88; idem, "Pope Urban II and the Idea of Crusade," *Studi Medievali* 36 (1995): 721–42, reprinted in *The Crusades and Latin Monasticism, 11th-12th Centuries*, article V.

88. Fulcher, *Historia*, pp. 132–33; Ryan, *History*, pp. 65–66.

89. D. M. Nicols, "Byzantium and the Papacy in the Eleventh Century," *Journal of Ecclesiastical History* 13 (1962): 1–19. Urban's predecessor Gregory VII (c. 1020–1085) was alarmed by the rapid advances of the Seljuk Turks after the battle of Mantzikert, and wrote several letters in the course of 1074 attempting to rally support for the Byzantines, hoping military support would translate into ecclesiastical reunion. *Das Register Gregors VII*, ed. Erich Caspar, Monumenta Germaniae Historica, 1: 69–71, trans. Ephraim Emerton, *The Correspondence of Pope Gregory VII*, pp. 22–23. In 1089, Urban II wrote to the Ecumenical Patriarch of Constantinople in an attempt to have his name re-instated on the diptychs in the Great Church in Constantinople. For

more western attitudes toward the east, see John France, *Victory in the East*, pp. 96–102.

90. Paul Magdalino has suggested that increased trade between the Levantine seaboard, particularly Antioch, fostered contact between Rome and eastern churches. In 1052, the new patriarch of Antioch, Peter, announced his election to Rome, a traditional gesture not done in many years. As Magdalino has pointed out, mercantile trade had grown tremendously in the eleventh century, as had pilgrimage traffic from the west. "The Byzantine Background to the First Crusade," This work was originally published by the Canadian Institute of Balkan Studies as a pamphlet, http://www.deremilitari.org/resources/articles/magdalino.htm.

91. *Das Register Gregors VII*, pp. 510–14; trans. in Emerton, *Correspondence*, pp. 157–58.

92. Marcus Bull, "Views of Muslims and Jerusalem in Miracle Stories, c. 1000–c. 1200: Reflections on the Study of the First Crusaders' Motivations," in *The Experience of Crusading*, vol. 1, *Western Approaches*, ed. Marcus Bull and Norman Housley, pp. 13–32.

93. Heinrich Hagenmeyer, *Epistulae et chartae ad historiam primi belli sacri spectantes*, p. 136.

Chapter 2. Close Encounters of the Ambiguous Kind: When Crusaders and Locals Meet

1. Cited by Michel le Syrien, *Chronique*, trans. and ed. J.-B. Chabot, vol. IV, p. 639; trans. vol. III, p. 278.

2. Christopher MacEvitt, "The *Chronicle* of Matthew of Edessa: Apocalypse, the First Crusade and the Armenian Diaspora," *Dumbarton Oaks Papers* 61 (2007): 254–96.

3. Anonymous, *Anonymi Auctoris Chronicon Ad Annum Christi 1234 Pertinens*, ed. J.-B. Chabot, Corpus Scriptorum Christianorum Orientalium; Scriptores Syri 82, t. 37, vol. II, text. This publication is an anastatic reproduction of a volume published by Chabot in 1916 under the same title, series III, t. XV, text. A third volume published in the same series under the same title, labeled vol. 354/t. 154 (1974), contains a French translation by Albert Abouna.

4. For Basil bar Shumana, see J.-B. Chabot, *Littérature syriaque*, pp. 122, 129–30; Gérard Dédéyan, Review of *Ananun Edesac'i, Zamanakagrut'yun (Chronicle of the Anonymous of Edessa)*, by Lewon H. Ter-Petrosyan, *Revue des études arméniennes* n.s. 17 (1983): 658–62.

5. Dorothea Weltecke, *Die "Beschreibung der Zeiten" von Mor Michael dem Grossen (1126–1199)*, Corpus Scriptorum Christianorum Orientalium 594, Subsidia, t. 110.

6. Albertus Aquensis [Albert of Aachen], "Historia Hierosolymitana," *Recueil des historiens des croisades: Historiens occidentaux*, 3: 265–713.

7. Radulfus Cadomensis [Ralph of Caen], "Gesta Tancredi in expeditione Hierosolymitana," *Receuil des historiens des Croisades: Historiens occidentaux*, 3: 587–716.

See the new translation by Bernard Bachrach and David Bachrach, *The Gesta Tancredi of Ralph of Caen A History of the Normans on the First Crusade*, and Jean-Charles Payen, "L'image du grec dans la chronique normande: sur un passage de Raoul de Caen," in *Images et signes de l'Orient dans l'Occident médiéval*, pp. 269–80.

8. Benedict of Edessa was probably ordained at Christmastime 1099, but did not reach his see until 1100. Bernard Hamilton, *The Latin Church in the Crusader States*, p. 16.

9. Greg Woolf, *Becoming Roman*.

10. Joshua Prawer, "The Armenians in Jerusalem Under the Crusaders," in *Armenian and Biblical Studies*, ed. Michael Stone, pp. 222–36; James H. Forse, "Armenians and the First Crusade," *Journal of Medieval History* 17 (1991): 13.

11. For Cilician independence in the late Roman period, see Noel Lenski, "Assimilation and Revolt in the Territory of Isauria, from the 1st Century B.C. to the 6th Century A.D.," *Journal of the Economic and Social History of the East* 42 (1999): 411–65.

12. Fulcher of Chartres [Fulcher Carnotensis], *Historia Hierosolymitana*, ed. Heinrich Hagenmeyer, pp. 202–3; trans. Frances Rita Ryan in *A History of the Expedition to Jerusalem*, p. 88.

13. Anonymous, *Gesta Francorum et aliorum Hiersolimitanorum*, ed. Rosalind Hill, p. 25.

14. Some historians have argued that Tancred and Baldwin's conquest of Cilicia was a plan approved by all the crusading princes; most recently John France argued that this was designed to isolate Antioch as part of an "Armenian strategy." France, *Victory in the East*, pp. 185–96, a notion Thomas Asbridge also considers. Asbridge, *The Creation of the Principality of Antioch, 1098–1130*, pp. 16–24. Others, however, saw this as a purely private enterprise on the part of Baldwin and Tancred. Steven Runciman, "The First Crusade: Constantinople to Antioch," in *A History of the Crusades*, ed. Kenneth Setton, vol. 1, *The First Hundred Years*, ed. Marshall Baldwin, pp. 296–302; Hans Eberhard Mayer, *The Crusades*, trans. John Gillingham, p. 48. Ralph of Caen suggested that Tancred went from his own initiative, but this suggestion deliberately contrasts Tancred's choice of the difficult road through the Taurus mountains with the main crusader army's choice of the easy road to Marash. Radulfus, "Gesta Tancredi," p. 629. Albert of Aachen claimed that the leaders of the crusade agreed, but his point in somewhat lost when Tancred is puzzled to see Baldwin at Tarsus (Approval of the leaders, Albert, "Historia," III, 3, p. 340; Tancred's surprise, III, 6, p. 343). It also seems that if that were the case, Tancred and Baldwin would have been accompanied by Byzantine troops to receive the cities that they conquered. Although Tancred and Baldwin's actions may have actually helped the larger crusade armies, little in their actions betrays an interest in the common goals of the crusade. Both seemed far more motivated by self-aggrandizement.

15. All dates given in this chapter relative to the crusade rely on Heinrich Hagenmeyer, "Chronologie de la première croisade (1094–1100)," *Revue de l'orient latin* 6 (1893): 214–93, 490–549; VII: 430–503, VIII: 318–82.

16. Radulfus, "Gesta Tancredi," p. 630. Unless otherwise noted, translations of Ralph are my own.

17. For Tancred's troop numbers, Radulfus, "Gesta Tancredi," p. 630; for Baldwin's, "Gesta Tancredi," p. 633.

18. On this point, most of the crusade chronicles agree. Albert of Aachen suggests that Baldwin's eloquent evocation of his brother Godfrey of Bouillon's power and influence led to his triumph over Tancred. Albert of Aachen, "Historia," III, 9, p. 345. The Anonymous "Gesta" had the citizens explicitly choose Tancred over Baldwin, and then gave Tancred the high-minded motive to leave because he had "no wish to plunder Christians," as Baldwin advocated. *Gesta*, pp. 24–5.

19. Radulfus, "Gesta Tancredi," pp. 636–67. Again, Albert of Aachen differs, suggesting that Adana was ruled by a Burgundian named Welf, "Historia," III, 10, pp. 345–46.

20. Albert describes her death after Baldwin conquers Tell Bashir, "Historia," III, 27, p. 358. It is unclear how long the garrisons remained; Tancred had to reconquer the area in 1101. Asbridge, *Principality*, p. 52.

21. Radulfus, "Gesta Tancredi," p. 634.

22. Radulfus, "Gesta Tancredi," p. 636.

23. Penny Cole, "'O God, the Heathen Have Come into Your Inheritance' (Ps. 78.1): The Theme of Religious Pollution in Crusade Documents, 1095–1188," in *Crusaders and Muslims in Twelfth-Century Syria*, ed. Maya Shatzmiller, pp. 84–111.

24. M. Dulaurier, ed., *Recueil des historiens des croisade: Documents arméniens*, vol. I, p. 33, note 2. Joseph Laurent argues that Ursinus, Oshin, and Aspietes (a figure in Anna Komnena's *Alexiad* many historians have identified as Oshin) are all different people. I find his argument separating Aspietes from Oshin convincing, but find the links between Oshin and Ursinus, if not compelling, at least persuasive. Joseph Laurent, "Arméniens de Cilicie: Aspiétès, Oschin, Ursinus," in *Études d'histoire arméniennes*, pp. 51–60.

25. For a history of the castle and a description of its recent condition, see F. C. R. Robinson and P. C. Hughes, "Lampron—Castle of Armenian Cilicia," *Anatolian Studies* 19 (1969): 183–207.

26. Samuel Anets'iots' [Samuel of Ani], *Havak'munk'i Grots Patmagrats*, roughly translated in Samouel d'Ani, "Tables Chronologiques," trans. Marie-Félicité Brosset, *Collection d'historiens arméniens*, 2nd ed., p. 453.

27. Once the crusaders moved on to Antioch, Oshin supported them with provisions, eager to have them move beyond Cilicia. One wonders if he directed his supplies to particular crusade leaders. Matt'eos Urhayets'i, *Zhamanakagrut'iwn*, p. 259; Matthew of Edessa, *Chronicle*, p. 167.

28. Albert of Aachen, "Historia," III, 5, p. 342.

29. Many Muslims also confused the Franks with the Byzantines during the First Crusade; Carole Hillenbrand, "The First Crusade: the Muslim Perspective" in *The First Crusade: Origins and Impact*, ed. Jonathan Phillips, p. 136. Ibn al-Athir preserves an account of a Frank who held a castle in the area of Hisn-Zaid in the period of Philaretos. *The Annals of the Saljuq Turks: Selections from al-Kamil fi'l Ta'rikh of 'Izz al-Din Ibn al-Athir*, trans. D. S. Richards, p. 245.

30. Ralph of Caen suggests that Baldwin received an invitation to come to Edessa while still in Tarsus; due to *lacunae* in the text, the identity of the inviter is unknown. Radulfus, "Gesta Tancredi," p. 637. Matthew of Edessa, who may well have

been a witness of Baldwin's arrival, says that Baldwin left the army with a hundred horsemen, but after conquering Turbessel (in Arabic, Tell Bashir) and other fortresses and leaving garrisons there, arrived in Edessa with only sixty knights. Matt'eos Urhayets'i, *Zhamanakagrut'iwn*, p. 260; Matthew of Edessa, *Chronicle*, p. 168. Fulcher does not record how many troops Baldwin had when he left the main army at Marash, but says that Baldwin had eighty knights with him when he entered Edessa. Presumably, he left some knights behind to defend Tell Bashir and Rawandan. Fulcher, *Historia*, pp. 210–11; Ryan, *History*, p. 90. Albert of Aachen, basing his account on the reports of other crusaders rather than personal experience, reported he left the army with 700, and arrived in Edessa with 200. Albert of Aachen, "Historia," III, 17, p. 350; 19, p. 352.

31. Albert of Aachen, "Historia." III, 17, p. 350. For a critique of Albert's account, comparing him to other chroniclers, see A. A. Beaumont, "Albert of Aachen and the County of Edessa," in *The Crusades and Other Historical Essays*, ed. Louis J. Paetow, pp. 101–38.

32. Albert of Aachen, "Historia." III, 17, p. 351.

33. According to Matthew of Edessa, he had land and castles in the area around Rawandan, Matt'eos Urhayets'i, *Zhamanakagrut'iwn*, p. 338; Matthew of Edessa, *Chronicle*, p. 220.

34. Albert of Aachen, "Historia," III, 17, p. 350.

35. Quoted in David Morray, "A Medieval Visit to the Castle of Al-Rawandan," *Anatolian Studies* 43 (1993): 137–42. Morray also gives a description of the condition of the castle in 1987. Claude Cahen also has a brief description; *La Syrie du Nord à l'époque des Croisades et la principauté franque d'Antioche*, pp. 117–18. The Latin name is Ravenel or Ravendal.

36. Albert of Aachen, "Historia," III, 17, p. 351.

37. Fulcher, *Historia*, p. 208; Ryan, *History*, p. 89.

38. Claude Cahen, *Pre-Ottoman Turkey*, trans. J. Jones-Williams, pp. 72–90. See also Cahen, "The Turkish Invasion: The Selchükids," in *A History of the Crusades*, ed. Kenneth Setton, vol. 1, *The First Hundred Years*, ed. Marshall Baldwin, chap. 5, pp. 135–76.

39. Albert of Aachen, "Historia," III, 18, p. 351. Dédéyan suggests P'er can be identified with Vahram Pahlavuni, but does not explain why; "Les princes arméniens de l'Euphratèse et l'Empire byzantin (fin XIe-milieu XIIe siècle)," in *Arménie et Byzance: histoire et culture*, p. 87.

40. Albert of Aachen, "Historia," III, 18, p. 351.

41. Albert of Aachen, "Historia," III, 18, p. 351.

42. John France, "The Fall of Antioch During the First Crusade," in *Dei gesta per Francos*, ed. Michel Balard, Benjamin Z. Kedar, and Jonathan Riley-Smith, pp. 13–20. The greatest challenge in studying the foundation of the principality of Antioch is the lack of sources. No figure comparable to Matthew of Edessa or the anonymous Syriac chronicler exists, and the Latin accounts focus on Edessa and Jerusalem. One chronicle, written by Walter, chancellor of the principality, does survive, but it is largely concerned with military matters in the years between 1114 and 1124.

43. It is unclear whether this is the case, or if the city chose to cooperate with Turkish forces.

44. Asbridge, *Principality*, pp. 28–30.

45. Rugia was probably the fortress later known as Chastel-Rouge. Asbridge, *Principality*, p. 30. The troops were under the direct command of Peter of Roaix. Anonymous, *Gesta Francorum*, p. 26.

46. John France, "The Departure of Tatikios from the Crusader Army," *Bulletin of the Institute of Historical Research* 44 (1971): 138–47.

47. Asbridge, *Principality*, pp. 31–34.

48. Carole Hillenbrand, *The Crusades: Islamic Perspectives*, pp. 44–46.

49. Albert, "Historia," V, 6–10, pp. 436–39.

50. Albert, "Historia," III, 21–25, pp. 353–57.

51. Albert, "Historia," III, 25, pp. 356–57.

52. This perhaps illustrates Christopher Tyerman's argument that modern historians (and thirteenth-century canonists) have a clearer idea of what a crusader was than those who participated in what we call the crusades. *The Invention of the Crusades*.

53. Usamah ibn-Munqidh, *An Arab-Syrian Gentleman and Warrior in the Period of the Crusades*, trans. Philip K. Hitti.

54. It is not clear what title T'oros used. Matthew of Edessa calls T'oros *kouropalates* most often, occasionally also using the Armenian word "ishkhan" which generally means "leader" or "prince." Fulcher of Chartres honors him with "princeps," Albert of Aachen refers to T'oros as "dux."

55. Albert of Aachen, "Historia," III, 19, p. 352. Most historians have followed Matthew of Edessa, and placed the initiative in T'oros' hands. The anonymous Edessan chronicler, on the other hand, suggested Edessa's citizens approached Baldwin. "When the townspeople heard that the Franks had come and camped in the district of Antioch, they approached Theodore [T'oros], son of Hetom and said to him, "We ask that you send for help from the Frankish soldiers to guard the city against the Turks." Theodore [T'oros] did not agree to this. But seeing that he could not defy the townsmen, and fearing that they would send for them [the Franks] against his will, he pretended to agree though he was not really pleased at their coming, and even more people in the city hated him." According to the chronicler, Godfrey sent his brother, who turned out to be the help the citizens desired, but T'oros feared. Baldwin thus may have been well aware that his presence in the city was welcomed by a portion of the citizenry, but not by T'oros. Anonymous, *Chronicon*, p. 41; trans. A. Abouna, p. 56.

56. Matt'eos Urhayets'i, *Zhamanakagrut'iwn*, p. 257; Matthew of Edessa, *Chronicle*, p. 166. The Muslim chronicler Ibn al-Athir believed that the Franks had gained control of Edessa "through correspondence." Hillenbrand, *Islamic Perspectives*, p. 56.

57. Fulcher, *Historia*, p. 212; Ryan, *History*, p. 91.

58. Matt'eos Urhayets'i, *Zhamanakagrut'iwn*, pp. 223–24; Matthew of Edessa, *Chronicle*, p. 147. Also see Jean-Claude Cheynet, "Les Arméniens de l'empire en Orient de Constantin X à Alexis Comnène (1059–1081)" in *L'Arménie et Byzance: histoire et culture*, p. 71.

59. Matthew called the leader of this plot by the name of Ishkhan, which means "prince" in Armenian, but Matthew stated that he tried to take power away from the

Armenians, suggesting he may have been Greek or Syrian. Matt'eos Urhayets'i, *Zhamanakagrut'iwn*, pp. 223–24; Matthew, *Chronicle*, p. 147.

60. Matt'eos Urhayets'i, *Zhamanakagrut'iwn*, p. 260; Matthew, *Chronicle*, p. 168.

61. Albert of Aachen, "Historia," III, 20, p. 352.

62. Albert of Aachen, "Historia," III, 21, p. 353.

63. Al-Faraj (in Armenian Alp'irak) was, according to Matthew, a grandson of the Seljuk general Kutulmish (in Armenian Ddlmsh), though that tie does not show up in any other source. Matt'eos Urhayets'i, *Zhamanakagrut'iwn*, p. 252; Matthew of Edessa, *Chronicle*, p. 163. Kutulmish was a cousin of the Seljuk Sultan Toghrul, who had entered Baghdad to rule at the caliph's invitation in the 1050s. Kutulmish's son Sulaiman (al-Faraj's father or uncle) established the Seljuk Sultanate of Rum, which ruled territory from Nicaea to Antioch before the First Crusade, and after became an Anatolian sultanate with its capital at Konya (ancient Iconium). See Cahen, *Pre-Ottoman Turkey*, pp. 72–90. The anonymous chronicler has a different account, suggesting that al-Faraj ('lpyrg in unvocalized Syriac) was sent to Edessa by the Seljuk prince Tutush. Al-Faraj was then poisoned by a Christian dancer and singer named Qira Gali. *Chronicon*, pp. 52–53; trans. A. Abouna, pp. 38–39.

64. Matthew of Edessa frequently refers to him as a Roman prince—"ishkan Horomots," in Armenian (Matt'eos Urhayets'i, *Zhamanakagrut'iwn*, p. 248), while specifically naming other local lords, such as Constantine of Gargar, as Armenian (*Zhamanakagrut'iwn*, p. 260). Philaretos, on the other hand, he specifically noted that he was Armenian by birth but belonged to "Roman faith" (*Zhamanakagrut'iwn*, p. 206). Likewise, Fulcher of Chartres, who had likely met him, labeled him a Greek (*Historia*, p. 210). Modern historians have assumed that "Greek" indicated that T'oros was a Melkite, and that his name, conspicuously Armenian, announced his ethnic background. Medieval ideas of identity and ethnicity, however, were linked to language and culture, not descent. The label "Greek," therefore, might refer either to T'oros' language, culture, religious affiliation, or some combination of these. Furthermore, he was only called "T'oros" in Armenian and Latin sources (though curiously Albert of Aachen never gives him a name); Syriac chroniclers referred to him as Theodoros, a fine Greek name; T'oros is simply the Armenian version of that name.

65. William Saunders, "The Greek Inscription on the Harran Gate at Edessa: Some Further Evidence," *Byzantinische Forschungen* 21 (1995): 301–4.

66. Anonymous, *Chronicon*, p. 54; trans. A. Abouna, p. 39.

67. J. B. Segal, *Edessa, "the Blessed City"*, p. 227.

68. Fulcher, *Historia*, pp. 213–14; Ryan, *History*, p. 91; Matt'eos Urhayets'i, *Zhamanagakrut'iwn*, pp. 261–2; Matthew of Edessa, Chronicle, pp. 169–70; Anonymous, *Chronicon*, p. 57; trans. A. Abouna. pp. 41–2.

69. Matt'eos Urhayets'i, *Zhamanakagrut'iwn*, p. 271; Matthew of Edessa, *Chronicle*, p. 175.

70. Matt'eos Urhayets'i, *Zhamanagakrut'iwn*, p. 233; Matthew of Edessa, *Chronicle*, p. 152.

71. Matt'eos Urhayets'i, *Zhamanagakrut'iwn*, p. 216; Matthew of Edessa, *Chronicle*, p. 143.

72. Fulcher, *Historia*, pp. 213–14; Ryan, *History*, p. 91.

73. Matt'eos Urhayets'i, *Zhamanagakrut'iwn*, pp. 261–62; Matthew of Edessa, *Chronicle*, pp. 169.

74. Many crusaders had relics that they either brought with them or acquired in Constantinople. Robert of Flanders carried an arm of St. George, acquired in Byzantium, with him. "Narratio quomodo relliquiae martyris Georgii ad nos Aquicinenses pervenerunt," in *Recueil des historiens des Croisades: Historiens occidentaux*, 5: 248–52. See also Jonathan Riley-Smith, *The First Crusade and the Idea of Crusading*, pp. 93–95.

75. T'ovma Vardapet Artsruni, *Patmut'iwn Tann Artsruneats'*; Thomas Artsruni, *History of the House of the Artsrunik'*, trans. Robert W. Thomson, p. 369. Hrip'sime helped convert Armenia in the early fourth century. What brought the relic to Edessa is unclear; however, Matthew of Edessa remembered when in 1092/3 "the Holy Cross of Varag and the Icon of the Holy Virgin Mary were brought to the city of Edessa, and so there was great rejoicing among the nation of Abgar. Deeply moved, all the inhabitants of Edessa collectively went forth to receive these holy objects and then brought them into the city with great pomp" (Matt'eos Urhayets'i, *Zhamanakagrut'iwn*, p. 242; Matthew of Edessa, *Chronicle*, p. 157.)

76. Albert of Aachen, "Historia," III, 21, p. 353. This ceremony has few parallels in Greek or Armenian sources. Adoption and fosterage, however, were a common custom among the *naxarar* clans of Armenia. Nobody, however, described the form of these adoptions, so we cannot determine whether this was in fact a traditional Armenian ritual. See Robert Bedrosian, *"Dayeakut'iwn* in Ancient Armenia," *Armenian Review* 37 (1984): 23–47. Travelers to the Caucasuses in the eighteenth and nineteenth centuries report "milkrelationships," adoptions between two adults, usually of the opposite sex, wherein the adoptee placed the nipple of the woman who was adopting him in his mouth. See Alexander Grigolia, "Milkrelationship in the Caucasus," *Bedi kartlisa* 41–42 (1962): 147–67.

77. Albert of Aachen, "Historia," III, 31; p.361. Many historians have named her "Arda," but there does not seem to be a textual basis for this name. See Ryan, *History*, p. 218, n. 4. If Taphnuz hoped to benefit from the position of his new son-in-law, he was sorely disappointed. Fearing Baldwin's greed, he fled Edessa not long after the marriage. It is curious that these details, which reflect so poorly on Baldwin's character, came from the observations of a fellow Frank. Matthew of Edessa, on the other hand, did not comment on the count's marriage or on the fate of his father-in-law.

78. "Bisant" is the western name for the Byzantine *nomisma*, a gold coin introduced by emperor Alexios Komnenos weighing approximately 4.55 grams.

Albert of Aachen remarked vaguely that Taphnuz was the brother of a certain Constentinus, who controlled strong castles in the mountains. Some historians have argued that this man was Constantine of Vahka, and that Taphnuz was a Latin misspelling of T'oros, his brother's name. If so, the marriage linked Baldwin with an Armenian family who won the Armenian leadership lottery, becoming the kings of Cilician Armenia in 1198. However, Costentinus can alternatively be identified with Constantine of Gargar. Matthew of Edessa described the role that Constantine of Gargar played in the revolt against T'oros; Albert similarly mentions the participation of a "Constentinus de montanis" in that revolt. Albert, "Historia," III, 12, p. 354. The close co-operation between Baldwin and Constantine of Gargar in both the attack in Samosata and the revolt against T'oros would suggest that this Constantine was the one to whom Albert referred. Rüdt-Collenberg strangely suggests that Constantine of Gargar is T'oros of Edessa's brother and related to Oshin of Lampron, but I find no textual support for this claim. Wipertus-Hugo Rüdt-Collenberg, *The Rupenides, Hethumides and Lusignans: The Structure of the Armeno-Cilician Dynasties*, p. 78. Michel Balard suggests she is the daugher of T'at'ul, Armenian ruler of Marash. *Croisades et Orient latin*, p. 53. For more on T'at'ul, see Chapter 3.

79. Albert of Aachen, "Historia," IV, 9, p. 395.

80. Albert of Aachen, "Historia," V, 14, p. 441.

81. Albert of Aachen, "Historia," V, 16, p. 442.

82. Albert of Aachen, "Historia," V, 17, p. 443. For punishment, see Nicole Gonthier, *Le châtiment du crime au moyen âge*, p. 145.

83. Albert of Aachen, "Historia," V, 17, p. 443. It is striking that this story comes from Albert of Aachen, but is not mentioned in Matthew of Edessa, who frequently accused the Franks of greed and was fascinated by stories of betrayal.

84. W. L. Warren, however, argues that the Norman conquest of Ireland was followed by a period of coexistence, before a "colonial" mentality began to dominate. "Church and State in Angevin Ireland," *Peritia* 12 (1999): 276–91.

Chapter 3. Images of Authority in Edessa

1. For the most recent argument about Daibert's relationship with Godfrey and Baldwin, see Alan Murray, *The Crusader Kingdom of Jerusalem: A Dynastic History, 1099–1125*. The establishment of Baldwin as king in Jerusalem is discussed further in Chapter 4.

2. As far as the sources allow a reconstruction of his actions, he continued with the rest of the crusader army to Jerusalem after the capture of Antioch. He joined Tancred in capturing Bethlehem (Fulcher, *Historia*, p. 278; Ryan, *History*, p. 115), and was wounded during the siege of the Holy City (Albert, "Historia," VI, 4, p. 468). He then returned north and took service with Bohemund in Antioch (Albert, "Historia," VII, 21, p. 527; Matt'eos Urhayets'i, *Zhamanakagrut'iwn*, p. 274; Matthew of Edessa, *Chronicle*, p. 177; Radulfus Cadomensis [Ralph of Caen], "Gesta Tancredi in expeditione Hierosolymitana," *Receuil des historiens des croisades: historiens occidentaux*, 3: 706).

3. Gérard Dédéyan, "L'argent et le pouvoir chez chefs arméniens de l'Euphratèse à l'époque de la première croisade" in *EYΨYXIA: mélanges offerts à Hélène Ahrweiler*, pp. 195–208.

4. Michael the Great reports that Hromgla was controlled by Kourtig, whom he describes as a governor for Kogh Vasil. Michel le Syrien, *Chronique*, vol. IV, pp. 595–96; trans. vol. III, p. 199.

5. Fulcher, *Historia*, p. 211; Ryan, *History*, p. 90.

6. The few studies of Edessa from an institutional perspective have presented Baldwin as replacing unruly and independent local lordship with a feudal system im-

ported wholesale from Europe, even suggesting that feudal bonds were stronger in the Latin East than in western Europe because all land was necessarily feudal through conquest. Monique Amouroux-Mourad, *Le comté d'Edesse*, p. 120. In fact, we know little about the governance of Edessa at any level. Recent work in the kingdom of Jerusalem has shown that it took decades before the obligations of knights and lords began to approach anything systematized. One would expect that in Edessa, where there was less stability in inheritance and a shorter institutional lifespan, the expectation of lordly military service would been been quite loose. Given the lack of evidence, one may doubt whether the County of Edessa was feudal at all. Furthermore, recent work by Susan Reynolds has pointed out that the term "feudal" has been used to cover such a variety of practices that the term has lost usefulness. Susan Reynolds, *Fiefs and Vassals*; see also her article on Jerusalem, "Fiefs and Vassals in Twelfth-Century Jerusalem: A View from the West," *Crusades* 1 (2002): 29–48. What the sources show is merely the granting of towns, cities, and fortresses, and the consequent expectation (though not obligation) of military service, a form of administrative and military organization well known outside western Europe. See also Christopher MacEvitt, "Christian Authority in the Latin East: Edessa in Crusade History," in *The Medieval Crusade*, ed. Susan Ridyard, pp. 71–83.

7. Anonymous, *Chronicon*, p. 63; trans. A. Abouna, p. 46.

8. Melitene and Edessa had many political ties. The unfortunate T'oros ruled Melitene for a few years before moving to Edessa, and he married another daughter of Gabriel. Michel le Syrien, *Chronique*; vol. IV, p. 581; trans. vol. III, pp. 173–74. Gabriel was probably Melkite. Willelmus Tyrensis, *Chronicon*, ed. R. B. C. Huygens, Corpus Christianorum Continuatio Mediaevalis 63, 10: 24, pp. 482–83, trans. in William of Tyre, *A History of Deeds Done Beyond the Sea*, trans. Emily Atwater Babcock and A. C. Krey, pp. 450–51. Matthew of Edessa mentioned neither the marriage nor Gabriel's faith or ethnicity. Michael the Great also called Gabriel a Greek, but whether this referred to both religion and language or just religion is unclear. *Chronique*, vol. IV, p. 589; trans. vol. III, p. 188. Albert of Aachen and Ibn al-Athir simply labeled him an Armenian. Albert, "Historia," VII, 27, p. 524; Ibn al-Athir, "Extrait de la chronique intituleé Kamel-altevarykh," *Recueil des historiens des croisades: Historiens orientaux*, 1: 203. The anonymous chronicler labeled him a Chalcedonian. *Chronicon*, p. 49; trans. A. Abouna, p. 36. William of Tyre calls him an Armenian by birth (*natio, lingua, habitus*) and Greek by faith (*Chronicon*, 10: 23 (24), pp. 452–53).

9. Fulcher, *Historia*, pp. 343–46; Ryan, *History*, p. 135.

10. The anonymous chronicler called Gabriel "the cursed one" for his treatment of Jacobites, and Michael the Great reported with satisfaction that, when Gabriel died, his body was thrown to the dogs. *Chronicon*, p. 63, trans. A. Abouna, p. 47; Michel le Syrien, *Chronique*, vol. IV, p. 590, trans. vol. III, pp. 188–89.

11. Anonymous, *Chronicon*, p. 62; trans. A. Abouna, p. 45.

12. The only reference to this marriage in a primary source was Orderic Vitalis, who stated that Levon was the uncle of Bohemund II's wife. Bohemund's wife was Alice, daughter of Baldwin II and Morfia of Melitene. If this statement is correct, the only way Levon could be her uncle was through marriage to a sister of Baldwin or Morfia. Ordericus Vitalis, *The Ecclesiastical History of Orderic Vitalis*, ed. and trans. Marjorie

Chibnall, XI, 29, pp. 134–35. However, Orderic's distance from northern Syria does not make him the most reliable source.

13. Anonymous, *Chronicon*, p. 64; trans. A. Abouna, p. 47; Michael the Great wrongly believed that Melitene was captured by Gümüshtigin immediately following the capture of Bohemund in 1100. Baldwin would not have married Morfia if her father were not still alive. Albert of Aachen indicated that Melitene came under Baldwin I's control following Gümüshtigin's raid (Albert, "Historia," VII, 27, p. 525). The anonymous account presents a synthesis of the two versions; he records that Gümüshtigin returned to besiege Melitene a second time, and successfully captured the city and killed Gabriel. The chronicler did not give a precise date for Melitene's capture; he placed it in his narrative between the crusade of 1101 and the Turkish siege of Saruj later that year.

14. Joscelin married twice, once to the daughter of Constantine, and once to Marie, sister of Roger of Antioch. The only evidence for the first marriage comes from William of Tyre, who states that Joscelin II's mother was a sister of Levon the Armenian. Willelmus Tyrensis, *Chronicon*, 14: 3, vol. 63A, p. 635; Babcock and Krey, *History*, vol. II, pp. 52–53. Joscelin I's second marriage probably occurred some time after his inheritance of the County of Edessa in the spring of 1118 and before Roger's death on 28 June 1119. As Joscelin II was born in 1113, the Armenian marriage must have been the first. Anonymous, *Chronicon*, pp. 78–79; trans. A. Abouna, p. 58.

15. Fulcher, *Historia*, p. 748; Ryan, *History*, p. 271.

16. Sokman was the son of Artuk ibn Aksub, who had been the Seljuk governor of Jerusalem. The family lost power there following the Fatimid seizure of the city in 1098. Sokman had captured Saruj in 1096, and installed his nephew Balak ibn Bahram as governor. Baldwin I captured Saruj from him (Albert names him Balas) in 1098. The center of Artukid power lay in eastern Iraq, around Mardin and Hisn Kayfa (modern Hasankeyf) on the northern Tigris, north of Nisibis. See Claude Cahen, "Le Diyar Bakr au temps des premiers Urtukides," *Journal Asiatique* 227 (1935): 219–76.

17. Matt'eos Urhayets'i, *Zhamanakagrut'iwn*, pp. 274–75; Matthew of Edessa, *Chronicle*, p. 178; Albert, "Historia," III, 24, p. 357. He was previously known as Fulcher of Chartres. In addition to the historian Fulcher of Chartres, Albert confusingly records the existence of a third Fulcher or Fulbert of Chartres dying in the army of Peter the Hermit (Albert, "Historia," I, 21, p. 288).

18. Matt'eos Urhayets'i, *Zhamanakagrut'iwn*, p. 296, Matthew of Edessa, *Chronicle*, p. 178.

19. The text refers to the bishop as "papios," a word Matthew uses only for Latin bishops, never Armenian ones. The word is not often used to refer to bishops. *Nor barkirk haykazean lezui (The New Armenian Dictionary)*; Matt'eos Urhayets'i, *Zhamanakagrut'iwn*, p. 275; Matthew of Edessa, *Chronicle*, p. 178.

20. Matt'eos Urhayets'i, *Zhamanakagrut'iwn*, p. 275; Matthew of Edessa, *Chronicle*, p. 178.

21. Ibn al-Qalanisi, who was a member of a leading Damascene family and was twice *ra'is* of the city, recorded this attack on Saruj in his chronicle and confirmed the massacres that followed the Frankish capture of the town, saying "the Franks arrived at Saruj, seized the city and killed or reduced into slavery its population." *Damas de*

1075 à 1154, trans. Roger Le Tourneau, p. 45. For a brief discussion of al-Qalanisi's biography and work, see Claude Cahen, *La Syrie du Nord à l'époque des croisades et la principauté franque d'Antioche*, pp. 38–40.

22. Abou l'Feda, "Tiré des annals des Abou l'Feda," *Recueil des historiens des Croisades: historiens orientaux*, 1: 6.

23. Ibn Athir, *Chronicle*, pp. 207–8. The *Mirat az-Zeman*, unlike other Arabic texts, noted that Sokman first had attacked the city and captured it. [Sibt ibn al-Djawzi], "Extrait du Mirat ez-Zèman," *Recueil des historiens des croisades: Historiens orientaux*, 3: 523. Sibt ibn al-Djawzi, however, was writing in the thirteenth century, though he did use other earlier accounts. In addition, the version used in the *Recueil* depends on a continuation of the work from the fourteenth century. See Claude Cahen, "Ibn al-Djawzi, Shams a-Din abu l'-Muzaffar Yusuf b. Kizoghlu, known as Sibt," *Encyclopedia of Islam*, ed. P. Bearman, Th. Bianquis, C. E. Bosworth, E. Van Donzel, and W. P. Heinrichs, ccessed online 26 January 2007, http://www.brillonline.nl/subscriber/entry?entry=islam_SIM-3140, accessed 26 January 2007.

24. Anonymous, *Chronicon*, pp. 65–66; trans. A. Abouna, p. 48.

25. Anonymous, *Chronicon*, p. 66; trans. A. Abouna, p. 49. Despite the descriptions of the massacre of at least the Muslim population, Ibn al-Athir recorded that in 1108 there were still 300 poor Muslims in Saruj, led by a Muslim who converted to Christianity. He also noted that the community still had mosques in which to worship, which Baldwin II allowed his Muslim allies to repair. Ibn al-Athir, *Chronicle*, p. 139.

26. This is not to suggest that Basil's is a "true" account and Mattthew's is false; Basil's story of the resistance of the Muslim citizens after Sokman's defeat might be a way to justify the massacre that Matthew and the Arabic sources recalled. It is unlikely, however, that Basil would have suggested that the local Christian population survived if they had not, as the Christian population of the city was probably in large proportion Jacobite.

27. Nor was the incident at Saruj the only event when Matthew suggested that Baldwin inexplicably massacred local Christians following his archbishop's orders. Following the defeat of Baldwin II at the hands of Tancred and Richard of Salerno in 1108, the citizens of Edessa, again with the aid of the Latin archbishop, seized control of the city to prevent Richard from capturing it. Matthew reported that when Baldwin made his way to the city, he assumed that the citizens had united against him and "proceeded to wantonly pillage everything in sight and to put out the sight of many innocent people" (Matt'eos Urhayets'i, *Zhamanakagrut'iwn*, p. 309; Matthew of Edessa, *Chronicle*, p. 202). The actions of the citizens were intended to preserve the city for Baldwin, as the cooperation of the Frankish archbishop indicated. On another occasion, Matthew accused the Franks of expelling the entire population of Edessa because Baldwin feared they city would revolt against him (Matt'eos Urhayets'i, *Zhamanakagrut'iwn*, pp. 354–56; Matthew of Edessa, *Chronicle*, pp. 212–13). Three days later, the population was allowed to return. Unsurprisingly, no other source recorded this event.

28. Orderic Vitalis, *The Ecclesiastical History*, X, 20; vol. V: 325.

29. Jonathan Riley-Smith, *The First Crusaders, 1095–1131*, pp. 169–95.

30. The Byzantines gained control of Lattakia (Laodicea) on the Syrian coast following the First Crusade, then lost it to Tancred in 1103, regained it in 1104 after Muslim armies crushed the Franks at the battle of Harran, and again lost it to Tancred in 1108 for the final time. Byzantine attempts to conquer Cilicia follow a similar outline. Only in the 1130s did the Byzantines gain significant influence in the area.

31. Matt'eos Urhayets'i, *Zhamanakagrut'iwn*, p. 338; Matthew of Edessa, *Chronicle*, p. 220. It is then particularly surprising to read Matthew's appraisal of Baldwin's character: "this Baldwin was one of the more illustrious members of the Frankish nobility: a valiant man and a warrior, exemplary in conduct, an enemy of sin, and by nature humble and modest; however, these good qualities were offset by his ingenious avariciousness in seizing and accumulating the wealth of others, his insatiable love for money, and his deep lack of generosity; as for the rest, he was very orthodox in his faith, and his ethical conduct and basic character were quite solid"(Matt'eos Urhayets'i, *Zhamanakagrut'iwn*, pp. 340–41; Matthew of Edessa, *Chronicle*, pp. 221–22).

32. Matt'eos Urhayets'i, *Zhamanakagrut'iwn*, p. 339; Matthew of Edessa, Chronicle, p. 221.

33. For more on this aspect of Matthew, see MacEvitt, "The *Chronicle* of Matthew of Edessa: Apocalypse, the First Crusade and the Armenian Diaspora," *Dumbarton Oaks Papers* 61 (2007): 254–96.

34. Fulcher, *Historia*, pp. 205–6; Ryan, *History*, p. 89. Albert of Aachen claims that the Turkish garrison fled when the crusaders approached the city. "Historia," III, 27, p. 357.

35. Matt'eos Urhayets'i, *Zhamanakagrut'iwn*, p. 272; Matthew of Edessa, *Chronicle*, p. 176; George T. Beech, "The Crusader Lordship of Marash in Armenian Cilicia, 1104–1149," *Viator* 27 (1996): 35–52.

36. Matt'eos Urhayets'i, *Zhamanakagrut'iwn*, p. 272; Matthew of Edessa, *Chronicle*, p. 176.

37. Matt'eos Urhayets'i, *Zhamanakagrut'iwn*, p. 278; Matthew of Edessa, *Chronicle*, p. 195. Yet already in 1104 Ralph of Caen was describing Joscelin as ruler of the city (Asbridge, *Principality*, p. 162). But in 1111 Richard of Salerno was ruling the city as a "knight of Tancred" (Beech, "Lordship of Marash," pp. 35–52). J.-C. Cheynet has suggested that T'at'ul left the city in response to Tancred's defeat of the Byzantine army in Cilicia in 1104. J.-C. Cheynet, "Thathoul, Archonte des Archontes," *Revue des études byzantines* 48 (1990): 233–42.

38. The title derives from the Persian royal title *shahnshah*, "king of kings" (Matt'eos Urhayets'i, *Zhamanakagrut'iwn*, p. 272; Matthew of Edessa, *Chronicle*, p. 176). The title "prince of princes" is not, as Ara Dostourian suggests, that of the Byzantine commander of Cilicia. Matthew of Edessa, *Chronicle*, p. 333.

39. J.-C. Cheynet, "Thathoul," pp. 233–42.

40. Anna Komnene thought that Marash was reoccupied by the Byzantine general Butumides in 1103, but her chronological and geographical distance from the events in Syria leave her an unreliable source for this episode. Anne Comnène, *Alexiade*, ed. and trans. Bernard Leib, XI, ix, vol. III, p. 41. For a defense of the *Alexiad* as a source for the First Crusade, see Peter Frankopan, "Perception and Projection of Prejudice:

Anna Comnena, the *Alexiad* and the First Crusade" in *Gendering the Crusades,* ed. Susan B. Edgington and Sarah Lambert, pp. 59–76.

41. Rustam Shukurov, "Turkoman and Byzantine Self-Identity: Some Reflections on the Logic of Title-Making in Twelfth- and Thirteenth-Century Anatolia," in *Eastern Approaches to Byzantium,* ed. Antony Eastmond, pp. 259–76.

42. For more on the connections between Matthew of Edessa and Kogh Vasil, see MacEvitt, "Matthew of Edessa."

43. Albert of Aachen seems to have thought that Kogh Vasil was a vassal of Antioch: around 1110 he listed him among the lords who responded to a summons from Tancred, along with Bagrat. "Historia," XI, 40, pp. 682–83.

44. Michel le Syrien, *Chronique,* vol. IV, p. 589; trans. vol. III, p. 187.

45. Matt'eos Urhayets'i, *Zhamanakagrut'iwn,* p. 324; Matthew of Edessa, *Chronicle,* p. 212. The Kamsarakans disappeared in the eighth century; possibly they lingered on as minor nobles, conscious of their former dignity, and thus showed up in twelfth-century Syria, but this is unlikely. Perhaps Vasil's wife did in fact have some distant claim to Kamsarakan ancestry, or more likely, to Pahlavuni heritage.

46. The Pahlavuni claim to Kamsarakan ancestry was dubious as well. The Pahlavuni family emerged only in the tenth century, yet claimed descent from St. Gregory the Illuminator, founder of Christianity in Armenia. Their surname evoked the Arsacid monarchy, Pahlav being both an area in Iran and the name of the two branches of the Arsacid family. Moses Khorenats'i [of Chorene], a historian whose writings have been dated anywhere from the fifth to the eighth century, records that both St. Gregory and the Kamsarakans were descended from the Iranian Pahlavids. Moses Khorenats'i, *History of the Armenians,* trans. Robert W. Thomson, II, 27, p. 165.

47. Matt'eos Urhayets'i, *Zhamanakagrut'iwn,* p. 294; Matthew of Edessa, *Chronicle,* p. 192.

48. Due to the religious and political confusions of the post-Mantzikert period, there were for a time four *kat'olikoi.* By 1104 only two remained—Barsegh and his uncle Gregory II. Matt'eos Urhayets'i, *Zhamanakagrut'iwn,* pp. 298–99; Matthew of Edessa, *Chronicle,* pp. 195–96.

49. Matt'eos Urhayets'i, *Zhamanakagrut'iwn,* p. 324; Matthew of Edessa, *Chronicle,* pp. 211–12.

50. For more on religious relations between Frankish and local Christians in Edessa, see Chapter 4.

51. Matt'eos Urhayets'i, *Zhamanakagrut'iwn,* pp. 306–7; Matthew of Edessa, *Chronicle,* pp. 200–201. Other chronicles do not mention these Armenian victories, and Matthew is likely exaggerating to some extent. Matthew also does not mention the many Franks in Kogh Vasil's service, as does Ibn al-Athir, *Chronicle,* p. 167.

52. Ralph of Caen credited Bohemund's release to Baldwin I and Bernard, Latin patriarch of Antioch. Radulfus, "Gesta Tancredi," p. 709. According to Albert of Aachen, Bohemund negotiated his release from Gümüshtigin by promising an alliance against the Byzantines and Kilij Arslan of Iconium. His relatives and friends in Antioch, Edessa, and Sicily paid the ransom. Albert of Aachen, "Historia," IX, 35–36, pp. 610–13. Ibn al-Athir recorded that Bohemund was released on the condition that he release the daughter of Yaghi-Siyan, the Seljuk governor of Antioch from whom the cru-

saders captured the city in 1098. Ibn Al-Athir, *Chronicle*, p. 60. None of the chronicles included Tancred as someone interested in his uncle's release.

53. Baldwin's contribution to Bohemond's ransom does not contradict this possibility. Baldwin, like the Byzantine emperor Alexios I Komnenos, was more interested in getting rid of Tancred than in rescuing Bohemund.

54. It is possible that this adoption did not actually happen, but was a rhetorical device used by Matthew to demonstrate the close relationship between Bohemund and Vasil, but the political relationship it represented was real. It is not mentioned in any other source (Matt'eos Urhayets'i, *Zhamanakagrut'iwn*, p. 294; Matthew of Edessa, *Chronicle*, p. 192). It is worth noting that Vasil did not have any natural children, and his heir at his death was his stepson, Vasil Dgha.

55. Matthew of Edessa, on the other hand, appeared uncertain whom to support in this conflict. On the one hand, Matthew favored Tancred, calling him a pious man, but he detested his lieutenant, Richard of Salerno. Yet, as discussed above, Matthew also saw Kogh Vasil as the leader of all Armenians, who confusingly fought on the side of the despised Baldwin. Matthew reserved his condemnations for Baldwin and Joscelin, for they "did a wicked thing, something that was not pleasing in the eyes of God," to ally with a Muslim. Matt'eos Urhayets'i, *Zhamanakagrut'iwn*, pp. 307–8; Matthew of Edessa, *Chronicle*, p. 201.

56. Matt'eos Urhayets'i, *Zhamanakagrut'iwn*, p. 322; Matthew of Edessa, *Chronicle*, p. 211.

57. Roger's father was Richard of Salerno, who had been held captive with Bohemund in 1100–1103. Richard was Tancred's cousin and had married Tancred's sister.

58. Galterius Cancellarius [Walter the Chancellor], *Bella Antiochena*, ed. Heinreich Hagenmeyer, p. 105. This text is translated in *Walter the Chancellor's "The Antiochene Wars"*, trans. Thomas S. Asbridge and Susan B. Edgington, p. 156. William of Tyre also refers to Roger's wife as Baldwin II's sister (Willelmus Tyrensis, *Chronicon*, XII, 9, p. 556; Babcock and Krey, *History*, vol. I, p. 528). Her name, Cecilia, is given in a charter of 1126, whereby she donated land near Mamistra to St. Mary of Josaphat. She is named "domina Tarsi," where she held land granted to her as the princess dowager of Antioch. Reinhold Röhricht, ed., *Regesta Regni Hierosolymitani; Addimentum*, p. 9.

59. Matt'eos Urhayets'i, *Zhamanakagrut'iwn*, p. 368; Matthew of Edessa, *Chronicle*, pp. 219–20. Vasil Dgha and his heirs may have continued to flourish in Byzantium under the name of Kokkovasileis.

60. Anonymous, *Chronicon*, p. 88; trans. A. Abouna, p. 66; Michel le Syrien, *Chronique*, vol. IV, p. 601, trans. vol. III, p. 210. Matthew recorded Michael's reconquest of Gargar from the Turks in 1124/5, but not his surrender of the fortress two years earlier. Matt'eos Urhayets'i, *Zhamanakagrut'iwn*, p. 359; Matthew of Edessa, *Chronicle*, p. 233.

61. Michael the Great recorded a confusing sequence of events in Gargar. He suggests that Michael abandoned the town, then reclaimed it, gave it to Joscelin, changed his mind and tried to recover it from Basil, and died accidentally. The Franks prevented Michael from dispossessing Vasil, but then somehow expelled him themselves. Vasil then allied with Levon, his son-in-law, (also Joscelin's brother-in-law) and attacked the Franks. Michel le Syrien, *Chronique*, vol. IV, p. 620, trans. vol. III, p. 244.

See also the continuator of Matthew of Edessa's chronicle. Grigor Erits' [Gregory the Priest], "Sharunkut'iwn," in *Zhamanakagrut'iwn*, p. 396; trans. in Gregory the Priest, "Continuation," in *Armenia and the Crusade*, trans. Ara Edmond Dostourian, p. 258.

62. Michael the Great claimed that Michael received a site called Sopharos in compensation. *Chronique*, vol. IV, p. 620, trans. vol. III, p. 244. For a summary of Dülük, see Hansgerd Hellenkemper, *Burgen der Kreuzritterzeit in der Grafschaft Edessa und im Königreich Kleinarmenien*, pp. 47–50.

63. The relationship of the person named Mahi (usually translated Mahuis), whom Matthew named lord of Dülük in 1124/5, to Michael is unclear (Matt'eos Urhayets'i, *Zhamanakagrut'iwn*, p. 357; Matthew of Edessa, *Chronicle*, p. 232). Gregory the Priest mentioned a relative of Mahi named Simon who attempted to seize 'Aintab (close to Dülük) from Joscelin II. Grigor Erits', "Sharunkut'iwn," pp. 370–71; Gregory the Priest, "Continuation," p. 242.

64. Bernard Hamilton, *The Latin Church in the Crusader States*, p. 29.

65. J. L. LaMonte, "Lords of Le Puiset on the Crusades," *Speculum* 17 (1942): 100–118.

66. Matt'eos Urhayets'i, *Zhamanakagrut'iwn*, p. 338; Matthew of Edessa, *Chronicle*, p. 220.

67. For Kahta, see Hellenkemper, *Burgen der Kreuzritterzeit*, p. 84.

68. Matt'eos Urhayets'i, *Zhamanakagrut'iwn*, p. 236; Matthew of Edessa, *Chronicle*, p. 154.

69. Albert of Aachen, "Historia," IX, 41, p. 616.

70. See Asbridge, *Principality*, p. 56.

71. Kemal ad-Din, "Chronique d'Alep," p. 592.

72. Ralph of Caen, "Gesta Tancredi," p. 712.

73. George Beech, "A Norman-Italian Adventurer in the East: Richard of Salerno 1097–1112," in *Anglo-Norman Studies XV: Proceedings of the XV Battle Conference*, ed. Marjorie Chibnall, pp. 25–40.

74. Anonymous, *Chronicon*, p. 70; trans. A. Abouna, p. 52.

75. Matt'eos Urhayets'i, *Zhamanakagrut'iwn*, p. 309; Matthew of Edessa, *Chronicle*, p. 202.

76. Matt'eos Urhayets'i, *Zhamanakagrut'iwn*, p. 302; Matthew of Edessa, *Chronicle*, p. 197.

77. Anonymous, *Chronicon* p. 70, trans. A. Abouna, p. 52.

78. Usama ibn Munqidh, *An Arab-Syrian Gentleman and Warrior in the Period of the Crusades*, trans. Philip K. Hitti: Armenian knights, p. 133, on status of knights, pp. 93–94.

79. Matt'eos Urhayets'i, *Zhamanakagrut'iwn*, p. 314; Matthew of Edessa, *Chronicle*, p. 205.

80. For a discussion of the use of the True Cross in the Kingdom of Jerusalem, see Alan V. Murray, "'Mighty Against the Enemies of Christ:' The Relic of the True Cross in the Armies of the Kingdom of Jerusalem," in *The Crusades and Their Sources*, ed. John France and William G. Zajac, pp. 217–38.

81. John Porteous, "Crusader Coinage with Greek or Latin Inscriptions," in *A History of the Crusades*, ed. Kenneth M. Setton, vol. 5, *The Impact of the Crusades on Eu-*

rope, ed. Harry W. Hazard and Norman P. Zacour, p. 365. See also D. M. Metcalf, *Coinage of the Crusades and the Latin East*, pp. 31–39.

82. Albert of Aachen, "Historia," VI, 38, p. 488.

83. Fulcher, *Historia*, p. 542; Ryan, *History*, p. 198.

84. Mattʿeos Urhayetsʿi, *Zhamanakagrutʿiwn*, p. 315; Matthew of Edessa, *Chronicle*, p. 206.

85. Mattʿeos Urhayetsʿi, *Zhamanakagrutʿiwn*, p. 346; Matthew of Edessa, *Chronicle*, p. 225.

86. Willelmus Tyrensis, *Chronicon*, vol. 63A, 14:3, p. 634; Babcock and Krey, *History*, vol. II, pp. 52–53.

87. C. J. F. Dowsett, "A Twelfth-Century Armenian Inscription at Edessa," in *Iran and Islam*, ed. C. E. Bosworth, pp. 197–227; for definition of the term, see *Nor barkirk haykazean*, s.v. "terapahutuin."

88. Anonymous, *Chronicon*, 305; trans. A. Abouna, 229.

89. Mattʿeos Urhayetsʿi, *Zhamanakagrutʿiwn*, pp. 53–55; Matthew of Edessa, *Chronicle*, pp. 229–30. William of Tyre claims that it was fifty men. Willelmus Tyrensis, *Chronicon*, XII, 17–20, pp. 566–71; Babcock and Krey, *History*, vol. I, pp. 539–45.

90. William of Tyre suggested this was a possibility.

91. Beech, "Lordship of Marash," pp. 45–47.

92. Grigor Eritsʿ, "Sharunkutʿiwn," p. 372; Gregory the Priest, "Continuation," p. 243.

93. Grigor Eritsʿ, "Sharunkutʿiwn," p. 374; Gregory the Priest, "Continuation," p. 245.

94. Grigor Eritsʿ, "Sharunkutʿiwn," p. 379; Gregory the Priest, "Continuation," p. 247.

95. Grigor Eritsʿ, "Sharunkutʿiwn," p. 380; Gregory the Priest, "Continuation," p. 248.

96. Grigor Eritsʿ, "Sharunkutʿiwn," p. 390; Gregory the Priest, "Continuation," p. 254.

97. Grigor Eritsʿ, "Sharunkutʿiwn," p. 391; Gregory the Priest, "Continuation," p. 255.

98. Grigor Eritsʿ, "Sharunkutʿiwn," p. 392; Gregory the Priest, "Continuation," p. 255.

99. Grigor Eritsʿ, "Sharunkutʿiwn," p. 392; Gregory the Priest, "Continuation," p. 255.

100. W. Neumann, "Drei mittelalter Pilgerschriften: II. Innominatus VI (Pseudo-Bela) *Österreichische Vierteljahresschrift für Katholische Theologie* 11 (1872): 397–438; trans. Audrey Stewart, *Anonymous Pilgrims I–VIII*, p. 51.

Chapter 4. Rough Tolerance and Ecclesiastical Ignorance

1. Albert of Aachen, "Historia," IV, 1, p. 433.

2. Fulcher, *Historia*, p. 264; Ryan, *History*, p. 111.

3. For a further discussion of Jacques de Vitry, see below.

4. Perhaps they were a Paulician group. Robertus Monachus, "Historia

Iherosolimitiana," *Recueil des historiens des croisades: historiens occidentaux*, 3: ch. 8, p. 745; Petrus Tudebodus, *Historia de Hierosolymitano itinere*, ed. John Hugh Hill and Laurita L. Hill, p. 41; Guitbertus Abbatis Novigenti, *Dei Gesta per Francos*, ed. R. B. C. Huygens, Corpus Christianorum Continuatio Mediaevalis 127A, 3: 92–93, p. 139; Anonymous, *Gesta Francorum et aliorum Hierosolimitanorum*, ed. and trans. Rosalind Hill, p. 8.

5. Anonymous, *Gesta Francorum*, pp. 20, 45, 49, 83.

6. Willelmus Tyrensis, *Chronicon*, ed. R. B. C. Huygens, Corpus Christianorum Continuatio Mediavalis 63, 22:11 (10), p. 1021.

7. Robert Bartlett, *The Making of Europe*, pp. 197–220.

8. Not included in this discussion is the large body of thirteenth-century legal texts from the Frankish Levant. For a discussion of these, see Chapter 5.

9. For a discussion of what this term may convey, see Joseph Nasrallah, "Syriens et Suriens," in *Symposium Syriacum 1972*, Orientalia Christiana Analecta 197, pp. 487–503; Johannes Pahlitzsch, *Graeci und Suriani im Palästina der Kreuzfahrerzeit*, pp. 181–88.

10. Amnon Linder, "Christian Communities in Jersusalem," in *The History of Jerusalem: The Early Muslim Period 638–1099*, ed. Joshua Prawer and Haggai Ben-Shammai, pp. 146–47; Sidney Griffith, "The Church of Jerusalem and the 'Melkites': The Making of an 'Arab Orthodox' Christian Identity in the World of Islam (750–1050 CE)," in *Christians and Christianity in the Holy Land: From the Origins to the Latin Kingdoms*, ed. Ora Limor and Guy G. Stroumsa, pp. 175–204.

11. For Israelites as Jacobites, Baldric of Dol, "Historia Jerosalimitana," *Recueil des historiens des croisades: Historiens occidentaux*, 4: 15.

12. *Peregrinationes Tres: Saewulf, John of Würzburg, Theodericus*, ed. R. B. C. Huygens, Corpus Christianorum Continuatio Mediaevalis 139, pp. 111, 136, 138.

13. *Peregrinationes Tres*, p. 152.

14. Benjamin Z. Kedar, "The *Tractatus de locis et statu terre ierosolimitane*," in *The Crusades and Their Sources*, ed. John France and William G. Zajac, pp. 111–31.

15. Jacques de Vitry, "Historia Hierosolimitana," in *Gesta Dei per Francos*, ed. Jacques Bongars, pp. 1089–95.

16. For further discussion of ways the thirteenth century was different from the twelfth, see Chapter 5.

17. Willelmus Tyrensis, *Chronicon*, vol. 63a, 20: 29, pp. 953–54; Babcock and Krey, *History*, II, p. 390. For further bibliography on Assassins, see Marshall Hodgson *The Order of the Assassins*.

18. Willelmus Tyrensis, *Chronicon*, vol. 63a, 22: 9 (8), pp. 1018–19.

19. Rainer Christoph Schwinges argues that William of Tyre displays "informal tolerance," acknowledging that Muslims too fought just wars against Christians. "William of Tyre, the Muslim Enemy, and the Problem of Tolerance," in *Tolerance and Intolerance: Social Conflict in the Age of the Crusades*, ed. Michael Gervers and James M. Powell, pp. 124–32.

20. Bernard Hamilton's masterful *The Latin Church in the Crusader States* has examined religious relationships from the political and ecclesiastical perspective of the

Latin clergy; my focus is instead on the indigenous clergy and monks of the Levant and their relationship to resident Christians—both Frankish and local.

21. Anonymous, *Chronicon*, p. 296; trans. A. Abouna, p. 222.

22. For the election of Abu Ghalib's brother Sa'id to the episcopate of Melitene and his subsequent murder by Gabriel, see Michel le Syrien, *Chronique*, vol. IV, pp. 585–87; trans. vol. III, pp. 185–86. For Michael's praise of the two brothers, see *Chronique*, vol. IV, p. 589; trans. vol. III, p. 190.

23. Anonymous, *Chronicon*, p. 300; trans. A. Abouna, p. 224.

24. Dorothea Weltecke has suggested that he can be identified with the translator who aided Stephen of Pisa in Antioch. "On the Syriac Orthodox in the Principality of Antioch During the Crusader Period," in *East and West in the Medieval Eastern Mediterranean*, ed. K. Ciggaar and M. Metcalf, pp. 95–124.

25. Michel le Syrien, *Chronique*, vol. IV, p. 600; trans. vol. III, p. 210.

26. Michel le Syrien, *Chronique*, vol. IV, p. 601; trans. vol. III, p. 212.

27. Michel le Syrien, *Chronique*, vol. IV, p. 587; trans. vol. III, p. 186. Michael names the caliph as Abu Jafar, likely a reference to al-Mustarshid (1118–1135), but Michael probably meant his predecessor al-Mustazhir (1094–1118).

28. For conflict as a source of social structure, see Patrick Geary, "Living with Conflicts in Stateless France: A Typology of Conflict Management Mechanisms, 1050–1200," in Geary, *Living with the Dead in the Middle Ages*, pp. 125–60.

29. Anonymous, *Chronicon*, p. 296; trans. A. Abouna, p. 222.

30. Michel le Syrien, *Chronique*, vol. IV, p. 601; trans. vol. III, p. 212.

31. According to both Michael the Great and the anonymous chronicler, the patriarch feuded with a prominent local Jacobite family, resulting in the excommunication of a deacon named Isaac, a member of the family. Isaac's family appealed to the ruler of Amida, who urged the patriarch to absolve the deacon. Isaac then craftily suggested that the governor should keep the aged patriarch in Amida, so that after his death he could seize his treasury. Michel le Syrien, *Chronique*, vol. IV, pp. 602, 610–11; trans. vol. III, pp. 213, 228; Anonymous, *Chronicon*, pp. 225–26; trans. A. Abouna, p. 301.

32. Anonymous, *Chronicon*, p. 301; trans. A. Abouna, p. 226.

33. Michel le Syrien, *Chronique*, vol. IV, pp. 610–11; trans. vol. III, p. 228; Anonymous, *Chronicon*, p. 302; trans. A. Abouna, p. 226.

34. Anonymous, *Chronicon*, pp. 298–300; trans. A. Abouna, pp. 223–24; Michel le Syrien, *Chronique*, vol. IV, pp. 610–611; trans. vol. III, p. 228. Nor was Joscelin's raid on Barsauma the last the monastery endured. Joscelin's son, Joscelin II, also raided the monastery in 1148, this time seizing a considerable quantity of gold and silver, including vessels for liturgical service. Joscelin had already lost Edessa to Nur al-Din, and was struggling to hold on to the western portion of his county, centered on Tell Bashir. The raid, however, was a sign of his desperation, not of a changed attitude toward Jacobites. Michel le Syrien, *Chronique*, vol. IV, pp. 642–43; trans. vol. III, pp. 283–85.

35. Anonymous, *Chronicon*, p. 303; trans. A. Abouna, p. 227; Michel le Syrien, *Chronique*, vol. IV, pp. 611–12; trans. vol. III, pp. 231–32. Michael also records that Joscelin prevailed on the new patriarch and assembled bishops to reinstate the bishop of Segestan, who had also been excommunicated. This bishop, however, seemed unwilling to remain in one place, and after having been transferred to Arsamosata, even-

tually traveled to Jerusalem and became a Templar. Segestan was the easternmost bishopric of the Jacobite church in the Middle Ages, distant from the centers of power. Consequently, it was not a popular assignment for ambitious clerics.

36. K'esun's bishop, Basil bar Shumana, grew disgusted with ecclesiastical politics and had conveniently withdrawn to a monastery. Michel le Syrien, *Chronique*, vol. IV, p. 617; trans. vol. III, p. 242.

37. Michel le Syrien, *Chronique*, vol. IV, p. 765; trans. vol. III, p. 477.

38. Michel le Syrien, *Chronique*, vol. IV, pp. 628–29; trans. vol. III, pp. 259–60.

39. Bernard Hamilton, *The Latin Church*, pp. 161–62.

40. Joshua Prawer, "Social Classes in the Crusader States: The 'Minorities,'" in *A History of the Crusades*, ed. Kenneth M. Setton, vol. 5, *The Impact of the Crusades on the Near East*, ed. Norman P. Zacour and Harry W. Hazard, p. 73.

41. Hugh Kennedy, "The Melkite Church from the Islamic Conquest to the Crusades: Continuity and Adaptation in the Byzantine Legacy," in *The 17th International Byzantine Congress*, pp. 325–343; also see Amnon Linder, "Christian Communities in Jersusalem," pp. 121–62.

42. Paul Riant, "Inventaire critique des lettres historiques de croisades-Appendice," *Archive de l'Orient latin* 1 (1881): 221. For a critical analysis of the letters and Simeon's position, see Johannes Pahlitzsch, "Symeon II. und die Errichtung der Lateinischen Kirche von Jerusalem durch die Kreuzfahrer," in *Militia Sancti Sepulcri: Idea e istituzioni*, ed. Kaspar Elm and Cosimo Damiano Fonseca, pp. 342–60.

43. Albert of Aachen, "Historia," VI, 29, p. 489.

44. Richard Barry Rose, "Pluralism in a Medieval Colonial Society: The Frankish Impact on the Melkite Community During the First Crusader Kingdom of Jerusalem, 1099–1187," App. 2. Anastasios wrote a treatise on fasting, "De jejunio gloriosissimae Deiparae," *Patrologia Graecae* 127, cols. 519–32.

45. "Disceptatio cum Achmed Saraceno," *Patrologia Graecae* 120, cols. 821–32. Another bishop of Gaza, Sulaiman al-Gazzi, was also a poet and a theologian. He can only be dated to sometime before 1116. Joseph Nasrallah, "Sulaïman al-Gazzi, évêque melchite de Gaza (XIe siècle)," *Oriens Christianus* 62 (1978): 144–57.

46. J. B. Segal, *Edessa, the "Blessed City"*, p. 238.

47. Albert of Aachen, "Historia," V, 1, p. 433.

48. Hamilton, *Latin Church*, p. 17. William of Tyre calls him "a true confessor of Christ." Willelmus Tyrensis, *Chronicon*, VI, 23, pp. 339–40, trans. in Babcock and Krey, *History*, 1: 297. It is possible that other Byzantine cities, such as Lattakia, also had Melkite bishops, although little record of them survives. For Lattakia, see Benjamin Z. Kedar, "Gerard of Nazareth, a Neglected Twelfth-Century Writer in the Latin East," *Dumbarton Oaks Papers* 37 (1983): 55–77.

49. Hamilton, *Latin Church*, pp. 179–80.

50. Dmitris Tsougarakis, *The Life of Leontios*; Rose, *Pluralism*, pp. 342–47.

51. Kirsopp Lake and Silva Lake, eds., *Dated Greek Minuscule Manuscripts to the Year 1200*, vol. 1, *Manuscripts at Jerusalem, Patmos and Athens*, Monumenta Palaeographica Vetera 1st ser., p. 12.

52. Without greater knowledge of Arabic Christian literature, I can little argue against Paul Khoury's dating of Paul's episcopacy. I do think it is at least a possibility

that Paul held office before the twelfth century. *Paul d'Antioche, évêque melkite de Sidon (XIIe s.)*, ed. and trans. Paul Khoury. Bernard Hamilton accepts the twelfth-century date (*Latin Church*, p. 183), but Claude Cahen expresses some doubts, *Orient et Occident au temps des croisades*, p. 214.

53. "Itinerarium regis Ricardi," in *Itinerarium Peregrinorum et Gesta Regis Ricardi*, vol. I, ed. William Stubbs, Rerum Britannicarum Medii Aevi Scriptores 38, V, 52, p. 376.

54. J. Delaville le Roulx, ed., *Cartulaire général de l'Ordre des Hospitaliers de S. Jean de Jérusalem*, vol. I, #443, pp. 306–8. This charter has been reproduced by Delaville le Roulx, "Trois chartres du XIIe siècle concernant l'ordre de St. Jean de Jerusalem," *Archives de l'Orient latin* 1(1881): 409–15.

55. Meron Benvenisti, *The Crusaders in the Holy Land*, pp. 189–94.

56. Denys Pringle, *The Churches of the Crusader Kingdom*, vol. 1, s.v. "Gaza," pp. 208–20. The church is a three-aisled basilica with four bays, measuring at least 32 by 20m.

57. The church measures 22.9m x 8.25m.

58. Martin A. Meyer, *History of the City of Gaza*, gives some sense of the city before 1948.

59. The see of Ascalon was transferred to Bethlehem in 1108. After the capture of Ascalon in 1153, Patriarch Fulcher appointed a bishop for Ascalon, but the bishop of Bethlehem successfully protested to the pope. Hans Eberhard Mayer, *Bistümer, Klöster und Stifte in Königreich Jerusalem*, Schriften der Monumenta Germaniae Historica 26, pp. 44–80.

60. For another example of conflict between different ecclesiastical institutions over tithes, see Ronnie Ellenblum, *Frankish Rural Settlement with the Latin Kingdom of Jerusalem*, pp. 106–12. The opportunity for such conflict is present whenever one institution owns property within the sphere of authority of another.

61. Delaville, "Trois chartres," 414–15. Claude Cahen has pointed to a similar example from the thirteenth century, where Latin priests leased a ruined church to a local Greek priest. "Un document concernant les melkites et les latins d'Antioche au temps des croisades," *Revue des études byzantines* 29 (1971): 285–92; reprinted in *Turcobyzantina et Oriens Christianus*.

62. Geneviève Bresc-Bautier, *Le Cartulaire du chapitre du Saint-Sépulcre de Jérusalem*, #142, pp. 275–78.

63. Pringle, *Churches*, s.v. "Bait Jibrin," pp. 95–101.

64. Bresc-Bautier, *Cartulaire*, #159, pp. 310–11.

65. Matt'eos Urhayets'i, *Zhamanakagrut'iwn*, pp. 275–76; Matthew of Edessa, *Chronicle*, pp. 178–79; Michel le Syrien, *Chronique*, vol. IV, p. 588; trans. vol. III, p. 190. The common historiographic gloss has been that this catastrophe was the result of the crusader expulsion from the Holy Sepulcher of local Christian clergy, who were the custodians of the secrets of the Holy Fire. Hamilton, *Latin Church*, p. 170. Scholars have since realized that the Melkite clergy were never in fact expelled, but the events of 1101 have not been reinterpreted. Prawer, "Social Classes in the Crusader States," p. 73. The Holy Fire was first recorded in 867 by the pilgrim Bernard the Wise (Bernardus Monachus), "Itinerarium Bernardi, monachi franci," in *Descriptiones Ter-*

rae Sanctae, ed. Titus Tobler, pp. 92–93. For more on the Holy Fire, see Otto Meinardus, "The Ceremony of the Holy Fire in the Middle Ages and To-Day," *Bulletin de la société d'archeologie copte* 16 (1961–62): 243–52; Marius Canard, "La destruction de l'église de la Résurrection par le Calife Hakim et l'histoire de la descente du feu sacré," *Byzantion* 35 (1965): 16–43.

66. Hamilton, *Latin Church*, pp. 53–56.

67. Fulcher, *Historia*, pp. 352–53; Ryan, *History*, p. 137.

68. Albert of Aachen, "Historia," VII, 48, p. 539. For Daibert's chronology, see Michael Matzke, *Daibert von Pisa: Zwischen, Pisa, Papst und erstem Kreuzzug*, pp. 207–20.

69. Albert of Aachen, "Historia," VII, 49, p. 540.

70. A breviary dated to sometime before 1184, discovered in the canonry of the Holy Sepulcher in Barletta, gives the liturgy for Holy Saturday and suggests that it should take place in the sixth hour. Charles Kohler, "Un rituel et un breviaire du Saint-Sépulcre de Jérusalem (XIIe–XIIIe siècle)," *Revue de l'Orient latin* 8 (1900/1901): 420–22.

71. Fulcher, *Historia*, pp. 831–84; translated in Daniel the Abbot, "The Pilgrimage of the Russian Abbot Daniel," trans. C. W. Wilson, *The Library of the Pilgrims' Palestine Text Society* 4, app. V, pp. 106–8.

72. The failure led some local Christians to question the motives of Latin ecclesiastics, but did not lead anyone to suggest that the Frankish presence in the Holy Land was contrary to divine will.

73. Matt'eos Urhayets'i, *Zhamanakagrut'iwn*, p. 276; Matthew of Edessa, *Chronicle*, p. 179.

74. Fulcher of Chartres, *Historia*, p. 368; Ryan, *History*, p. 143.

75. Albert of Aachen, "Historia," IX, 17, p. 600; trans. Hamilton, *Latin Church*, p. 56.

76. Comte Melchior de Vogüé, *Les Églises de la Terre Sainte*, p. 88.

77. Benjamin Z. Kedar, "Latins and Oriental Christians in the Frankish Levant," in *Sharing the Sacred: Religious Contacts and Conflicts in the Holy Land: First–Fifteenth Centuries CE*, ed. Arieh Kofsky and Guy G. Stroumsa, p. 219.

78. Fulcher, *Historia*, p. 665; Ryan, *History*, p. 242.

79. Icelandic pilgrims recorded by the middle of the twelfth century that services were offered every other day in "Hebrew," which is probably Greek but perhaps Syriac or Arabic. Benjamin Z. Kedar and Chr. Westergård-Nielsen, "Icelanders in the Crusader Kingdom of Jerusalem: A Twelfth-Century Account," *Mediaeval Scandinavia* 11 (1978–79): 193–211.

80. *Peregrinationes Tres*, p. 152. Once again we see the separation of Melkites into Greeks and Syrians.

81. *Peregrinationes Tres*, p. 153.

82. *Peregrinationes Tres*, p. 157.

83. Daniel the Abbot, "The Life and Journey of Daniel, Abbot of the Russian Land," in *Jerusalem Pilgrimage, 1099–1185*, ed. John Wilkinson, Joyce Hill, and W. F. Ryan, pp. 120–71.

84. Daniel the Abbot, "Journey," p. 166.

85. Higher in this context can suggest higher status, or lower, since it also places the lamp farther from the place where Jesus' body lay.

86. Daniel the Abbot, "Journey," pp. 168–69.

87. Some have suggested that he is identical with Meletios, archbishop of Gaza and Gibelin.

88. *Gastina* is a confusing Latin term, found largely in the Levant, which seems to correspond with the Arabic term "khirbet," and designates land that perhaps once was a village but has reverted to agricultural land.

89. Bresc-Bautier, *Le Cartulaire du Saint-Sépulcre*, #133, pp. 259–60; this sale is confirmed by Pope Alexander III in 1168. #146, p. 285. For more on this transaction, see Hans Eberhard Mayer, *Bistümer, Klöster und Stifte*, pp. 406–11.

90. We do not know enough about the Armenian community in Jerusalem to understand how Melisende might have supported that community. Some have suggested that she played a major role in the construction of the Armenian church of St. James in the city. Nurith Kenaan-Kedar, "Armenian Architecture in Twelfth-Century Crusader Jerusalem," *Assaph Studies in Art History* 3 (1998): 77–91.

91. Johannes Pahlitzsch, "St. Maria Magdalena, St. Thomas und St. Markus: Tradition und Geschichte dreier syrisch-orthodoxer Kirchen in Jerusalem," *Oriens Christianus* 81 (1997): 82–106.

92. Abbé Martin, "Les premiers croisés et les syriens jacobites de Jérusalem," *Journal Asiatique* 8 (1889): 43; trans. in Andrew Palmer, "The History of the Syrian Orthodox in Jerusalem, Part Two Queen Melisende and the Jacobite Estates," *Oriens Christianus* 76 (1992): 78. The scribe notes the joy of the Melkites when the Jacobites lost their property, as the Melkites had already lost theirs.

93. Martin, "Les premiers croisés," p. 46; trans. Palmer, "The History of the Syrian Orthodox," p. 79. Another property dispute arose between the Jacobites and the canons of the Holy Sepulcher over the villages of Ramatha and Hadessa, which was resolved in 1161, though we do not know what the resolution was. Bresc-Bautier, *Le Cartulaire du Saint-Sépulcre*, #131, p. 258. The invocation of Melisende's mother, Morfia, is ironic, given how much Jacobite sources detested her father, Gabriel of Melitene, and rejoiced at his death. See Chapter 2.

94. Andrew Palmer suggests that their claim to this village was dubious. Palmer, "History of the Syrian Orthodox," p. 87.

95. Abbé Martin, "Les premiers croisés," p. 41.

96. Bartlett, *The Making of Europe*, p. 96.

97. Bianca Kühnel has suggested that "crusader" art can be seen as a deliberate integration of the "local past" with the present. See "'Crusader Art'—An Art Historical Term," in *Crusader Art of the Twelfth Century: A Geographical, an Historical, or an Art Historical Notion?*, pp. 155–68.

98. Pringle, *Churches*, s.v. "Ascalon," vol. 1, pp. 63–64.

99. Yahya ibn-Sa'id, "Histoire," ed. and trans. J Kratchkovsky and A. Vasiliev, *Patrologia Orientalis* 17, fasc. 5, [21], p. 719.

100. Bresc-Bautier, *Cartulaire*, #49, pp. 132–34.

101. Joscelin III had usufruct of the entire inheritance, but by the thirteenth century, control of the property had reverted to all the heirs. Rafael Frankel, "Topographical Notes on the Territory of Acre in the Crusader Period," *Israel Exploration Journal* 38 (1988): 249–72; Hans Eberhard Mayer, "Die Seigneurie de Joscelin und der Deutsche Orden," in *Die Geistlichen Ritterorden Europas*, ed. Josef Fleckenstein and

Manfred Hellmann, Vorträge und Forschungen 26, pp. 171–216. For the site's later history, see Aharon Layish, "'Waqfs' and Sufi Monasteries in the Ottoman Policy of Colonization: Sultan Selim I's 'waqf' of 1516 in Favour of Dayr al-Asad," *Bulletin of the School of Oriental and African Studies* 1(1987): 61–89.

102. Pringle, *Churches*, s.v. "al-Ba'ina, Dair al-Asad," vol. 1, pp. 80–93.

103. Ernest Strehlke, ed., *Tabulae Ordinis Theutonici*, #12, p. 12. The name "St. George" is a Latin addition to the older name of al-Ba'ina. This style of nomenclature—adding a saint's name to a village—was common in Frankish Palestine. For example, in Latin documents the village of 'Abud is named Casale Sancti Mariae after the local church dedicated to the Virgin. Another example is the Castrum Sancti Helie, named for a Byzantine church dedicated to Elijah. Ellenblum, *Frankish Settlement*, p. 130.

104. Henri Michelant and Gaston Raynaud, eds., "Les sains pèlerinages," in *Itinéraires à Jérusalem et descriptions de la Terre Sainte*, p. 104. Another thirteenth-century text, however, says that they are "black monks," suggesting that they were Benedictines. Certain architectural characteristics indicate that it was designed to serve a Melkite community, particularly the existence of single cells in which the monks would live, rather than a communal living area such as the Benedictines favored.

105. Denys Pringle has pointed out that while this eremitic arrangement might indicate that the house belonged to the Carthusians, there is no evidence they ever had a house in the Holy Land. Another option would be the semi-eremitic Carmelites, but they were not established as an order until the thirteenth century. Pringle, *Churches*, s.v. "al-Ba'ina, Dair al-Asad," vol. 1, pp. 80–93.

106. Ellenblum, *Frankish Rural Settlement*, p. 169.

107. Ellenblum, *Frankish Rural Settlement*.

108. Charles Kohler, "Chartes de l'abbaye de Notre-Dame de la vallée de Josaphat," *Revue de l'Orient latin* 7 (1900): 113–15.

109. Hamilton, *Latin Church*, p. 72; Hans Eberhard Mayer, *Bistümer, Klöster und Stifte*, p. 81.

110. Henri-François Delaborde, *Chartes de Terre Sainte provenant de l'abbaye de Notre-Dame de Josaphat*, # 50, pp. 87–88.

111. Pringle, *Churches*, s.v. "Church of St. George," vol. 2, pp. 356–57.

112. Yizhar Hirschfeld, "The Anchor Church at the Summit of Mt. Berenice, Tiberias," *Biblical Archaeologist* 57 (1994): 122–33.

113. Robert Taft, *The Byzantine Rite*, p. 64, n. 31.

114. Ellenblum, *Frankish Rural Settlement*, pp. 125–28. Ellenblum points out that the same situation occurred at Mi'ilya as well.

115. Pringle, *Churches*, s.v. "at-Taiyiba," vol. 2, pp. 340–44.

116. Fra Niccolò da Poggibonsi, *Libro d'Oltramare*, p. 81.

117. Sylvester Saller, O.F.M., *Excavations at Bethany (1949–1952)*; Pringle, *Churches*, s.v. "Bethany," vol. 1, pp. 122–37.

118. Pringle, *Churches*, s.v. "Nazareth," vol. 2, pp. 116–20, 139.

119. Pringle, *Churches*, s.v. "Mount Tabor," vol. 2, pp. 63–66, 70–76.

120. Joannis Phocae, "Descriptio terrae sanctae," *Patrologia Graecae* 133, cols. 960–61.

121. Pringle, *Churches*, s.v. "Lydda," vol. 2, pp. 9–27.

122. Pringle, *Churches*, s.v. "Mount Tabor," vol. 2, pp. 63–66, 70–76.

123. Benjamin Z. Kedar, "Convergences of Oriental Christian, Muslim and Frankish Worshippers: The Case of Saydnaya," in *De Sion exibit lex et verbum domini de Hierusalem: Essays on Medieval Law, Liturgy and Literature in Honour of Amnon Linder*, ed. Yitzak Hen, pp. 59–69.

124. Willibaldus, "Vita seu potius hodoeporicon sancti Willibaldi," in *Descriptiones Terrae Sanctae ex seculo VIII. IX. XII. et XV.*, ed. Titus Tobler, pp. 34–45.

125. Saewulf did not visit the monastery, but knew of the priory of St. Sabas within the walls of Jerusalem, which belonged to the monastery. *Peregrinationes Tres*, p. 71.

126. Charles Jean Melchior de Vogüé, *Les Églises*, appendix, "De situ urbis Jerusalem," p. 429. See P. C. Boeren, *Rorgo Fretellus de Nazareth et sa description de la Terre Sainte: histoire et édition du texte*. For more on Fretellus and the difficulties of the text, see Rudolf Hiestand, "Un centre intellectuel en Syrie du Nord? notes sur la personnalité d'Aimery d'Antioche, Albert de Tarse et *Rorgo Fretellus*," *Moyen Age* 100 (1994): 7–36.

127. Cyril of Scythopolis, *Kyrillos von Skythopolis*, ed. Eduard Schwartz, pp. 136–37; trans. in Cyril of Scythopolis, *Lives of the Monks of Palestine*, trans. R. M. Price, pp. 146–47.

128. Kohler, "Un rituel et un breviaire," p. 431.

129. It is also possible that the author consulted a translation of Cyril in Palestine or in Europe. I have been able to find two unpublished Latin manuscripts including versions of the *Vita Sabae* that date from before the thirteenth century. At this point, however, I do not know if they contain the same miracles as those recorded in the pilgrimage account. One account is an eleventh-century manuscript in a Beneventuan hand in the manuscript library in Naples. Albert Poncelet, "Catalogus Codicum Hagiographicorum Latinorum Bibliothecarum Neapolitarum," *Analecta Bollandiana* 30 (1911): 158. The second manuscript is twelfth century, in the Vatican Library. Albert Poncelet, *Catalogus Codicum Hagiographicorum Latinorum Bibliothecae Vaticanae*, vol. 11, *Subsidia Hagiographica*, p. 441.

130. As an example, see Erich Poppe and Bianca Ross, eds., *The Legend of Mary of Egypt in Medieval Insular Hagiography*.

131. Maria Kouli, trans., "Life of St. Mary of Egypt," in *Holy Women of Byzantium*, ed. Alice-Mary Talbot, pp. 65–93.

132. H. Donner, "Die Palästinabeschreibung des Epiphanius Monachus Hagiopolita," *Deutscher Verein zur Erforschung Palästinas* 87 (1971): 68; trans. in Epiphanius the Monk, "The Holy City and the Holy Places," in *Jerusalem Pilgrims Before the Crusades*, ed. John Willkinson, p. 117.

133. P. Geyer, "Antonini Placentini Itinerarium," *Itineraria et Alia Geographica*, Corpus Christianorum, Series Latina 175, p. 139.

134. *Peregrinationes Tres*, p. 66.

135. "Anonymous Pilgrim II"; "Anonymous Pilgrim V," in *Anonymous Pilgrims I–VIII*, ed. A. Stewart, Palestine Pilgrims' Text Society 6, pp. 12, 23.

136. Steven Runciman, *History of the Crusades*, 3: 474.

137. Michel le Syrien, *Chronique*, vol. IV, p. 602, trans. vol. III, XV, xiv, p. 212

Chapter 5. The Legal and Social Status of Local Inhabitants in the Frankish Levant

1. J. Delaville le Roulx, ed., *Cartulaire général de l'Ordre des Hospitaliers de S. Jean de Jérusalem*, vol. I, #470, pp. 322–33.

2. A vast literature exists on these issues; I give here only the most recent and general overviews. Jonathan Riley-Smith, *The Feudal Nobility and the Kingdom of Jerusalem, 1174–1277*; Joshua Prawer, *Crusader Institutions*; Claude Cahen, *Orient et occident au temps des croisades*; Hans Eberhard Mayer, "Latins, Muslims and Greeks in the Latin Kingdom of Jerusalem," *History* 63 (1978): 175-92, reprinted in *Probleme des lateinischen Königreichs Jerusalem*, article VI; Jonathan Riley-Smith, "The Survival in Latin Palestine of Muslim Administration," in *The Eastern Mediterranean Lands in the Period of the Crusades*, ed. P. M. Holt; Jean Richard, "Agricultural Conditions in the Crusader States," in *A History of the Crusades*, ed. Kenneth M. Setton, vol. 5, *The Impact of the Crusades on the Near East*, ed. Norman P. Zacour and Harry W. Hazard, pp. 251–66; Joshua Prawer, "Social Classes in the Crusader States: The 'Minorities,'" in ibid., pp. 59–115; Jean Richard, "La seigneurie franque en Syrie et à Chypre: modèle oriental ou modèle occidental?" in *Seigneurs et Seigneuries au Moyen Âge*, pp. 155–66.

3. Jean d'Ibelin, "Le livre de Jean d'Ibelin," *Recueil des historiens des croisades: Lois*, vol. 1, p. 114; Geoffroy Le Tort, "Livre de Geoffroy Le Tort," ibid., vol. 1, ch. 32, p. 443; Philippe de Navarre, "Livre de Philippe de Navarre," ibid., vol. 1, ch. 28, p. 501. The condition that certain roles can only be filled by men "de la loy de Rome" can be found throughout the legal texts.

4. See Bernard Hamilton, "King Consorts of Jerusalem and Their Entourages," in *Die Kreuzfahrerstaaten als multikulturelle Gesellschaft*, ed. Hans Eberhard Mayer, pp. 13–24.

5. The possible exceptions are Aimery of Lusignan, who had been in the Latin East since the 1170s, and John of Ibelin, who was regent in the period 1205 to 1210 and was born a member of the most prominent local Frankish family. For a discussion of the divide between the twelfth and the thirteenth centuries from the perspective of lordly land tenure and the relationship between the king and his nobles, see Peter Edbury, "Fiefs and Vassals in the Kingdom of Jerusalem: From the Twelfth Century to the Thirteenth," *Crusades* 1 (2002): 49–62.

6. Peter Edbury, *John of Ibelin and the Kingdom of Jerusalem*.

7. Philippe de Navarre, "Livre de Phillipe de Navarre," in *Recueil des historiens des croisades: Lois* (Paris, 1841), vol. 1, ch. 47, pp. 521–23; Peter Edbury, "Law and Custom in the Latin East: *Les Letres dou Sepulcre*," in *Intercultural Contacts in the Medieval Mediterranean*, ed. Benjamin Arbel, pp. 71–79.

8. Jean d'Ibelin, "Livre," p. 27; trans. in Peter W. Edbury, *John of Ibelin*, p. 100.

9. Jonathan Riley-Smith, for example, dates the *établissement* concerning the con-

fiscation of fiefs to the reign of Baldwin II. "Further Thoughts on Baldwin II's *établissement* on the Confiscation of Fiefs," in *Crusade and Settlement*, ed. Peter Edbury, pp. 176–79. Maurice Grandeclaude provided the first list of assizes that might be dated to the first kingdom of Jerusalem; at the end of the list he tentatively added an assize concerning *villains* (Jean d'Ibelin, "Livre," ch. 251; p. Philippe de Navarre, "Livre," pp. 535–36) and another on the freeing of serfs "Livre des assises des bourgeois," *Recueil des historiens des croisades: Lois*, vol. 2, ch. 207, p. 140). Neither suggests that non-Latin Christians suffer any legal disabilities. "Liste d'assises remontant au premier royaume de Jérusalem (1099–1187)," in *Mélanges Paul Fournier*, pp. 329–45; Jean d'Ibelin, "Livre," ch. 251, p. 403.

10. Joshua Prawer commented that "in addition to presenting the dangers of anachronisms, because they project thirteenth-century realities (even if they are faithfully reproduced), into the twelfth century, the use of legal treatises as the principal sources for the constitutional history of the Latin Kingdom creates the illusion of a fossilized constitution." Prawer, *Crusader Institutions*, p. 9.

11. Riley-Smith, *Feudal Nobility*; Edbury, *John of Ibelin*; Prawer, *Crusader Institutions* passim.

12. Ronnie Ellenblum, *Frankish Rural Settlement in the Latin Kingdom of Jerusalem*, pp. 20–22. In comparison, recent work has suggested that the conversion of substantial numbers of Copts did not occur until the Fatimid period. See John Iskander, "Islamization in Medieval Egypt: The Copto-Arabic 'Apocalypse of Samuel' as a Source for the Social and Religious History of Medieval Copts," *Medieval Encounters* 4 (1998): 219–27. Tamer el-Leithy's dissertation discredits the notion of large-scale conversion before the thirteenth century and provides a useful critique of the literature about conversion in the medieval Middle East. "Coptic Culture and Conversion in Medieval Cairo, 1293–1524 A.D."

13. Prawer, *Crusader Institutions*, p. 202.

14. Interesting in this regard is the discussion over Jewish "serfdom" in the thirteenth century. Although few would argue that Jews had the same status as Christian agricultural laborers, the language of serfdom was employed as an analogy. See J. A. Watt, "The Jews, the Law and the Church: The Concept of Jewish Serfdom in Thirteenth-Century England," in *The Church and Sovereignty*, ed. Diana Wood, pp. 153–72.

15. For a brief discussion of the necessity for greater precision in the use of the terms "serf" and "serfdom," see János Bak, "Serfs and Serfdom: Words and Things," *Review* 4 (1980): 3–18.

16. Claude Cahen, "La communauté rurale dans le monde musulman médiéval," in *Les communautés rurales*, 3: 9–27.

17. Prawer, *Crusader Institutions*, p. 197.

18. Claude Cahen, "Notes sur l'histoire des croisades et de l'Orient latin II: le régime rural syrien au temps de la domination franque," *Bulletin de la faculté des letters de Strasbourg* 29 (1951): 286–310; reprinted in *Turcobyzantina et Oriens Christianus*; Prawer, *Crusader Institutions*, p. 205.

19. Nizam al-Mulk, *The Book of Government or Rules for Kings*, trans. Hubert Darke, p. 32.

20. There is some evidence that it was used in Syria, although whether Syria en-

compasses Palestine in this discussion is unclear. Hassanein Rabie, *The Financial System of Egypt*, p. 46.

21. *Encyclopaedia of Islam*, 2nd ed., s.v. "ikta."

22. Delaville le Roulx, ed., *Cartulaire Général des Hospitaliers*, vol. I, #20, pp. 21–22.

23. For example, Geneviève Bresc-Bautier, *Le Cartulaire du chapitre du Saint-Sépulcre de Jérusalem*, #36, pp. 103–5.

24. *Encyclopaedia of Islam*, 2nd ed., s.v. "musha." Crusader historians heretofore have been hesitant to give a decisive judgment—Riley-Smith and Prawer seem equivocal, while Cahen is cautiously in favor. Riley-Smith, *Feudal Nobility*, p. 41; Prawer, *Crusader Institutions*, pp. 187–95; Cahen, "Notes sur l'histoire," p. 295.

25. Jeremy Johns, *Arabic Administration in Norman Sicily*, pp. 43, 47. For more on the status of peasants in Norman Sicily, and discussion of the Greek, Latin, and Arabic terms used to describe them, see Annliese Nef, "Conquêtes et reconquêtes médiévales: la Sicile normande est-elle une terre de reduction en servitude généralisée?" in *Mélanges de l'École Française de Rome (Moyen Âge)* 112, 2: 579–607.

26. For slavery in the Latin East, see Charles Verlinden, *L'esclavage dans l'Europe médiévale*, 2: 964–77. During the initial conquests that established the kingdom, the inhabitants of captured cities such as Caesarea were often sold into slavery; Fulcher, *Historia*, p. 403; Ryan, *History*, p. 154; and the redemption of captives was a concern of Jewish and Muslim communities throughout the twelfth century. The Jewish communities of Egypt struggled to rescue fellow Jews who had been captured by the crusaders soon after the fall of Jerusalem in 1099. S. D. Goitein, *A Mediterranean Society*, 5: 372–79. Continuing battles and raids on Muslim lands ensured a bountiful, if erratic, supply of slaves. The Spanish traveler Ibn Jubayr testified to the concern for the redemption of Maghrebi slaves shown by pious Damascene merchants, Ibn Jubayr, *The Travels of Ibn Jubayr*, trans. R. J. C. Broadhurst, pp. 322–33, and Usama ibn-Munqidh, both friend and foe to the Franks, recorded the numerous occasions on which he purchased Muslim slaves from the Franks. Usamah ibn-Munqidh, *An Arab-Syrian Gentleman and Warrior in the Period of the Crusades*, trans. Philip K. Hitti, pp. 110–12. For female captives, see Yvonne Friedman, "Women in Captivity and Their Ransom During the Crusader Period," in *Cross Cultural Convergences in the Crusader Period*, ed. Michael Goodich, Sophia Menache, and Sylvia Schein, pp. 75–88.

27. Prawer at one point suggests the peasants are "ad glebam adscripti," but at another point he emphasizes that their servile condition was personal. Prawer, *Crusader Institutions*, p. 204–5.

28. William Chester Jordan, *From Servitude to Freedom: Manumission in the Sénonais in the Thirteenth Century*; Paul R. Hyams, *Kings, Lords and Peasants in Medieval England*; R. H. Hilton, *The Decline of Serfdom in Medieval England*; M. L. Bush, ed., *Serfdom and Slavery: Studies in Legal Bondage*; Walter Goffart, *Caput and Colonate: Towards a History of Late Roman Taxation*, pp. 66–90.

29. The phrase "heredes eorum" or "suis" appears frequently. See Bresc-Bautier, *Le Cartulaire du Saint-Sépulcre*, #78, pp. 183–85; #111, pp. 231–32; #156, pp. 305–6; Delaville le Roulx, eds., *Cartulaire général des Hospitaliers*, vol. I, #470, pp. 322–3.

30. Ibn Jubayr, *Travels*, p. 317.

31. One twelfth-century charter does mention a tax "qui vulges cavages dicitur." It

is unclear whether this is *chevage* or *kharaj*, the Muslim land tax. Comte de Marsy, "Fragment d'un cartulaire de l'ordre de Saint Lazare, en Terre-Sainte," *Archives de l'Orient latin* 2 (1884): #9, p. 130. Paul Sidelko argues that there is no connection between Muslim tax practices and those of the Franks. "Muslim Taxation Under Crusader Rule," in *Tolerance and Intolerance*, ed. Michael Gervers and James M. Powell, pp. 65–74.

32. Jean d'Ibelin, "Livre," ch. 254, pp. 405–6.

33. Emmanuel Sivan, "Réfugiés syro-palestiniens au temps des croisades," *Revue des études islamiques* 35 (1967): 135–48; Benjamin Z. Kedar, "The Subjected Muslims of the Frankish Levant," in *Muslims Under Latin Rule*, ed. James M. Powell, pp. 135–74; reprinted in *The Franks in the Levant, 11th to 14th Centuries*. For more on this fascinating community, see Daniella Talmon-Heller, "The Shaykh and the Community—Popular Hanabalite Islam in 12th-13th Century Jabal Nablus and Jabal Qasyun," *Studia Islamica* 79 (1994): 103–20; Benjamin Z. Kedar, "Some New Sources on Palestinian Muslims Before and During the Crusades," in *Die Kreuzfahrerstaaten als multikulturelle Gesellschaft*, ed. Hans Eberhard Mayer, pp. 129–40; Joseph Drory, "Hanabalis of the Nablus Region in the Eleventh and Twelfth Centuries," *Asian and African Studies* 22 (1988): 93–112. Less helpful is Hadia Dajani-Shakeel's "Displacement of the Palestinians During the Crusades," *Muslim World* 68 (1978): 157–75.

34. Delaville le Roulx, ed., *Cartulaire général des Hospitaliers*, vol. I, #783, pp. 491–96.

35. Johns, *Arabic Administration*, p. 146.

36. Delaville le Roulx, ed., *Cartulaire général des Hospitaliers*, vol. I, #648, pp. 436–37.

37. Prawer admitted this was not an easy charter to interpret. *Crusader Institutions*, p. 213.

38. It is interesting that in the charter of 1183 cited above, Bohemund donated a piece of land with its knights and villeins. This suggests that the donation of villeins with their villages is not a clear sign of servility. Delaville le Roulx, ed., *Cartulaire général des Hospitaliers*, vol. I, #783, p. 492.

39. Ibn Jubayr, *Travels*, p. 317.

40. The few examples we have of *corvées* in the Latin East date to the thirteenth century. One twelfth-century charter from the monastery of St. Mary of Jehosaphat mentions the commutation of labor services for a monetary payment, but both the date and provenance of this charter are unclear, as we have only a French translation of an eighteenth-century copy of the medieval cartulary. Charles Kohler, "Chartes de l'abbaye de Notre-Dame de la vallée de Josaphat en Terre-Sainte (1108–1291)," *Revue de l'Orient latin* 7 (1900): #10, pp. 120–21.

41. Ibn Jubayr, *Travels*, p. 316.

42. Jonathan Riley-Smith, "Some Lesser Officials in Latin Syria," *English Historical Review* 87 (1972): 10–11; Riley-Smith, *Feudal Nobility*, pp. 47–49; Prawer, *Crusader Institutions*, pp. 207–8.

43. Delaville le Roulx, ed., *Cartulaire général des Hospitaliers* #457, pp. 313–14. We have no way of knowing what religion 'Abd al-Masih and George were, but the latter's name, that of a Christian saint, suggests that they were Christian. This uncertainty applies for nearly every individual discussed in this chapter.

44. Marsy, "Fragment d'un cartulaire," #7, p. 128.

45. Delaville le Roulx, ed., *Cartulaire général des Hospitaliers*, #530–32, pp. 363–64.

46. Kohler, "Chartes de l'abbaye de Notre-Dame," #39, pp. 147–48.

47. Delaborde, ed., *Chartes de Terre Sainte*, #43, p. 91.

48. Bresc-Bautier, *Cartulaire*, #111, pp. 231–32.

49. Jean d'Ibelin, "Livre," ch. IV, p. 26.

50. Susan Reynolds has said generally about the legal arrangements of the kingdom of Jerusalem that "unless the kingdom was far ahead of the West, the working out of boundaries between different jurisdictions and the formulation of rules about them would not have been anything like complete by 1187." "Fiefs and Vassals in Twelfth-Century Jerusalem," *Crusades* 1 (2002): 29–48.

51. Willelmus Tyrensis, *Chronicon*, ed. R. B. C. Huygens, Corpus Christianorum Continuo Mediaevalis 63A, 22: 16 (15), p. 1029; Babcock and Krey, *History of Deeds Done Beyond the Sea*, vol. II, pp. 470–71. Jean Richard has speculated that eastern Christians may also have may also have made up part of the turcopoles, the troops who were in origin converted Turks. "Les Turcopoles au service des royaumes de Jérusalem et de Chypre: Musulmans convertis ou chrétiens orientaux?" *Revue des études islamiques* 54 (1986): 261–70.

52. Joseph Hajjar, "The Influence of Muslim Society on Church Law in the Arab East," *Concilium* 5 (1996): 66–80.

53. Joshua Prawer, *The History of the Jews in the Latin Kingdom of Jerusalem*, pp. 97–98 n. 13. For a detailed description of the functioning of such courts in Egypt, see S. D. Goitein, *Mediterranean Society*, vol. 2, *The Community*, pp. 311–45.

54. A. Papadopoulos-Kerameus, *Analekta Hierosolymitikes Stachyologias*, 2: 252–53. For a reproduction of this page of the manuscript, see Kirsopp and Silva Lake, eds., *Dated Greek Minuscule Manuscripts to the Year 1200*, vol. 1, *Manuscripts at Jerusalem, Patmos, and Athens*, Monumenta Palaeographica Vetera 1st ser., pl. 16.

55. Bresc-Bautier, *Le Cartulaire du Saint-Sépulcre*, #95, pp. 212–13.

56. "Livre des Assises des cours des bourgeois," vol. II, ch. 61–65, pp. 54–55; ch. 95, p. 96.

57. We have no evidence of Frankish settlement at Betheri, making it more likely that George is indigenous. Delaville le Roulx, ed., *Cartulaire général de des Hospitaliers*, vol. I, #495, p. 341. For other local Christians serving as scribes, see George Syrianus and his brother David, both scribes, in Delaville le Roulx, *Les archives, la bibliothèque et le trésor de l'ordre de Saint-Jean de Jérusalem à Malte*, ed. J. Delaville le Roulx, fasc. 32, *Bibliothèque des écoles françaises d'Athènes et de Rome*, #61, pp. 153–54.

58. Delaville le Roulx, ed., *Cartulaire général de des Hospitaliers*, vol. I, #516–18, pp. 352–53.

59. Riley-Smith, "Some Lesser Officials," p. 23.

60. The only historian to consider these individuals as significant in any way is Jean Richard, *The Latin Kingdom of Jerusalem*, trans. Janet Shirley, 1: 140–43.

61. Delaborde, ed., *Chartes de Notre-Dame de Josaphat*, #14, pp. 40–41.

62. Reinhold Röhricht, ed., *Regesta Regni Hierosolymitani*, #130, p. 32.

63. Delaville le Roulx, ed., *Cartulaire général des Hospitaliers*, vol. I, #84, p. 79. This was confirmed in #225, p. 173.

64. Röhricht, *Regesta*, #237, p. 60; Bresc-Bautier, *Cartulaire du Saint-Sépulcre*, #59, p. 151.

65. Bresc-Bautier, *Cartulaire du Saint-Sépulcre*, #88, pp. 201–3, #131, pp. 257–58.

66. Delaville le Roulx, ed., *Cartulaire général des Hospitaliers*, vol. I, #312, pp. 225–26. A certain Thomas Hernium shows up as a brother among the Templars, who may be from the same family. Marsy, "Fragment d'un cartulaire," #5, p. 126.

67. He first shows up as "Arrabi" in 1122. Delaville le Roulx, ed., *Cartulaire général des Hospitaliers*, vol. I, #59, p. 49; see also Bresc-Bautier, *Cartulaire du Saint-Sépulcre*, #44, pp. 121–22; #47, pp. 129–31; #51, pp. 137–38. See also Richard, *Latin Kingdom*, 1: 141.

68. Delaville le Roulx, ed., *Cartulaire général des Hospitaliers*, vol. I, #354, p. 245.

69. Delaville le Roulx, ed., *Cartulaire général des Hospitaliers*, vol. I, #495, p. 341; Delaborde, ed., *Chartes de Terre Sainte*, #32, pp. 78–79. Riley-Smith, *Feudal Nobility*, p. 10.

70. Another example of local Christians bearing Frankish names is Arnulf, son of Bernard the Syrian. Bresc-Bautier, *Cartulaire du Saint-Sépulcre*, #68, p. 165.

71. As marshal, he witnessed many charters. For a few examples, see Bresc-Bautier, *Cartulaire du Saint-Sépulcre*, #26, 30, 32, 34, 38; Delaville le Roulx, ed., *Cartulaire général des Hospitaliers*, vol. I, #77, p. 73; Marsy, "Fragment d'un cartulaire," #3, p. 125. The frequency with which he appeared in the charter lists suggests that Prawer's conclusion that "the office never attained any real importance" might need to be revised. *The Crusaders' Kingdom: European Colonialism in the Middle Ages*, p. 124. C. K. Slack mentions Sa'd in his discussion of royal *familiares*, but does not discuss his religion. "Royal Familiares in the Latin Kingdom of Jerusalem, 1100–1187," *Viator* 22 (1991): 24.

72. Bresc-Bautier, *Cartulaire du Saint-Sépulcre*, #36, pp. 103–5.

73. Bresc-Bautier, *Cartulaire du Saint-Sépulcre*, #38, p. 109.

74. A seventeenth-century redaction of Hospitaller charters records the existence in 1181 of Sade, the *ra'is* of the Saracens of Tyre, along with his brother William, leaving it unclear whether Sade was Muslim or Christian. J. Delaville de la Roulx, "Inventaire de pièces de Terre Sainte de l'ordre de l'Hôpital," *Revue de l'Orient latin* 3 (1895): #140, p. 66.

75. Myriam Greilsammer, ed., *Le livre au roi*, ch. 9, pp. 157–58.

76. Jean Richard, "*Cum omni raisagio montanee . . .* à propos de la cession du Crac aux Hospitaliers," in *Itinéraires d'Orient: hommages à Claude Cahen*, ed. Raoul Curiel and Rika Gyselen, pp. 187–94; Delaville le Roulx, ed., *Cartulaire général des Hospitaliers*, vol. I, #144, p. 117.

77. Delaville le Roulx, ed., *Cartulaire général des Hospitaliers*, vol. I, #783, pp. 491–96.

78. Bresc-Bautier, *Cartulaire du Saint-Sépulcre*, #36, pp. 103–5; #131, p. 358. For another Salem who is certainly indigenous, see #43, p. 120.

79. Bresc-Bautier, *Cartulaire du Saint-Sépulcre*, #88, pp. 201–3.

80. Bresc-Bautier, *Cartulaire du Saint-Sépulcre*, #77, p. 182.

81. Delaville le Roulx, ed., *Cartulaire général des Hospitaliers*, vol. I, #312, p. 225.

82. Marsy, "Fragment d'un cartulaire," #6, p. 127.

83. Bresc-Bautier, *Cartulaire du Saint-Sépulcre*, #41, pp. 113–15.

84. By an assise of 1162, all fief-holders took an oath of homage to the king directly, and thus enjoyed the privilege of attending the high court.

85. Queen Melisende is the one monarch who seems to have chosen simply "regina Jherusolimorum." See Bresc-Bautier, *Cartulaire du Saint-Sépulcre*, #35, 36, 37; Delaville le Roulx, ed., *Cartulaire général des Hospitaliers*, vol. I, #191.

Chapter 6. The Price of Unity-Ecumenical Negotiations and The End of Rough Tolerance

1. Ancyra (A.D. 314), Antioch (272), Sardica (342), Gangra (345), Laodicea (364), and Carthage (255).

2. The inscription acknowledged the aid of Ralph, Latin bishop of Bethlehem, and Amalric, king of Jerusalem. Lucy-Anne Hunt, "Art and Colonialism: The Mosaics of the Church of the Nativity in Bethlehem (1169) and the Problem of 'Crusader Art,'" *Dumbarton Oaks Papers* 45 (1991): 69–85; Jaroslav Folda, *The Art of the Crusaders in the Holy Land, 1098–1187*, pp. 347–64; Andrew Jotischky, "Manuel Comnenus and the Reunion of the Churches: The Evidence of the Conciliar Mosaics in the Church of the Nativity in Bethlehem," *Levant* 26 (1994): 207–24.

3. Joannis Phocae, "Descriptio Terrae Sanctae," *Patrologiae Graecae* 133: 943. For other discussions of Manuel's artistic patronage in the Holy Land, see A. M. Weyl-Carr, "The Mural Paintings of Abu Ghosh and the Patronage of Manuel Comnenus in the Holy Land," in *Crusader Art in the Twelfth Century*, ed. Jaroslav Folda, pp. 215–34.

4. Runciman suggests that this was largely an informal authority. Steven Runciman, "The Byzantine 'Protectorate' in the Holy Land," *Byzantion* 18 (1948): 207–15.

5. Jonathan Phillips, *Defenders of the Holy Land*, pp. 100–139.

6. William of Tyre, for example, believed that the Greek guides furnished to the German army deliberately led the crusaders astray and then abandoned them in the middle of the Turkish territories. Willelmus Tyrensis, *Chronicon*, ed. R. B. C. Huygens, Corpus Christianorum Continuatio Mediaevalis vol. 63A, 16: 21, pp. 744–75; trans. Emily Babcock and A. C. Krey, *History of Deeds Done Beyond the Sea*, vol. II, p. 169.

7. Paul Magdalino, *The Empire of Manuel I Komnenos*.

8. D. M. Nicols, "Byzantium and the Papacy in the Eleventh Century," *Journal of Ecclesiastical History* 13 (1962): 1–19.

9. Boso, "Alexander III," *Le Liber Pontificalis*, ed. L. Duchesne, vol. II, p. 415; see also Werner Ohnsorge, *Die Legaten Alexanders III*, pp. 69–90; John G. Rowe, "Alexander II and the Jerusalem Crusade: An Overview of Problems and Failures" in *Crusaders and Muslims in Twelfth-Century Syria*, ed. Maya Shatzmiller, pp. 112–32.

10. Magdalino, *Manuel I Komnenos*, pp. 36–41.

11. Ioannis Cinnamus, *Epitome*, ed. Augustus Meineke, Corpus Scriptorum Historiae Byzantinae 26, pp. 187–88; John Kinnamos, *Deeds of John and Manuel Comnenus*, trans. Charles M. Brand, p. 143.

12. Michel le Syrien, *Chronique*, vol. IV, p. 607 (inside column), trans. vol. III. p. 222.

13. For more on the complicated reasons for Ralph's deposition, see Bernard

Hamilton, "Ralph of Domfront, Patriarch of Antioch (1135–40)," *Nottingham Medieval Studies* 18 (1984): 1–21; Rudolf Hiestand, "Ein neuer Bericht über das Konzil von Antiochia 1140," *Annuarium historiae conciliorum* 19 (1987): 314–50.

14. Willelmus Tyrensis, *Chronicon*, vol. 63A, 15: 18, p. 699; trans. Babcock and Krey, *History of Deeds*, vol. II, p. 122.

15. The only Armenian account of this council survives in a somewhat garbled narrative in Samuel of Ani, a late twelfth-century chronicler, which betrays no sign that Gregory was forced to attend the council. Samuel Anets'iots' (Samuel of Ani), *Havak'munk' i Grots Patmagrats'*, pp. 122–23; trans. Marie-Félicité Brosset in *Collection d'historiens arméniens*, vol. 2, p. 457.

16. Michel le Syrien, *Chronique*, p. 626; trans. vol. III, XVI, 10, p.256.

17. Michel le Syrien, *Chronique*, vol. IV, p. 626; trans. vol. III, p. 256.

18. See note 12..

19. A letter from the Armenian patriarch Gregory II to John II Komnenos has been published, but we do not know what provoked the letter, nor what response it received. Jean Darrouzès, "Trois documents de la controverse gréco-arménienne, " *Revue des études Byzantines* 48 (1990): 89–153.

20. Otto of Freising, *Chronica sive Historia de duabus civitatibus*, ed. Adolf Hofmeister, Scriptores Rerum Germanicarum 45, VII, 32, p. 361; trans. in Otto, Bishop of Freising, *The Two Cities: A Chronicle of Universal History to the Year 1146 A. D.*, trans. Charles Christopher Mierow, p. 441. This may well be part of western expectations of finding another Christian power in the East other than Byzantium, which manifested itself also in the story of Prester John.

21. Otto, *Chronica*, pp. 361–62; Otto, *Two Cities*, pp. 441–42.

22. Nerses Shnorhali, brother of the *kat'olikos* Gregory III, composed a poem at approximately the same time as this embassy to the pope, in which he laments the fall of Edessa to Zengi. Speaking as Edessa herself, Nerses addresses Rome, saying "Quickly reach out your hand to me, who lie bound in the house of captivity, and take revenge unforgivingly on the enemy who has taken me prisoner. " Theo M. van Lint, "*Lament on Edessa* by Nerses Snorhali, " in *East and West in the Crusader States II*, ed. Krijnie Ciggaar and Herman Teule, p. 51. Edessa similarly addresses the other ecclesiastical centers of Christianity, asking Constantinople also for revenge, but only prayers from Jerusalem and Alexandria, while Antioch receives only reproaches for not having aided Edessa.

23. Several articles have been published discussing these negotiations. Pascal Tekeyan, *Controverses christologiques en Arméno-Cilicie dans la seconde moitié du XIIe siècle (1165–1198)*, Orientalia Christiana Analecta 124; Charles A. Frazee, "The Christian Church in Cilician Armenia: Its Relations with Rome and Constantinople to 1198," *Church History* 45 (1976): 166–84; Boghos Levon Zekiyan, "Un dialogue oecuménique au XIIe siècle: les pourparlers entre le Catholicos St. Nerses Snorhali et le légat impérial Théorianos en vué de l'union des églises arménienne et byzantine, " in *Actes du XVe congrès international d'études Byzantines*, vol. 4, pp. 420–41; Gérard Dédéyan, "Le rôle complémentaire des frères Pahlawuni, Grigor III Catholicos et saint Nerses Snorhali Catholicos, dans le rapprochement avec les Latins à l'époque de la chute d'Édesse (c. 1139–1150)," *Revue des études arméniennes* 33 (1992): 237–52.

24. Garegin A. Kat'olikos (Hovsepian), *Yishatakarank' Dzeragrats (Collection of Manuscripts)*, #187, col. 386; see also Gérard Dédéyan, "Les colophons de manuscrits arméniens comme sources pour l'histoire des Croisades, " in *The Crusades and Their Sources*, ed. John France and William G. Zajac, p. 104.

25. Nerses Shnorhali, *Endhanrakan Tultk' (Collected Letters)*, p. 96. These letters have been loosely translated into Latin, Joseph Cappelletti, *Sancti Nersetis Clajensis Armeniorum Catholici Opera*, vol. 1, Ep. IV, p. 182. His letter suggests that he had some sort of anti-Armenian treatise in front of him as he wrote, for he refutes specific accusations against the Armenians.

26. Nerses, *Endhanrakan*, p. 97; Cappelletti, Ep. IV, p. 183.

27. Hrant Khatchadourian, "The Christology of St. Nerses Shnorhali in Dialogue with Byzantium," *Miscellanea Francescana* 78 (1978): 413–34.

28. This letter is preserved only in an Armenian translation. Nerses, *Endhanrakan*, pp. 107–9.

29. Nerses, *Endhanrakan*, pp. 109–30; Cappelletti, pp. 195–230.

30. Nerses, *Endhanrakan*, p. 144.

31. Nerses, *Endhanrakan*, p. 145; Cappelletti, Ep. VII, pp. 231–38.

32. Theorianos, "Disputatio cum Armeniorum Catholico, " *Patrologiae Graecae* 133: 114–298.

33. Nerses, *Endhanrakan*, p. 155; Cappelletti, Ep. VIII, pp. 239–40.

34. Boghos Levon Zekiyan, "Les relations arméno-byzantines après la mort de St. Nersès Snorhali, " *Jahrbuch der Österreichischen Byzantinistik* 32, 4 (1982): 331–37.

35. Known today as Rumkale, in the past thousand years it has gone by several names, including Qala'at ar-Rum, Kala Roumaita, and Ranculat. For more on the history and topography of the site, see Hansgerd Hellenkemper, *Burgen der Kreuzritterzeit in der Grafschaft Edessa und im Königreich Kleinarmenerien*, pp. 51–61; for its position in the greater Euphrates valley, see Anthony Comfort, Catherine Abadie-Reynal and Rifat Ergeç, "Crossing the Euphrates in Antiquity: Zeugma Seen from Space," *Anatolian Studies* 50 (2000): 99–126.

36. For more on the Pahlavunis, see Christopher MacEvitt, "The *Chronicle* of Matthew of Edessa: Apocalypse, the First Crusade and the Armenian Diaspora," *Dumbarton Oaks Papers* 61 (2007): 254–96; Avedis Sanjian, "Gregory Magistros: An Armenian Hellenist" in *TO ΕΛΛΗΝΙΚΟΝ: Studies in Honor of Speros Vyronis, Jr.*, vol. 2, *Byzantinoslavica, Armeniaca, Islamica, the Balkans and Modern Greece*, ed. Jelisveta Stanojevich Allen et al., pp. 131–58; Maurice Leroy, "Grégoire Magistros et les traductions arméniennes d'auteurs grecs," *Annuaire de l'Institut de philologie et d'histoire orientales* 3 (1935): 263–94; B. L. Chukaszyan, "Échos de legendes épiques iraniennes dans les 'lettres' de Grigor Magistros," *Revue des études arméniennes* 1 (1964): 321–29.

37. Robert Thomson, "*Vardapet* in the Early Armenian Church," *Le Muséon* 75 (1962): 367–84. Perhaps the closest parallel were Islamic '*ulama*', who similarly played an interpretative role within the community. For the possibility that the '*ulama*' also played a quasi-sacerdotal role of serving as an intermediary between God and man, see A. Kevin Reinhart, "Transcendence and Social Practice: *Muftis* and *Qadis* as Religious Interpreters," *Annales Islamologiques* 27 (1993): 5–28.

38. The prestige of the *vardapet*s can be seen in the pages of Matthew of Edessa; his chronicle of political events was frequently leavened with accounts of holy men, almost all of them *vardapet*s. In contrast, Matthew hardly ever mentioned bishops, aside from the *kat'olikos*.

39. Gregorius Bar Hebraeus, *Chronicon Ecclesiasticum*, ed. J.-B. Abbeloos and T. J. Lamy, vol. 2, pp. 535–42. French translation in Michel le Syrien, *Chronique*, vol. III, XIX, pp. 329–30.

40. Barhebraeus, *Chronicon Ecclesiasticum*, vol. II, p. 546, French translation in Michel le Syrien, *Chronique*, vol. III, XIX, p. 332.

41. Andrew Palmer, "The History of the Syrian Orthodox in Jerusalem," *Oriens Christianus* 75 (1991): 34.

42. Albert Failler, "Le patriarche d'Antioche Athanase Ier Manassès (1157–1170), " *Revue des études byzantines* 51 (1993): 63–75.

43. The anonymous chronicle of 1234 proclaimed that Michael had even been enthroned on the chair of Peter in Antioch's cathedral. Michael, however, makes no such claim for himself, though as noted above, the portion of his chronicle dealing with his early patriarchate has been lost. Anonymous, *Chronicon*, p. 307; trans. A. Abouna, p. 230. See also Bernard Hamilton, "Aimery of Limoges, Latin Patriarch of Antioch (c. 1142–c. 1196) and the Unity of the Churches," in *East and West in the Crusader States*, ed. Krijnie Ciggaar and Herman Teule, 2: 1–12. For further discussion of the Jacobite patriarchs sitting in the patriarchal chair, see Dorothea Weltecke, "On the Syriac Orthodox in the Principality of Antioch During the Crusader Period," in *East and West in the Medieval Eastern Mediterranean*, ed. Krijnie Ciggaar and M. Metcalf, pp. 95–124.

44. Unfortunately, this treatise does not survive. Michel le Syrien, *Chronique*, vol. IV, p. 718; trans. vol. III, pp. 377–38.

45. Dorothea Weltecke, "The World Chronicle of Patriarch Michael the Great (1126–1199): Some Reflections," *Journal of Assyrian Academic Studies* 11 (1997): 6–29.

46. Bar Hebraeus, *Chronicon Ecclesiasticum*, vol. II, p. 549; trans. in Michel le Syrien, *Chronique*, vol. III, p. 334.

47. Michel le Syrien, *Chronique*, vol. IV, pp. 723–24; trans. vol. III, pp. 386–87. For more on Theodoros, see Hubert Kaufold, "Zur syrischen Kirchengeschichte des 12. Jahrhunderts: Neue Quellen über Theodoros bar Wahbun," *Oriens Christianus* 74 (1990): 115–51.

48. Bar Hebraeus, *Chronicon Ecclesiasticum*, vol. II, pp. 577–89.

49. Theorianus, "Disputatio," col. 295.

50. Bar Hebraeus, *Chronicon Ecclesiasticum*, vol. II, pp. 581–84.

51. Michel le Syrien, *Chronique*, vol. IV, pp. 703–4; trans. vol. III, XIX, x, pp. 351–52.

52. Although Michael's depiction of the theologically confused Armenians draws on a Jacobite stereotype, I believe the Syriac account reflected authentic bewilderment among certain Armenians. Michel le Syrien, *Chronique*, vol. IV, pp. 704–5; trans. vol. III, pp. 351, 353–54.

53. Sidney Griffith, "Dionysius bar Salibi on the Muslims" in *IV Symposium Syriacum 1984: Literary Genres in Syriac Literature*, ed. H. J. W. Drijvers, R. Lavenant S. J., C. Molenberg, and G. J. Reinink, Orientalia Christiana Analecta 229, pp. 353–65.

54. Patrick van der Aalst, "Denis Bar Salibi, polémiste, " *Proche-Orient Chrétien* 9 (1959): 10–23.

55. Dionysius bar Salibi, "Against the Melchites," in *Woodbrooke Studies*, ed. A. Mingana, vol. 1, p. 82; trans. p. 46. See also Herman Teule, *"It is not right to call ourselves Orthodox and the others heretics*: Ecumenical Attitudes in the Jacobite Church in the Time of the Crusades," in *East and West in the Crusader States*, ed. Krijnie Ciggaar and Herman Teule, 2: 13–28.

56. Dionysius, "Against the Melchites," p. 69, trans. p. 26.

57. Dionysius, "Against the Melchites, " p. 69, trans. p. 26.

58. Dionysius, "Against the Melchites," p. 72, trans. p. 31.

59. Dionysius, "Against the Melchites," p. 70, trans. p. 27.

60. Dionysius does support diversity of a certain sort in Christianity. "The fact that people of every country pray differently, and have something which singles them out from the rest, goes to their credit, first because it indicates the wealth of their devotions and spiritual vigor, and secondly because it is a sign of the incomprehensibility of God who wishes to be glorified in different ways in different countries and towns." Dionysius, "Against the Melchites," p. 73, trans. p. 34.

61. Dionysius, "Against the Melchites," p. 90, trans. p. 61.

62. Dionysius, "Against the Melchites," p. 70, trans. p. 28.

63. Dionysius, "Against the Melchites," p. 74; trans. p. 39.

64. Dionysius, "Against the Melchites," p. 74; trans. p. 39. Dionysius also states that "God removed the kingdom from the Franks and bestowed it on the Greeks." "Against the Melchites," p. 82, trans. p. 48.

65. Dionysius bar Salibi, "Against the Armenians," in *Woodbrooke Studies*, ed. A. Mingana, vol. 4, p. 71, trans. p. 7.

66. For its earlier history among the Armenians, see Jean Meyendorff, "L'Aphartodocétisme en Arménie: un imbroglio doctrinal et politique," *Revue des études arméniennes* 23 (1992): 27–37.

67. Dionysius, "Against the Armenians, " p. 71, trans. pp. 8–9.

68. Dionysius, "Against the Armenians, " p. 100, trans. p. 54.

69. Dionysius, "Against the Armenians, " p. 85, trans. p. 32.

70. Gregory Bar Hebraeus, *Chronography*, trans. Ernest A. Wallis Budge, 1: 283.

71. Nerses Klaietsi [Nerses Shnorhali], *Élégie sur la prise d'Édesse*, ed. D. J. Zohrab, p. 83; trans. in Theo M. van Lint, "*Lament on Edessa* by Nerses Snorhali," in *East and West in the Crusader States*, ed. Krijnie Cignaar and Herman Teule, p. 100.

72. Nerses Klaietsi, *Élégie*, p. 84; trans. van Lint, "Lament," p. 101.

73. Nerses Klaietsi, *Élégie*, pp. 86–87; trans. van Lint, "Lament," p. 103.

Bibliography

Primary Sources

Abou 'l-Feda. "Résumé de l'histoire des croisades tiré des annals des Abou 'l-Feda." In *Recueil des historiens des croisades: Historiens orientaux*. Paris: Imprimerie nationale, 1872. 1: 1–186.

Albertus Aquensis [Albert of Aachen]. "Historia Hierosolymitana." In *Recueil des historiens des croisades: Historiens occidentaux*. Paris: Imprimerie nationale, 1879. 4: 265–713.

Al-Muqaddasi. *The Best Divisions for Knowledge of the Regions*. Trans. Basil Anthony Collins. Reading: Centre for Muslim Contribution to Civilisation: Garnet, 1994.

Amato di Montecassino. *Storia de' Normanni*. Rome: Istituto Storico Italiano per il Medio Evo, 1935.

Amatus of Montecassino. *The History of the Normans*. Trans. Prescott N. Dunbar. Woodbridge: Boydell, 2004.

Anastasios of Caesarea. "De jejunio gloriosissimae Deiparae." *Patrologia Cursus Completus: Series Graeco-Latina* 127: 519–32. Paris, 1864.

Annales Altahenses Maiores. Ed. Wilhelm von Giesebrecht and Edmund von Oefele. Monumenta Germaniae Historica, Scriptores 4. Hannover: Hahnsche Buchhandlung, 1979.

Anne Comnène [Anna Komnene]. *Alexiade*. Ed. and trans. Bernard Leib. Paris: Les Belles Lettres, 1937.

Anonymous. *Gesta Francorum et aliorum Hiersolimitanorum*. Ed. and trans. Rosalind Hill. London: Thomas Nelson, 1962.

Anonymous of 1234. *Anonymi Auctoris Chronicon Ad Annum Christi 1234 Pertinens*. Ed. J.-B. Chabot, vol. 82/t. 37; trans. Albert Abouna, vol. 354/t. 154. Corpus Scriptorum Christianorum Orientalium; Scriptores Syri II, text. Louvain: Imprimerie Orientaliste, 1953, 1974.

Anonymous Pilgrims I–VIII: Eleventh and Twelfth Centuries. Trans. Audrey Stewart. Library of the Palestine Pilgrims' Texts 6. London: Palestine Pilgrims' Text Society, 1894.

Aristakes de Lastivert [Aristakes Lastivertts'i]. *Récit des malheurs de la nation arménienne*. Trans. Haïg Berbérian and Marius Canard. Bruxelles: Éditions de Byzantion, 1973.

Aristakes Lastivertts'i. *Patmut'iwn*. Venice: I Tparani Srboyn Ghazaru, 1901.

Baldric of Dol. "Historia Jerosolimitana." In *Recueil des historiens des croisades: Historiens occidentaux*. Paris: Imprimerie nationale, 1879. 4: 1–111.

Benjamin of Tudela. *The Itinerary of Benjamin of Tudela*. Malibu, Calif.: Pangloss Press, 1987.

Bernard the Wise [Bernardus Monachus]. "Itinerarium Bernardi, monachi franci." In *Descriptiones Terrae Sanctae*, ed. Titus Tobler. Leipzig: J.C. Hinrichs'sche Buchhandlung, 1874. 85–99.

Bongars, Jacques. *Gesta dei per Francos*. Hanoviae: Typis Wechelianis, apud heredes I. Aubrii, 1611.

Boso. "Alexander III." *Le Liber Pontificalis.*, ed. L. Duchesne. Paris: Ernest Thorin, 1892. 2: 387–446.

Bresc-Bautier, Geneviève, ed. *Le Cartulaire du chapitre du Saint-Sépulcre de Jérusalem*. Paris: Librairie Orientaliste Paul Guethner, 1984.

Cappelletti, Joseph. *Sancti Nersetis Clajensis Armeniorum Catholici Opera*. Venice: Typis PP. Mechistaristarum in insula S. Lazari, 1833.

Chahan de Cirbied, Jacques. "Notice de deux Manuscrits Arméniens, de la Bibliothèque impériale, nos. 95 et 99, contenant l'histoire écrite par *Mathieu Eretz*, et Extrait relatif à l'histoire de la première croisade." In *Notices et Extraits des Manuscripts de la Bibliothèque impériale, et autres bibliothèques*. Paris: Imprimerie impériale, 1813. 9: 275–364.

Cyril of Scythopolis. *Kyrillos von Skythopolis*. Ed. Eduard Schwartz. Leipzig: Hinrichs, 1939.

———. *Lives of the Monks of Palestine*. Trans. R. M. Price. Kalamazoo, Mich.: Cistercian Publications, 1991.

Daniel the Abbot. "The Pilgrimage of the Russian Abbot Daniel." Trans. C. W. Wilson in *The Library of the Pilgrims' Palestine Text Society*. London, 1895. Reprint New York: AMS Press, 1971.

———. "The Life and Journey of Daniel, Abbot of the Russian Land." In *Jerusalem Pilgrimage, 1099–1185*, ed. John Wilkinson, Joyce Hill, and W. F. Ryan. London: Hakluyt Society, 1988. 120–71.

Darrouzès, Jean. "Trois documents de la controverse gréco-arménienne." *Revue des études byzantines* 48 (1990): 89–153.

Delaborde, Henri-François, ed. *Chartres de Terre Sainte provenant de l'abbaye de Notre-Dame de Josaphat*. Paris: Thorin, 1880.

Delaville le Roulx, J., ed. *Les archives, la bibliothèque et le trésor de l'Ordre de Saint-Jean de Jérusalem à Malte*. Bibliothèque des écoles françaises d'Athènes et de Rome 32. Paris: Thorin, 1883.

———. *Cartulaire général de l'Ordre des Hospitaliers de S. Jean de Jérusalem*. Paris: Leroux, 1894. 4 vols.

———. "Inventaire de pièces de Terre Sainte de l'ordre de l'Hôpital." *Revue de l'Orient latin* 3 (1895): 36–106.

———. "Trois chartres du XIIe siècle concernant l'ordre de St. Jean de Jerusalem." *Archives de l'Orient latin* 1(1881): 409–15.

Dionysius bar Salibi. *The Work of Dionysius Barsalibi Against the Armenians*. Ed. Alphonse Mingana. Woodbrooke Studies: Christian Documents in Syriac, Arabic, and Gershuni 4. Cambridge: W. Heffer and Sons, 1931.

———. "Against the Melchites." In *Barsalibi's Treatise Against the Melchites*..., ed. Alphonse Mingana. Woodbrooke Studies: Christian Documents in Syriac, Arabic, and Gershuni 1. Cambridge: Heffer and Sons, 1927. 1: 17–95.

Donner, Herbert. "Die Palästinabeschreibung des Epiphanius Monachus Hagiopolita." *Deutscher Verein zur Erforschung Palästinas* 87 (1971): 42–91.

Epiphanius the Monk. "The Holy City and the Holy Places." In *Jerusalem Pilgrims Before the Crusades*, ed. John Wilkinson. Warminster: Aris and Phillips, 1977.

Fretellus. *Rorgo Fretellus de Nazareth et sa description de la Terre Sainte: histoire et édition du texte*. Ed. Petrus Cornelis Boeren. Amsterdam: North-Holland, 1980.

Fulcherius Carnotensis [Fulcher of Chartres]. *Historia Hierosolymitana*. Ed. Heinrich Hagenmeyer. Heidelberg: Carl Winters, 1913.

Fulcher of Chartres. *A History of the Expedition to Jerusalem*. Trans. Frances Rita Ryan. Knoxville: University of Tennessee Press, 1969.

Galterius Cancellarius [Walter the Chancellor]. *Bella Antiochena*. Ed. Heinreich Hagenmeyer. Innsbruck: Wagner'schen Universistäts-Buchshandlung, 1896.

Garegin A. Kat'olikos [Hovsepian]. *Yishatakarank' Dzeragrats' (Collection of Manuscripts)*. Antelias: Armenian Katholicate of Cilicia Press, 1951.

Geoffroy Le Tort. "Livre de Geoffroy Le Tort." In *Recueil des historiens des croisades: Lois*. Paris: Imprimerie royale, 1841. 1: 435–50.

Georgius Cedrenus. *Historiarum Compendium*. Ed. Immanuel Bekker. Corpus Scriptorum Historiae Byzantinae. Bonn: Ed. Weberi, 1838.

Geyer, P., ed. "Antonini Placentini Itinerarium." *Itineraria et Alia Geographica*. Corpus Christianorum, Series Latina 175. Turnhout: Brepols, 1965. 127–74.

Gregorius Bar Hebraeus. *Chronicon Ecclesiasticum*. Ed. J.-B. Abbeloos and T. J. Lamy. Paris: Maisonneuve, 1874. 2 vols.

Gregory Bar Hebraeus. *Chronography*. Trans. Ernest A. Wallis Budge. London: Oxford University Press. 2 vols.

Gregory VII. *Das Register Gregors VII*. Ed. Erich Caspar. Monumenta Germaniae Historica, Epistolae Selectae 2. Berlin: Weidmannsche Buchhandlung, 1920. 2 vols.

Gregory VII. *The Correspondence of Pope Gregory VII*. Trans. Ephraim Emerton. New York: Columbia University Press, 1932.

Gregory the Priest. "Continuation." In *Armenia and the Crusade*, trans. Ara Edmond Dostourian. Lanham, Md.: University Press of America, 1993. 241–80.

Greilsammer, Myriam, ed. *Le livre au roi*. Paris: Académie des Inscriptions et Belles-Lettres, 1995.

Grigor Erits' [Gregory the Priest]. "Sharunkut'iwn." In *Zhamanakagrut'iwn*. Vagharshapat, 1898. 369–429.

Guitbertus Abbatis Novigenti. *Dei gesta per Francos*. Ed. R. B. C. Huygens. Corpus Christianorum Continuatio Mediaevalis 127A. Turnhout: Brepols, 1994.

Hagenmeyer, Heinrich. *Epistulae et chartae ad historiam primi belli sacri spectantes*. Innsbruck: Wagner'sche Universitäts-Buchhandlung, 1901. Reprint Hildesheim: Georg Olms, 1973.

Ibn al-Athir. "Extrait de la chronique intitulée Kamel-altevarykh." In *Recueil des historiens des croisades: Historiens orientaux*. Paris: Imprimerie nationale, 1872. 1: 190–774.

———. *The Annals of the Saljuq Turks: Selections from al-Kamil fi'l Ta'rikh of 'Izz al-Din Ibn al-Athir*. Trans. D. S. Richards. London: Routledge Curzon, 2002.

———. *The Chronicle of Ibn al-Athir for the Crusading Period from* Al-Kamil fi'l-Ta'rikh. *Part I, The Years 491–541/1097–1146: The Coming of the Franks and the Muslim Response*. Trans. D. S. Richards. Crusade Texts in Translation 13. Aldershot: Ashgate, 2006.

[Ibn al-Djawzi, Sibt]. "Extrait du Mirat ez-Zèman." In *Recueil des historiens des croisades: Historiens orientaux*. Paris: Imprimerie nationale, 1884. 3: 517–70.

Ibn al-Qalanisi. *Damas de 1075 à 1154*. Trans. Roger Le Tourneau. Damascus: Institut français de Damas, 1952.

Ibn Jubayr. *The Travels of Ibn Jubayr*. Trans. R. J. C. Broadhurst. London: Jonathan Cape, 1952.

Ioannis Cinnamus [John Kinnamos]. *Epitome*. Ed. Augustus Meineke. Corpus Scriptorum Historiae Byzantinae 26. Bonn: Weberi, 1836.

"Itinerarium regis Ricardi." In William Stubbs, ed., *Chronicles and Memorials of the Reign of Richard I*, vol. 1, *Itinerarium peregrinorum et gesta regis Ricardi*. Rerum Britannicarum Medii Aevi Scriptores 38. London: Longman, Green, 1864. Reprint Wiesbaden: Kraus, 1964.

Jacques de Vitry. "Historia Hierosolimitana." In *Gesta dei per Francos*, ed. Jacques Bongars. Hanoviae: Typis Wechelianis, apud heres I. Aubrii, 1611.

Jean d'Ibelin. "Livre de Jean d'Ibelin." In *Recueil des historiens des croisades: lois*. Paris: Imprimerie royale, 1841. 1: 7–432.

Joannis Phocae. "Descriptio Terrae Sanctae." *Patrologia Cursus Completus: Series Graeco-Latina* 133, ed. J.-P. Migne. Paris, 1864. Reprint Turnhout: Brepols, 1977. 925–62.

John Kinnamos. *Deeds of John and Manuel Comnenus*. Trans. Charles M. Brand. New York: Columbia University Press, 1976.

Kemal ed-Din. "Extraits de la chronique d'Alep." In *Recueil des historiens des croisades: Historiens orientaux*. Paris: Imprimerie nationale, 1884. 1: 677–732.

Kohler, Charles. "Chartes de l'abbaye de Notre-Dame de la vallée de Josaphat en Terre-Sainte (1108–1291)." *Revue de l'Orient Latin 7* (1899): 108–222.

Kouli, Maria, trans. "Life of St. Mary of Egypt." In *Holy Women of Byzantium: Ten Saints' Lives in English Translation*, ed. Alice-Mary Talbot. Washington, D.C.: Dumbarton Oaks Research Library and Collection, 1996. 65–93.

Lake, Kirsopp and Silva Lake, eds. *Dated Greek Minuscule Manuscripts to the Year 1200*. Vol. 1, *Manuscripts at Jerusalem, Patmos, and Athens*. Monumenta Palaeographica Vetera 1st ser. Boston: American Academy of Arts and Sciences, 1934.

Lambert von Hersfeld. *Lamperti Monachis Hersfeldensis Opera*. Ed. Oswald Holder-Egger. Monumenta Germaniae Historica, Scriptores 38. Hannover: Impensis Bibliopoli Hahniani, 1894.

Leontios Makhairas. *Recital Concerning the Sweet Land of Cyprus entitled "Chronicle"*. Ed and trans. R. M. Dawkins. Oxford: Clarendon Press, 1932. 2 vols.

"Livre des assises des cour des bourgeois." In *Recueil des historiens des croisades: Lois*. Paris: Imprimerie royale, 1843. 2: 5–226.

Marsy, Arthur de. "Fragment d'un cartulaire de l'ordre de Saint Lazare, en Terre-Sainte." *Archives de l'Orient latin 2* (1884): 121–57.

Martin, Abbé. "Les premiers croisés et les syriens jacobites de Jérusalem." *Journal Asiatique* 8 (1889): 33–79.

Matt'eos Urhayets'i [Matthew of Edessa]. *Zhamanakagrut'iwn.* Vagharshapat, 1898.

Matthew of Edessa. *Armenia and the Crusades: Tenth to Twelfth Centuries: The Chronicle of Matthew of Edessa.* Trans. Ara Edmond Dostourian. Lanham, Md.: University Press of America, 1993.

Mavrogordato, John, ed. and trans. *Digenes Akrites.* Oxford: Clarendon Press, 1956.

Michael Attaleiates. *Historia.* Ed. Immanuel Bekker. Corpus Scriptorum Historiae Byzantinae. Bonn: Weberi, 1853.

Michaud, Joseph. *Bibliothèque des croisades.* 4 vols. Paris: Chez A. J. Ducollet, Libraire-éditeur, 1829.

Michel le Syrien [Michael the Syrian, Michael the Great]. *Chronique.* Trans. and ed. J.-B. Chabot. Paris: Leroux, 1905. 4 vols.

Michelant, Henri and Gaston Raynaud, eds. "Les sains pèlerinages." In *Itinéraires a Jérusalem et descriptions de la Terre Sainte.* Geneva: Jules-Guillaume Fick, 1882. 104–104[7].

Mingana, Alphonse. "A Charter of Protection Granted to the Nestorian Church in A.D. 1138, by Muktafi II, Caliph of Baghdad." *Bulletin of the John Rylands Library* 10 (1926): 127–33.

Moses Khorenats'i. *History of the Armenians.* Trans. Robert W. Thomson. Cambridge, Mass.: Harvard University Press, 1978.

Movses Dasxuranci [Daskhurants'i, Kaghankatuats'i]. *History of the Caucasian Albanians.* Trans. C. J. F. Dowsett. London: Oxford University Press, 1961.

Movses Kaghankatuats'i. *Patmut'iwn Aghuanits 'Aghkharhi.* Ed. Varag Arak'elyan. Erevan: Haykakan SSH GA Hratarakch'ut'yun, 1983.

"Narratio quomodo relliquiae martyris Georgii ad nos Aquicinenses pervenerunt." In *Recueil des historiens des croisades: Historiens occidentaux.* Paris: Imprimerie nationale, 1895. 5: 248–52.

Nerses Klaietsi [Shnorhali]. *Élégie sur la prise d'Édesse.* Ed. D. J. Zohrab. Paris: Librairie orientale de Dondey-Dupré père et fils, 1878.

Nerses Shnorhali. *Endhanrakan Tultk' (Collected Letters).* Jerusalem, 1871.

Neumann, W. "Drei mittelalter Pilgerschriften: II. Innominatus VI. (Pseudo-Beda)." *Österreichische Vierteljahresschrift für katholische Theologie* 11 (1872): 397–438.

Niccolò da Poggibonsi. *Libro d'Oltramare.* Jerusalem: PP. Francescani, 1945.

Nizam al-Mulk. *The Book of Government or Rules for Kings.* Trans. Hubert Darke. London: Routledge and Kegan Paul, 1960.

Nor barkirk' haykazean. Venice, 1837.

Omont, H. "Manuel de conversation arménien-latin du Xe siècle." *Bibliothèque de l'école de chartes* 43 (1882): 563–64.

Ordericus Vitalis. *The Ecclesiastical History of Orderic Vitalis.* Ed. and trans. Marjorie Chibnall. Oxford: Clarendon Press, 1978. 6 vols.

Otto of Freising. *Chronica sive Historia de duabus civitatibus.* Ed. Adolf Hofmeister. Scriptores Rerum Germanicarum 45. Hannover: Impensis Bibliopolii Hahnani, 1912.

Otto, Bishop of Freising. *The Two Cities: A Chronicle of Universal History to the Year 1146 A. D.* Trans. Charles Christopher Mierow. New York: Columbia University Press, 1928.

Papadopoulos-Kerameus, Athanasios. *Analekta Hierosolymitikes Stachyologias.* St. Petersburg: Typographeion V. Kirvaoum, 1891–1898. Anastatic reprint Brussels: Culture et Civilisation, 1963. 5 vols.

P'awstos Buzand. *Epic Histories.* Trans. Nina Garsoïan. Cambridge: Cambridge University Press, 1989.

Paul of Antioch. *Paul d'Antioche, évêque melkite de Sidon (XIIe s.).* Ed. and trans. Paul Khoury. Beirut: Imprimerie Catholique, 1965.

Peregrinationes Tres: Saewulf, John of Würzburg, Theodericus. Ed. R. B. C. Huygens. Corpus Christianorum Continuatio Mediaevalis 139. Turnhout: Brepols, 1994.

Petrus Tudebodus. *Historia de hierosolymitano itinere.* Ed. John Hugh Hill and Laurita L. Hill. Paris: Librairie orientaliste Paul Guethner, 1977.

Philippe de Navarre. "Livre de Philippe de Navarre." In *Recueil des historiens des croisades: Lois.* Paris: Imprimerie royale, 1841. 1: 469–571.

Pseudo-Methodius. *Die Apokalypse des Pseudo-Methodius die ältesten Griechischen und Lateinischen Übersetzungen.* Ed. W. J. Aerts and G. A. A. Kortekaas. Corpus Scriptorum Orientalium 569, Subsidia t. 97. Louvain: Peeters, 1998. 2 vols.

Radulfus Cadomensis [Ralph of Caen]. "Gesta Tancredi in expeditione Hierosolymitana." In *Recueil des historiens des croisades: Historiens occidentaux.* Paris: Imprimerie impériale, 1866. 3: 587–716.

Ralph of Caen. *The Gesta Tancredi of Ralph of Caen: A History of the Normans on the First Crusade.* Trans. Bernard Bachrach and David Bachrach. Aldershot: Ashgate, 2005.

Raymond d'Aguilers. *Le "Liber" de Raymond d'Aguilers.* Ed. John Hugh Hill and Laurita L. Hill. Paris: Librairie Orientaliste Paul Guethner, 1969.

Riant, Paul. "Inventaire critique des lettres historiques de croisades—Appendice." *Archive de l'Orient latin* 1 (1881): 1–224.

Robertus Monachus. "Historia Iherosolimitiana." In *Recueil des historiens des croisades: Historiens occidentaux.* Paris: Imprimerie impériale, 1866. 3: 717–882.

Rodulfus Glaber. *Historiarum libri quinque.* Ed. and trans. John France and Paul Reynolds. Oxford: Clarendon Press, 1989.

Röhricht, Reinhold, ed. *Regesta regni Hierosolymitani: addimentum.* Oeniponti: Libraria Academica Wageriana, 1893.

Samonas. *Disceptatio cum Achmed Saraceno de corpore ac sanguine Domini in Eucharistia.* 1781. *Patrologia Cursus Completus: Series Graeco-Latina* 120, ed. J.-P. Migne. 821–32.

Samouel d'Ani [Samuel Anets'iots']. "Tables Chronologiques." Trans. Marie-Félicité Brosset. In *Collection d'historiens arméniens.* St. Petersburg: Imprimerie de l'Académie impériale des sciences, 1874. Reprint Amsterdam: APA-Philo Press, 1979. 1: 340–83.

Samuel Anets'iots' [Samuel of Ani]. *Havak'munk'i Grots Patmagrats.* Ejmiacin, 1893.

Stephen of Taron [Étienne Asolik de Taròn; Step'anos Taronets'i]. *Histoire universelle.* Trans. Frederic Macler. Paris: Imprimerie natiônale, 1917.

————. [Step'anos Taronets'i]. *Patmut'iwn*. Ed. M. Malchasian. St. Petersburg: Tparani N. Skorokhodovi, 1885.

————. *Des Stephanos von Taron Armenische Geschichte*. Trans. Heinrich Gelzer and August Burckhardt. Leipzig: B. G. Teubner, 1907.

Strehlke, Ernest, ed. *Tabulae Ordinis Theutonici*. Berlin: Weidmann, 1869. Reprint Toronto: University of Toronto Press, 1975.

Theorianos. "Disputatio cum Armeniorum Catholico." *Patrologia cursus completus: Series Graeco-Latina* 133, ed. J.-P. Migne. Paris, 1864. Reprint Turnhout: Brepols, 1977. 114–298.

Thomas Artsruni. *History of the House of the Artsrunik'*. Trans. Robert W. Thomson. Detroit: Wayne State University Press, 1985.

Tovma Vardapet Artsruni. *Patmut'iwn Tann Artsruneats'*. Ed. K. P. Patkanov. St. Petersburg: Tparani N. Skorokhodovi, 1887.

Tsougarakis, Dimitris, trans. *The Life of Leontios*. Leiden: Brill, 1993.

Usamah ibn Munqidh. *An Arab-Syrian Gentleman and Warrior in the Period of the Crusades*. Trans. Philip K. Hitti. New York: Coumbia University Press, 1929. Reprint Princeton, N.J.: Princeton University Press, 1987.

Walter the Chancellor [Galterius Cancellarius]. *Walter the Chancellor's "The Antiochene Wars"*. Trans. Thomas S. Asbridge and Susan B. Edgington. Aldershot: Ashgate, 1999.

Willelmus Tyrensis. *Chronicon*. Ed. R. B. C. Huygens. Corpus Christianorum Continuatio Mediaevalis 63. Turnhout: Brepols, 1986. 2 vols.

William of Tyre. *A History of Deeds Done Beyond the Sea*. Trans. Emily Atwater Babcock and A. C. Krey. New York: Columbia University Press, 1943. 2 vols.

Willibaldus. "Vita seu potius hodoeporicon sancti Willibaldi." In *Descriptiones Terrae Sanctae ex seculo VIII. IX. XII. Et XV.*, ed. Titus Tobler. Leipzig: J. C. Hinrichs'sche Buchhandlung, 1874. 1–76.

Yahya ibn-Sa'ïd. *Histoire de Yahya Ibn-Sa'id d'Antioche*. Ed. and trans. J. Kratchkovsky and A. Vasiliev. Patrologia Orientalis 18, 23, ed. R. Graffin and F. Nau. Paris: Firmin-Didot, 1924–32.

Secondary Literature

Abulafia, David. "Introduction: Seven Types of Ambiguity, c. 1100–c. 1500." In *Medieval Frontiers: Concepts and Practices*, ed. Nora Berend and David Abulafia. Aldershot: Ashgate, 2002. 1–34.

Adontz, Nicolas. *Études Arméno-Byzantines*. Lisbon: Livararia Bertrand, 1965.

Alexander, Paul. *Byzantine Apocalyptic Tradition*. Berkeley: University of California Press, 1985.

Amouroux-Mourad, Monique. *Le comté d'Édesse*. Paris: Librairie Orientaliste Paul Geuthner, 1988.

Angold, Michael. "The Byzantine State on the Eve of the Battle of Manzikert." *Byzantinische Forschungen* 41 (1991): 9–34.

———. "Knowledge of Byzantine History in the West: The Norman Historians (Eleventh and Twelfth Centuries)." *Anglo-Norman Studies* 25 (2002): 19–33.

Arutjunova-Fidanjan, V. A. "The Ethno-Confessional Self-Awareness of Armenian Chalcedonians." *Revue des études arméniennes* 21 (1988–89): 345–63.

Asbridge, Thomas. *The Creation of the Principality of Antioch, 1098–1130*. Woodbridge: Boydell, 2000.

Bak, János. "Serfs and Serfdom: Words and Things." *Review* 4 (1980): 3–18.

Balard, Michel. *Croisades et Orient latin*. Paris: Armand Colin, 2001.

Bartlett, Robert. *The Making of Europe: Conquest, Colonization, and Cultural Change, 950–1350*. Princeton, N.J.: Princeton University Press, 1993.

Baum, William and Dietmar Winkler. *The Church of the East: A Concise History*. London: Routledge Curzon, 2003.

Bearman, P., Th. Bianquis, C.E. Bosworth, E. van Donzel and W.P. Heinrich, eds. *Encyclopaedia of Islam*. Online ed. Leiden: Brill, 2006.

Beaumont, A. A. "Albert of Aachen and the County of Edessa." In *The Crusades and Other Historical Essays: Presented to Dana C. Munro by His Former Students*, ed. Louis J. Paetow. New York: F.S. Crofts, 1928. 101–38.

Bedrosian, Robert. "*Dayeakut'iwn* in Ancient Armenia." *Armenian Review* 37 (1984): 23–47.

Beech, George T. "The Crusader Lordship of Marash in Armenian Cilicia, 1104–1149." *Viator* 27 (1996): 35–52.

———. "A Norman-Italian Adventurer in the East: Richard of Salerno 1097–1112." In *Anglo-Norman Studies XV: Proceedings of the XV Battle Conference*, ed. Marjorie Chibnall. Woodbridge: Boydell Press, 1992. 25–40.

Benvenisti, Meron. *The Crusaders in the Holy Land*. New York: Macmillan, 1970.

Boojamra, J. L. "Christianity in Greater Syria: Surrender and Survival." *Byzantion* 67 (1997): 148–78.

Brock, Sebastian. "The 'Nestorian' Church: A Lamentable Misnomer." *Bulletin of the John Rylands University Library of Manchester* 78, 3 (1996): 23–35.

Buck, Christopher. "The Identity of the Sabi'un: An Historical Quest." *Muslim World* 74 (1984): 172–86.

Bull, Marcus. "Views of Muslims and Jerusalem in Miracle Stories, c. 1000–c. 1200: Reflections on the Study of the First Crusaders' Motivations." In *The Experience of Crusading: Western Approaches*, ed. Marcus Bull and Norman Housley. Cambridge: Cambridge University Press, 2003. 1: 13–32.

Bush, M. L., ed. *Serfdom and Slavery: Studies in Legal Bondage*. London: Longmans, 1996.

Cahen, Claude. "La communauté rurale dans le monde musulman médiéval." In *Les communautés rurales*, vol. 3, *Asie et Islam*. Paris: Dessain et Tolra, 1982. 9–27.

———. "Le Diyar Bakr au temps des premiers Urtukides." *Journal Asiatique* 227 (1935): 219–76.

———. "Un document concernant les melkites et les latins d'Antioche." *Revues des études Byzantines* 29 (1971): 285–92. Reprinted in Claude Cahen, *Turcobyzantina et Oriens Christianus*. London: Variorum Reprints, 1974.

———. "Indigènes et croisés." *Syria* 15 (1934): 351–60. Reprinted in Cahen, *Turcobyzantina et Oriens Christianus*. London: Variorum Reprints, 1974.

———. "Une inscription mal comprise concernant le rapprochement entre Maronites et Croisés." In *Medieval and Middle Eastern Studies in Honor of A. S. Atiya*, ed. Sami A. Hanna. Leiden: Brill, 1972. 62–64.

———. "Notes sur l'histoire des croisades et de l'Orient latin II: le regime rural syrien au temps de la domination franque." *Bulletin de la faculté des letters de Strasbourg* 29 (1951): 286–310. Reprinted in Claude Cahen, *Turcobyzantina et Oriens Christianus*. London: Variorum Reprints, 1974.

Cahen, Claude. "Ibn al-Djawzi, Shams a-Din abu l'-Muzaffar Yusuf b. Kizoghlu, Known as Sibt." *Encyclopedia of Islam*, ed. P. Bearman, Th. Bianquis, C. E. Bosworth, E. Van Donzel, and W. P. Heinrichs. Online ed. Leiden: Brill, 2006. http://www.brillonline.nl/subscriber/entry?entry=islam_SIM-3140, accessed 26 January 2007.

———. *Orient et Occident au temps des croisades*. Paris: Éditions Aubier Montaigne, 1983.

———. *Pre-Ottoman Turkey*. Trans. J. Jones-Williams. London: Sidgwick and Jackson, 1968.

———. *La Syrie du Nord à l'époque des croisades et la principauté franque d'Antioche*. Paris: Librairie Paul Guethner, 1940.

———. "The Turkish Invasion: The Selchükids." In *A History of the Crusades*, ed. Kenneth Setton, vol. 1, *The First Hundred Years*, ed. Marshall Baldwin. Philadelphia: University of Pennsylvania Press, 1955. 135–76.

Canard, Marius. "La destruction de l'église de la Résurrection par le Calife Hakim et l'histoire de la descente du feu sacré." *Byzantion* 35 (1965): 16–43.

Chabot, J.-B. *Littérature syriaque*. Paris: Librairie Bloud et Gay, 1934.

Chamchiam, Michael. *History of Armenia*. 2 vols. Trans. Johannes Avdall. Calcutta: Bishop's College Press, 1827.

Charanis, Peter. *The Armenians in the Byzantine Empire*. Lisbon: Livraria Bertrand, [1963].

Cheynet, Jean-Claude. "Les arméniens de l'empire en Orient de Constantin X à Alexis Comnène (1059–1081)." In *L'Arménie et Byzance: histoire et culture*. Paris: Publications de la Sorbonne, 1996. 67–78.

———. "Mantzikert: un désastre militaire?" *Byzantion* 50 (1980): 410–438.

———. *Pouvoir et contestations à Byzance (963–1210)*. Paris: Publications de la Sorbonne, 1990.

———. "La résistance aux Turcs en Asie Mineure entre Manzikert et la Première Croisade." In EYψYXIA: *mélanges offerts à Hélène Ahrweiler*. Paris: Publications de la Sorbonne, 1998. 1: 131–47.

———. "Thathoul, Archonte des Archontes." *Revue des études byzantines* 48 (1990): 233–242.

Cheynet, Jean-Claude and Jean-François Vannier. *Études prosopographiques*. Paris: Publications de la Sorbonne, 1986.

Chukaszyan, B. L. "Échos de legendes épiques iraniennes dans les «lettres» de Grigor Magistros." *Revue des études arméniennes* 1 (1964): 321–29.

Ciggaar, Krijnie N. *Western Travellers to Constantinople*. Leiden: Brill, 1996.

Cohen, Mark R. "What Was the Pact of 'Umar? A Literary-Historical Study." *Jerusalem Studies in Arabic and Islam* 23 (1999): 100–157.

Cole, Penny. "'O God, the Heathen Have Come into Your Inheritance' (Ps. 78.1): The Theme of Religious Pollution in Crusade Documents, 1095–1188." In *Crusaders and Muslims in Twelfth-Century Syria*, ed. Maya Shatzmiller. Leiden: Brill, 1993. 84–111.

Comfort, Anthony, Catherine Abadie-Reynal, and Rifat Ergeç. "Crossing the Euphrates in Antiquity: Zeugma Seen from Space." *Anatolian Studies* 50 (2000): 99–126.

Conder, Claude. *The Latin Kingdom of Jerusalem 1099 to 1291 A.D.* London: Committee of the Palestine Exploration Fund, 1897.

Conrad, L. I. "Varietas Syriaca: Secular and Scientific Culture in the Christian Communities of Syria After the Arab Conquest." In *After Bardaisan: Studies on Continuity and Change in Syriac Christianity in Honour of Professor Hans J. W. Drijvers*, ed. G. J. Reinink and A. C. Klugkist. Leuven: Uiteverij Peeters, 1999. 85–105.

Constable, Giles. "The Historiography of the Crusades." In *The Crusades from the Perspective of Byzantium and the Muslim World*, ed. Angeliki Laiou and Roy Parviz Mottahedeh. Washington, D.C.: Dumbarton Oaks Research Library and Collection, 2001. 1–22.

Cowdrey, H. E. J. "Pope Urban II and the Idea of Crusade." *Studi Medievali* 36 (1995): 721–42. Reprinted in *The Crusades and Latin Monasticism, 11th–12th Centuries*. Aldershot: Ashgate, 1999.

———. "Pope Urban II's Preaching of the First Crusade." *History* 55 (1970): 177–88.

Dachévytch, Yaroslav. "Les Arméniens en Islande." *Revue des études arméniennes* 20 (1986–87): 321–36.

Dagron, Gilbert. "Minorités ethniques et religieuses dans l'Orient byzantin à la fin du Xe et au XIe siècle: l'immigration syrienne." *Travaux et mémoirés* 6 (1976): 177–216.

Dajani-Shakeel, Hadia. "Displacement of the Palestinians During the Crusades." *Muslim World* 68 (1978): 157–75.

Dédéyan, Gérard. Review of *Ananun Edesac'i, Zamanakagrut'yun (Chronicle of the Anonymous of Edessa)*, by Lewon H. Ter-Petrosyan. *Revue des études arméniennes* n.s. 17 (1983): 658–62.

———. "L'argent et le pouvoir chez chefs arméniens de l'Euphratèse à l'époque de la première croisade." In EYΨYXIA: *mélanges offerts à Hélène Ahrweiler*. Paris: Publications de la Sorbonne, 1998. 1: 195–208.

———. *Les arméniens entre grecs, musulmans et croisés: études sur les pouvoirs arméniens dans le proche-orient méditerranéen (1068–1150)*. Lisbon: Fundação Calouste Gulbenkian, 2003.

———. "Les colophons de manuscrits arméniens comme sources pour l'histoire des croisades." In *The Crusades and Their Sources*, ed. John France and William G. Zajac. Aldershot: Ashgate, 1998. 89–109.

———. "L'immigration arménienne en Cappadoce au XIe siècle." *Byzantion* 45 (1975): 41–117.

———. "Mleh le Grand, Stratège de Lykandos." *Revue des études arméniennes* 15 (1981): 73–102.

———. "Les princes arméniens de l'Euphratèse et l'Empire byzantin (fin XIe-milieu XIIe siècle)." In *L'Arménie et Byzance: histoire et culture*. Paris: Publications de la Sorbonne, 1996. 79–88.

———. "Le rôle complémentaire des frères Pahlawuni, Grigor III Catholicos et saint Nerses Snorhali Catholicos, dans le rapprochement avec les latins à l'époque de la chute d'Édesse (c. 1139–1150)." *Revue des études arméniennes* 33 (1992): 237–52.

———. "Le rôle des arméniens en Syrie du nord pendant la reconquête byzantine (vers 945–1031)." *Byzantinische Forschungen* 25 (1999): 248–84.

Der Nersessian, Sirarpie. *The Armenians*. London: Thames and Hudson, 1969.

De Vries-van der Velden, Eva. "Psellos, Romain IV Diogénès et Mantzikert." *Byzantinoslavica* 58 (1997): 274–308.

Dowsett, C. J. F. "A Twelfth-Century Armenian Inscription at Edessa." In *Iran and Islam*, ed. C. E. Bosworth. Edinburgh: Edinburgh University Press, 1984. 197–222.

Drory, Joseph. "Hanabalis of the Nablus Region in the Eleventh and Twelfth Centuries." *Asian and African Studies* 22 (1988): 93–112.

Edbury, Peter. "Fiefs and Vassals in the Kingdom of Jerusalem: from the Twelfth Century to the Thirteenth." *Crusades* 1 (2002): 49–62.

———. *John of Ibelin and the Kingdom of Jerusalem*. Woodbridge: Boydell, 1997.

———. "Law and Custom in the Latin East: *Les Letres dou Sepulcre.*" In *Intercultural Contacts in the Medieval Mediterranean*, ed. Benjamin Arbel. Portland, Ore.: Frank Cass, 1996. 71–79.

El-Leithy, Tamer. "Coptic Culture and Conversion in Medieval Cairo, 1293–1524 A.D." Ph.D. dissertation, Princeton University, 2005.

Ellenblum, Ronnie. *Frankish Rural Settlement in the Latin Kingdom of Jerusalem*. Cambridge: Cambridge University Press, 1998.

———. "Were There Borders and Borderlines in the Middle Ages? The Example of the Latin Kingdom of Jerusalem." In *Medieval Frontiers: Concepts and Practices*, ed. David Abulafia and Nora Berend. Aldershot: Ashgate, 2002. 105–19.

Erdmann, Carl. *The Origin of the Idea of Crusade*. Trans. Marshall W. Baldwin and Walter Goffart. Princeton, N.J.: Princeton University Press, 1977.

Failler, Albert. "Le patriarche d'Antioche Athanase Ier Manassès (1157–1170)." *Revue des études byzantines* 51 (1993): 63–75.

Favreau-Lilie, Marie-Luise. "'Multikulturelle Gesellschaft' oder 'Persecuting Society'? 'Franken' und 'Einheimishe' im Königreich Jerusalem." In *Jerusalem im Hoch- und Spätmittelalter*, ed. Dieter Bauer, Klaus Herbers, and Nikolas Jaspert. Frankfurt: Campus Verlag, 2001. 55–93.

Fawaz, Leila Tarazi. *Merchants and Migrants in Nineteenth-Century Beirut*. Cambridge, Mass.: Harvard University Press, 1983.

———. *An Occasion for War: Civil Conflict in Lebanon and Damascus in 1860*. Berkeley: University of California Press, 1994.

Fiey, Jean Maurice. *Chrétiens syriaques sous les Abbasides surtout à Bagdad*. Corpus Scriptorum Christianorum Orientalium 420, Subsidia t. 59. Louvain: Secrétariat du Corpus SCO, 1980.

Folda, Jaroslav. *The Art of the Crusaders in the Holy Land, 1098–1187*. Cambridge: Cambridge University Press, 1995.

Forse, James H. "Armenians and the First Crusade." *Journal of Medieval History* 17 (1991): 13–22.

France, John. "The Departure of Tatikios from the Crusader Army." *Bulletin of the Institute of Historical Research* 44 (1971): 138–47.

———. "The Fall of Antioch During the First Crusade." In *Dei gesta per Francos*, ed. Michel Balard, Benjamin Z. Kedar, and Jonathan Riley-Smith. Aldershot: Ashgate, 2001. 13–20.

———. *Victory in the East.* Cambridge: Cambridge University Press, 1994.

Frankel, Rafael. "Topographical Notes on the Territory of Acre in the Crusader Period." *Israel Exploration Journal* 38 (1988): 249–72.

Frankopan, Peter. "Perception and Projection of Prejudice: Anna Comnena, the *Alexiad*, and the First Crusade." In *Gendering the Crusades*, ed. Susan B. Edgington and Sarah Lambert. New York: Columbia University Press, 2002. 59–76.

Frazee, Charles A. "The Christian Church in Cilician Armenia: Its Relations with Rome and Constantinople to 1198." *Church History* 45 (1976): 166–84.

Friedman, Yvonne. "Women in Captivity and Their Ransom During the Crusader Period." In *Cross Cultural Convergences in the Crusader Period*, ed. Michael Goodich, Sophia Menache, and Sylvia Schein. New York: Peter Lang, 1995. 75–88.

Garsoïan, Nina. *L'église arménienne et le grand schisme d'Orient.* Corpus Scriptorum Christianorum Orientalium 574, Subsidia, t. 100. Louvain: Peeters, 1999.

———. "Quelques précisions préliminaires sur le schisme entre les églises byzantine et arménienne au sujet du concile de Chalcédoine II: La date et les circonstances de la rupture." In *L'Arménie et Byzance: histoire et culture.* Publications de la Sorbonne Série Byzantina Sorbonensia 12. Paris: Centre de recherches d'histoire et de civilisation byzantines, 1996. 99–112.

Geary, Patrick. "Living with Conflicts in Stateless France: A Typology of Conflict Management Mechanism, 1050–1200." In *Living with the Dead in the Middle Ages*. Ithaca, N.Y.: Cornell University Press, 1994. 125–60.

Gervers, Michael and Ramzi Jibran Bikhazi, eds. *Indigenous Christian Communities in Islamic Lands: Eighth to the Eighteenth Centuries.* Papers in Medieval Studies 9. Toronto: Pontifical Institute of Mediaeval Studies, 1990.

Gibbon, Edward. *The History of the Decline and Fall of the Roman Empire.* London: Methuen, 1898. 6 vols.

Goffart, Walter. *Caput and Colonate: Towards a History of Late Roman Taxation.* Toronto: University of Toronto Press, 1974.

Goitein, S. D. *A Mediterranean Society.* Berkeley: University of California Press, 1988. 5 vols.

Gonthier, Nicole. *Le châtiment du crime au moyen âge.* Rennes: Presses Universitaires de Rennes, 1998.

Gouillard, Jean. "Gagik II, défenseur de la foi arménienne." *Travaux et mémoires* 7 (1979): 399–418.

Grandeclaude, Maurice. "Liste d'assises remontant au premier royaume de Jérusalem (1099–1187)." In *Mélanges Paul Fournier.* Paris: Recueil Sirey, 1929. 329–45.

Gray, Patrick. "Theological Discourse in the Seventh Century: The Heritage from the Sixth Century." *Byzantinische Forschungen* 26 (2000): 219–28.

Griffith, Sidney. "The Church of Jerusalem and the 'Melkites': The Making of an 'Arab Orthodox' Christian Identity in the World of Islam (750–1050 CE)." In *Christians* and *Christianity in the Holy Land: From the Origins to the Latin Kingdoms*, ed. Ora Limor and Guy G. Stroumsa. Turnhout: Brepols, 2006. 175–204.

———. "Dionysius bar Salibi on the Muslims." In *IV Symposium Syriacum 1984: Literary Genres in Syriac Literature*, ed. H. J. W. Drijvers, R. Lavenant S. J., C. Molenberg, and G. J. Reinink. Orientalia Christiana Analecta 229. Rome: Pont. Institutum Studiorum Orientalium, 1987. 353–65.

———. "Faith and Reason in Christian Kalam: Theodore Abu Qurrah on Discerning the True Religion." In *Christian Arabic Apologetics During the Abbasid Period (750–1258)*, ed. Samir Khalil Samir and Jørgen S. Nielsen. Leiden: Brill, 1994. 1–43.

———. "'Melkites,' 'Jacobites' and the Christological Controversies in Arabic in Third/Ninth Century Syria." In *Syrian Christians Under Islam*, ed. David Thomas. Leiden: Brill, 2001. 9–55.

———. "The Monk in the Emir's *Majlis*: Reflections on a Popular Genre of Christian Literary Apologetics in Arabic in the Early Islamic Period." In *The Majlis: Interreligious Encounters in Medieval Islam*, ed. Hava Lazarus-Yafeh, Mark R. Cohen, Sasson Somekh, and Sidney Griffith. Wiesbaden: Harrassowitz, 1999. 13–65.

———. "The 'Philosphical Life' in Tenth-Century Baghdad: The Contribution of Yahya Ibn 'Adi's *Kitab tahdhib al-akhlaq*." In *Christians at the Heart of Islamic Rule: Church Life and Scholarship in 'Abbasid Iraq*, ed. David Thomas. Leiden: Brill, 2003. 129–49.

Grigolia, Alexander. "Milkrelationship in the Caucasus." *Bedi kartlisa* 41–42 (1962): 147–67.

Grousset, René. *Histoire de l'Arménie, des origines à 1071*. Paris: Payot, 1947.

Hagenmeyer, Heinrich. "Chronologie de la première croisade (1094–1100)." *Revue de l'orient latin* 6 (1893): 214–293, 490–549; 7: 430–503; 8: 318–82.

Hajjar, Joseph. "The Influence of Muslim Society on Church Law in the Arab East." *Concilium* 5 (1996): 66–80.

Hamilton, Bernard. "Aimery of Limoges, Latin Patriarch of Antioch (c. 1142–c. 1196) and the Unity of the Churches." In *East and West in the Crusader States II*, ed. Krijnie Ciggaar and Herman Teule. Leuven: Uitgeverij Peeters, 1999. 1–12.

———. "King Consorts of Jerusalem and Their Entourages." In *Die Kreuzfahrerstaaten als multikulturelle Gesellschaft*, ed. Hans Eberhard Mayer. Munich: Oldenbourg, 1997. 13–24.

———. *The Latin Church in the Crusader States*. London: Variorum, 1980.

———. "Ralph of Domfront, Patriarch of Antioch (1135–40)." *Nottingham Medieval Studies* 18 (1984): 1–21.

Hayden, Robert. "Antagonistic Tolerance: Competitive Sharing of Religious Sites in South Asia and the Balkans." *Current Anthropology* 43 (2002): 205–31.

Hellenkemper, Hansgerd. *Burgen der Kreuzritterzeit in der Grafschaft Edessa und im Königreich Kleinarmenien*. Bonn: Rudolf Habelt Verlag, 1976.

Heyd, David, ed. *Toleration*. Princeton, N.J.: Princeton University Press, 1996.

Hiestand, Rudolf. "Un centre intellectuel en Syrie du Nord? Notes sur la personalité d'Aimery d'Antioche, Albert de Tarse et *Rorgo Fretellus*." *Le Moyen Age* 100 (1994): 7–36.

———. "Ein neuer Bericht über das Konzil von Antiochia 1140." *Annuarium historiae conciliorum* 19 (1987): 314–50.

Hillenbrand, Carole. *The Crusades: Islamic Perspectives*. New York: Routledge, 2000.
———. "The First Crusade: The Muslim Perspective." In *The First Crusade: Origins and Impact*, ed. Jonathan Phillips. Manchester: Manchester University Press, 1997. 130–41.
Hilton, R. H. *The Decline of Serfdom in Medieval England*. New York: St. Martin's Press, 1969.
Hirschfeld, Yizhar. "The Anchor Church at the Summit of Mt. Berenice, Tiberias." *Biblical Archaeologist* 57 (1994): 122–33.
Hodgson, Marshall. *The Order of the Assassins*. New York: AMS Press, 1980.
———. *The Venture of Islam*. Chicago: University of Chicago Press, 1974. 3 vols.
Holmes, Catherine. "'How the East Was Won' in the Reign of Basil II." In *Eastern Approaches to Byzantium: Papers from the Thirty-Third Spring Symposium of Byzantine Studies, University of Warwick, Coventry, March 1999*, ed. Anthony Eastmond. Aldershot: Ashgate, 2001. 41–56.
Hoyland, Robert G. *Seeing Islam as Others Saw It*. Studies in Late Antiquity and Early Islam 13. Princeton, N.J.: Darwin Press, 1997.
Hunt, Lucy-Anne. "Art and Colonialism: The Mosaics of the Church of the Nativity in Bethlehem (1169) and the Problem of 'Crusader Art.'" *Dumbarton Oaks Papers* 45 (1991): 69–85.
Hyams, Paul R. *Kings, Lords and Peasants in Medieval England*. Oxford: Clarendon Press, 1980.
Irwin, Robert. "Orientalism and the Early Development of Crusader Studies." In *The Experience of Crusading*, ed. Peter Edbury and Jonathan Phillips. Cambridge: Cambridge University Press, 2003. 1: 214–30.
Iskander, John. "Islamization in Medieval Egypt: The Copto-Arabic 'Apocalypse of Samuel' as a Source for the Social and Religious History of Medieval Copts." *Medieval Encounters* 4 (1998): 219–27.
Janin, R. "Les Francs au service des Byzantins." *Echos d'Orient* 29 (1930): 61–72.
Johns, Jeremy. *Arabic Administration in Norman Sicily: The Royal Diwan*. Cambridge: Cambridge University Press, 2002.
Jones, Lynn. "The Church of the Holy Cross and the Iconography of Kingship." *Gesta* 33, 2 (1994): 104–17.
Joranson, Einar. "The Great German Pilgrimage of 1064–5." In *The Crusades and Other Historical Essays*, ed. Louis Paetow. New York: Crofts, 1928. 3–43.
Jordan, William Chester. *From Servitude to Freedom: Manumission in the Séonais in the Thirteenth Century*. Philadelphia: University of Pennsylvania Press, 1986.
Jotischky, Andrew. "Manuel Comnenus and the Reunion of the Churches: The Evidence of the Conciliar Mosaics in the Church of the Nativity in Bethlehem." *Levant* 26 (1994): 207–24.
Kaufold, Hubert. "Zur syrischen Kirchengeschichte des 12. Jahrhunderts: Neue Quellen über Theodoros bar Wahbun." *Oriens Christianus* 74 (1990): 115–51.
Kazhdan, Alexander. "The Armenians in the Byzantine Ruling Class Predominantly in the Ninth Through the Twelfth Centuries." In *Medieval Armenian Culture*, ed. Thomas J. Samuelian and Michael E. Stone. Chico, Calif.: Scholars Press, 1984. 439–51.

Kedar, Benjamin Z. "Convergences of Oriental Christian, Muslim and Frankish Worshippers: The Case of Saydnaya." In *De Sion exibit lex et verbum domini de Hierusalem: Essays on Medieval Law, Liturgy and Literature in Honour of Amnon Linder*, ed. Yitzak Hen. Turnhout: Brepols, 2001. 59–69.

————. *Crusade and Mission.* Princeton, N.J.: Princeton University Press, 1984.

————. "The Frankish Period." In *The Samaritans*, ed. A. D. Crown. Tübingen: Mohr, 1989. 82–94.

————. "Gerard of Nazareth, a Neglected Twelfth-Century Writer in the Latin East." *Dumbarton Oaks Papers* 37 (1983): 55–77.

————. "Latins and Oriental Christians in the Frankish Levant." In *Sharing the Sacred: Religious Contacts and Conflicts in the Holy Land: First-Fifteenth Centuries CE*, ed. Arieh Kofsky and Guy G. Stroumsa. Jerusalem: Yad Izhak Ben Zvi, 1998. 208–22.

————. "On the Origins of the Earliest Laws of Frankish Jerusalem: The Canons of the Council of Nablus, 1120." *Speculum* 74 (1999): 310–35.

————. "Some New Sources on Palestinian Muslims Before and During the Crusades." In *Die Kreuzfahrerstaaten als multikulturelle Gesellschaft*, ed. Hans Eberhard Mayer. Munich: Oldenbourg, 1997. 129–40.

————. "The Subjected Muslims of the Frankish Levant." In *Muslims Under Latin Rule*, ed. James M. Powell. Princeton, N.J.: Princeton University Press, 1990. 135–74. Reprinted in *The Franks in the Levant, 11th to 14th Centuries*. Aldershot: Variorum, 1993.

————. "The *Tractatus de locis et statu terre ierosolimitane*." In *The Crusades and Their Sources*, ed. John France and William G. Zajac. Aldershot: Ashgate, 1998. 111–31.

Kedar, Benjamin Z. and Chr. Westergård-Nielsen. "Icelanders in the Crusader Kingdom of Jerusalem: A Twelfth-Century Account." *Mediaeval Scandinavia* 11 (1978–79): 193–211.

Kenaan-Kedar, Nurith. "Armenian Architecture in Twelfth-Century Crusader Jerusalem." *Assaph Studies in Art History* 3 (1998): 77–91.

Kennedy, Hugh. "The Melkite Church from the Islamic Conquest to the Crusades: Continuity and Adaptation in the Byzantine Legacy." In *The 17th International Byzantine Congress*. New Rochelle, N.Y.: Aristide D. Caratzas, 1986. 325–43.

Khatchadourian, Hrant. "The Christology of St. Nerses Shnorhali in Dialogue with Byzantium." *Miscellanea Francescana* 78 (1978): 413–34.

Kohler, Charles. "Un rituel et un breviaire du Saint-Sépulcre de Jérusalem (XIIe-XIIIe siècle)." *Revue de l'Orient latin* 8 (1900/01): 383–500.

Kohlberg, Etan and Benjamin Z. Kedar. "A Melkite Physician in Frankish Jerusalem and Ayyubid Damascus: Muwaffaq al-Din Ya'qub b. Siqlab." *Asian and African Studies* 22 (1988): 113–26.

Kühnel, Bianca. "'Crusader Art'—An Art Historical Term." In *Crusader Art of the Twelfth Century: A Geographical, an Historical, or an Art Historical Notion?* Berlin: Gebr. Mann Verlag, 1994. 155–68.

Laiou, Angeliki. "The Many Faces of Medieval Colonialism." In *Native Traditions in the Postconquest World*, ed. Elizabeth Hill Boone and Tom Cummins. Washington, D.C.: Dumbarton Oaks, 1998. 13–30.

LaMonte, J. L. "Lords of Le Puiset on the Crusades." *Speculum* 17 (1942): 100–118.

Lamoreaux, John C. "Early Eastern Christian Responses to Islam." In *Medieval Christian Perceptions of Islam*, ed. John Victor Tolan. New York: Garland, 1996. 3–32.

Laurent, Joseph. "Arméniens de Cilicie: Aspiétès, Oschin, Ursinus." In *Études d'histoire arméniennes*. Louvain: Éditions Peeters, 1971. 51–60.

———. "Byzance et Antioche sous le curopalate Philarète." *Revue des études arméniennes* 9 (1929): 61–72. Reprinted in *Études d'histoire arménienne*. Louvain: Éditions Peeters, 1971. 148–59.

———. "Des grecs aux Croisés: Étude sur l'histoire d'Édesse entre 1071 et 1098." *Byzantion*, I (1924): 367–449. Reprinted in *Études d'histoire arménienne*. Louvain: Éditions Peeters, 1971. 61–128.

Layish, Aharon. "'Waqfs' and Sufi Monasteries in the Ottoman Policy of Colonization: Sultan Selim I's 'Waqf' of 1516 in Favour of Dayr al-Asad." *Bulletin of the School of Oriental and African Studies* 1 (1987): 61–89.

Lenski, Noel. "Assimilation and Revolt in the Territory of Isauria, from the 1st Century B.C. to the 6th Century A.D." *Journal of the Economic and Social History of the East* 42 (1999): 411–65.

Leroy, Maurice. "Grégoire Magistros et les traductions arméniennes d'auteurs grecs." *Annuaire de l'Institut de philologie et d'histoire orientales* 3 (1935): 263–94.

Lilie, Ralph-Johannes. *Byzantium and the Crusader States, 1096–1204.* Trans. J. C. Morris and Jean E. Ridings. Oxford: Clarendon Press, 1993.

Linder, Amnon. "Christian Communities in Jerusalem." In *The History of Jerusalem: The Early Muslim Period 638–1099*, ed. Joshua Prawer and Haggai Ben-Shammai. New York: New York University Press, 1996. 121–62.

MacEvitt, Christopher. "The *Chronicle* of Matthew of Edessa: Apocalypse, the First Crusade and the Armenian Diaspora." *Dumbarton Oaks Papers* 61 (2007): 254–96.

———. "Christian Authority in the Latin East: Edessa in Crusader History." In *The Mediaeval Crusade*, ed. Susan Ridyard. Woodbridge: Boydell, 2004. 71–83.

Magdalino, Paul. "The Byzantine Background to the First Crusade." deremilitari.org., http://www.deremilitari.org/resources/articles/magdalino.htm, accessed 10 May 2007.

———. *The Empire of Manuel I Komnenos.* Cambridge: Cambridge University Press, 1993.

Manandian, H. A. *The Trade and Cities of Armenia in Relation to Ancient World Trade.* Trans. Nina G. Garsoïan. Lisbon: Livraria Bertrand, 1965.

Maranci, Christina. *Medieval Armenian Architecture.* Louvain: Peeters, 2001.

Matzke, Michael. *Daibert von Pisa: Zwischen, Pisa, Papst und erstem Kreuzzug.* Sigmaringen: Jan Thorbecke, 1998.

Mayer, Hans Eberhard. *Bistümer, Klöster und Stifte in Königreich Jerusalem.* Schriften der Monumenta Germaniae Historica 26. Stuttgart: Anton Hiersemann, 1977.

———. *The Crusades.* Trans. John Gillingham. 2nd ed. Oxford: Oxford University Press, 1990.

———. "Latins, Muslims and Greeks in the Latin Kingdom of Jerusalem." *History* 63 (1978): 175–92. Reprinted in *Probleme des lateinischen Königreichs Jerusalem.* London: Variorum, 1983.

———. "Die Seigneurie de Joscelin und der Deutsche Orden." In *Die Geistlichen Ritterorden Europas*, ed. Josef Fleckenstein and Manfred Hellmann. *Vorträge und Forschungen.* Sigmaringen: Jan Thorbecke Verlag, 1980. 26: 171–216.

Meinardus, Otto. "The Ceremony of the Holy Fire in the Middle Ages and To-Day." *Bulletin de la société d'archeologie copte* 16 (1961–62): 243–52.

Metcalf, D. M. *Coinage of the Crusades and the Latin East.* London: Royal Numismatic Society, 1995.

Meyendorff, Jean. "L'aphartodocétisme en Arménie: un imbroglio doctrinal et politique." *Revue des études arméniennes* 23 (1992): 27–37.

Meyer, Martin A. *History of the City of Gaza.* New York: Columbia University Press, 1907.

Michaud, Joseph. *Histoire des croisades.* 7th ed. Paris: Furne, Jouvet, 1867.

Moore, Robert. *Formation of a Persecuting Society: Power and Deviance in Western Europe, 950–1250.* Oxford: Blackwell, 1987.

Morray, David. "A Medieval Visit to the Castle of Al-Rawandan." *Anatolian Studies* 43 (1993): 137–42.

Muldoon, James. "Tolerance and Intolerance in the Medieval Canon Lawyers." In *Tolerance and Intolerance: Social Conflict in the Age of the Crusades*, ed. Michael Gervers and James M. Powell. Syracuse, N.Y.: Syracuse University Press, 2001. 117–23.

Munro, Dana Carleton. *The Kingdom of the Crusaders.* New York: Appleton-Century, 1935. Reprinted Port Washington, N.Y.: Kennikat Press, 1966.

———. "The Speech of Pope Urban II at Clermont, 1095." *American Historical Review* 11 (1905–6): 231–42.

Murray, Alan. "'Mighty Against the Enemies of Christ:' The Relic of the True Cross in the Armies of the Kingdom of Jerusalem." In *The Crusades and Their Sources*, ed. John France and William G. Zajac. Aldershot: Ashgate, 1998. 217–38.

———. *The Crusader Kingdom of Jerusalem: A Dynastic History, 1099–1125.* Oxford: Unit for Prosopographical Research, 2000.

Mutafian, Claude. *La Cilicie au carrefour des empires.* Paris: Les Belles Lettres, 1988. 2 vols.

Nasrallah, Joseph. "Sulaïman al-Gazzi, évêque melchite de Gaza (XIe siècle)." *Oriens Christianus* 62 (1978): 144–57.

———. "Syriens et Suriens." In *Symposium Syriacum 1972: célébré dans les jours 26–31 octobre 1972 à l'Institut pontifical oriental de Rome: rapports et communications.* Orientalia Christiana Analecta 197. Rome: Pontificium Orientalium Studiorum, 1974. 487–503.

Nederman, Cary J. and John Christian Laursen, eds. *Difference and Dissent: Theories of Tolerance in Medieval and Early Modern Europe.* Lanham, Md.: Rowman and Littlefield, 1996.

Nef, Annliese. "Conquêtes et reconquêtes médiévales: la Sicile normande est-elle une terre de reduction en servitude généralisée?" In *Mélanges de l'École Française de Rome: Moyen Âge, temps modernes.* 112, 2: 579–607.

Nicols, D. M. "Byzantium and the Papacy in the Eleventh Century." *Journal of Ecclesiastical History* 13 (1962): 1–19.

Nirenberg, David. *Communities of Violence: Persecution of Minorities in the Middle Ages.* Princeton, N.J.: Princeton University Press, 1996.

Ohnsorge, Werner. *Die Legaten Alexanders III.* Berlin: Mathiesen Verlag, 1928. Reprinted Vaduz: Kraus, 1965.

Oikonomides, Nicholas. "L'organisation de la frontière orientale de Byzance aux Xe–IXe siècles et le Taktikon de l'Escurial." In *Actes du XIVe Congrès international d'Études Byzantines*. Bucarest, 1974. 1: 285–302.

Pagels, Elaine. *The Origin of Satan*. New York: Vintage Books, 1995.

Pahlitzsch, Johannes. "Georgians and Greeks in Jerusalem (1099–1310)." In *East and West in the Crusader States III*, ed. Krignie Ciggaar and Herman Teule. Leuven: Uitgeverij Peeters, 2003. 35–51.

———. *Graeci und Suriani im Palästina der Kreuzfahrerzeit*. Berlin: Duncker und Humblot, 2001.

———. "St. Maria Magdalena, St. Thomas und St. Markus: Tradition und Geschichte dreier syrisch-orthodoxer Kirchen in Jerusalem." *Oriens Christianus* 81 (1997): 82–106.

———. "Symeon II. und die Errichtung der Lateinischen Kirche von Jerusalem durch die Kreuzfahrer. " In *Militia Sancti Sepulcri: Idea e istituzioni*, ed. Kaspar Elm and Cosimo Damiano Fonseca. Vatican City: [s.n.], 1998. 342–60.

Palmer, Andrew. "The History of the Syrian Orthodox in Jerusalem." *Oriens Christianus* 75 (1991): 16–43.

———. "The History of the Syrian Orthodox in Jerusalem, Part Two: Queen Melisende and the Jacobite Estates." *Oriens Christianus* 76 (1992): 74–94.

———. *Monk and Mason on the Tigris Frontier*. Cambridge: Cambridge University Press, 1990.

Payen, Jean-Charles. "L'image du grec dans la chronique normande: sur un passage de Raoul de Caen." In *Images et signes de l'Orient dans l'Occident médiéval*, Aix-en-Provence: Université de Provence, 1982, 269–80.

Phillips, Jonathan. *Defenders of the Holy Land*. Oxford: Clarendon Press, 1996.

Poncelet, Albert. "Catalogus Codicum Hagiographicorum Latinorum Bibliothecarum Neapolitarum." *Analecta Bollandiana* 30 (1911): 137–236.

———. *Catalogus Codicum Hagiographicorum Latinorum Bibliothecae Vaticanae*. Vol. 11, *Subsidia Hagiographica*. Brussels: Socios Bollandianos, 1910.

Poppe, Erich and Bianca Ross, eds. *The Legend of Mary of Egypt in Medieval Insular Hagiography*. Portland, Ore.: Four Courts Press, 1996.

Porteous, John. "Crusader Coinage with Greek or Latin Inscriptions." In *A History of the Crusades*, ed. Kenneth M. Setton, vol. 6, *The Impact of the Crusades on Europe*, ed. Harry W. Hazard and Norman P. Zacour. Madison: University of Wisconsin Press, 1989. 354–87.

Prawer, Joshua. "The Armenians in Jerusalem Under the Crusaders." In *Armenian and Biblical Studies*, ed. Michael Stone. Jerusalem: St. James Press, 1976.

———. *Crusader Institutions*. Oxford: Clarendon Press, 1980. 222–36.

———. *The Crusaders' Kingdom: European Colonialism in the Middle Ages*. New York: Praeger, 1972.

———. *The History of the Jews in the Latin Kingdom of Jerusalem*. Oxford: Clarendon Press, 1988.

———. "Social Classes in the Crusader States: The 'Minorities.' " In *A History of the Crusades*, ed. Kenneth M. Setton, vol. 5, *The Impact of the Crusades on the Near East*, ed.

Norman P. Zacour and Harry W. Hazard. Madison: University of Wisconsin Press, 1985. 59–115.

Pringle, Denys. *The Churches of the Crusader Kingdom of Jerusalem: A Corpus.* Cambridge: Cambridge University Press, 1993–.

Rabie, Hassanein. *The Financial System of Egypt.* London: Oxford University Press, 1972.

Rapp, Stephen H., Jr. "Christian Caucasian Dialogues: Glimpses of Armeno-K'art'velian Relations in Medieval Georgian Historiography." In *Peace and Negotiation: Strategies for Coexistence in the Middle Ages and the Renaissance,* ed. Diane Wolfthal. Turnhout: Brepols, 2000. 163–78.

Redgate, A. E. *The Armenians.* Oxford: Blackwell, 1998.

Reinhart, A. Kevin. "Transcendence and Social Practice: *Muftis* and *Qadis* as Religious Interpreters." *Annales Islamologiques* 27 (1993): 5–28.

Rey, Emmanuel. *Les colonies franques de Syrie aux XIIe et XIIIe siècles.* Paris: Alphonse Picard, 1883.

Reynolds, Susan. *Fiefs and Vassals: The Medieval Evidence Reinterpreted.* Oxford: Oxford University Press, 1994.

———. "Fiefs and Vassals in Twelfth-Century Jerusalem: a View from the West." *Crusades* 1 (2002): 29–48.

Richard, Jean. "Agricultural Conditions in the Crusader States." In *A History of the Crusades,* ed. Kenneth M. Setton, vol. 5, *The Impact of the Crusades on the Near East,* ed. Norman P. Zacour and Harry W. Hazard. Madison: University of Wisconsin Press, 1985. 251–66.

———. *"Cum omni raisagio montanee . . . à propos de la cession du Crac aux Hospitaliers."* In *Itinéraries d'orient: hommages à Claude Cahen,* ed. Raoul Curiel and Rika Gyselen. Bures-sur-Yvette: Groupe pour l'Étude de la Civilisation du Moyen-Orient, 1994. 187–94.

———. *The Latin Kingdom of Jerusalem.* Trans. Janet Shirley. 2 vols. Amsterdam: North-Holland, 1979.

———. "La seigneurie franque en Syrie et à Chypre: modèle oriental ou modèle occidental?" In *Seigneurs et seigneuries au moyen-âge: actes du 117e congrès national des sociétés savantes, Clermont-Ferrand, 1992.* Paris: Éditions du C.T.H.S., 1993. 155–66.

———. "Les Turcoples au service des royaumes de Jérusalem et de Chypre: Musulmans convertis ou chrétiens orientaux?" *Revue des études islamiques* 54 (1986): 261–70.

Riley-Smith, Jonathan. *The Feudal Nobility and the Kingdom of Jerusalem, 1174–1277.* Hamden: Archon, 1973.

———. *The First Crusade and the Idea of Crusading.* Philadelphia: University of Pennsylvania Press, 1986.

———. *The First Crusaders, 1095–1131.* Cambridge: Cambridge University Press, 1997.

———. "Further Thoughts in Baldwin II's *établissement* on the Confiscation of Fiefs." In *Crusade and Settlement,* ed. Peter Edbury. Cardiff: University College Cardiff Press, 1985. 176–80.

———. "Some Lesser Officials in Latin Syria." *English Historical Review* 87 (1972): 1–26.

———. "The Survival in Latin Palestine of Muslim Administration." In *The Eastern Mediterranean Lands in the Period of the Crusades*, ed. P. M. Holt. Warminster: Aris and Phillips, 1977. 9–12.

Robinson, F. C. R. and P. C. Hughes. "Lampron—Castle of Armenian Cilicia." *Anatolian Studies* 19 (1969): 183–207.

Rose, Richard Barry. "Pluralism in a Medieval Colonial Society: The Frankish Impact on the Melkite Community During the First Crusader Kingdom of Jerusalem, 1099–1187." Ph.D. dissertation, Graduate Theological Union, 1980.

Rowe, John G. "Alexander II and the Jerusalem Crusade: An Overview of Problems and Failures." In *Crusaders and Muslims in Twelfth-Century Syria*, ed. Maya Shatzmiller. Leiden: Brill, 1993. 112–32

Rüdt-Collenberg, Wipertus-Hugo. *The Rupenides, Hethumides and Lusignans: The Structure of the Armeno-Cilician Dynasties*. Paris: Klincksieck, 1963.

Runciman, Steven. "The Byzantine 'Protectorate' in the Holy Land." *Byzantion* 18 (1948): 207–15.

———. "The First Crusade: Constantinople to Antioch." In *A History of the Crusades*, ed. Kenneth Setton, vol. 1, *The First Hundred Years*, ed. Marshall Baldwin. Philadelphia: University of Pennsylvania Press, 1955. 280–307.

———. *A History of the Crusades*. 3 vols. Cambridge: Cambridge University Press, 1951.

Russell, James. *Zoroastrianism in Armenia*. Cambridge, Mass.: Harvard University Department of Near Eastern Languages and Civilizations, 1987.

Rustow, Marina. *Toward a History of Jewish Heresy: The Jews of Egypt and Syria, 980–1100*. Ithaca, N.Y.: Cornell University Press, forthcoming.

Saller, Sylvester, O.F.M. *Excavations at Bethany (1949–1952)* . Jerusalem: Franciscan Press, 1957.

Sanjian, Avedis. "Gregory Magistros: An Armenian Hellenist." In *TO ΕΛΛΗΝΙΚΟΝ: Studies in Honor of Speros Vryonis, Jr.*, vol. 2, *Byzantinoslavica, Armeniaca, Islamica, the Balkans and Modern Greece*, ed. Jelisveta Stanojevich Allen et al. New Rochelle, N.Y.: Aristide D. Caratzas, 1993. 131–58.

Saunders, William. "The Greek Inscription on the Harran Gate at Edessa: Some Further Evidence." *Byzantinische Forschungen* 21 (1995): 301–4.

Schwab, Raymond. *L'auteur des Mille et une Nuits: vie d'Antoine Galland*. Paris: Mercure de France, 1964.

Schwinges, Rainer Christoph. "William of Tyre, the Muslim Enemey, and the Problem of Tolerance." In *Tolerance and Intolerance: Social Conflict in the Age of the Crusades*, ed. Michael Gervers and James M. Powell. Syracuse, N.Y.: Syracuse University Press, 2001. 124–32.

Segal, J. B. *Edessa, "the Blessed City"*. Oxford: Clarendon Press, 1970.

Sevcenko, Nancy. "The Monastery of Mount Sinai and the Cult of St. Catherine." In *Byzantium, Faith, and Power (1261–1557): Perspectives on Late Byzantine Art and Culture*, ed. Sarah Brooks. New York: Metropolitan Museum of Art, forthcoming.

Sharf, Andrew. "Armenians and Byzantines in the Time of Alexios I Komnenos." In *Confrontation and Coexistence*, ed. Pinhas Artzi. Bar-Ilan Studies in History. Ramat Gan, Israel: Bar-Ilan University Press, 1984. 101–22.

Sidelko, Paul L. "Muslim Taxation Under Crusader Rule." In *Tolerance and Intolerance: Social Conflict in the Age of the Crusades*, ed. Michael Gervers and James M. Powell. Syracuse, N.Y.: Syracuse Unversity Press, 2001. 65–74.

Sivan, Emmanuel. "Réfugiés syro-palestiniens au temps des croisades." *Revue des études islamiques* 35 (1967): 135–48.

Slack, C. K. "Royal Familiares in the Latin Kingdom of Jerusalem, 1100–1187." *Viator* 22 (1991): 15–68.

Smail, R. C. *Crusading Warfare (1097–1193)*. Cambridge: Cambridge University Press, 1956.

Smith, Jonathan K. "What a Difference a Difference Makes." In *"To See Ourselves as Others See Us": Christians, Jews, "Others" in Late Antiquity*, ed. Jacob Neusner and Ernest S. Frerichs. Chico, Calif.: Scholars Press, 1985. 3–48.

Stevenson, William. *The Crusaders in the East*. Cambridge: Cambridge University Press, 1907.

Stow, Kenneth R. *Alienated Minority: The Jews of Medieval Latin Europe*. Cambridge, Mass.: Harvard University Press, 1992.

Suny, Ronald Grigor. *The Making of the Georgian Nation*. Bloomington: Indiana Unversity Press, 1994.

Swanson, Mark N. "The Martyrdom of 'Abd al-Masih, Superior of Mount Sinai (Qays al-Ghassani)." In *Syrian Christians Under Islam*, ed. David Thomas. Leiden: Brill, 2001. 107–29.

Taft, Robert. *The Byzantine Rite*. Collegeville, Md.: Liturgical Press, 1992.

Talmon-Heller, Daniella. *"The Cited Tales of the Wondrous Doings of the Shaykhs of the Holy Land* by Diya' al-Din Abu 'Abd Allah Muhammad b. 'Abd al-Wahid al Maqdisi (569/1173–643/1245): Text, Translation and Commentary." *Crusades* 1 (2002): 111–54.

———. "The Shaykh and the Community—Popular Hanabalite Islam in 12th–13th Century Jabal Nablus and Jabal Qasyun." *Studia Islamica* 79 (1994): 103–20.

Tardieu, Michel. "Sabiens coraniques et sabiens de Harran." *Journal Asiatique* 274 (1986): 1–44.

Tekeyan, Pascal. *Controverses christologiques en Arméno-Cilicie dans la seconde moitié du XIIe siècle (1165–1198)*. Orientalia Christiana Analecta 124. Rome: Pontificium Institutum Orientalium Studiorum, 1939.

Ter-Ghewondyan, Aram. *The Arab Emirates in Bagratid Armenia*. Trans. Nina G. Garsoïan. Lisbon: Livraria Bertrand, 1976.

Teule, Herman. *"It Is Not Right to Call Ourselves Orthodox and the Others Heretics*: Ecumenical Attitudes in the Jacobite Church in the Time of the Crusades." In *East and West in the Crusader States II*, ed. Krijnie Ciggaar and Herman Teule. Leuven: Uitgeverij Peeters, 1999. 13–28.

Thomson, Robert. "Crusades Through Armenian Eyes." In *The Crusades from the Perspective of Byzantium and the Muslim World*, ed. Angeliki E. Laiou and Roy Parviz Mottahedeh. Washington, D.C.: Dumbarton Oaks Research Library and Collection, 2001. 71–82.

———. "'History' in Medieval Armenian Historians." In *Eastern Approaches to Byzantium*, ed. Antony Eastmond. Aldershot: Ashgate, 2001. 89–99.

———. *"Vardapet* in the Early Armenian Church." *Le Muséon* 75 (1962): 367–84.

Troupeau, Gérard. "Églises et chrétiens dans l'Orient musulman." In *Histoire du chris-tianisme des origins à nos jours*, ed. Jean-Marie Mayeur et al., vol. 4, *Évêques, moines et empéreurs (610–1054)* . Paris: Desclée, 1993. 375–456.

Tyerman, Christopher. *Fighting for Christendom: Holy War and the Crusades*. Oxford: Oxford University Press, 2004.

———. *The Invention of the Crusades*. Houndsmill: Macmillan, 1998.

Van der Aalst, Patrick. "Denis Bar Salibi, polémiste." *Proche-Orient Chrétien* 9 (1959): 10–23.

Van Donzel, E. "Were There Ethiopians in Jerusalem at the Time of Saladin's Conquest in 1187?" In *East and West in the Crusader States II*, ed. Krijnie Ciggaar and Herman Teule. Leuven: Uitgeverij Peeters, 1999. 125–30.

Van Lint, Theo M. "*Lament on Edessa* by Nerses Snorhali." In *East and West in the Crusader States II*, ed. Krijnie Cignaar and Herman Teule. Leuven: Uitgeverij Peeters, 1999. 29–106.

Van Rompay, Lucas. "Society and Community in the Christian East." In *The Cambridge Companion to the Age of Justinian*, ed. Michael Maas. Cambridge: Cambridge University Press, 2005. 239–66.

Verlinden, Charles. *L'esclavage dans l'Europe médiévale*. Ghent: Riksuniversiteit te Gent, 1977. 2 vols.

Vogüé, Comte Melchior de. *Les églises de la Terre Sainte*. Paris: Librairie de Victor Didron, 1860.

Walker, Paul E. "The 'Crusade' of John Tzimisces in the Light of New Arabic Evidence." *Byzantion* 47 (1977): 301–27.

Warren, W. L. "Church and State in Angevin Ireland." *Peritia* 12 (1999): 276–91.

Watt, J. A. "The Jews, The Law and the Church: The Concept of Jewish Serfdom in Thirteenth-Century England." In *The Church and Sovereignty*, ed. Diana Wood. Oxford: Blackwell, 1991. 153–72.

Weltecke, Dorothea. *Die "Beschreibung der Zeiten" von Mor Michael dem Grossen (1126–1199)* . Corpus Scriptorum Christianorum Orientalium 594, Subsidia, t. 110. Leuven: Peeters, 2003.

———. "On the Syriac Orthodox in the Principality of Antioch During the Crusader period." In *East and West in the Medieval Eastern Mediterranean*, ed. K. Ciggaar and M. Metcalf. Leuven: Uitgeverij Peeters, 2006. 95–124.

———. "The World Chronicle of Patriarch Michael the Great (1126–1199): Some Reflections." *Journal of Assyrian Academic Studies* 11 (1997): 6–29.

Weyl-Carr, A. M. "The Mural Paintings of Abu Ghosh and the Patronage of Manuel Comnenus in the Holy Land." In *Crusader Art in the Twelfth Century*, ed. Jaroslav Folda. Jerusalem: British Archaeological Reports, 1982. 215–34.

Whittow, Mark. *The Making of Byzantium, 600–1025*. Berkeley: University of California Press, 1996.

Wolff, Robert Lee. "How the News Was Brought from Byzantium to Angoulême; or, The Pursuit of a Hare in an Ox Cart." *Byzantine and Modern Greek Studies* 4 (1978): 139–89.

Woolf, Greg. *Becoming Roman: The Origins of Provincial Civilization in Gaul*. Cambridge: Cambridge University Press, 1998.

Yarnley, C. J. "Philaretos: Armenian Bandit or Byzantine General?" *Revue des ètudes arméniennes* n.s. 9 (1972): 331–53.

Zekiyan, Boghos Levon. "Un dialogue oecuménique au XIIe siècle: les pourparlers entre le Catholicos St. Nerses Snorhali et le légat impérial Théorianos en vue de l'union des églises arménienne et Byzantine." In *Actes du XVe congrès international d'études Byzantines—Athènes, Septembre 1976*. Athens: Association Internationale des Études Byzantines, 1980. 4: 420–41.

———. "Les relations arméno-byzantines après la mort de St. Nersès Snorhali." In *16. Internationaler Byzantinistenkongress, Wien, 4.–9. Okt. 1981: Akten. Jahrbuch der Österreichischen Byzantinistik* 32, 4 (1982): 331–37.

Index

intermarriage, 146; and land, 143–47; Muslim status under Franks, 148; segregationalist model, 137–38; and servile conditions, 145, 149, 219 nn.26–27; in Palestine, 144–49

P'er (local warlord), 61–62, 76

Persian Empire, 30–32, 186 n.7

Persian language, 37

Peter Hermenius (local knight), 153

Peter the Venerable, 13

Petros, *kat'olikos*, 27

Phantasiasts, 175

Philaretos, 41–43, 190 n.58; and city of Edessa, 41–42, 53, 66, 68–69, 190 n.60; death, 68–69; effect on Armenian church, 42; effect on Armenian dynasties, 42, 190–91 n.63; effect on Jacobite church, 191 n.64; loss of power, 42, 55; Matthew of Edessa on, 190 n.60, 198 n.64; principalities established in Syria and Cilicia, 41–42; rule of Marash, 83

Piacenza pilgrim, 134

pilgrims to Holy Land, 45, 47, 132–35; interest in nonbiblical sacred events, 132; interest in St. Sabas, 132–33, 216 nn.125, 129; and legend of St. Mary the Egyptian, 133–34; and Mar Saba monastery, 132–33; meeting locals, 133; and mixed Latin-local communities in Palestine, 132–34; pre-crusade focus on exclusively biblical events, 132; references to local Muslims, 47; and rhetoric of heresy, 100–104; text evidence of shared Melkite-Latin shrines, 131; textual erasure of Jacobite representation, 103–4

Prawer, Joshua, 13–14, 16–17, 110–11, 137, 142, 218 n.10

Pringle, Denys, 128, 131

Pseudo-Methodius, 28

Qartmin monastery, 33, 37

Qenneshre monastery, 33

Rabbanite communities, 11

ra'is. See *ru'asa*

Ralph of Caen: on Baldwin's arrival in Edessa, 195 n.30; on captivity of Bohemund, 205 n.52; on conquest of Cilicia, 56–58, 194 n.14; on establishment of

Frankish county of Edessa, 53, 56–58; on Joscelin as ruler of Marash, 204 n.37; on Tancred, 53

Ralph of Domfront, patriarch, 162

Rawandan, 60–62, 75–76

Raymond of Poitiers, prince of Antioch, 94, 161

Raymond of St. Gilles (of Toulouse), 5, 64

Recueil des historiens des croisades, 14

relics and symbols: Armenian Christianity, 70, 90–92, 199 n.75; Baldwin II's new coin, 91; crusaders, 70, 199 n.74; Franks' adoption of Armenian, 90–92; Holy Cross of Varag, 70, 91–92, 199 n.75; Holy Lance, 91; True Cross, 91, 112

religious communities of Levant, 7–12; Jewish, 11–12; liturgical/cultural distinctions, 8; Maronite, 9, 105; Muslim, 10–11, 105–6; Nestorian, 10, 31–32, 47, 103–4; other Christian, 9–10. See also Armenian tradition; Jacobites; Melkites

Rey, Emmanuel, 15–17

Reynald, prince of Antioch, 160–61

Richard II of Normandy, duke, 46

Richard of Salerno, 83, 90, 203 n.27, 204 n.37, 206 nn.55, 57

Richard I the Lion-heart, king, 2, 112

Ridvan of Aleppo, 60–61, 64, 89

Riley-Smith, Jonathan, 16–17, 80, 137, 149–50, 154, 217–18 n.9

Rmbarat (Frankish mercenary), 41

Robert of Paris (papal legate), 119

Roger of Antioch, prince, 87, 107–8, 202 n.14, 206 n.57

Romanos IV Diogenes, 40–41, 46

Rome: named in pre-crusade Armenian histories, 44, 191 n.74

rough tolerance, 21, 22: as alternative to segregationalist model, 21; and "antagonistic tolerance," 184 n.52; characteristics allowing existence, 22–24; as differing from *convivencia*, 25; as differing from *dhimmi* system, 24; ecumenical negotiations and disappearance, 176–77; and establishment of Frankish county of Edessa, 73; and localization (of violence), 23–24; as new mode of interaction between local Christians and Franks, 2–3, 21–26; and permeability, 23, 132, 138; roots, 24–25; and silence, 22–23, 102

Acknowledgments

In researching and writing on rough tolerance, I have experienced far more of the tolerance than of the roughness. My deepest debts are the earliest. Julia Smith introduced me to medieval history at Trinity College, and taught me how to read primary sources critically. At Princeton University, I had the good fortune to work with Peter Brown, whose generosity and kindness, shared by his wife Betsy, sustained me through the many ups and downs of graduate life. His work embodies an ideal few can achieve. William Chester Jordan showed me how to be both a teacher and a scholar, and how to approach both the past and other scholars with respect and an open mind. Michael Gaddis, Jennifer Hevelone-Harper, Emily Kadens, Anne Lester, Jarbel Rodriguez, Lisa Bailey, and Holly Grieco provided social and intellectual support during the research for this book. In particular, Kim Bowes, Meri Clark, Jaclyn Maxwell, and Kevin Uhalde made those years among the most stimulating and happiest of my life. The support of the staff of Dumbarton Oaks Research Library, in particular Irene Vaslef, was invaluable. The director, Alice-Mary Talbot and the other junior fellows—Cecily Hilsdale, Sarah Brooks, Warren Woodfin, and Elena Boeck—created an atmosphere of collegiality and hard work. Sy Gitin and the staff of the Albright Institute in Jerusalem opened up a world for me that straddled walls and borders, and provided crucial time for reflection on my approach to Syrian and Palestinian history, as did a generous one-month NEH fellowship at the Vatican Film Library at St. Louis University.

My colleagues at Dartmouth College in the Religion Department welcomed me into their community and made room for a historian among scholars of religion. Their influence can be seen throughout this book.

Cecilia Gaposchkin welcomed me to Dartmouth, and strengthened my book in the course of many enjoyable conversations. The staff of Baker-Berry Library has been tireless in finding and copying nineteenth-century editions of Armenian texts for me, as well as other equally frustrating tasks. Tia Kolbaba, Carole Hillenbrand, Edward Peters, Jonathan Riley-Smith and the anonymous outside reader for the press have all given valuable comments, which I have tried to incorporate into the book. The errors that remain indubitably my own. Finally, my thanks go to the American Academy of Rome, particularly to the director Carmela Vircillo Franklin, where I have completed the final draft of the manuscript.

The financial support of many institutions has been instrumental in my ability to complete this project. I must thank Princeton University, the Department of History, the Program in the Ancient World, the Group for the Study of Late Antiquity, and the Center for the Study of Religion for earlier financial support. Funding from the National Endowment for the Humanities, Dumbarton Oaks Research Library, W. F. Albright Institute, and American Academy of Rome supported writing the book. Not least has been the support of my family—my parents Mike and Annie Laurie, my sister Amanda, and my aunt and uncle David and Mary Ann Kenedy. Their kindness, joy, and love have been with me every day.

Stories of
Coming Home